PRAISE FOR

THE KING ARTHUR BAKING COMPANY BIG BOOK OF BREAD

"The very best cookbooks display an enthusiastic compulsion to get every recipe right, and that means each recipe is tested until all doubt is removed; but they're also written with sensitivity to the needs, wants, and even emotions of the home cook and baker. *The King Arthur Baking Company Big Book of Bread* succeeds wonderfully! I love the scope. This book covers a broad expanse of breads extending well beyond the basics, and it deserves to be in handy reach of any novice or experienced home baker!"

—**KEN FORKISH**, author of *Flour, Water, Salt, Yeast*; *Evolutions in Bread*; and *Let's Make Bread!*

"It can be hard to find a bread book that is as authoritative and comprehensive as it is accessible and easy to follow, but *The King Arthur Baking Company Big Book of Bread* checks every box. It's packed with all the information any novice needs to bake bread successfully, written and presented in a simple and manageable way. The wide breadth of recipes covers everything from flatbreads and buns to babkas and baguettes, with plenty of creative touches throughout. It's truly a bread book for every baker."

—**CLAIRE SAFFITZ**, author of the *New York Times* bestsellers *Dessert Person* and *What's for Dessert*

"'Big' is an understatement when describing this book! From tender flatbreads to crusty loaves of sourdough, *The King Arthur Baking Company Big Book of Bread* contains an immense wealth of knowledge and dives deep into all the beautiful and delicious things you can make with flour, yeast, and water. This is a must-have for any baker and bread lover!"

—**KRISTINA CHO**, author of *Mooncakes and Milk Bread: Sweet & Savory Recipes Inspired by Chinese Bakeries*

"When King Arthur tells you how to bake bread, you better listen. The vast *Big Book of Bread* from the King Arthur Baking Company—renowned worldwide for their flour—is basically a master class on baking everything from flour tortillas to pita bread to lavash to pain au levain to sticky buns. Bake from here and pretty soon you'll be known as the king or queen of baking the world's breads."

—**NANCY SILVERTON**, author of the *New York Times* bestseller *The Cookie That Changed My Life*

"What an adventure of a book! It's both a celebration and an investigation of bread, and it makes baking breads from all over the world accessible to everyday bakers. I've made space on my kitchen shelf for this book, as I know I'll be reaching for it over and over again."

—**BETTY LIU**, author of *My Shanghai* and *The Chinese Way*

THE KING ARTHUR
BAKING COMPANY

BIG
BOOK
OF
BREAD

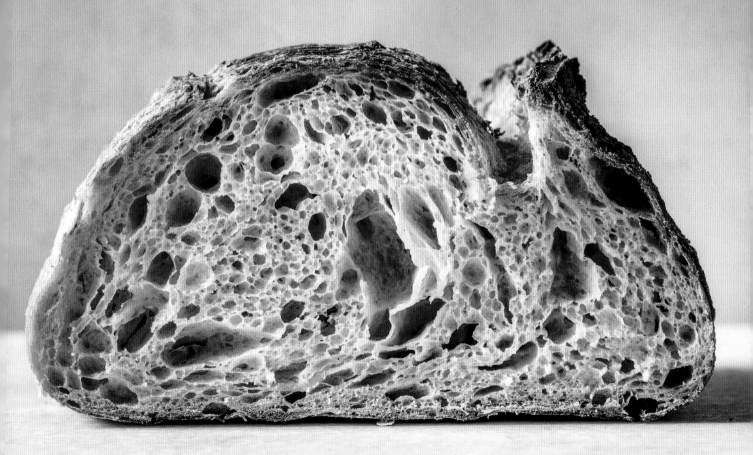

PAIN DE CAMPAGNE, PAGE 205

BIG
BOOK
OF
BREAD

125+ RECIPES FOR EVERY BAKER

JESSICA BATTILANA, MARTIN PHILIP, AND MELANIE WANDERS

PHOTOGRAPHY BY ED ANDERSON

SIMON
ELEMENT

NEW YORK   LONDON   TORONTO   SYDNEY   NEW DELHI

TOURTE AU SEIGLE, PAGE 225

Contents

14 — The Essentials

57 — Flatbreads

119 — Pan Breads

395 — Things to Make with Bread

443 — Flour Primer

YEASTED BAGUETTES, PAGE 262

Introduction

There are all sorts of bread bakers in the world. Some of us make the same simple pan bread week in and week out, a loaf we slice for morning toast and use for sandwiches, the recipe committed to memory. Some of us wait for the holidays before we pull out all the stops, twisting rich, sweet dough into chocolate babkas and making big pans of fluffy yeasted dinner rolls.

There are bread bakers who patiently feed and nurture their sourdough cultures to make loaves with dark brown crusts. Bakers who can't resist baking one loaf, then another, and then another, tweaking it every time on a quest for perfection. Bakers who have no interest at all in sourdough but who want to make their own golden, soft hamburger buns, bubbly naan, or bagels, having decided once and for all that a homemade version of any of those is so much better than the alternative.

For those bakers, and every other baker and baker-to-be, we've written this book. It is our first-ever book devoted solely to bread.

When we initially conceived the idea of a book focused on bread, we knew we wanted to make a wide-ranging book. Bread is made and eaten the world over, and we felt that this book should reflect the global tradition of bread baking.

But first we had to establish some parameters, including the most obvious: What did we consider bread? Quick breads like banana bread and biscuits, we decided, were out; we narrowed our definition to include only doughs leavened with yeast or sourdough culture. Or did we? Once we started to consider all the amazing unleavened flatbreads we loved (which, by our own somewhat arbitrary guidelines, didn't have a place in this book), we revised our thinking and expanded our definition—and our recipe list.

Working from that list, we began to bake bread. A *lot* of bread. In our Vermont test kitchen—and in our home kitchens, too—we formed loaves, shaped flatbreads, proofed pan breads, and baked sourdough of all kinds. Two of our expert bakers, Martin Philip and Melanie Wanders, led the recipe development charge, each baking hundreds of loaves over the course of eighteen months. As they baked, their minds were ever on the home baker: Can you make this bread in a home oven? Can it be made with yeast *and* sourdough culture? What equipment is essential for breadmaking, and what's optional? And the biggest question: Was the payoff for a particular bread worth the effort required to make it? Once we felt a recipe was ready, we asked less experienced bread bakers to give it a spin; the questions that emerged from those cross-tests helped us further refine the recipes.

Because of all this baking, we were never far from a slice of sourdough toast slathered with butter and jam, a jar of crunchy crackers for snacking, a pillowy piece of brioche, a crisp-crusted baguette, or a potato-stuffed flatbread. Not only did it make for very good eating but it also allowed us to marvel on a near-daily basis about the myriad styles of bread you can make using essentially the same three ingredients: flour, water, and salt.

In these pages you'll find unleavened flatbreads that can be made in thirty minutes and naturally leavened loaves that ferment overnight in the fridge. You'll find chewy bagels (page 284) and fluffy focaccia (page 58) and loaves of rye bread (page 143). You'll find recipes for breads that you might make once a year, and others that you can make weekly. Our hope is not only that you discover recipes that work for you, that become go-tos you make often and easily, but also that you become a bread baker with developed instincts who can do it all, baking whatever kind of bread you want, whenever you want. Of course, breadmaking is both art and science, and it takes some practice to get good at it. Devote that time and you'll be well on your way to great bread. And if you need more guidance, this book explains in detail the fundamental skills needed to bake great bread at home, outlines the essential tools you need to get started and to further hone your craft, and provides information about the best ingredients to use (hint: great bread starts with great flour). We've also included QR codes that link to instructional videos so you can see demonstrations of frequently used techniques.

Our hope is that you'll use this book to start baking a loaf of simple white bread (page 120) each week, so you always have some at the ready for toast and sandwiches. Maybe you'll make the outrageously delicious giant sticky bun (page 391) for one special breakfast every year. Or perhaps you'll fall down the sourdough rabbit hole, working to perfect your pain au levain (page 201). You might make pita bread (page 69) for dinner tonight and watch with wonder as it puffs miraculously in the oven. Whatever you make, whether it's your first loaf of homemade bread or your hundredth, consider this book your trusted partner.

The Essentials

TOOLS

At an excavation site in Jordan's Black Desert, an archaeologist made a stunning discovery. In addition to two well-preserved structures and stone tools, resting near what was once a firepit, she found the charred remains of a flatbread—evidence that the people who lived in the area more than fourteen thousand years ago were bakers.

The discovery was important for countless reasons, but we mention it here, in the Tools section, as evidence of something else: You don't need fancy tools to make bread. The Natufians, the ancient tribe who likely lived near the archaeologist's site, did not have steam-injected ovens, scales, or a baker's peel—and as a pre-agricultural society, they didn't even have cultivated grains.

And yet they made bread anyway.

The list of must-have tools for breadmaking is short. You likely already have what you *really* need, such as mixing bowls and a wooden spoon; you may already have a good scale and thermometer, two tools we consider essential. As you develop as a baker, you might find you want to add some things to your kit, as the right tool can make things easier and perhaps even more pleasant. But you do not need to "gear up" to make bread successfully at home or to have fun doing so.

Below are some of the tools we find handy. If you do buy anything, we suggest purchasing the best quality you can comfortably afford so that it lasts a long time.

SCALE

A scale makes it easy and convenient to weigh your ingredients, which is the most precise way to bake. Yes, technically you can use measuring cups, but baking by volume can have highly variable results. It may not seem like a few extra tablespoons of water or flour would make a huge difference, but relatively little imprecisions can result in a dough that's too wet and soft to shape, or breads that are dense instead of tender. Because baking by weight is our preference—and the preference of all professional bakers—we consider a scale absolutely imperative. You'll also note that the recipes in this book list the gram amounts for each ingredient first, followed by the volumetric equivalent. If you're measuring flour by volume, you'll have more accuracy if you gently spoon it into a measuring cup, then sweep off any excess.

Bottom line: if you are going to buy one tool you don't already have, it should be a scale. Good scales are not expensive and a scale with a 10-pound capacity is sufficient. The most common kitchen scales often don't register very small amounts (a few grams of salt or yeast, for example). Don't worry about it. You can use volumetric measurements (i.e., ⅛ teaspoon) for those quantities.

MIXING BOWLS/DOUGH RISING BUCKETS

You need something in which to mix your bread dough. This can be a large bowl (made of glass or metal, which are light) or something made of food-grade plastic, often sold as "dough rising buckets." The buckets, which are available in round and square shapes, come with snap-on lids and stack nicely. You can also see into them, which makes it easy to check on the dough as it rises.

LOAF AND PULLMAN PANS

For most of the pan breads in this book, you'll need a sturdy loaf pan with straight edges. We use the standard 8½ × 4½ × 2⅝-inch metal loaf pans, which conduct heat well so your loaves brown evenly. A few recipes, like the Pain de Mie (page 132) and the Tiger Milk Bread (page 169) call for a Pullman loaf pan, which is a metal pan with high, straight sides and comes in two sizes, 9 × 4 × 4-inch (called a half Pullman pan) and 13 × 4 × 4-inch. The Pullman pans have lids, so you can make a perfectly square loaf.

BENCH KNIFE

A bench knife is a dull, flat, straight-edged metal blade, typically 4 to 6 inches wide, with a wooden or plastic handle. It is a baker's best friend. You'll use it to divide dough, transfer ingredients efficiently from one place to another, and scrape your work surface clean, which is essential when kneading by hand.

PLASTIC BOWL SCRAPER

This is just a bendable piece of food-grade plastic that makes scraping every last bit of dough or batter from a bowl a cinch. It's also great for folding dough during bulk fermentation. They're cheap, and while they aren't absolutely vital, once you use one you'll wonder how you ever lived life without it.

LAME

A baker's lame (pronounced *lahm*) is a handle made to hold a metal razor used to score loaves of bread before they're baked (see Scoring, page 46). Some have fixed blades (that can be replaced when they become dull), while other models allow you to use the razor either straight or curved, depending on what kinds of scores you're trying to make. While you could simply use a razor blade to score your loaf (or, in a pinch, a sharp knife), the handle makes it easier to achieve the correct angle and score faster (and cleaner).

SCISSORS

In addition to its more obvious uses, we use a pair of heavy-duty kitchen shears to score seeded breads; a smaller pair is nice for detailed work or cutting rolls.

DIGITAL AND INFRARED THERMOMETERS

Thermometers are another breadmaking tool we consider essential. Use a digital thermometer to check the temperature of the water you're adding to your dough, to monitor the temperature of your dough (and the room!) during bulk fermentation, and to take the guesswork out of determining whether your bread is truly done as it approaches the end of its baking time. An infrared thermometer can be used to gauge the temperature of your baking stone or steel, and can typically read temperatures up to around 1,000°F.

PROOFING BASKETS AND BAKER'S LINEN

Once dough has been shaped, it needs to rise a second time before it's baked. Pan loaves rise directly in the pan, but free-form loaves such as boules require a vessel that can support them vertically; otherwise your loaf will spread outward, resulting in a flatter, denser loaf of bread. Proofing baskets (also called bannetons or brotforms) or baker's linen (also called couches) provide this support. Proofing baskets are available in various sizes; we like the ones that come with a cloth liner because it prevents your formed loaf from sticking to the basket. A 9 × 3-inch round basket is perfect for round boules, and oval proofing baskets that measure 9 × 6 × 3 inches are good for bâtards. You can also make a reasonable facsimile of a round proofing basket with a mixing bowl or colander and a flour-dusted kitchen towel, but a couple of proper proofing baskets will make your life easier.

A baker's linen is a large piece of flax cloth. The cloth is floured, the shaped dough is placed on it, and the cloth is folded to provide support to the rising dough, just as a proofing basket does. The notable difference, of course, is that proofing baskets come in limited shapes and sizes, whereas a baker's linen can be folded in myriad ways to provide support to long, thin loaves, like baguettes, and squat, square loaves, like ciabatta, as well as rolls.

Baker's linens and proofing basket liners should never be washed; simply shake them out to remove the excess flour. If any dough sticks, allow it to dry,

DUSTING A PROOFING BASKET OR COUCHE

The primary purpose of dusting proofing baskets and linens with flour is to prevent sticking. The best tool for dusting baskets is a fine-mesh sieve that applies flour in a slow, even coating. Add flour to the sieve, then drum your fingers on the edge of the sieve so the flour flows through freely. Dust the basket or linen evenly and thoroughly, extending the dusting up the sidewalls of baskets. The application should be just enough to prevent the dough from sticking during proofing, but not so heavy that the finished loaf will be caked with raw flour.

then scrape it off. We recommend storing your couche and proofing basket liners in a zip-top bag in the freezer between uses.

BAKING STONE OR STEEL

A baking stone (made from ceramic) or steel (made from a thick plate of heavy-gauge steel) conducts and holds heat well, transforming a home oven, with its typical hot and cold spots, into something more akin to a hearth, in which heat is distributed evenly. Place the stone or steel in the oven when you preheat it (or at least 30 minutes before baking), so that when you load your unbaked loaves, they get a sudden burst of heat, which aids in oven spring (see page 46). The heat from the stone or steel also helps brown the bottom crust.

Baking stones and steels are also great for pizza and other flatbreads, too. Even breads that are baked in a pan can benefit from the boost of bottom heat a stone or steel provides. (They are also a secret weapon for pies—no soggy bottoms!)

COVERED BAKER

A cast-iron combo cooker or large enameled cast-iron Dutch oven is a useful bread baking vessel, especially if you have a gas oven (see To Bake Hearth Loaves in a Gas Oven, page 51). They conduct heat well and trap the steam that occurs naturally as bread bakes, improving its oven spring (see page 46) and crust. As with baking stones and steels, the covered baker should be preheated along with your oven. For more details on baking in a covered baker, see Baking (page 48).

BAKER'S PEEL AND TRANSFER PEEL

A baker's peel—also known as a pizza peel—is helpful for transferring loaves of bread into and out of the oven. Made of metal or wood with handles of varying lengths, they make it easier to position a loaf on a baking stone or steel without burning your arms and can be used midbake to rotate a loaf for even browning. If you bake in a covered baker (see Baking, page 48), you don't need a peel.

A transfer peel, as the name suggests, helps transfer longer or more elongated loaves, such as baguettes and ficelles, from the baker's linen to the baker's peel or baking stone or steel. These are typically pieces of thin wood about 4 inches wide and 16 inches long. You can make one from a scrap of wood (it doesn't need to be fancy) or a piece of sturdy cardboard.

SHOWER CAPS

The shower cap industry owes a debt to bakers: We use them to cover bowls of dough or loaves of bread as they rise in their proofing baskets. The elasticized edge helps create a nice seal, and unlike plastic wrap, they're reusable. They also keep the air out, which is critical; if you cover rising dough with something permeable, like a towel, you risk the dough drying out and forming a skin, which will inhibit its rise. Of course, if you haven't been to a hotel recently (which is when we typically stock up), you can use a clean nonperforated plastic bag instead.

FINE-MESH SIEVE

We use a metal fine-mesh sieve to dust a fine, even coating of flour in our proofing baskets (see page 17) and a smaller one for dusting the tops of the loaves.

MEASURING SPOONS

Since many scales aren't sensitive enough to register small amounts, you can measure small quantities of ingredients like salt and yeast with measuring spoons.

ROLLING PIN

A straight wooden rolling pin is a useful tool; it's nice to have a smaller one (about 6 inches), which is helpful for rolling out flatbreads, as well as a longer one.

TAPE MEASURE OR RULER

Many of the recipes in this book instruct you to roll your dough to particular dimensions, or to proof it until it rises a certain height above the top of the pan. Use a tape measure or ruler to eliminate guesswork.

WOODEN SPOON OR DOUGH WHISK

When mixing dough by hand, we like to use the handles of sturdy wooden spoons. Why the handle? It mixes efficiently, but because it does not have the surface area of the spoon's bowl, there's less opportunity for the dough to cling to it (which means less cleaning for you). Alternatively, you can use a dough whisk, a flat, circular-ish coil of concentric rings made from stiff wire and attached to a long handle.

RIMMED BAKING SHEETS

Invest in heavy-duty metal sheet pans, which resist warping. The half-sheet pan size (18 × 13 × ¾ inch) is the one we use most commonly (it's perfect for focaccia), but quarter-sheet pans (13 × 9 × ¾ inch) are also incredibly useful; we use them to toast nuts, or as seed trays when coating a loaf.

SHEET PAN COVERS

Also called sheet pan lids, these heavy-duty, reusable plastic covers snap onto sheet pans and are a more sustainable (not to mention more functional) alternative to plastic wrap.

PASTRY BRUSHES

We like pastry brushes with natural bristles and wooden handles for brushing butter or egg wash on the tops of loaves.

PAN SPRAY

Though technically not a tool, pan spray (also called pan release), an aerosolized vegetable oil spray, prevents sticking, and we use it frequently to grease pans and work surfaces.

KEY TECHNIQUES

In the pages that follow, we outline each step of our breadmaking process, explain *why* we do it, and teach you *how* to do it. Every recipe in this book cross-references this section.

MIXING

WHAT IS IT?

Mixing is made up of two essential stages: incorporation of ingredients and dough development. In plainest terms, mixing is the act of combining the bread dough ingredients and stirring them together until you no longer see any bits of dry flour, then working the dough (by hand or machine) until it begins to develop strength.

WHY DO WE DO IT?

Mixing initiates gluten development and builds strength in your dough. Gluten is a protein present in some grains including wheat, barley, and rye. When you mix a grain that contains gluten with water, it kick-starts gluten development by causing the proteins to link. That, in turn, creates a stretchy glutinous web that will trap the gases expelled by the yeast (a single-celled organism that's part of the fungi kingdom). Yeast needs oxygen to reproduce and when it's in the bread dough, where there isn't any oxygen, it stops reproducing. Instead, it starts to eat: Sugar (sucrose and fructose) is its favorite food. If there is sugar in the dough, that's what the yeast eats first; once that's gone, yeast converts the starch in flour into sugar—thus, flour is capable of providing yeast with a continuous food source.

The by-products of this yeast feeding frenzy are carbon dioxide, alcohol, and organic acids. The carbon dioxide released by yeast is trapped in bread dough's elastic web of gluten; think of blowing up a balloon. This is what helps bread rise and makes it light and airy, rather than hard and dense. The alcohol and organic acids, meanwhile, disperse throughout the dough, enhancing baked bread's flavor.

That glutinous web that results from mixing (as well as your choice of flour and how you treat your dough in the steps that follow) also contributes to dough strength. Dough strength is important: It gives your loaves shape and structure. And it all starts with mixing: Once you combine flour and water, the gluten proteins lock together in long chains (think back to your days of linking arms for Red Rover). Mixing initiates gluten development and dough strength building, and these processes continue throughout the breadmaking process, from kneading or folding through bulk fermentation and right up until you shape your loaf.

HOW DO WE DO IT?

Begin by combining the water (and sourdough culture or preferment, if the recipe uses them) and flour (and yeast, if using) in a large bowl (1, 2). It's often easier to incorporate dry ingredients if you add them to the wet,

MIXING BY HAND

MIXING BY MACHINE

because you're less likely to end up with any dry pockets at the bottom or edges of the bowl. If the dough is being mixed by hand, use a flexible bowl scraper, the handle of a wooden spoon, or a dough whisk to mix the flour into the water (3), periodically scraping down the sides and bottom of the bowl until there are no dry spots (4, 5). If the dough is being mixed by machine, the ingredients are combined in the bowl of a stand mixer, then mixed on low speed with the dough hook until combined and no dry flour remains (6).

Once the initial mix is done, the dough sometimes rests for a short period (see Autolyse, page 24), during which time the flour hydrates. Following the rest period, the dough moves on to the second phase of mixing, which is when dough development begins. In this phase, strength is built in the dough in a variety of ways, including kneading (either by hand or by machine).

KNEADING

WHAT IS IT?

Kneading (by hand or machine) is one way to develop dough strength and elasticity.

WHY DO WE DO IT?

Dough strength is achieved through development, whether active or passive. We need a strong dough; it aids a good rise, supports oven spring (see page 46), and affects internal structure and loaf volume.

When you first mix your dough, it will look like a shaggy mass. But with time, kneading, and/or folding, structure begins to develop.

HOW DO WE DO IT?

Turn your dough out onto a lightly floured surface (1). Using your hands, fold the dough back onto itself (2, 3). With the center of your hand, push the dough away from you (4). Turn the dough 90 degrees and repeat (5), flouring the surface as necessary, until the dough is smooth and bounces back when pressed with a floured finger (6).

To knead by machine, combine the ingredients in the bowl of a stand mixer and mix with the dough hook as instructed in the recipe.

We often use a fourth, hybrid approach, in which we allow the dough to sit for an extended time, occasionally folding it (see page 30) to build strength. Folding builds strength in the dough in much the same way kneading by hand or machine does, while also preserving some of the developing open structure that will show up in your baked bread as an open crumb. Folding by hand also allows the baker to actually touch the dough and get a feel for how it's developing; as the dough strengthens, it will feel firmer and less slack.

KNEADING BY HAND

KNEADING BY MACHINE

THE WINDOWPANE TEST

WHAT IS IT?

The windowpane test is one way of assessing your dough's development. As you knead dough, you "exercise" the gluten, both strengthening it and aligning the strands into a complex web. The stronger and more elastic the web is, the more thinly it can stretch without breaking, and the higher your bread will rise. The windowpane test lets you see just how strong and elastic your dough is at any point.

WHEN DO WE DO IT?

The windowpane test is especially useful for doughs that get almost all of their development from kneading (especially kneading in a stand mixer) rather than the passage of time. This includes enriched doughs, such as Japanese Milk Bread (page 165) or Brioche (page 377). Adding butter, sugar, and egg weakens these doughs, so they require a longer kneading time. If they aren't fully developed before shaping, the resulting breads could leak butter or be dense.

HOW DO WE DO IT?

When you think your dough is sufficiently kneaded, grab a piece about the size of a Ping-Pong ball. Flatten it between your fingers. Very gently pull on opposite ends to stretch out the middle.

As you pull, the dough in the center will become thinner and thinner until at some point it tears. This may happen almost immediately (meaning your dough is underdeveloped), or the dough may stretch so far you can see light through it; this is called "achieving the windowpane."

WINDOWPANE TEST

AUTOLYSE

Autolyse is a rest period that takes place after the ingredients are mixed. In a "true" autolyse, only the flour and water in a bread recipe are combined (but, notably, not the sourdough culture/yeast, salt, or any of the other ingredients in the dough), followed by a 20- to 60-minute rest period. After the rest, the remaining ingredients are added and the kneading (or folding) begins.

During this rest period, two enzymes present in flour—protease and amylase—begin their work. The protease enzymes degrade the protein in the flour, which makes the dough more extensible (stretchy). The amylase enzymes turn the flour's starch into sugars that the yeast can consume, starting gluten development and shortening kneading time. Strictly speaking, an autolyse includes just the flour and water in a bread recipe. Salt can tighten the gluten structure, as can the fermentation brought about by the addition of yeast or sourdough culture. Since these ingredients work against the development of extensibility, they are omitted from a true autolyse.

Autolyse also allows the flour to fully hydrate, which is particularly useful when working with whole-grain flour. In whole-grain breads, the rest period softens the bran in the flour. Bran's sharp edges can act like razors in your bread dough, cutting the gluten network and leading to breads that can be dense or less high-rising.

In recipes where we think a rest period benefits the bread, our approach—call it "autolyse light"—calls for mixing all the ingredients together—including the culture and/or yeast, and the salt—until homogenous, and then letting the dough rest for a short time before kneading or folding it. In our testing, we didn't find that holding back yeast, culture, or salt made much of a difference; but giving the dough a rest period, during which time the flour fully hydrates and gluten development begins, did have a notably positive impact on the dough. It also avoids some of the key disadvantages of a "true" autolyse—namely, the challenge of incorporating sourdough culture, salt, and yeast into fully hydrated flour, which can be like trying to mix pancake batter into a brick. The other disadvantage to autolyse: the increased probability that you'll forget to add the salt and yeast altogether. (No one wants unsalted, unleavened loaves!)

When you return to your dough after it has rested, you will notice that it is more workable than it was 20 minutes earlier. Dough that's undergone a rest period *feels* good. It has a soft and yielding strength and is easier to work with.

BULK FERMENTATION OR THE FIRST RISE

WHAT IS IT?

After the dough is mixed, it must sit to get stronger and grow in volume. This is referred to as the first rise, or bulk fermentation.

WHY DO WE DO IT?

As we noted earlier, the by-products of fermentation (that is, the by-products of yeast eating the sugars in dough) are organic acids, which gives the dough flavor and strength, and carbon dioxide, which gives the dough volume and lightness.

HOW DO WE DO IT?

Bulk fermentation is a mostly hands-off process. After mixing the dough and, if the recipe requires it, folding it (see Folding, page 30), the dough is covered and left alone, with some monitoring for temperature (see Maintaining Temperature during Bulk Fermentation, page 29) and some attention to time.

In each recipe we give approximate times for bulk fermentation. These should be considered guidelines: Various factors, such as temperature, humidity, and even the container in which the dough is rising can affect the length of the rise, or bulk fermentation. It's better to use your senses to assess a dough's readiness rather than the clock. At the end of bulk fermentation, your dough should have risen significantly, feel smoother than when you started, and, if you give it a tug, show resistance and elasticity. You can also give the bowl a little shake: A nicely risen, well-aerated dough will jiggle. These are all signs that the dough has fermented sufficiently and is strong enough to be divided and preshaped. An important note: Covering your dough with a draped kitchen towel is not a sufficient cover—your dough will dry out, forming a skin that will inhibit its rise. Use an airtight lid, a shower cap (see page 18), or plastic wrap instead (see The Right Way to Cover Dough and Rising Loaves, page 28).

TEMPERATURE

Temperature is as important to good bread as your ingredients. Dough, as well as sourdough culture (see page 187), is impacted by shifts in temperature. If you've ever watched dough sluggishly rise in a cold kitchen or race along in one that's too warm, then you know how true this can be. When considering temperature, you need to think not only about the air temperature but also about the temperature of the flour, the preferment (see page 193) if the recipe calls for one, and the water you use to mix the dough. You can't control all of these factors, but you can manipulate a few of them, and those manipulations can completely change your bread's outcome.

Bakers use what's called Desired Dough Temperature (DDT), a calculation that takes into consideration these factors, plus something called the "friction factor," which accounts for the heat created when a dough is mixed by either machine or hand. Presuming the ambient temperature of your kitchen, flour, and preferment are all the same—that is, "room temperature"—and challenging to manipulate, the easiest variable to control is the temperature of the water you use in the initial dough mix.

If it's very cold in your kitchen, use warmer water when you mix your bread dough. If it's very hot in your house, use cooler water. The goal is to get the dough to the optimal temperature for the type of bread you're making, and then to *keep it there*.

To determine what temperature water you should add to your dough, see Calculating Desired Dough Temperature (page 27) for the formula. If the idea of precisely calculating DDT feels overwhelming, however, here's the important takeaway: Bread doughs are at their best—ferment properly, rise well, bake up beautifully—when they are at the optimal temperature *at the end of the mixing stage*, and when you *maintain* that temperature all the way from the mix through bulk fermentation. So, in addition to the formula, we offer these at-a-glance guidelines for doughs that are mixed by hand (for doughs mixed by machine for a longer period, like Brioche (page 377) or Japanese Milk Bread (page 165), subtract 5°F to account for the heat generated by mechanical mixing).

Take your air temperature:

If the ambient temperature is 60°F, use 100°F–110°F water.

If the ambient temperature is 65°F, use 95°F–105°F water.

If the ambient temperature is 70°F, use 85°F–95°F water.

If the ambient temperature is 75°F, use 75°F–85°F water.

In general, wheat-based doughs should be between 74°F and 78°F at the end of the mix time. This may sound counterintuitive, given that yeast likes temperatures in the 90°F range. Dough at that temperature would, however, ferment too quickly, at the expense of flavor development. By aiming for a happy medium, you get the best of both worlds: bread with good rise and good flavor. The exception to this general rule is naturally leavened breads made with a high proportion of rye, which benefit from a dough temperature in the 80°F to 86°F range.

If you've used the correct temperature of water relative to the ambient temperature, at the end of mixing your dough should fall in the 74° to 78°F temperature range. But if it doesn't, all is not lost: It simply means that you're going to need to warm (or cool) it for the bulk fermentation. We'll get into this in greater detail later, but in short: Place cool doughs in warmer ambient conditions and consider extending the time of the bulk fermentation. Place warm doughs in a cooler ambient condition (like the fridge) and consider shortening the time of the bulk fermentation.

TIME

Time is the third leg of the three-legged stool of fermentation and, like temperature and the amount and type of leaven, it's a factor that can be controlled by the baker.

In recipes for low-knead, naturally leavened breads (like Pain de Campagne, page 205) that contain relatively little sourdough culture, the length of bulk fermentation is quite long, often overnight. A slow, cold rise (typically an overnight rise in the refrigerator) encourages the yeast to produce acetic and lactic acid, while simultaneously developing the structure of the bread. The more acid, the more flavorful the bread.

For other recipes that rely solely on commercial yeast for rise (or a combination of culture and yeast), like the (Not So) Basic White Sandwich Bread (page 120), the fermentation time may be shorter, because adding commercial yeast introduces more yeast cells (in addition to your culture's wild yeast) to the mix, causing it to rise more quickly. A shorter fermentation means less time for the bacteria to produce the acids that are responsible for flavor (but flavor can be added in other ways, too, including flour choice and add-ins, so a bread that has a shorter fermentation period can still be plenty flavorful). Recipes are designed the way they are for many reasons. Some contain more yeast and longer fermentation; some use sourdough culture and 2 hours of bulk fermentation. There are endless possibilities. All the recipes in this book are formulated for optimal fermentation in the times provided if the baker is also mindful of temperature.

CALCULATING DESIRED DOUGH TEMPERATURE

For many home bakers, simply aiming for dough temperatures of 74°F to 78°F is sufficient. But for bakers looking for a bit more precision, there is a calculation to guide you.

Assume you have a desired dough temperature in mind (see Temperature, page 25). To determine the optimal water temperature, we will multiply your desired DDT by 3 for a straight dough (that is, one made without a preferment; see page 193) and by 4 if using a preferment. The result will be the total temperature factor (TTF). To determine the ideal water temperature, we simply subtract the sum of the known ingredients from the TTF. So:

TTF – (room temperature + flour temperature + preferment temperature) = required water temperature

Here's an example: Suppose you want your dough to end up at 75°F, and that it's a dough made without a preferment. You've used your thermometer to determine the temperature of both your flour and the room (both 65°F) and added those numbers together (130°F). And you've multiplied your Desired Dough Temperature by 3 to get your Total Temperature Factor (225). To figure out what temperature water to use in your mix, all you need to do is simple subtraction: 225 – 130 = 95. To reach the DDT, you'd want to use water that's 95°F when mixing your dough.

The friction factor noted earlier is not a considerable factor when making just a loaf or two of bread by machine, although if the recipe calls for a long machine mix—as in the case of Brioche (page 377) or Japanese Milk Bread (page 165)—you may want to reduce your water temperature by 5°F to account for the heat generated during the longer mix.

THE RIGHT WAY TO COVER DOUGH AND RISING LOAVES

Covering your dough and shaped loaves correctly is an important part of the breadmaking process. For best results, you want to cover rising dough during bulk fermentation with a nonporous, tight-fitting lid that will keep the dough from becoming too cool or developing a skin. Similarly, you want to ensure that rising loaves are well covered, while also leaving room for the dough to expand.

DO

For bowls of rising dough, plastic wrap works fine. Note that if you're using plastic wrap to cover shaped loaves, spray it with pan spray first, then cover the bread with the greased side toward the dough to avoid sticking.

If you want something you can reuse, silicone bowl covers are a good option for bowls of dough, as are shower caps, which you can use to cover both bowls of dough and loaves rising in loaf pans or proofing baskets.

You can also use a large pot lid or a sheet pan over a bowl of proofing dough—just make sure the seal is tight enough to prevent any air movement.

Or you can set the entire bowl of dough (or a shaped loaf or pan of rolls) inside a clean, unscented trash bag, which can be reused multiple times (and then eventually for its intended purpose).

DON'T

Use a towel to cover your dough. The porous material allows heat to escape, causing the dough to lose temperature, and also allows air *in*, drying out your dough and creating a skin that inhibits rising, shaping, and, eventually, baking. The result? Poorly fermented dough that bakes up as squat, dense bread.

MAINTAINING TEMPERATURE DURING BULK FERMENTATION

For optimal dough (and optimal bread), you want to control the dough temperature during bulk fermentation, just as you did during the mixing phase. If, for example, you take your dough's temperature at the end of the mixing phase (we suggest doing so, using a digital thermometer) and discover that it's a bit cooler or warmer than is optimal (74°F to 78°F), there are several ways to bring it to the right temperature:

TO WARM UP COOL DOUGH

Put your rising dough near a radiator or stove, on the top of the fridge (surprisingly warm!), or the inside of your (turned off) oven with the oven light on. Or you might spin your dryer (empty) for a couple minutes to warm it up, then turn it off and pop your container of dough inside.

Place your rising dough on a heating pad (set on low), in a temperature-controlled proofing box, or in your microwave, with a cup of steaming water tucked in beside it (a homemade proofing box!).

You may have heard that wrapping your bowl of dough in a towel or blanket will warm it up. A sweet idea, tucking in your dough baby like that, but while it will help to slow heat dissipation from your dough, the dough itself generates little heat, and if your room is cold the dough will eventually cool down, too.

TO COOL DOWN WARM DOUGH

With a too-cool dough, you're doing whatever you can to encourage it along. But with a too-warm dough, you want to prevent it from racing along, developing too much volume, and overproofing before it's had time to develop the structure and flavor that comes from controlled bulk fermentation.

Find a cool spot for your dough, such as the steps to your basement (if you have one) or near an open window.

Place the dough in a cooler lined with ice packs.

Popping your dough into the fridge will work, too, but fridges are very cold—usually about 37°F, and it'll slow fermentation dramatically, so we suggest you only do it for the first 30 minutes of bulk fermentation, then return the dough to room temperature for the remainder of the time.

FOLDING

WHAT IS IT?
Folding is a technique used to add strength to the dough during the first rise or bulk fermentation.

WHY DO WE DO IT?
Folding the dough during bulk fermentation is a gentle way to develop the gluten network and add strength to the dough; a strong gluten network helps ensure a bread that has good structure and shape.

HOW DO WE DO IT?
In many of the recipes in this book, the instructions will indicate that you should "fold" the dough during the bulk fermentation. It will specify either "bowl folds" or "coil folds." Typically, a recipe will instruct you to perform folds every 15 or so minutes for the first hour of bulk fermentation. With each successive round of folding, you'll see the dough transform from something shaggy and soft to something that's smoother, tighter, and noticeably stronger. Perform the rounds of folding at the intervals specified in the recipe (don't worry if you're a few minutes late—it's not that time-sensitive), but also use your senses to determine if your dough is ready for preshaping. After all the prescribed folds, one way to check the strength of your dough is to grab a piece of it and gently stretch. If it tears easily, the dough may still be a bit weak (another way to say that the gluten is still underdeveloped), and would benefit from another round or two of folding.

BOWL FOLD

BOWL FOLD

With wet hands, reach into the bowl, grab the underside of a section of dough, and gently stretch it upward until you begin to feel resistance (1), then fold it over the top of the mass of dough (2). Rotate the bowl 90 degrees (a quarter-turn) and repeat until you've done a full rotation, then turn the dough over so the folds are underneath.

With wet hands, reach under the dough and gently stretch the middle upward until the dough releases from the bowl or pan (1). Roll it forward off your hands, allowing it to fold over (or "coil") onto itself (2). Rotate the bowl or pan 90 degrees (a quarter-turn) and repeat (3). Continue performing this folding action until the dough feels like it won't stretch and elongate easily, usually four to five times.

COIL FOLD

DIVIDING AND PRESHAPING

WHAT IS IT?

Dividing, which takes place after bulk fermentation, is the act of cutting one large piece of dough into two (or more) equal pieces. Preshaping is the step that comes after dividing the dough but before the final shaping into a loaf. It's used to bring any small pieces of dough together into one and form a smooth skin on the outside of the dough piece.

WHY DO WE DO IT?

Dividing dough into smaller pieces makes it more manageable (and helps us achieve the final bread shape we desire). Preshaping adds strength to the dough, removes any large gas bubbles that may remain after fermentation, and gives dough uniformity, which will, in turn, support good final shaping. The most common preshaped form is a loose ball, or what bakers refer to as a "round." The preshape can also be long or tubular. In general, the preshape will mimic the bread's final shape in nature. For example, a round preshape for round or oval loaves, and a tubular preshape for baguettes. After a rest of 10 to 15 minutes, most preshaped doughs will be ready for final shaping.

On a lightly floured surface, gently pat the dough to remove any large bubbles, then stretch the outside edges of the dough slightly away from its center (1). Next, fold the edges of the dough back to its center (2), working your way around the entire dough piece in five or six sections, and press down to gently seal. You will notice that the motion is not unlike the folding motion performed during bulk fermentation (see Folding, page 30). Set the preshaped dough to rest on a lightly floured surface, seam side down (3) and covered to prevent a skin from forming, and let it rest for 10 to 15 minutes before shaping.

PRESHAPE A
ROUND

PRESHAPE A TUBE ··

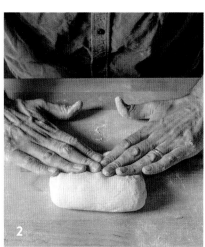

On a lightly floured surface, gently pat the dough to remove any large bubbles and stretch it into a rough round. Next, fold the sides toward the middle, pressing down to lightly seal (1). Beginning with the top edge, fold the dough one-third of the way toward the edge closest to you and pat again to seal (2). Repeat this process two times, sealing as you go. Set the dough to rest on a lightly floured surface, seam side down (3) and covered to prevent a skin from forming, and let it rest for 10 to 15 minutes before shaping.

PRESHAPE A
TUBE

SHAPING

WHAT IS IT?

Shaping is the act of forming the dough by hand into its final shape.

WHY DO WE DO IT?

When you shape bread dough, you're making it the basic shape of the bread you want to bake. You're also developing surface tension, which gives the loaf more volume and an even exterior.

HOW TO SHAPE A BOULE

Shaping a round boule is similar to the preshaping process for a round:

Begin with a preshaped round of dough that has relaxed for 10 to 15 minutes. Place seam side up on a lightly floured surface.

Pull the edges of the round of dough upward and outward slightly (1), then fold toward the center (2, 3), pressing gently to seal (4). Repeat this process, working your way around the entire round until the dough tightens noticeably.

When you've made your way around the dough, flip it seam side down (5).

Using cupped hands and keeping them in contact with the work surface, wrap your hands gently around the side of the dough farthest from you and gently drag the dough toward your body (6). The dough should slightly stick to the work surface; the resulting tension should tuck the dough under the mass. If the dough slides instead of sticking slightly,

SHAPE A BOULE

scrape some of the flour off your work surface or wipe your work surface with a damp towel and try again.

Repeat the dragging two to three times (7, 8); avoid the inclination to overwork the dough. If tears or small rips appear, stop—you've reached the stretching capacity of the dough.

Place seam side up in a proofing basket (see page 16).

HOW TO SHAPE A BÂTARD

The bâtard shape is an elliptical form, longer than a boule but shorter (and much wider) than a baguette.

Begin with a preshaped round of dough that has relaxed for 10 to 15 minutes. With the seam side up, on a lightly floured surface, pat it into a thick rectangle with one of the long sides facing you. Fold in the sides, overlapping them slightly (1, 2).

Using both hands like paddles, with your fingers pointed toward each other, fold the top of the dough down just a bit at the top to begin a small roll (3), pressing the seam to seal with your fingers (4).

Next, use both hands to begin rolling the dough down toward your body (5), using both thumbs to press the dough into itself (6) and tuck the ends in as you roll the dough along until it has been formed into a long cylinder (7). Beginning in the middle of the form and applying gentle pressure, roll your hands outward toward the ends of the dough, elongating and tapering it slightly as you go. Repeat until the dough is the desired length, pinch the ends closed, then place seam side up in an oval proofing basket (8, 9).

SHAPE A
BÂTARD

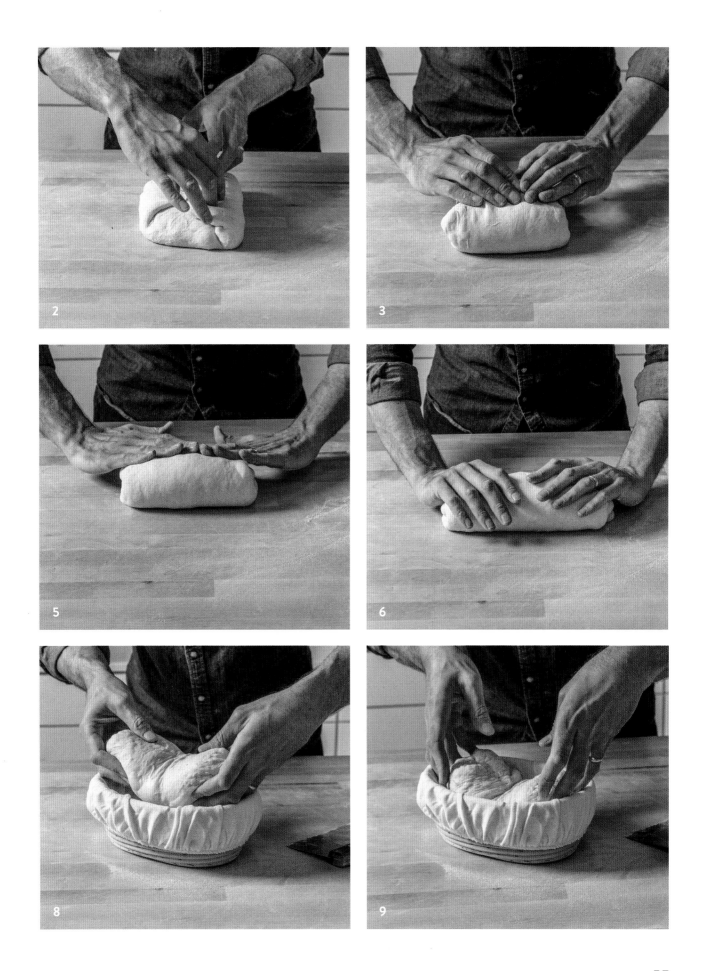

HOW TO SHAPE PAN LOAVES

The pan loaf is the most forgiving to shape and therefore easiest for the beginner. Doughs that are baked in a pan are generally lower in total hydration. Less hydration (less water) means dough releases from your hands and the shaping surface more easily, and as it will rise and bake in a pan, the dough has the support of the vessel.

Begin with a preshaped round of dough that has relaxed for 10 to 15 minutes. Place it seam side up on a lightly floured surface and pat gently to remove any bubbles that formed during the rest period (1), then pat into a 12 × 8-inch rectangle with a long side facing you (2). Fold the short sides of the rectangle into the center (3), overlapping them slightly and pressing gently to seal (4), then gently flatten with your palm.

Beginning with the side farthest from you, fold the dough one-third of the way toward you and pat gently to seal (5).

Next, fold the dough down half of the way toward you and press gently to seal (6).

Finally, fold the dough toward you once more, all the way to the edge of the dough closest to you (7). Roll the loaf seam side up and pinch the seam to seal (8), then roll the loaf gently to even it out and place in the prepared loaf pan, seam side down (9).

SHAPE A
PAN LOAF

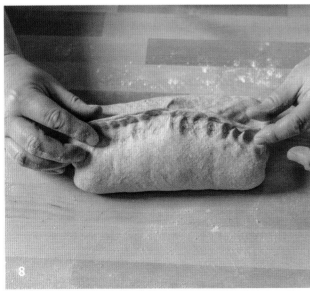

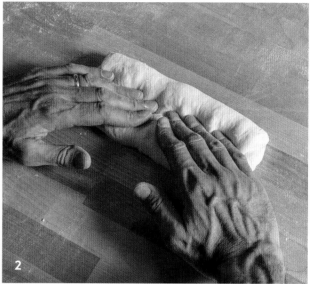

HOW TO SHAPE BAGUETTES

Begin with a preshaped tube of dough that has relaxed for 10 to 15 minutes. Start by flattening the preshaped dough into a rectangle (1). With a long side facing you, and starting at the edge farthest from you, fold the dough two-thirds of the way toward yourself along the long, east-west axis, then press gently to seal (2).

Turn the dough 180 degrees and repeat the fold: Take the edge of dough farthest from you and fold two-thirds of the way down, pressing gently to seal. At this point, the dough piece should be 6 to 8 inches in length.

Next, fold the dough in half along the long, east-west axis, bringing the far side to the edge nearest to you (3). Press gently to seal either with your fingertips or the heel of your palm. During this process, the dough will naturally elongate slightly.

SHAPE A
BAGUETTE

Now it's time to roll. Beginning in the middle of the tubular dough piece with the seam side down, roll the dough back and forth with a cupped hand (4). At first, the shape will look like a dog bone, with a thin middle and thicker ends. This is normal.

Next, starting in the center of the narrow middle section, bring both hands in and roll gently back and forth, moving your hands outward toward the tips as you do so (5, 6), evening out the high spots while in motion; the dough should be 15 to 17 inches long. (If your baking stone or steel is smaller, you can roll the baguettes a bit shorter so they'll fit on the stone or steel.)

Once you reach the end of the dough piece, apply a slight amount of pressure to taper the ends between your palms and the work surface (7).

Once shaped (8), loaves should be placed seam side up on a lightly dusted baker's linen or couche (see page 17) to rise before baking.

Note: If, when you go to shape, you feel like the dough is fighting you, resisting the elongation process, give it a few more minutes to further relax and then try again. A good baguette should be coaxed, not forced.

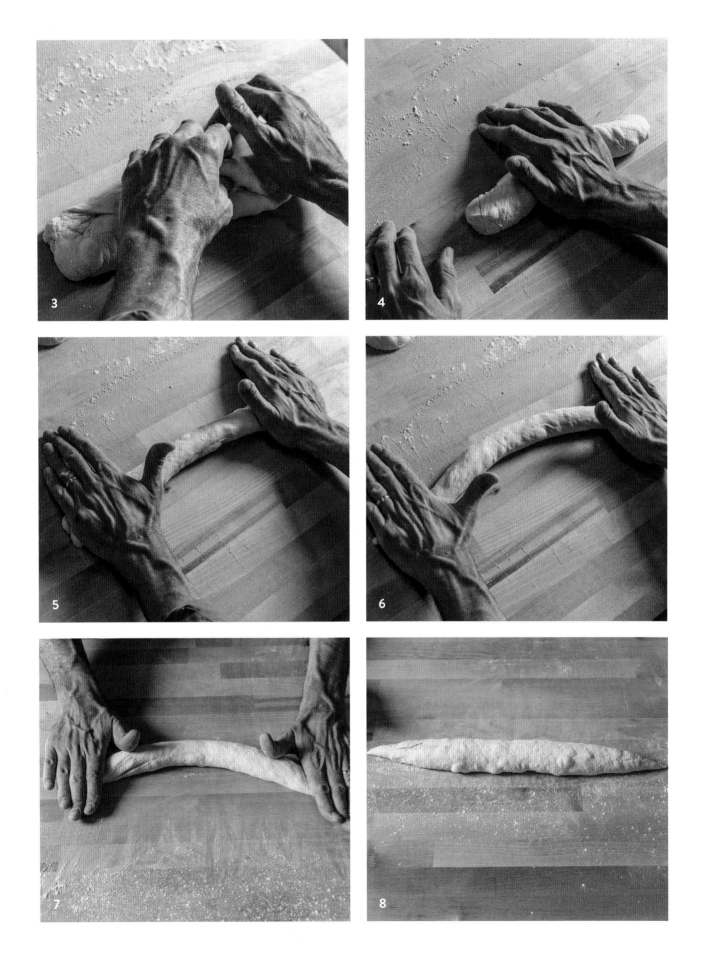

HOW TO SHAPE ROLLS

Rolls may be shaped using the same steps used to shape larger pieces of dough. You may make tiny boules, short bâtards, or miniature baguettes (see Petits Pains, page 341).

For a classic round roll, begin by dividing the dough, then preshape each portion into rounds (1, 2). Place seam side down on an unfloured work surface and using a cupped hand, roll each piece of dough against the work surface to tighten the round and develop surface tension (3, 4, 5). (If your roll is sliding instead of catching on the surface, scrape off any excess flour and wipe the work surface with a damp towel and continue.)

Shaped rolls (6) can rise in pans, on flour-dusted baker's linen, or on parchment-lined baking sheets. Cover to protect the dough from drying out.

SHAPE
ROLLS

PROOFING

Bread recipes typically call for two rises, or proofs: The first is the bulk fermentation when the dough rises in the bowl (we talk about how to assess the proof at the beginning of the section on bulk fermentation on page 25). The second rise takes place after the dough has been shaped, such as when a pan bread proofs directly in the loaf pan, or a hearth loaf in a proofing basket. While you have some wiggle room with the first rise, the timing of the second rise needs to be more accurate to get a nice full loaf. If baked before it's fully proofed, the bread will have a constricted crumb structure. If the dough is over-proofed, the loaf might collapse in the oven, resulting in a loaf with a dense, gummy center, or a pan loaf with a large gap between crust and crumb.

We give a time range for both the first and second rises, but because kitchen conditions can vary, time isn't always the best way to measure your dough's readiness. The water temperature (see Temperature, page 25) used to make the dough, the temperature and humidity in the room where it's rising, the size of dough pieces, the vessel holding it, and how it was shaped all impact the rise. With so many variables in play, think of the times provided in a recipe as a guideline rather than a hard and fast rule. Getting to know the look and feel of proofed dough will be your key to successfully nailing both rises.

HOW TO KNOW WHEN BREAD IS PROPERLY PROOFED AND READY TO BE BAKED

BREADS BAKED IN LOAF PANS

We recommend baking once the dough has reached 1 inch over the lip of the pan at the center of the loaf. Don't guess—measure. Use a ruler to check your dough periodically to ensure your dough isn't under- or overproofed (and make sure that you're using the size of loaf pan specified in the recipe). You can also combine this measurement with the poke test (see below).

FREE-FORM BREADS SUCH AS ROLLS, BOULES, OR BÂTARDS (AND FOR PAN LOAVES, TOO!)

Use the poke test: Lightly flour your finger and poke the dough down about ½ inch. If the indent slowly starts to fill in, it's ready to bake. If it pops back out quickly, give it a bit more time. (If the indent remains, it's a sign that your dough may be overproofed—get it into the oven as soon as possible!) Start poke-testing your dough toward the beginning of the rise-time window specified in the recipe. If the temperature and humidity in your kitchen are high, it's likely your dough will rise faster than you expect. On the flip side, expect longer rise times when the air is cold and dry. Either way, testing early is better than missing your ideal window. Properly proofed bread dough will feel light, almost marshmallowy. For dough that's proofing in a proofing basket, you can also lift the proofing basket and give it a mild shake; the dough should wobble gently.

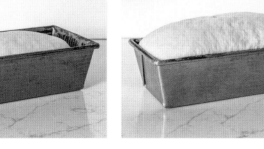

UNDERPROOFED   PERFECTLY PROOFED   OVERPROOFED

SCORING

WHAT IS IT?

Scoring is the act of making light cuts on the surface of proofed loaves just before baking.

WHY DO WE DO IT?

Scoring is both decorative and functional. According to legend, in the days when loaves from many households were baked in communal ovens, scoring was used for identification, like an edible name tag. But loaves weren't then (and aren't now) only scored for decoration. Scoring also has an essential function: It allows the bread to continue to rise in the oven, and directs that rising. If you don't score your loaf, it won't rise fully and properly, and will be dense, with a constricted interior structure (what bakers call "alveolar structure"). Scoring is not (usually) necessary in pan loaves, because the pan itself provides structure, allowing the bread to rise in a more controlled way.

It works like this: When we put bread into a preheated oven, the fermentation process speeds up, quickly producing gases (and expanding gases already present in the dough) that push against the taut surface of the bread created during shaping. This is called "oven spring." If we don't score the loaf, and there is adequate strength when the loaf goes into the oven, the bread will likely burst in a weak spot and create an unsightly rupture. Scoring helps direct and control where those ruptures occur, so gas can escape and allow the dough to continue to rise, resulting in a bread with a nice crumb structure.

SCORING
A BÂTARD

SCORING A
BOULE

HOW DO WE DO IT?

Scoring takes some practice. You want to score deeply and quickly enough to cleanly cut through the dough's surface, but not so deep that you're pressing hard on the dough, potentially degassing it. Once you begin cutting, you need to cut decisively, pulling the razor through to make a clean cut. Most bread bakers score the dough with a baker's lame (see Tools, page 16) or very sharp knife. You can make utilitarian cuts or elaborate decorative ones; that's up to you. Straight blades are ideal for straight cuts, while curved blades are best for scoring to produce what's called an "ear," which is a flap of dough that lifts up from the bread, becoming deliciously browned and crusty.

If using a straight blade, hold it perpendicular to the surface of the dough and slash with speed and purpose. If using a curved blade, hold the blade at a 30-degree angle to the surface of the dough and make a cut using the corner of the blade; the angling will prevent the back corner of the blade from dragging as you cut. Aim for a cut ¼ to ½ inch deep; if your score is too shallow, the cut might fuse together in the oven before the loaf has the chance to rise to its full potential.

If scoring a loaf with lots of add-ins or crust treatments, such as grains, seeds, or fruit, it can be easier to use a pair of scissors to make cuts in the surface of the dough. If you're new to scoring, it makes sense to stick to simple, more functional slashes. But as you get to know your dough and have a feel for scoring, you might try more elaborate designs, such as those on the facing page.

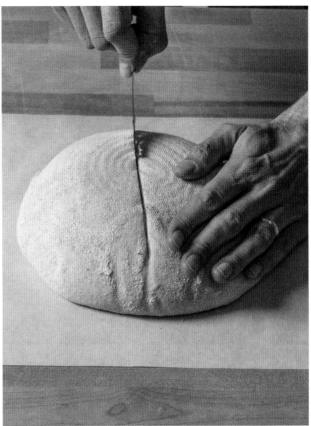

Different Ways to Score Your Bread

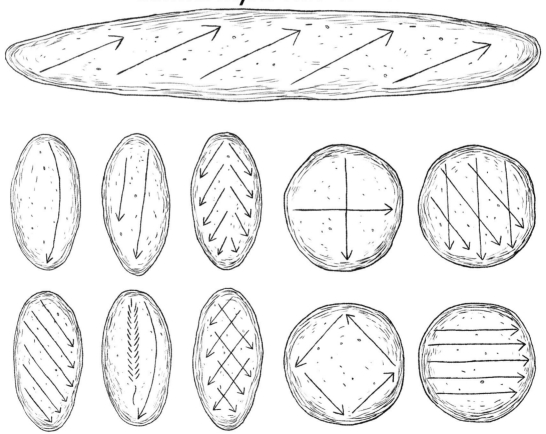

BAKING

Professional bakeries achieve enviable golden, crusty hearth breads with ovens that have special features like steam-injection capabilities and rotating racks that make baking beautiful bread easy. Obviously, home ovens don't have those same trappings, but there are a few tricks that make a home oven more like a professional one:

BAKING STONE OR STEEL

Place a baking stone or steel on the center rack for an hour while preheating the oven: It conducts heat well and replicates the hot oven floor of a deck oven (an oven with a solid heated floor or "deck" on which loaves are baked directly). Unglazed masonry tiles do the trick here, too. When your loaves are loaded onto the baking stone or steel, steam can be added to the oven using one of the methods described in the Steaming section (page 50).

COVERED BAKER

Use a covered baker with a well-fitted lid; cast-iron Dutch ovens work well, but you can also use two-piece vessels made of cast iron or ceramic that are specifically made for baking bread. Place the pot and its lid in the oven while it's preheating. Cast-iron holds heat well, and the lid traps steam generated by the baking bread, which aids with oven spring (see page 46) and helps give your loaf a crisp crust. Toward the end of the bake time, the lid is removed to promote crust browning.

HYBRID METHOD

If you don't have a Dutch oven but want to trap more steam around your bread, you can also try a hybrid approach: Load your bread directly onto a baking stone or steel and then invert a heatproof bowl over it for all or a portion of the bake time. This will help capture the steam generated by your loaf. As with the Dutch oven, the bowl can be removed at the end of the baking time in order to brown the crust more deeply.

STEAMING

WHAT IS IT?

The act of introducing moisture to the oven while your bread bakes.

WHY DO WE DO IT?

Steam is critical for achieving expansive, open-crumbed loaves with a golden, crisp crust. If you bake bread in a dry oven, the crust quickly sets, which prevents the dough from expanding to its full potential, leading to loaves with a denser crumb. If you introduce steam at the start of the bake, the crust remains moist and pliable and the loaf can stretch and expand before the crust sets, resulting in a lighter, more open crumb.

Steam also helps gelatinize starches on the loaf's exterior. That helps it brown and creates an especially crispy, flavorful, and shiny loaf.

Note: While steam is necessary for some types of loaves, particularly crusty hearth loaves, there are times when you don't want—or need—to add steam, such as when you're baking loaves with an egg wash, or when you want a bread with a soft and tender crust (like most of the loaves in the Pan Breads chapter, pages 119 to 182).

HOW DO WE DO IT?

To steam your oven, set a large cast-iron skillet below your baking stone or steel when you preheat the oven. Take care not to set the pan directly below the bread, but rather a little to the side so that the steam can rise and doesn't just hit the bottom of the stone or steel. After you load your bread into the oven, immediately pour a cup or so of warm water into the preheated cast-iron skillet and quickly close the door so the steam doesn't escape. (If you don't have a cast-iron skillet, you can pick up some lava rocks at your local hardware store and set the lava rocks in a 9- or 10-inch cake pan, preheat as described above, then pour water directly onto the lava rocks. Both methods work equally well. If you use the cake pan, consider an old or used one because the heat and water may cause it to warp.)

Note: Now that we've convinced you of the merits of steam, some bad news. If you have a gas oven, it's very hard to add sufficient steam. By design, gas ovens vent out effluence, meaning whatever steam you add is very quickly vented out of the oven chamber. But all is not lost; there is a workaround.

TO BAKE HEARTH LOAVES IN A GAS OVEN

Use a preheated covered baker, such as a Dutch oven. The lidded vessel traps the steam that escapes from the loaf as it bakes, becoming a kind of self-steaming oven. Slip a few ice cubes between the parchment beneath your loaf and the pan to give the loaf an extra initial burst of steam. Don't skip the parchment—otherwise the extra water from the melting ice may cause your bread to stick to the pot.

Most of the loaves in this book that would benefit from steam can also be made in a covered baker; the most notable exceptions are baguettes (pages 259 to 263) and some of the buns and rolls in the Buns, Bagels & Rolls chapter (pages 283 to 350). That doesn't mean you can't bake these breads at home if you have a gas oven; it just means that you need to manage your expectations for how they'll turn out, likely with a softer, more matte crust and a denser interior.

BAKER'S MATH:
IT ISN'T JUST FOR PROS

For home bakers, especially beginning home bakers, baker's math (aka baker's percentages) can seem confusing at first. But in professional baking it's lingua franca, and understanding it will make you a better baker.

Baker's math is a ratio system. All ingredients are expressed as a percentage of the flour. The total weight of flour is always treated as 100%, and all the other ingredients are a ratio of that. Baker's math allows you to think about dough as a formula, rather than a recipe. Note that the total is always going to be more than 100% because the ratio is constructed around flour, which is always 100%. This is the part of baker's math that throws people off.

While ingredient amounts change with different batch sizes, the ratios—that is, the relationship among the flour, water, salt, yeast, and other ingredients—will always remain the same.

Here's an example of a simple formula using baker's percentages:

INGREDIENT	%	WEIGHT
FLOUR	100%	1,000 GRAMS
WATER	66%	660 GRAMS
SALT	2%	20 GRAMS
YEAST	1.2%	12 GRAMS

How did we arrive at these numbers? Well, remember that flour is 100%. In the example above, the flour weighs 1,000 grams. To determine the percentage of the other ingredients, we divide each one by the weight of the flour (1,000 grams), then multiply the result (which is in decimal form) by 100 to convert it to a percent.

So, in the example at left, for the water: we divided 660 grams by 1,000 grams, which is 0.66. We multiplied that by 100 to get the percentage, 66%. We followed the same formula for the salt and yeast. Salt: 20 grams ÷ 1,000 grams = 0.02 × 100, or 2%. Yeast: 12 grams ÷ 1,000 grams = 0.012 × 100, or 1.2%.

Baker's math is indispensable for scaling recipes up or down. For example, if you wanted to triple the batch above, you'd first triple the flour amount to 3,000 grams, and then calculate the other ingredients based on the percentages. To determine the water, you'd multiply the total flour weight by 66%: 3,000 grams × 0.66 = 1,980 grams water. For salt, the calculation would be 3,000 × 0.02 = 60 grams. And for yeast, it would be 3,000 × 0.012 = 36 grams.

Baker's math is also a useful tool for assessing the characteristics of a dough at a glance, and for troubleshooting. If you routinely calculate the percentage of hydration (see Hydration, page 54) in a bread dough, you will have a benchmark for how an 80% hydration dough looks, feels, and behaves. If you're mixing an 80% hydration dough and it has a different texture than you're accustomed to, you'll know something is off.

Important things to remember about baker's math:

FLOUR IS ANY type of flour used in the recipe, including all-purpose, bread flour, whole wheat, rye flour, '00', even gluten-free flour. Rolled oats and other flaked products, such as rye chops, and cracked grains, such as corn grits, are generally not categorized as flour. Nor is sugar.

WHEN CALCULATING hydration, the primary baker's math consideration is the amount of water in the recipe, or other liquids that contain a majority portion of water, such as milk, coffee, or wine. While it's true that many ingredients (such as eggs or oil) will change a dough's consistency, when we calculate hydration we do not include those ingredients in the total (see more about calculating and adjusting hydration on page 54). Fats—even liquid fats, like oil or melted butter—are not considered when calculating hydration. They simply don't contain significant quantities of water, a key requirement for gluten formation. The same goes for liquid sweeteners (like honey or maple syrup).

INGREDIENTS SUCH as honey and syrup, butter, or oats or seeds can (and should) still be expressed in a ratio by calculating them against the flour weight. Using a dough example with 1,000 grams flour: If our recipe calls for 40 grams of honey, the percentage of honey in baker's math is 4% (40 divided by 1,000 = 0.04 ×100 = 4%). If a recipe uses a preferment (see page 193), you have to take into account the flour and water amounts in the preferments when you're calculating total flour and hydration. You do not, however, have to account for the flour and water used in the culture you might add to a preferment because it's such a small amount.

INCLUSIONS, SUCH as nuts or dried fruit, aren't considered a part of the "formula," and the decision to include them is ultimately guided by flavor preferences. But it's helpful to think about the functional impact of the ingredients that you add. There's a sweet spot where the ingredients support the flavor without weighing down the bread's structure too much. With denser breads, the percentage of add-ins like dried fruit and nuts can go quite high (up to 40%), but with more open-crumbed breads, structure will be compromised if you add too much stuff. A good rule of thumb is the percentage of the additions should be between 20% and 30% of the total flour weight.

FOR "SOAKERS" (presoaked quantities of water and grain sometimes included in a recipe), break out the amount of water used in a soaker, rather than group it with the water used to mix the final dough. It is still considered part of the total hydration.

HYDRATION

In breadmaking, hydration refers to the total quantity of moisture in a bread dough. Hydration affects doughs at every step of the breadmaking process, from how we mix and develop strength to how we fold, shape, and even bake. Water in bread dough enables fermentation, hydrates starches and proteins, and positively impacts texture, flavor, and crumb. If you understand hydration, you'll bake better bread.

High ratios of water, when combined with active fermentation and good gluten development (through time, mixing, and folds), have the potential to significantly open the crumb (or the "alveolar structure") of loaves. Strong, wet doughs spring well in the oven, forming nice "ears" and, if given time in cold fermentation, a blistered crust. But for many, the most coveted feature of high-hydration loaves is their dramatically open crumb or alveolar structure. In other words, it's all about the holes.

We quantify a dough's hydration by using a ratio found by dividing the total weight of water by the total weight of flour in a given recipe (for more on this, see Baker's Math, page 52).

The ratio of the two numbers (water to flour), written as a percentage, mathematically expresses what is referred to as hydration. High hydration refers to doughs that are often in excess of 80% hydration. In some cases, hydration may actually exceed 100% due to the thirsty needs of high-protein or whole-grain flours (such as bread flour or whole wheat flour). Knowing hydration is like checking the weather before setting out on a road trip. It prepares you for the conditions ahead. Bakers often refer to high-hydration doughs, or doughs that have more water than flour, like the Pan de Cristal (page 330), as "slack," because it presents as, well, slack and sticky. Slack doughs usually require some adjustments in how they're handled, from the type of folds used during fermentation to the way the loaves are shaped and moved.

At the other end of the spectrum are doughs that fall around 60% hydration, which would be considered low-hydration or "stiff." A stiff dough may require less folding or other handling during fermentation.

Let's look at an example recipe:

Flour: 1,000 grams

Water: 750 grams

Salt: 20 grams

Yeast: 10 grams

In the recipe above, the water is 750 grams and flour is 1,000 grams, so the total hydration of the dough is 750 ÷ 1,000, or 75%.

Another example: If a recipe has the same weight of flour and water (let's say 750 grams of each), then the hydration would be 100%.

To be accurate in your calculation of hydration, make sure to account for all the liquid in a recipe, including any water that is used in a preferment (see page 193) or soaker (presoaked grain) if that recipe calls for either, or both.

Other ingredients that contain significant water content, however, such as eggs or fresh fruit, are typically not considered as part of the hydration percentage in breadmaking. But that doesn't mean they shouldn't be considered at all; it's useful to think about the functional impacts of each of these ingredients as well.

For example, in baker's math terms, Brioche Dough (page 377) is often 50% butter, 50% whole eggs, and 10% water or milk. While the hydration percentage looks extremely low—too low to even hydrate the flour, yeast, or sugar—the dough still works beautifully. Why? Because the eggs are roughly 75% water, and the butter also contains around 18% water.

The way hydration is calculated doesn't change with flour types. So, 1,000 grams of flour and 750 grams of water will always be 75% hydration;

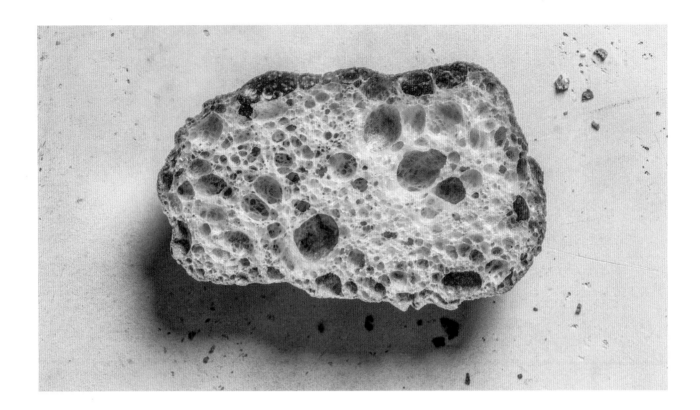

it doesn't matter if the flour is rye, whole wheat, buckwheat, or gluten-free. However, whole-grain flours are "thirstier," and doughs made with whole-grain flours typically require more water. As a result, a dough made with all-purpose flour and hydrated at 75% will feel significantly softer than an equally hydrated whole wheat dough.

For flour percentages, the best practice is to only include the milled product of grains. While cocoa powder, dry milk powder, potato flour, freeze-dried fruit powders, and other ingredients do absorb water from the dough, we do not consider them as part of the flour percentage. But, as with water content in eggs, do always consider the impact of any ingredient on hydration.

If your bread comfort zone revolves around sturdy pan loaves, flatbreads, or enriched breads, you may find higher-hydration doughs take some getting used to, but they are worth the practice. Often sticky, these doughs benefit from a delicate touch and may require new techniques, like folding rather than kneading (see Folding, page 30) and loose shaping. They also require multiple hours between the

preferment, extended bulk fermentation (see page 29), and cool overnight rise, and, often, longer bake times.

Lower-hydration doughs include loaves that look better with definition (such as challah), bagels, pretzels, or even a structured sandwich loaf that you don't want full of holes: The comparatively closed crumb structure and toothy chew of a lower-hydration dough is sometimes exactly what you want.

Hydration is one of the dials that a baker can adjust at any point. It's something that professional bakers tweak in small degrees while mixing, adding a little water if a dough feels "thirsty" or holding some back if necessary, depending on the season (flour traps more moisture in humid weather) or flour composition (see the earlier note about whole-grain flours being thirstier).

Flatbreads

FOCACCIA

MIX	BULK FERMENTATION	SHAPE	BAKE
5 MIN	2 HOURS	30 MIN	23–36 MIN

TIME: ABOUT 3 HOURS

MAKES ONE 18 × 13-INCH FOCACCIA

735 grams (6 cups plus 2 tablespoons) unbleached all-purpose flour

510 grams (2¼ cups) warm water (see Temperature, page 25)

37 grams (3 tablespoons) olive oil, plus more for the pan and drizzling

16.5 grams (2¾ teaspoons) fine salt

6 grams (2 teaspoons) instant yeast

Flaky sea salt, such as Maldon, for sprinkling

This simple recipe for focaccia can be made easily in an afternoon and yields a sheet pan of wonderfully plush, tender, open-crumbed bread with a golden, bubbly crust. For the crispiest crust, use a generous amount of olive oil, both in the pan and drizzled on top, and sprinkle with coarse salt before baking. Though this focaccia is flavorful enough to stand alone, it also can be used to make a supreme sandwich. If you want to add toppings to your focaccia (such as cherry tomatoes, olives, fresh herbs, or thinly sliced onions), add them to the dimpled dough just before baking.

MAKE THE DOUGH: In a large bowl, combine the flour, water, olive oil, salt, and yeast and mix with the handle of a wooden spoon until no dry spots remain; the dough will be shaggy and sticky (see Mixing, page 20).

Bulk fermentation or the "first rise" (see page 25) will take 2 hours. During that time, you'll tend to the dough four times (directions follow), folding the dough every 15 minutes for the first hour. Then the dough will rest, covered and undisturbed, for the final hour.

BULK FERMENT THE DOUGH: Once you've mixed the dough, cover and let stand for 15 minutes. Using a wet hand, perform 8 to 10 bowl folds (see Bowl Fold, page 30), or until the dough resists stretching. Cover and let rest 15 minutes, then repeat the bowl folds. As you perform the folds, you'll notice the dough smooth out, gain strength, and become more elastic. Cover and let rest another 15 minutes. Repeat the bowl folds, cover, and let rest 15 minutes more. Repeat the bowl folds one final time (for a total of four times). Cover and let rest until the dough has increased significantly in volume and is very puffy and marshmallowy, about 1 hour.

Arrange racks in the upper and lower third of the oven and preheat the oven to 450°F. Generously oil an 18 × 13-inch rimmed baking sheet.

SHAPE THE DOUGH: Using a plastic bowl scraper, gently ease the dough out of the bowl onto the prepared pan and turn to coat with oil. Cover and let stand for 30 minutes. Using your fingertips, dimple the dough, pressing it evenly into the pan and all the way to the corners. If the dough resists stretching, re-cover and let rest 15 minutes longer so the gluten can relax. Drizzle a few tablespoons of oil over the top of the focaccia, then sprinkle with coarse salt.

BAKE THE FOCACCIA: Bake on the lower rack for 22 to 24 minutes, rotating the pan front to back halfway through. After 22 to 24 minutes, turn the oven to broil and move the pan to the upper rack and broil until the top is deeply browned, 1 to 2 minutes, keeping a close eye on it so it doesn't burn.

Slide the focaccia out of the pan and let cool on a wire rack. Transfer to a cutting board and cut into squares. Focaccia is best eaten the same day it's baked. Store leftovers well wrapped at room temperature; reheat in a low oven.

FOCACCIA DI RECCO

MIX	SHAPE	BAKE
25 MIN	20 MIN	20–24 MIN

········ TIME: ABOUT 1 HOUR ········

MAKES TWO 14- TO 16-INCH THIN FOCACCE

370 grams (3 cups plus 3 tablespoons) '00' flour, plus more for dusting

227 grams (1 cup) warm water (see Temperature, page 25)

25 grams (2 tablespoons) extra-virgin olive oil, plus more for drizzling

9 grams (1½ teaspoons) fine salt

198 grams (7 ounces) cow or buffalo milk mozzarella cheese, torn into bite-size pieces

Flaky sea salt, such as Maldon, for topping

This thin, crispy, cheese-filled focaccia hails from the coastal Italian region of Liguria. There, it's baked on hammered copper sheets in blazing pizza ovens, reaching blistered perfection in minutes. For a home version, we mimic the conditions as best we can by cranking the oven up as high as it will go and baking the focaccia on a thin round metal pizza pan set directly on a pizza stone or steel, which ensures that the focaccia gets crispy on both the bottom and the top. This dough, made with finely milled '00' flour (which is used in some pizza recipes, too), is a pleasure to work with, stretching easily until nearly translucent, and browning beautifully in the oven.

MAKE THE DOUGH: In a stand mixer bowl, combine the flour, water, olive oil, and salt. Using the dough hook attachment, mix on medium speed until the ingredients come together into a smooth ball, about 10 minutes. Cover and let stand 15 minutes.

Preheat the oven to 550°F (or as hot as it will get; some ovens only go up to 500°F, in which case you may just have to bake the focaccia slightly longer). If using a baking stone or steel, preheat it along with the oven.

DIVIDE AND SHAPE: Divide the dough into 4 equal portions (each about 157 grams) and gently shape each portion into a round (see Shaping, page 34). Cover with an inverted bowl to prevent the dough from drying out. Flour a work surface and rolling pin and roll one piece of dough into a round about 10 inches in diameter.

STRETCH THE DOUGH: Transfer the dough to a round, flat, rimless pizza pan that's 14 to 16 inches in diameter. Gently stretch the dough to the edges of the pan, anchoring one side by pulling it over the pan's edge to aid the stretching. Continue stretching until the dough is paper thin and overhanging the pan on all sides by about 1 inch. Dot the dough with half of the cheese.

On the floured work surface, roll a second piece of dough into a 10-inch round, then lay over the cheese. Pulling gently, stretch the dough so that it entirely covers the cheese and extends past the edge of the pan by 1 inch. Gently roll your rolling pin over the edge of the pan to cut off the overhanging dough, then roll the edge to form a twisted rope edge. Using your thumb and forefinger, pinch the top piece of dough in a few spots to tear open irregular holes, which will allow the steam from the cheese to escape.

BAKE THE FOCACCIA: Place the pan directly on the baking stone or steel and bake until the focaccia is browned, blistered, and cracker-like on top and bottom, 10 to 12 minutes.

Remove from the oven, let cool 1 minute, then slide off the pan onto a cutting board, drizzle with a bit of olive oil, and sprinkle with flaky salt and cut into squares or wedges. Eat while hot, then repeat with the remaining dough and cheese to make a second focaccia.

This is best eaten hot and fresh from the oven, but you can store leftover cooled focaccia well wrapped in the refrigerator for up to 2 days. Reheat on a parchment-lined baking sheet in a 400°F oven until warmed through, about 5 minutes.

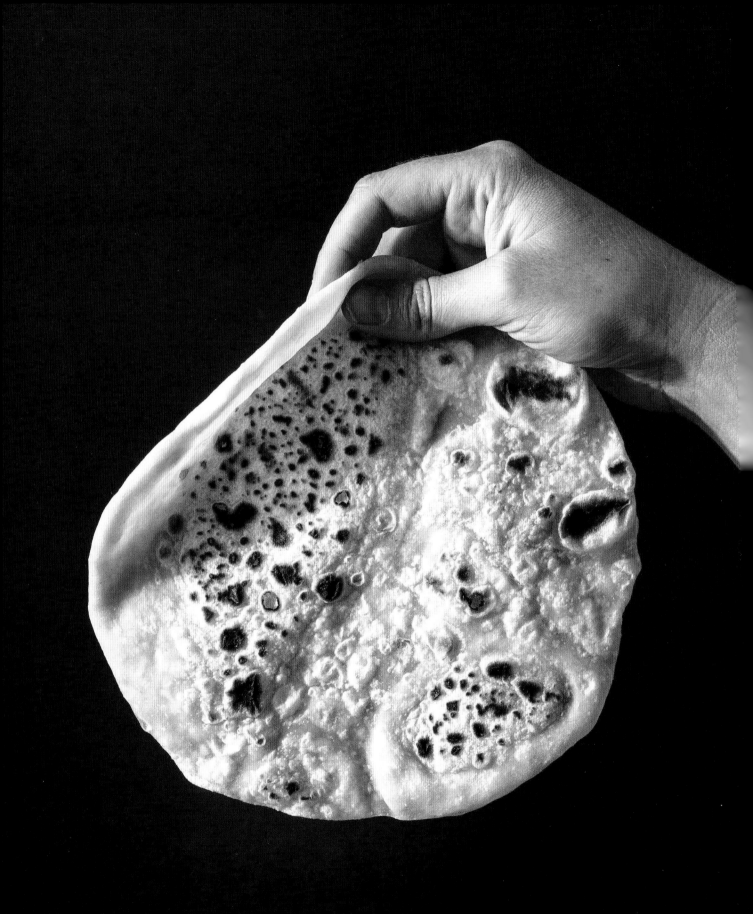

FLOUR TORTILLAS

MIX	PRESHAPE	REST	SHAPE	COOK
10 MIN	5 MIN	30 MIN	10 MIN	8 MIN

TIME: ABOUT 1 HOUR

MAKES EIGHT 8-INCH TORTILLAS

300 grams (2½ cups) unbleached bread flour, plus more for dusting

3 grams (½ teaspoon) fine salt

57 grams (4 tablespoons) lard or solid refined coconut oil

170 grams (¾ cup) warm water (see Temperature, page 25)

NOTE: To keep your tortillas (and other flatbreads) circular: When rolling, start from the center, working out in one direction away from you, then from the center working back toward you; rotate the dough one-eighth turn (45 degrees) in between each roll, which helps ensure the dough isn't sticking and maintains its round shape; a quarter-turn (90 degrees) will give you a square shape instead.

Surprisingly easy (and quick) to make at home, these tortillas are tender, flaky, and slightly chewy, and will forever ruin you for store-bought. Flour tortillas are traditionally made with lard, which makes them especially rich, but we found refined coconut oil works well, too. The higher protein level of bread flour makes the tortillas both easy to roll out and strong enough to be folded around your favorite fillings without tearing.

MAKE THE DOUGH: In a medium bowl, combine the flour and salt. Using your hands, work in the lard or coconut oil until no visible pieces of fat remain. Add the water, mixing to form a shaggy mass. Turn the mixture out onto a lightly floured surface and knead until a smooth, cohesive, slightly tacky dough forms, 3 to 5 minutes. Divide the dough into 8 equal portions (each about 65 grams). Gently shape each piece into a round (see Shaping, page 34), cover, and let rest for 30 minutes.

ROLL AND COOK THE TORTILLAS: Meanwhile, preheat a 10- to 12-inch nonstick or cast-iron skillet over medium heat until a few water drops flicked on the surface sizzle and almost immediately evaporate.

Working with one piece of dough at a time, on a lightly floured surface, roll it out into an 8-inch round. Using a pastry brush, lightly brush off any excess flour. When you have a few tortillas rolled out, start cooking; while the first few cook you can continue to roll the remaining.

Cook the tortilla until bubbles form on the top and some light brown spots begin to form on the bottom, about 30 seconds. Flip and cook for 30 seconds more on the second side. The tortilla will puff and the bottom will be leopard-spotted. Wrap the cooked tortilla in a clean, dry kitchen towel, stacking them as you go.

Let leftover tortillas cool completely before wrapping and refrigerating. Reheat tortillas on a preheated nonstick or cast-iron skillet until warmed through, about 20 seconds per side, or wrap tortillas in a clean kitchen towel and heat in the microwave in 5-second increments.

TORTILLAS DE MAÍZ

CORN TORTILLAS

MIX	REST	SHAPE	COOK
5 MIN	30 MIN	10 MIN	30 MIN

TIME: ABOUT 1¼ HOURS

MAKES SIXTEEN 5-INCH TORTILLAS

233 grams (2½ cups) masa harina

Pinch of fine salt

378 grams (1⅔ cups) warm water (see Temperature, page 25)

Pliant, aromatic, and deeply corn-y in flavor, fresh homemade corn tortillas are a revelation. They're also fun to make, and a great project for kids, who like smashing the balls of masa into thin rounds. It's helpful to have a tortilla press to form the tortillas, a small investment that will quickly pay off when you start making tortillas on regular rotation (which you will, because they are so good!). If you're just an occasional tortilla maker, you can also use a heavy skillet to flatten the disks of dough; just take care that you press down evenly. Use these for tacos, of course, or just serve a warm stack of them alongside chili, soup, or rice and beans. Day-old tortillas can be fried into tortilla chips.

MAKE THE DOUGH: In a large shallow bowl, combine the masa harina and salt. Add the warm water, then, holding your hand in a clawlike fashion (which helps to incorporate the wet and dry ingredients evenly and helps prevent the dough from sticking to your hand), mix to form a cohesive dough, eventually folding the soft dough over itself. It should be smooth and semifirm, similar in texture to Play-Doh. If the dough sticks to your hands and feels wet, add more masa harina ½ teaspoon at a time. If you roll a piece into a ball and squeeze it and the edges crack, knead in more water ½ teaspoon at a time and test again. Cover and let rest for 30 minutes; this gives the masa time to fully hydrate.

Toward the end of resting time for the tortilla dough, heat a cast-iron or nonstick skillet, griddle, or comal over medium to medium-high heat. The surface temperature should be between 375°F and 385°F. If you have an infrared thermometer (see page 16), use that to check the surface temperature; if not, scatter a few drops of water on the pan—they should sizzle and evaporate almost immediately on contact. Cut two round or square pieces of food-safe plastic—from a plastic produce or zip-top bag—to a size about ½ inch larger than the diameter of your tortilla press.

Set aside.

Recipe continues

SHAPE THE TORTILLAS: Divide the dough into 16 equal portions (about the size of a Ping-Pong ball; 35 to 40 grams each) and roll each piece into a ball. Place the balls on a clean work surface and cover them with plastic or a damp kitchen towel to keep them moist.

Working with one ball of dough at a time, sandwich it in the center of the two pieces of plastic. Place the plastic-enclosed dough on the bottom plate of a tortilla press. Gently squeeze the handle of the press until the dough is $\frac{1}{8}$ to $\frac{1}{16}$ inch thick and about 5 inches in diameter. To achieve a nicely round tortilla, jiggle the handle of your press just as you near the bottom. You may need to press it a couple of times to get the desired thinness.

COOK THE TORTILLAS: Peel away the top piece of plastic from the tortilla, invert the tortilla onto your hand, and carefully peel off the bottom piece of plastic.

Gently lay the tortilla down in the hot skillet. Don't worry if it isn't perfectly flat (you'll get better as you practice), and don't try to move it, which will cause it to tear. Cook the tortilla until it releases easily from the pan and its color has lightened and become opaque, about 30 seconds; you don't want the tortilla to brown or become freckled at this point.

Using a spatula or your fingers, flip the tortilla and cook it until the bottom edges start to brown and some freckles appear, about 1 minute more.

Flip the tortilla one more time and cook until it puffs, 10 to 15 seconds. If the tortilla doesn't puff on its own, gently press it a few times near the center with a dry kitchen towel. Once it puffs, let the tortilla cook until fully set and soft, 15 to 20 seconds longer. Remove the tortilla from the heat and wrap it in a clean kitchen towel or transfer it to a cloth-lined tortillero (tortilla warmer).

Repeat the pressing and cooking process with the remaining dough. Corn tortillas are best eaten fresh and warm, but leftovers can be stored, wrapped in a kitchen towel and sealed in a plastic bag, for 2 to 3 days, or frozen for 2 to 3 months. To reheat, preheat a cast-iron or nonstick pan, griddle, or comal for 5 minutes over medium heat and warm the tortillas for about 1 minute on each side.

PITA BREAD

MIX	BULK FERMENTATION	PRESHAPE	REST	SHAPE	BAKE
10 MIN	1 HOUR	5 MIN	15 MIN	10 MIN	24–32 MIN

············· TIME: ABOUT 2¼ HOURS ·············

MAKES EIGHT 7-INCH PITAS

360 grams (3 cups) unbleached all-purpose flour, plus more for dusting

9 grams (1½ teaspoons) fine salt

8 grams (2 teaspoons) sugar

6 grams (2 teaspoons) instant yeast

241 grams (1 cup plus 1 tablespoon) warm water (see Temperature, page 25)

25 grams (2 tablespoons) olive oil

It's always a thrill to watch a piece of dough inflate into a magnificent pita balloon. These versatile breads can be made in the oven or on the stovetop (see Variation), and while they'll keep for up to 2 days and can be frozen for longer storage, it's hard to beat the experience of tearing into a warm pita. If you'd like, you can substitute whole wheat flour for some of the all-purpose flour (see Variation).

MAKE THE DOUGH: In a medium bowl, combine the flour, salt, sugar, and yeast. Add the water and oil, mixing with the handle of a wooden spoon to form a cohesive, slightly sticky dough. On a lightly floured surface, knead the dough by hand until smooth and springy, about 5 minutes. Place the dough back in the bowl, cover, and let rest until noticeably puffy, about 1 hour.

Meanwhile, arrange a rack in the top third of the oven and preheat the oven to 500°F with a baking stone or steel on the rack.

DIVIDE AND PRESHAPE: Transfer the dough to a lightly floured surface. Gently pat the dough into a flat round, then divide it into 8 equal portions (each about 81 grams). Gently preshape each piece of dough into a round (see Preshaping, page 32), then cover and let rest at room temperature for 15 minutes.

ROLL AND BAKE THE PITA: On a lightly floured surface, roll out each piece of dough into a 7-inch round about ⅛ inch thick. Place 2 pieces of rolled-out dough on a lightly floured baker's peel or an inverted baking sheet, then slide off the peel onto the preheated baking stone or steel. Bake until the pitas have puffed and the tops look set (they will not take on much color), 3 to 4 minutes.

Using tongs or a peel, carefully remove the pitas from the oven. Stack the baked pitas on a clean kitchen towel, wrapping them to cover.

Recipe continues

This keeps the pitas pliable and warm. Eat warm or cool completely before storing them in an airtight container at room temperature for up to 2 days. Freeze for longer storage.

VARIATIONS

WHOLE-GRAIN PITA: Use a combination of 180 grams (1½ cups) unbleached all-purpose flour and 177 grams (1½ cups) golden wheat flour. Depending on how you measure your flour and if you live in a dry climate or not, you may need to add up to 14 grams (1 tablespoon) additional water to create a soft, slightly sticky dough. Proceed with the recipe as written.

STOVETOP PITA: Make and roll the dough as directed. Preheat a dry 8- or 10-inch cast-iron skillet over medium-high heat for 7 to 10 minutes, or until the surface temperature is about 450°F. If your cast-iron skillet smokes slightly when preheating, turn on your stove's fan or open a window when making this recipe. Carefully place one pita in the pan and cook 1½ to 2 minutes per side. The pita may not puff completely using this method since you only have heat coming from one side, but the pita will be equally delicious.

LAVASH

MIX	BULK FERMENTATION	PRESHAPE	REST	SHAPE	BAKE
10 MIN	1 HOUR	5 MIN	1 HOUR	30 MIN	8–24 MIN

MAKE THE PREFERMENT (1 HOUR BEFORE)

TIME: ABOUT 4 HOURS

MAKES 8 LARGE LAVASH

PREFERMENT

150 grams (1¼ cups) unbleached all-purpose flour

156 grams (½ cup plus 3 tablespoons) warm water (see Temperature, page 25)

1.5 grams (½ teaspoon) instant yeast

DOUGH

174 grams (1½ cups) '00' flour

180 grams (1½ cups) unbleached all-purpose flour

17 grams (1 tablespoon plus 1 teaspoon) olive oil

6 grams (1 teaspoon) fine salt

1.5 grams (½ teaspoon) instant yeast

170 grams (¾ cup) warm water (see Temperature, page 25)

Lavash is a staple of Armenian culture, but, like all great recipes, knows nothing of borders and is found in the neighboring countries of Iran, Turkey, and Azerbaijan. Typically, it's made with a small amount of dough saved from the previous day's bake (a preferment called pâte fermentée), which adds flavor and improves its keeping quality. But since most home bakers aren't baking lavash daily, here we use a simple yeasted preferment—it provides all the benefits of the pâte fermentée but is more practical. A combination of all-purpose and finely milled '00' flour gives the oversize flatbread its pliant texture, which is especially desirable since lavash is typically used to wrap up grilled kebabs or vegetables and cheese. In Armenia, lavash is baked in a tonir, a large underground oven that is lined with clay tiles. A wood fire burns at the bottom, and the unbaked lavash are slapped on the walls of the oven, where they bake in minutes, developing their signature leopard-spotted appearance. Lacking a tonir at home, we adapted the method, using a preheated baking stone or steel and the broiler to emulate the tonir's blistering heat. Do your best to roll the lavash thinly and uniformly so they bake evenly. For foldable lavash, bake them for only a few minutes. If you prefer a crisp, cracker-like lavash, add a few minutes to the baking time (see Variation). Lavash also form the base for Fattoush (page 426).

MAKE THE PREFERMENT: In a medium bowl, combine the flour, water, and yeast, mixing until no dry spots remain and a wet, sticky dough forms. Cover and let rest at room temperature for 1 hour; the preferment will look smoother than when it was first mixed, and some small bubbles will be visible.

MAKE THE DOUGH: Add the '00' flour, all-purpose flour, oil, salt, yeast, and water to the bowl with the preferment. Mix until a mostly cohesive dough with a few dry bits forms. Transfer the dough to a lightly floured

Recipe continues

work surface and knead until the dough is smooth and springy, 5 to 8 minutes. The dough will be slightly sticky at first, then will smooth out. Add just enough additional flour to keep the dough from sticking to your hands and work surface. Use a bench knife to scrape up any dough that sticks to your work surface; this will reduce the amount of extra flour you need to add. Cover and let the dough rest at room temperature for 1 hour. The dough will be relaxed but will not rise much or spring back when pressed with a floured finger.

DIVIDE AND PRESHAPE: Transfer the dough to an unfloured work surface and divide it into 8 equal portions (each about 107 grams). Preshape each piece of dough into a loose round (see Preshaping, page 32) and place seam side down on a lightly dusted work surface or baking sheet. Cover and let rest 1 hour at room temperature; this will make it easier to roll out thinly.

While the dough is resting, preheat the oven to 500°F with a baking stone or steel placed on the bottom rack.

SHAPE AND BAKE THE LAVASH: Working with one piece of dough at a time, roll it out on a lightly floured surface into a 13 × 9-inch oval. As the dough gets thinner, it may resist stretching. If this happens, flour the backs of your hands and drape the dough over them. Gently stretch the dough by pushing one hand away from you while pulling the other hand toward you. Stretch the dough as evenly and thinly as possible; the edges will be slightly thicker than the center. Brush off any excess flour.

When the first flatbread is ready to bake, switch the oven to broil. Transfer the dough to a lightly floured baker's peel or an inverted baking sheet, then slide it off the peel onto the preheated baking stone or steel. Broil until the lavash is blistered and puffed and light brown spots appear on top of the bread, 1 to 2 minutes; do not flip. Using tongs or a peel, carefully remove the lavash from the oven. Stack the baked lavash on a clean kitchen towel, wrapping to cover. Continue shaping, baking, and stacking the remaining lavash, leaving your oven on broil the whole time.

Lavash is best eaten the day it is baked. If there are crisp areas on the flatbread after cooling, spritz them lightly with water, cover with a towel, and let rest for 30 minutes. The lavash will absorb the water, soften, and become pliable.

Fold any leftovers and store in a plastic bag at room temperature to keep them soft, up to 2 days; if they seem dry, you can spritz with water as described above.

VARIATION

CRISP LAVASH CRACKERS: Roll and stretch the dough as directed, then broil the lavash as described until it is covered in brown spots and dry, 2 to 3 minutes. Allow the flatbreads to cool on a wire rack, uncovered; they'll continue to crisp as they cool. Once cool, break the flatbread into crackers for serving.

GÖZLEME

STUFFED AND PAN-FRIED TURKISH FLATBREAD

MIX	REST	PRESHAPE	2ND REST	SHAPE	COOK
10 MIN	30–60 MIN	10 MIN	15–30 MIN	30 MIN	40–48 MIN

······· TIME: ABOUT 2½ HOURS ·······

MAKES EIGHT 10-INCH FILLED FLATBREADS

DOUGH

400 grams (3⅓ cups) unbleached all-purpose flour, plus more for dusting

6 grams (1 teaspoon) fine salt

198 grams (¾ cup plus 2 tablespoons) warm water (see Temperature, page 25)

57 grams (¼ cup) cold milk, whole preferred

FILLING

142 grams (one 5-ounce) container fresh baby spinach, finely chopped

½ large white or yellow onion, finely chopped (about 125 grams)

3 large scallions, white parts only, finely chopped (about 20 grams)

5 sprigs fresh flat-leaf parsley, finely chopped

4 sprigs fresh dill, finely chopped

2 teaspoons sweet paprika

1 teaspoon ground cumin

½ teaspoon fine salt

½ teaspoon freshly ground black pepper

Ingredients continue

These stuffed flatbreads are found throughout Turkey, where they're made with different fillings, ranging from spiced ground lamb to cheese to chocolate. This version combines spinach, green herbs, and a combination of feta and mozzarella cheese for the perfect balance of salty and creamy. The unleavened dough is folded around the filling and then pan-fried until the dough is cooked through and the flatbread is crispy and irresistible. These are a bit of a project, so it's a nice thing to do assembly line–style with a friend. Or break up the process over 2 days, making the filling one day and the dough the next, then filling and pan-frying just before you want to serve.

MAKE THE DOUGH: In a large bowl, combine the flour, salt, water, and milk, mixing with the handle of a wooden spoon until no dry patches remain and a cohesive dough forms. Transfer the dough to a very lightly floured surface and knead until the dough springs back when lightly pressed with your finger, 5 to 8 minutes. Add just enough flour to keep the dough from sticking. If you find the dough is sticking, scraping the work surface clean of any sticky dough will speed up the process and reduce the amount of flour required for kneading. The dough will have a texture similar to soft modeling clay, though its surface may not be completely smooth. Return the dough to the bowl, cover, and let rest for 30 minutes to 1 hour. The dough will be relaxed but will not have risen at all, and when pressed with a floured finger will not spring back.

WHILE THE DOUGH RESTS, MAKE THE FILLING: In a large bowl, combine the spinach, onion, scallions, parsley, dill, paprika, cumin, salt, black pepper, and pepper flakes (if using). Using your hands, toss, then rub the ingredients together to soften the spinach and distribute the ingredients evenly. Stir in the feta and set the filling aside.

Recipe continues

A few pinches of red pepper flakes (optional)

113 grams (4 ounces) feta cheese, crumbled (1 cup)

227 grams (8 ounces) shredded mozzarella cheese (2 cups), divided

50 grams (¼ cup) olive oil, for brushing

DIVIDE, SHAPE, AND FILL THE GÖZLEME: Lightly flour a work surface, then use a plastic bowl scraper to ease the dough out of the bowl onto the work surface. Divide the dough into 8 equal portions (each about 82 grams). Gently preshape the pieces into rounds (see Preshaping, page 32) and place seam side down on a lightly floured surface. Cover and let rest for 15 to 30 minutes.

Preheat the oven to 200°F. Line two rimmed baking sheets with parchment paper and set near the stove.

Working with one piece of dough at a time, roll it out on a lightly floured surface into a 10-inch round. If the dough is shrinking back before you've gotten it to the correct dimension, set it aside to rest, covered, for 5 to 10 minutes while you work on rolling out more pieces of dough. Continue this pattern, going back to the first prerolled piece of dough once you've rolled them all out partially; the brief rest should make it possible for you to more easily roll it out to 10 inches. The dough will be thin enough to almost see through.

Evenly spread 56 grams (2 to 3 tablespoons) filling over the bottom half of the round, leaving a ½-inch border along the edge. Sprinkle 28 grams (¼ cup) mozzarella cheese over the filling. Fold the top of the round down over the filling to create a half-moon shape, then pinch the edges to seal. Set the filled flatbread on the prepared baking sheet, then continue rolling, filling, and shaping the remaining flatbreads.

COOK THE GÖZLEME: When all the flatbreads are filled, preheat a 10- to 12-inch nonstick or cast-iron skillet over medium heat until a few water drops flicked on the surface sizzle and almost immediately evaporate. Brush the pan with a bit of olive oil, then add a gözleme (or 2, if your pan is large enough to accommodate 2 in a single layer). Cook, pressing down on the top of the flatbread intermittently to keep it from puffing up and to keep it in contact with the hot pan, until browned spots appear on the bottom of the flatbread, about 2 minutes. Brush the top of the gözleme with olive oil, then flip, brush the other side with olive oil, and cook until browned spots appear on the bottom, about 2 minutes. Flip again and cook an additional 1 to 2 minutes on each side until the gözleme are crisp and the edges no longer look opaque. Transfer to a lined baking sheet and keep warm in the oven while you cook the remaining gözleme. Serve warm.

Any leftovers will keep, tightly wrapped and refrigerated, for 2 to 3 days, or can be frozen for up to 2 weeks. Thaw overnight in the refrigerator and reheat in a 350°F oven until warmed through, about 5 minutes.

SFEEHA HALABY

ALEPPAN-STYLE MEAT FLATBREAD

MIX	BULK FERMENTATION	SHAPE	REST	SHAPE	BAKE
10 MIN	1 HOUR 30 MIN	10 MIN	20 MIN	10 MIN	40–48 MIN

TIME: ABOUT 3 HOURS

MAKES FOUR 10-INCH FLATBREADS

DOUGH

330 grams (2¾ cups) unbleached bread flour

75 grams (½ cup plus 2 tablespoons) unbleached all-purpose flour, plus more for dusting

9 grams (1½ teaspoons) fine salt

4.5 grams (1½ teaspoons) instant yeast

3 grams (¾ teaspoon) sugar

284 grams (1¼ cups) warm water (see Temperature, page 25)

25 grams (2 tablespoons) olive oil

TOPPING

1 large tomato (158 grams), finely chopped (1 cup)

1 small red onion (142 grams), finely chopped (1 cup)

2 to 3 garlic cloves (14 grams) peeled and finely chopped (1 tablespoon)

28 grams (2 tablespoons) full-fat yogurt

20 grams (1 tablespoon) pomegranate molasses

Ingredients continue

These thin, crispy flatbreads are topped with a spiced meat mixture (typically lamb, though ground beef can also be used) that's thinly spread across the dough. This recipe is typical of the versions served in Syria, but similar breads exist in Lebanon, Turkey, and Armenia, where they're called lahm bi ajeen or lahmacun. After baking, the flatbread is garnished with sweet pomegranate seeds and toasted pine nuts, which add sweetness and crunch.

MAKE THE DOUGH: In a large bowl, combine the bread flour, all-purpose flour, salt, yeast, sugar, water, and olive oil. Mix with the handle of a wooden spoon until a shaggy dough forms, then transfer it to a floured work surface and knead until the dough is soft, smooth, and elastic, 8 to 10 minutes. The dough will be sticky at first but will smooth out quickly; to make it easier to handle, use a bench knife to scrape the dough from your work surface as you knead, which will speed up the process and reduce the amount of flour required for kneading (adding too much flour at this stage can make your flatbread denser). Return the dough to the bowl, cover, and let rest at room temperature until doubled in size, about 1½ hours.

Alternatively, in a stand mixer bowl, combine the dough ingredients. Using the dough hook attachment, mix on medium-low until a shaggy dough forms. Scrape down the bowl as necessary, then increase the speed to medium and mix until the dough is smooth, elastic, and cleans the sides of the bowl, 5 to 8 minutes. Cover the bowl and let rest at room temperature until doubled in size, about 1½ hours.

MEANWHILE, PREPARE THE TOPPING: Place the tomato in a sieve set over a small bowl to drain any excess liquid. In a medium bowl, combine the onion, garlic, yogurt, molasses, tahini, salt, coriander, allspice, cinnamon, and pepper. Gently knead the meat into the spice mixture

Recipe continues

16 grams (1 tablespoon) tahini

9 grams (1½ teaspoons) fine salt

1 teaspoon ground coriander

½ teaspoon ground allspice

½ teaspoon ground cinnamon

¼ teaspoon freshly ground black pepper

227 grams (8 ounces) ground lamb or beef

½ small red Fresno or jalapeño chile (6 grams), seeded and finely chopped (2 teaspoons)

20 grams (2 tablespoons) semolina flour or yellow cornmeal, for dusting

GARNISH

44 grams (¼ cup) pomegranate seeds

36 grams (¼ cup) toasted pine nuts

15 grams (¼ cup) roughly chopped fresh parsley

with your hands until just incorporated. Fold in the tomato and chile (if using).

Arrange racks in the upper and lower thirds of the oven and preheat the oven to 500°F with a baking stone or steel on the lower rack.

DIVIDE AND SHAPE: Lightly flour a work surface, then use a plastic bowl scraper to ease the dough out of the bowl onto the work surface. With a bench knife or a knife, divide the dough into 4 equal portions (each about 182 grams). Shape the dough into rounds (see Shaping, page 34), transfer to a flour-dusted baking sheet, cover, and let rest at room temperature for 20 minutes.

ROLL AND BAKE THE SFEEHA: Have ready four pieces of parchment paper. Working with one piece of dough at a time, lightly dust each round of dough with flour and then roll it out into a 10-inch round. Dust the parchment with semolina or cornmeal, then transfer one piece of rolled dough to each sheet of parchment. Divide the filling into 4 equal portions (each about 156 grams/½ cup). Scoop a portion of the meat mixture onto the rolled-out dough and using your fingers and palm, spread the paste into a thin, even layer, leaving a ⅛-inch border around the edges.

Using a baker's peel or an inverted baking sheet to aid you, transfer the sfeeha (still on the parchment) to the baking stone or steel and bake until the bottom is golden brown and crisp, about 5 minutes. Transfer the sfeeha to the top rack and bake until the edges are golden brown and the topping is sizzling, an additional 5 to 7 minutes. Remove from the oven, transfer to a cutting board, and garnish with pomegranate seeds, pine nuts, and parsley. Cut into wedges while still warm and serve.

Store leftover sfeeha in an airtight container up to 2 days. Reheat on a parchment-lined baking sheet in a 400°F oven for 5 minutes or until warmed through.

CHAPATI

WHOLE WHEAT INDIAN FLATBREAD

MIX	REST	SHAPE	COOK
10 MIN	20 MIN	10 MIN	12–16 MIN

······· TIME: ABOUT 1 HOUR ·······

MAKES EIGHT 8-INCH CHAPATI

184 grams (1½ cups plus 2 tablespoons) golden wheat flour (see page 449)

80 grams (½ cup plus 3 tablespoons) '00' flour, plus more for dusting

2 grams (scant ½ teaspoon) fine salt

184 grams (¾ cup plus 1 tablespoon) warm water (see Temperature, page 25), plus more as needed

Chapati are unleavened whole wheat flatbreads eaten throughout the Indian subcontinent that are made with chakki atta flour, a finely milled stone-ground high-protein whole wheat flour. Western whole wheat, by contrast, is coarser, and we found in our testing that substituting it 1 to 1 for atta flour didn't yield great results. Further tinkering led us to a combination of golden wheat flour, which contributes strength and flavor, and finely milled '00' flour, which lends tenderness. The result? A flatbread that is soft, easily tearable, and has chapati's characteristic bubbles.

Most chapati contain little to no salt, as they're typically served alongside highly seasoned dishes. As per tradition, we've chosen to keep the amount of salt on the lower end, but feel free to increase the amount to suit your taste.

MAKE THE DOUGH: In a medium bowl, combine the golden wheat flour, '00' flour, and salt. Add the water, mixing with the handle of a wooden spoon to form a sticky dough. On a lightly floured surface, knead the dough by hand until smooth and springy, 5 to 8 minutes. The dough will be sticky at first but will smooth out quickly. Using a bench knife to scrape the work surface clean of any sticky dough will speed up the process and reduce the amount of flour required for kneading. Return the dough to the bowl, cover, and let rest 20 minutes at room temperature.

DIVIDE AND SHAPE: Transfer the dough to a lightly floured surface and divide it into 8 equal portions (each about 56 grams). Gently shape each piece of dough into a round, then cover.

Recipe continues

Preheat a 10- to 12-inch nonstick or cast-iron skillet over medium heat until a few water drops flicked on the surface sizzle and almost immediately evaporate.

ROLL AND COOK THE CHAPATI: Working with one piece of dough at a time, roll it out into an 8-inch round on a lightly floured work surface. Use a pastry brush to brush off any excess flour. We find it's easiest when we get in a bit of a groove, rolling out one chapati while another cooks.

Cook the chapati one at a time until some light brown spots begin to form on the bottom, about 30 seconds. Flip the chapati and continue cooking on the second side until light brown spots form there, too. Flip the chapati again and cook, gently pressing down on the chapati using the back of a spatula, which will encourage it to puff, 30 to 60 more seconds. Wrap the cooked chapati in a clean kitchen towel, stacking them as you go, so that they stay warm and pliable until ready to serve. Chapati are best eaten right away.

To store, cool leftover chapati completely, then wrap and refrigerate. Reheat on a preheated griddle pan or cast-iron skillet until warmed through, about 20 seconds per side. (Alternatively, wrap chapati in a clean kitchen towel and heat in the microwave in 10-second increments.)

NAAN

MIX	BULK FERMENTATION	PRESHAPE	2ND RISE	SHAPE	BAKE
10 MIN	1 HOUR	5 MIN	20 MIN	10 MIN	8–16 MIN

········ TIME: ABOUT 2 HOURS ········

MAKES EIGHT 8-INCH NAAN

DOUGH

180 grams (1½ cups) unbleached all-purpose flour, plus more for dusting

90 grams (¾ cup) unbleached bread flour

6 grams (1 teaspoon) fine salt

4.5 grams (1½ teaspoons) instant yeast

4 grams (1 teaspoon) sugar

142 grams (½ cup plus 2 tablespoons) warm water (see Temperature, page 25)

70 grams (5 tablespoons) full-fat Greek yogurt

28 grams (2½ tablespoons) ghee, store-bought or homemade (recipe follows), melted

TO COOK AND FINISH

28 grams (2½ tablespoons) ghee, melted, plus more for serving

6 grams (2 teaspoons) nigella seeds (optional)

15 grams (¼ cup) chopped fresh cilantro (optional)

Flaky sea salt, such as Maldon (optional)

Plush, soft, and tender, with a bit of tanginess from yogurt, these naan are a pleasure to make (and eat!). They are also quick and simple enough that with only a modest amount of preplanning, you can have fresh naan on the table in time for dinner. Though naan are typically baked on the walls of a super-heated tandoor oven, since most of us don't have access to one, we developed a stovetop cooking method that yields good results.

MAKE THE DOUGH: In a medium bowl, combine the all-purpose flour, bread flour, salt, yeast, and sugar. Add the ghee, yogurt, and water and mix with the handle of a wooden spoon until no dry spots of flour remain. Transfer the dough to a lightly floured surface and knead until the dough is smooth and elastic, 6 to 8 minutes; the dough will be slightly tacky. Return the dough to the bowl, cover, and let rise until doubled in size, about 1 hour.

Alternatively, in a stand mixer bowl, combine the all-purpose flour, bread flour, salt, yeast, sugar, water, yogurt, and ghee. Using the dough hook attachment, mix on medium-low speed until a shaggy dough forms. Increase the speed to medium and continue mixing until the dough is smooth and elastic and pulls away from the sides of the bowl, about 5 minutes. Cover and let rise until doubled in size, about 1 hour.

DIVIDE AND SHAPE: Turn the dough out onto a lightly floured surface and divide it into 8 equal portions (each about 65 grams). Shape each piece of dough into a round (see Shaping, page 34), then cover with plastic wrap and let rest for 20 minutes.

ROLL AND COOK THE NAAN: On a lightly floured surface, roll out each piece of dough into an 8-inch round. Preheat a 10-inch nonstick or cast-iron skillet over medium-high heat until a few water drops flicked on the surface sizzle and almost immediately evaporate. Cook the naan one at a time until bubbles form on top and light brown spots appear

Recipe continues

HOMEMADE GHEE

Ghee is clarified butter. As the water and milk solids have been removed, it has a higher smoke point and is shelf stable. To make ghee, the butter is first melted and then cooked until the milk solids begin to brown. The browned milk solids are then strained out. That bit of browning infuses the remaining clarified butter with a wonderful nutty flavor. You can buy jars of ghee, but it's also easy to make your own.

113 grams (8 tablespoons)
unsalted butter

In a small saucepan, melt the butter over medium-low heat. The butter will eventually begin to simmer. Carefully skim off and discard any foam that forms on top. Continue skimming until the butter is clear and the milk solids have sunk to the bottom and just started to brown.

Remove the pot from the heat and allow to cool for a few minutes. Carefully strain the clarified butter through cheesecloth or a coffee filter. Store at room temperature for up to 1 month.

on the bottom, 40 to 50 seconds. Flip the naan and continue cooking on the second side until the bottom has light brown spots, an additional 30 to 40 seconds (begin rolling the second naan while the first cooks). Transfer to a plate and lightly brush both sides with ghee. Wrap the cooked naan in a clean, dry, lint-free kitchen towel. Repeat with the remaining naan, stacking them in the towel as they're cooked. Brush the naan with additional ghee. If desired, top them with a sprinkling of nigella seeds, chopped cilantro, and flaky salt. Eat while still warm.

ALOO PARATHA
SPICED POTATO-STUFFED FLATBREAD

MIX	REST	PRE-SHAPE	2ND REST	SHAPE	COOK
30 MIN	20–30 MIN	5 MIN	20 MIN	30 MIN	22–26 MIN

·········· TIME: ABOUT 2¾ HOURS ··········

MAKES FOUR 9-INCH PARATHAS

DOUGH

120 grams (1 cup) unbleached all-purpose flour, plus more for dusting

113 grams (1 cup) golden wheat flour

3 grams (½ teaspoon) fine salt

12 grams (1 tablespoon) ghee, store-bought or homemade (page 85), melted, or vegetable or other neutral oil

156 grams (½ cup plus 3 tablespoons) warm water (see Temperature, page 25)

FILLING

2 medium russet potatoes (about 454 grams/1 pound)

4 medium shallots (about 168 grams), finely chopped

60 grams fresh cilantro leaves (1 cup packed), chopped

2 to 3 Indian green chiles (10 to 15 grams) or an equal weight of jalapeño or serrano, seeded and minced

6 grams (2 teaspoons) chaat masala (see Notes)

6 grams (1 teaspoon) fine salt

Ingredients continue

We've yet to meet a potato-filled flatbread we didn't love (carbs on carbs!), but this pan-fried Indian version is especially good: A little crispy on the exterior, with a potato filling that's spiced with cilantro, minced fresh green chiles, chili powder, and chaat masala (see Notes). Typical of Northern India, where parathas are often eaten for breakfast, the unleavened dough is rolled out, filled with the cooked potato mixture, then rolled out a second time, enclosing the potato within the dough. If you want to stock your freezer with ready-to-cook parathas (and trust us, you do), we've given instructions for parcooking (see Notes).

MAKE THE DOUGH: In a medium bowl, combine the all-purpose flour, golden wheat flour, salt, and ghee; the mixture will look clumpy. Add the water, mixing with the handle of a wooden spoon to form a shaggy dough. Cover and let rest at room temperature for 20 minutes. This resting period allows the flours to hydrate and makes hand-kneading easier and less sticky.

Transfer the dough to a lightly floured surface and knead by hand until the dough is smooth and elastic, about 5 minutes. Cover and let rest while you prepare the filling, 20 to 30 minutes.

MEANWHILE, MAKE THE FILLING: Prick the potatoes all over with a fork and place them on a microwaveable plate. Microwave until fork-tender, about 8 minutes. (Alternatively, bake the potatoes on a parchment-lined baking sheet in a preheated 400°F oven until tender, about 45 minutes.)

Set the potatoes aside to cool for 10 minutes, then peel them. Roughly chop the potato flesh and transfer it to a ricer or medium-gauge wire-mesh sieve. Press the cooked potato through the ricer or sieve into a large bowl. Set aside, uncovered, to cool. (If you have neither ricer nor sieve, you can also grate the peeled potatoes on the large holes of a box grater.)

Recipe continues

½ teaspoon Kashmiri chili powder or ¼ teaspoon cayenne pepper plus ¼ teaspoon sweet paprika

FOR COOKING AND SERVING

33 grams (3 tablespoons) ghee, store-bought or homemade (page 85), melted, or vegetable or other neutral cooking oil, for cooking

Lime wedges (optional)

Minced Indian green chiles (optional)

Mango pickle or achaar (optional)

Plain yogurt (optional)

Coconut chutney (optional)

NOTES:

Chaat masala is an Indian spice blend that gets its tangy flavor from the inclusion of green mango powder.

To parcook parathas: After assembling the parathas, cook for 1½ minutes on each side, but do not brush with ghee. Transfer to a wire rack to cool completely, then separate with parchment paper and place in an airtight container to freeze.

To cook parathas from frozen: Brush with ghee and extend cooking time as needed until heated through.

Measure out 300 grams/2½ cups riced potatoes; any extra can be saved for another use.

Add the shallots, cilantro, chiles, chaat masala, salt, and Kashmiri chili powder to the riced potatoes, mixing to combine. Divide the filling into 4 equal portions (each about 138 grams/1 cup loosely packed). Shape each portion into a puck 3 inches wide by 1 inch thick. Set aside.

DIVIDE AND SHAPE: Divide the dough into 4 equal pieces (each about 100 grams). Preshape each piece of dough into a ball (see Preshaping, page 32). Using a cupped hand on an unfloured area of your work surface, shape each piece of dough into a taut round (see Shaping, page 34). Cover the pieces of dough with a damp towel to keep them from drying out and let rest for 20 minutes. The rest will make it easier to roll out the parathas.

ROLL AND FILL THE PARATHAS: Lightly flour a work surface. Beginning with the first piece of dough that you preshaped, roll it into an 8- to 9-inch round. Place a puck of potato filling in the center of the round. Starting at 12 o'clock, fold the dough down toward the center of the filling. Continue to work around the dough in this fashion, pleating and pinching the dough around the filling, enclosing it. Try to avoid overlapping the dough too much at the center, as this can cause the middle of the paratha to be doughy.

Dust your work surface with flour, then reroll the sealed paratha into a 9-inch circle. Continue rolling, filling, and rerolling the remaining parathas. Lightly dust each paratha with flour as you go and stack them, separating them with parchment paper, and cover with a damp towel.

COOK THE PARATHAS: Preheat a 10- to 12-inch nonstick or cast-iron skillet over medium heat until a few water drops flicked on the surface sizzle and almost immediately evaporate. Cook one paratha at a time, undisturbed, until the underside looks dry and is just starting to take on light spots of color, about 90 seconds. Flip, then brush the cooked side with melted ghee. Cook the second side for another minute, then flip and brush that side with ghee. Continue cooking and flipping the paratha until it starts to puff and the exterior is evenly speckled with deep brown spots, an additional 3 to 4 minutes. Cook the remaining parathas in the same manner, stacking and wrapping them in a clean, dry, lint-free kitchen towel as you go.

Serve warm with lime wedges, minced chiles, mango pickle, achaar, yogurt, or coconut chutney, if desired.

88   BIG BOOK OF BREAD

BANANA PURI

FRIED BANANA FLATBREAD

			PRE-SHAPE	2ND REST	SHAPE	FRY
MIX	REST					
10 MIN	4 HOURS		10 MIN	20 MIN	15 MIN	24 MIN

TIME: ABOUT 5 HOURS

MAKES 12 PURI

227 grams (8 ounces) ripe yellow bananas (about 2 medium Cavendish bananas or 3 to 4 Indian bananas; see headnote), peeled

28 grams (2 tablespoons) demerara sugar or granulated sugar

4.5 grams (¾ teaspoon) fine salt

43 to 57 grams (3 to 4 tablespoons) full-fat yogurt (not Greek)

248 grams (2 cups plus 1 tablespoon) unbleached all-purpose flour, plus more for dusting

78 grams (½ cup plus 3 tablespoons) golden wheat flour (see page 449)

½ teaspoon ground cumin

¼ teaspoon baking soda

Vegetable or other neutral oil, for deep-frying (about 1,188 grams/6 cups)

Laced with cumin and fried in hot oil until puffed, these banana puri, also known as mangalore buns, are more savory than sweet. They are a wonderful snack on their own, but you can serve them as part of an Indian meal, with coconut chutney and sambhar. In India, where these puri originate, they are typically made with banana varieties that we don't have easy access to in the States, including Elaichi, Poovan, and Lady Finger. Those varieties are a bit less sweet than the typical yellow Cavendish banana we find here, but we found that the recipe still worked well (and tasted great) with regular grocery store bananas.

MAKE THE DOUGH: In a medium bowl, combine the bananas, sugar, and salt and mash with the back of a fork or potato masher until the mixture is as smooth as possible. Only very small pieces of banana, if any, should remain visible. Stir in 43 grams (3 tablespoons) of the yogurt. Add the all-purpose flour, golden wheat flour, cumin, and baking soda, stirring to form a slightly sticky dough. Depending on the ripeness of your bananas, you may need to add an additional 14 grams (1 tablespoon) yogurt (for less ripe bananas) or additional all-purpose flour (for more ripe bananas) to bring the dough together.

Transfer the dough to an unfloured work surface and, using lightly oiled hands, knead until a stiff yet tacky dough forms, about 5 minutes. If the dough sticks to the work surface, use a bench knife to scrape the surface, then continue kneading. When finished, the dough will be slightly elastic, though its surface may not be completely smooth. Return the dough to the bowl, cover, and let rest at room temperature for 4 hours. (Alternatively, you can refrigerate the dough overnight, 12 to 16 hours.)

If your dough has been refrigerated, let it come to room temperature for 1 hour.

Recipe continues

DIVIDE AND SHAPE: Lightly flour a work surface and use a plastic bowl scraper to ease the dough out of the bowl onto the work surface. Divide the dough into 12 equal portions (each about 53 grams). Preshape the pieces into rounds (see Preshaping, page 32), then cover with a barely damp, lint-free kitchen towel to rest for 20 minutes.

HEAT THE OIL: Line a rimmed baking sheet with paper towels and set a wire rack on top of the paper towels. Set near the stove. Pour 1½ inches oil into a 10- to 12-inch-wide pan that's at least 3 inches deep—such as a Dutch oven or a karahi (Indian wok)—and heat over medium heat until it registers 365°F on a digital or deep-frying thermometer.

MEANWHILE, ROLL THE PURI: Working with one piece of dough at a time on a lightly floured surface, roll it into a 4-inch round slightly less than ¼ inch thick. Set the rounds aside, slightly overlapped and covered with the damp towel, as you wait for the oil to heat.

FRY THE PURI: Working with one puri at a time, carefully lower the edge of the dough round into the hot oil, then release it away from you. Add a second and third puri to the oil. The puri will sink to the bottom and then float to the surface and begin to inflate. Use a metal spatula or spider/skimmer to lightly press down on the puri, which will encourage them to puff. Fry the puri on the first side until deep golden brown, about 30 seconds, then flip and fry on the second side until evenly deep golden brown, about 30 seconds more. Transfer the finished puri to the wire rack. Continue frying the remaining puri in batches, letting the oil return to temperature between batches. If the rolled dough rounds shrink while resting, gently roll them out again to 4 inches in diameter before frying.

Serve immediately.

SCALLION PANCAKES

MAKES 8 PANCAKES

DOUGH

300 grams (2½ cups) unbleached all-purpose flour, plus more for dusting

6 grams (1 teaspoon) fine salt

170 grams (¾ cup) boiling water (212°F)

DIPPING SAUCE

4 large scallions (63 grams/ ½ bunch), white parts only, finely chopped (reserve the green tops for the pancakes)

8 grams (1-inch piece) fresh ginger, peeled and finely grated

9 grams (1 tablespoon) white sesame seeds

28 grams (2 tablespoons) soy sauce or tamari

14 grams (1 tablespoon) rice vinegar

14 grams (1 tablespoon) water

13 grams (2 teaspoons) maple syrup

12 grams (1 tablespoon) sesame oil

Ingredients continue

A staple of many Chinese restaurant menus, these scallion pancakes are made with a boiling water dough. When you add boiling water to flour, rather than being absorbed by the protein in the flour, it's absorbed into the starch molecules. That means the proteins in flour that are responsible for creating gluten (gliadin and glutenin) don't get the water they need for strong gluten formation. In practical terms, this means the dough is easy to roll and doesn't spring back, which is key in a recipe like this one, where the flatbreads are rolled, brushed with fat, coiled, and rolled again, which is what gives them their distinctive flaky layers.

Cookbook author Hetty Lui McKinnon, who developed this recipe, cooks her scallion pancakes in a hot skillet lightly filmed with oil, though for an extra-crispy version, you can also shallow-fry them in a more generous amount of oil. In either case, don't skip the gingery dipping sauce.

MAKE THE DOUGH: In a medium bowl, combine the flour and salt. Wet a clean kitchen towel, then wring it out and place the towel under the bowl to prevent it from moving while you are mixing. Simultaneously stream in the boiling water while stirring the mixture with the handle-end of a wooden spoon or pair of chopsticks. The mixture will be lumpy. Carefully use a plastic bowl scraper to fold the dough over itself until it begins to hold together. (The dough will be very warm.)

Turn the dough out onto a clean work surface and knead until the dough is smooth, about 5 minutes. Return the dough to the bowl, cover, and let rest at room temperature for 30 minutes.

MEANWHILE, MAKE THE DIPPING SAUCE: In a small bowl, combine the scallion whites, ginger, sesame seeds, soy sauce or tamari, rice vinegar, water, maple syrup, and sesame oil and stir to combine. Cover and set aside at room temperature for serving.

Recipe continues

PANCAKES

4 large scallions, green parts only, sliced into rings

149 grams (¾ cup) vegetable or other neutral oil, divided

17 grams (1 tablespoon plus 1 teaspoon) sesame oil

Fine sea salt, for sprinkling

PREPARE THE PANCAKE INGREDIENTS: Set the scallion greens aside in a small bowl. Combine 50 grams (¼ cup) of the neutral cooking oil and the sesame oil in a separate small bowl. Set aside.

DIVIDE AND SHAPE: Lightly flour a work surface and use a plastic bowl scraper to ease the dough out of the bowl onto the work surface. Divide the dough into 8 equal portions (each about 60 grams). Shape each piece of dough into a smooth ball by rolling it in your hands, then cover with a damp cloth.

ROLL THE PANCAKES: Line a rimmed baking sheet with parchment paper. Working with one piece of dough at a time, roll it out into a thin round 6 to 7 inches in diameter. Brush a very thin layer of the sesame oil mixture over the dough (too much and it can make the subsequent rolling more difficult), then roll it into a log. Wind the log into a coil, tucking the end underneath. Gently press down on the coil with your palm to slightly flatten it, then cover again with a damp towel while you work through the remaining dough.

Working with one coil of dough at a time, gently flatten the coil with the palm of your hand, then roll it into a thin 6- to 7-inch diameter round. Brush the dough with a very thin layer of the sesame oil mixture, then sprinkle with 4 grams (scant 1 tablespoon) of the sliced scallion greens and a pinch of salt. Roll the dough up into a thin cylinder again, then wind into a coil, tucking the end underneath. Gently press down on the coil with your palm to slightly flatten it, then cover again with a damp towel while you work through the remaining dough.

Roll each filled coil one final time into a thin 6- to 7-inch round. This repeated process of rolling, coiling, then rolling again creates layers in the dough. Lightly brush the top of each pancake with a bit of the sesame oil mixture, then set on the prepared baking sheet and cover; separate the scallion pancakes with layers of parchment paper to prevent them from sticking together. Repeat with the remaining coils of dough, oiling and stacking as you go. Keep the stack of pancakes covered with the damp towel to prevent them from drying out.

FRY THE PANCAKES: Preheat a 10-inch nonstick or cast-iron skillet over medium heat until a few water drops flicked on the surface sizzle and almost immediately evaporate. Add 12 grams (1 tablespoon) neutral oil to the skillet. Gently place one pancake in the pan and cook. Using a spatula, gently press the pancake onto the hot surface. After about 2 minutes the top of the pancake will turn an opaque color and bubbles will start to appear. The bottom of the pancake will be crisp and golden brown in spots. Flip the pancake over and continue cooking in the same manner, gently pressing it onto the hot skillet surface until it's deep golden brown and crispy, an additional 2 minutes. Transfer the pancake to a paper towel to absorb any excess oil, then to a wire rack to cool slightly. You may need to adjust your heat up and down while cooking to ensure the pancakes are thoroughly cooked without overbrowning. Continue cooking the remaining pancakes, adding 12 grams (1 tablespoon) additional oil to the pan between each batch.

Cut into wedges and serve hot with the dipping sauce. Scallion pancakes are best eaten right after they're cooked.

SPICY CHIVE AND EGG GUŌ KUĪ

CHIVE-AND-EGG-STUFFED FLATBREAD

MIX — 10 MIN | REST — 1 HOUR | SHAPE — 30 MIN | FRY AND BAKE — 22 MIN

TIME: ABOUT 2 HOURS

MAKES SIX 3-INCH FLATBREADS

DOUGH

263 grams (2 cups plus 3 tablespoons) unbleached all-purpose flour, plus more for dusting

5 grams (scant 1 teaspoon) fine salt

4.5 grams (1½ teaspoons) instant yeast

4 grams (1 teaspoon) sugar

170 grams (¾ cup) warm water (see Temperature, page 25)

12 grams (1 tablespoon) vegetable oil or other neutral oil

FILLING

24 grams (2 tablespoons) vegetable oil or other neutral oil, divided

2 large eggs (100 grams), beaten

1 large clove garlic (8 grams), minced

½ teaspoon crushed Sichuan peppercorns

1 teaspoon red pepper flakes

1½ teaspoons doubanjiang (spicy fermented broad bean paste; optional)

Guō kuī are circular Chinese pan-fried flatbreads that originated in Shanxi but are also commonly found in the Sichuan region. The Chinese characters themselves translate directly to "pot helmet," a reference to the fact these flatbreads look like small pot lids. These coiled buns are golden brown and crispy on the exterior and fluffy within and are typically layered with either sweet fillings (brown sugar) or savory ones (spiced ground meat). In this recipe, developed for us by Betty Liu, author of *My Shanghai*, the filling is a spicy mixture of garlic chives and scrambled eggs, which Betty says is not exactly traditional but is nevertheless wildly delicious and intensely fragrant. If you want a less spicy filling, reduce the amount of doubanjiang, or omit it entirely. Chinese garlic chives can be found at Asian markets or well-stocked supermarkets. If you can't find them, a combination of scallions and chives can be substituted.

MAKE THE DOUGH: In a medium bowl, combine the flour, salt, yeast, sugar, and water and stir the mixture with the handle of a wooden spoon. As the dough begins to come together into a shaggy mass, stream in the oil. Continue working the mixture in the bowl until you have a cohesive dough with no dry patches.

Transfer the dough to a lightly floured surface and knead until the dough is smooth and elastic, about 8 minutes. The dough will be sticky at first but will smooth out quickly; to make it easier to handle, use a bench knife to scrape the dough off your work surface as you knead, which will speed up the process and reduce the amount of flour required for kneading (adding too much flour at this stage can make your guō kuī denser). Because this is a relatively small amount of dough, it doesn't quite have enough volume to make using a stand mixer for mixing and kneading efficient, therefore we recommend mixing and kneading by hand. Return the dough to the bowl, cover, and let rest until it is puffy though not necessarily doubled in size, about 1 hour.

227 grams (8 ounces) Chinese garlic chives, trimmed and cut into ¼-inch pieces

1 teaspoon sugar

Scant ½ teaspoon fine salt

½ teaspoon ground white pepper

1 teaspoon soy sauce

½ teaspoon sesame oil

24 grams (2 tablespoons) vegetable oil or other neutral oil, for cooking

While the dough rises, heat a well-seasoned wok or 10- to 12-inch nonstick skillet over medium-high heat. Add 12 grams (1 tablespoon) of the oil and when the oil is hot, add the eggs and quickly scramble. As soon as the eggs start to set, remove the pan from the heat and transfer the eggs to a medium bowl. Use a spatula to break up the eggs into small pieces. Set aside.

Wipe out the wok or skillet and set over medium-high heat. Add the remaining 12 grams (1 tablespoon) oil, the garlic, Sichuan peppercorns, pepper flakes, and doubanjiang (if using). Cook until the mixture is fragrant and the doubanjiang paste has softened and is no longer clumpy, about 30 seconds. Remove from the heat, add the garlic chives, and stir to combine; the residual heat will soften them. Add the garlic chive mixture to the eggs and mix to combine. Wipe the skillet clean with a paper towel. You will use it to cook the guō kuī.

In a small bowl, whisk together the sugar, salt, white pepper, soy sauce, and sesame oil. Pour this over the garlic chive and egg mixture. Stir to combine.

Preheat the oven to 400°F. Line a rimmed baking sheet with parchment paper.

DIVIDE, ROLL, AND FILL THE DOUGH: Lightly flour a work surface and use a plastic bowl scraper to ease the dough out of the bowl onto the work surface. Gently flatten the dough into a rectangle and divide it into 6 equal portions (each about 75 grams). Working with one piece of dough at a time and keeping the remaining dough pieces covered so they don't dry out, roll out the dough into an 8 × 4-inch rectangle. Set the rectangle with a short side facing you. Spread 58 grams (¼ cup) filling into a thin layer on the rectangle leaving a ½-inch border on all sides. Fold the long sides of the dough in toward the center to partially cover the filling, then, starting at the short side closest to you, roll the dough up into a 3-inch-long cylinder. Pinch to seal. Stand the cylinder up on one end and, using your palm, gently press it down into a 2-inch-thick disk. Some of the filling may squeeze out where the dough is thin; that's OK. Just keep going and add any escaped filling to the next bun. Repeat with the remaining dough and filling.

FRY THE GUŌ KUĪ: Once all of the guō kuī are formed, press down on each disk once more until it is about 3 inches in diameter and 1 inch thick. Return the wok or nonstick skillet to medium-low heat and add

Recipe continues

12 grams (1 tablespoon) of the oil. Place 3 flatbreads in the pan in a single layer and cook until the bottoms are golden brown, 2 to 3 minutes. Flip and continue cooking until the second sides are golden brown, an additional 2 to 3 minutes. Transfer to the prepared baking sheet. Add another 12 grams (1 tablespoon) oil to the skillet and cook the remaining 3 guō kuī and transfer them to the baking sheet.

Place the baking sheet in the oven and bake for 10 minutes. Remove from the oven and let cool 5 minutes before serving.

Store leftover guō kuī in an airtight container up to 3 days. Reheat flatbreads in a 400°F oven for 8 to 10 minutes or until warmed through.

SESAME DÀ BĬNG

YEASTED SESAME BREAD

MIX	BULK FERMENTATION	SHAPE	FRY
10 MIN	1–1½ HOURS	15 MIN	30 MIN

TIME: ABOUT 2½ HOURS

MAKES 1 LOAF

DOUGH

248 grams (2 cups plus 1 tablespoon) unbleached all-purpose flour, plus more for dusting

170 grams (¾ cup) warm water (see Temperature, page 25)

12 grams (1 tablespoon) sugar

4.5 grams (1½ teaspoons) instant yeast

3 grams (½ teaspoon) fine salt

14 grams (1 tablespoon) unsalted butter, melted and cooled slightly

FOR THE YOU SU (SESAME OIL PASTE)

30 grams (¼ cup) unbleached all-purpose flour

36 grams (3 tablespoons) sesame oil

13 grams (2 teaspoons) maple syrup or 8 grams (2 teaspoons) sugar

1½ teaspoons five-spice powder

Dà bĭng means "big bread," and is so named because it's thick and fluffy. In Shanghai, large-format dà bĭng, nearly a foot in diameter, are cut into wedges, like pizza, and sold as street food, often alongside hot soy milk or soup. Our dinner-plate-size version is encrusted in sesame seeds, with striations of fragrant sesame oil and five-spice powder paste within. This bread is pan-fried in a covered skillet, so it steams and crisps simultaneously. Monitor the heat as the bread cooks; you want it brown without charring and cooked long enough that it's baked all the way through.

MAKE THE DOUGH: In a medium bowl, combine the flour, water, sugar, yeast, and salt and mix with the handle of a wooden spoon until a shaggy dough forms. Stream in the melted butter and continue mixing and kneading in the bowl until a soft, sticky dough forms. Transfer the dough to a lightly floured surface and continue kneading until the dough is smooth and elastic, 5 to 8 minutes. The dough will be sticky at first but will smooth out quickly; to make it easier to handle, use a bench knife to scrape the dough off your work surface as you knead, which will speed up the process and reduce the amount of flour required for kneading (adding too much flour at this stage can make your bread denser). Return the dough to the bowl, cover, and let rest in a warm place for 30 minutes.

Alternatively, in a stand mixer bowl, combine the flour, water, sugar, yeast, and salt and, using the dough hook attachment, mix on medium-low speed until a shaggy dough forms. With the mixer running, stream in the melted butter, then continue mixing until the dough is smooth and elastic and pulls away from the sides of the bowl, about 5 minutes. Cover and let rest in a warm place for 30 minutes.

With a lightly floured hand, deflate the dough and then perform 6 to 8 bowl folds (see Folding, page 30) or until the dough resists stretching.

Ingredients continue

Recipe continues

¼ teaspoon fine salt

¾ teaspoon freshly ground black pepper

1 large egg white (35 grams)

27 grams (3 tablespoons) white sesame seeds

24 grams (2 tablespoons) vegetable or other neutral oil

Round out the dough and place it seam side down, then cover and let rise until very puffy and doubled in size, 30 minutes to 1 hour.

MEANWHILE, MAKE THE SESAME OIL PASTE: In a small bowl, whisk together the flour, sesame oil, maple syrup (or sugar), and five-spice powder until the mixture is smooth. Set aside.

ASSEMBLE THE DÀ BǏNG: Use a plastic bowl scraper to gently ease the dough out of the bowl onto a lightly floured work surface, then use a rolling pin to roll it into an 18 × 12-inch rectangle. Set the rectangle with a long side facing you. Spread the sesame oil paste over the dough, leaving a 1-inch border on the long side farthest away from you. Sprinkle the salt and pepper over the sesame paste. Starting with the long side closest to you, roll the dough into a log. Pinch the edge to seal, then place it seam side down. Cover and let rest for 5 minutes.

Starting at one end, gently coil the log into a spiral, pinching the end and tucking it under the spiral so that it doesn't unravel when transferring it to the pan to cook. Using your hands or a rolling pin, gently flatten the entire spiral to about 1 inch thick. Brush the top of the spiral with egg white, then generously sprinkle the sesame seeds over the top to coat, pressing down lightly to ensure they are adhered.

FRY THE DÀ BǏNG: In a 10-inch nonstick pan, heat the oil over medium-high heat. When the oil is shimmering, carefully transfer the coiled dough to the pan with the sesame seed side up. Reduce the heat to low, cover with a lid, and cook the bread until the bottom is golden brown, about 15 minutes, peeking at the underside occasionally to ensure it's not browning too much. If it's taking on too much color, reduce the heat.

Uncover, flip the bread, cover again, and continue cooking over low heat until the sesame seed side is golden brown, about 10 minutes. Uncover, then flip the bread one more time so that the sesame seed side is up and cook for 5 more minutes uncovered. When tapped, the bread should sound hollow and feel light for its size.

Remove the bread from the pan and transfer it to a cutting board to rest for 10 minutes. Using a serrated knife, cut the bread into 8 wedges. This bread is best served warm. Store leftover bread in an airtight container for up to 2 days. To reheat the bread, wrap it in foil, then place it in a preheated 350°F oven until heated through, 5 to 8 minutes.

SCHÜTTELBROT

TYROLEAN RYE FLATBREAD

MIX	BULK FERMENTATION	SHAPE	BAKE
5 MIN	1–1½ HOURS	20 MIN	35–40 MIN

MAKE THE PREFERMENT (12–16 HOURS BEFORE)

········ TIME: ABOUT 18 HOURS ········

MAKES FOUR 8-INCH FLATBREADS

PREFERMENT

28 grams (2 tablespoons) sourdough culture (see page 187)

120 grams (1 cup plus 2 tablespoons) whole rye flour

120 grams (generous ½ cup) cold water (55°F to 60°F)

DOUGH

80 grams (½ cup plus 3 tablespoons) unbleached all-purpose flour

136 grams (1¼ cups plus 1 tablespoon) whole rye flour, divided, plus more for dusting

½ teaspoon fine salt

½ teaspoon fennel seeds, coarsely ground

½ teaspoon caraway seeds, coarsely ground

150 grams (½ cup plus 3 tablespoons) cold water (55°F to 60°F)

These exceptionally craggy, crunchy sourdough flatbreads, spiced with fennel and caraway seeds, hail from the mountainous border region between Austria and Italy. They're made with a rye flour preferment (as well as a majority of rye flour in the dough), which gives them a pleasant tanginess and, because the dough is so wet and sticky, they employ an unusual shaping technique. Rather than being rolled, the dough is shaken and bounced during shaping (*schüttelbrot* translates to "shaken bread"), resulting in irregularly shaped flatbreads with craggy surfaces.

DAY 1

MAKE THE PREFERMENT: The evening before you want to bake, make the preferment. Combine the sourdough culture, rye flour, and water in a medium bowl, mixing until no dry spots remain. The mixture will be thick and pasty. Cover and let stand at room temperature overnight, 12 to 16 hours.

DAY 2

MAKE THE DOUGH: Add the all-purpose flour, 30 grams (¼ cup plus 1 tablespoon) rye flour, salt, fennel seeds, caraway seeds, and water to the preferment. Mix well until a smooth, wet, and sticky dough forms. Cover and let rest at room temperature for 1 to 1½ hours. The dough may have some small bubbles, but will not have risen much, if at all.

Meanwhile, evenly space the racks in the oven and preheat to 375°F. Line two baking sheets with parchment paper and set aside.

SHAPE THE FLATBREADS: Place the remaining 106 grams (1 cup) rye flour in a shallow, wide bowl. Using a muffin scoop or a ⅓-cup measuring cup that has been dipped in water, scoop one portion of dough into the pile of rye flour. With a cupped hand, gently turn the dough over to coat

Recipe continues

both sides with flour. Transfer the dough to an 8-inch cardboard cake round (or the removable bottom of a 9-inch tart pan covered with parchment paper) that has been lightly dusted with rye flour.

Holding the round with the dough at a 45-degree angle, gently shake and bounce the round to move the dough toward the edge farthest away from you. Rotate the round between one-eighth and one-quarter of a turn, then repeat the motion of gently shaking, bouncing, and rotating the round until the dough is fairly round in shape and about 6 inches in diameter and ¼ inch thick. Slide the dough onto the prepared baking sheet. Repeat this process with the remaining dough, placing three flatbreads on each baking sheet.

BAKE: Bake the flatbreads until the edges are one shade darker than the centers and the centers feel firm and barely yield to gentle pressure, 35 to 40 minutes. Turn off the oven, leaving the door closed, and let the flatbreads cool completely in the oven.

Break flatbreads into pieces to serve. The flatbreads will keep in an airtight container for up to 2 weeks.

TUNNBRÖD

RYE FLATBREAD

MIX	BULK FERMENTATION	PRESHAPE	SHAPE	BAKE
5 MIN	1 HOUR	5 MIN	10 MIN	16 MIN

TIME: ABOUT 2 HOURS

MAKES EIGHT 6- TO 7-INCH SOFT FLATBREADS

195 grams (1½ cups plus 2 tablespoons) unbleached all-purpose flour, plus more for dusting

53 grams (½ cup) whole rye flour

4 grams (2 teaspoons) fennel seeds, coarsely ground

1 teaspoon instant yeast

½ teaspoon fine salt

28 grams (2 tablespoons) unsalted butter, melted

199 grams (¾ cup plus 2 tablespoons) warm milk (see Temperature, page 25), whole preferred

We love the versatility of tunnbröd, which is a staple flatbread in Sweden. The dough can be cooked in a skillet on the stovetop, resulting in a pliable, tender bread that can be used as a wrap (in Sweden, street food versions are filled with mashed potatoes and hot dogs!). Or it can be rolled more thinly and baked in the oven until crisp and cracker-like (see Variation). It's amazing how this dough can become two different things just by rolling and cooking it more. Early recipes for tunnbröd were made with barley, rye, or oats; we've opted for a combination of all-purpose and whole rye flours for optimal foldability and flavor. We enrich the dough with butter and milk, which helps keep the breads tender. Fennel seeds are a traditional addition to tunnbröd. But if you're fennel-averse they can be omitted.

MAKE THE DOUGH: In a large bowl, combine the all-purpose flour, rye flour, fennel seeds, yeast, and salt. Add the melted butter and milk and mix with the handle of a wooden spoon to form a cohesive, slightly sticky dough. Transfer the dough to a lightly floured surface and knead by hand until smooth and springy, about 5 minutes. The dough will be tacky. Place the dough back in the bowl, cover, and let rest at room temperature for 1 hour.

DIVIDE AND PRESHAPE: Use a plastic bowl scraper to gently ease the dough out of the bowl onto a lightly floured work surface. Divide the dough into 8 equal portions (each about 60 grams). Gently preshape each piece into a round (see Preshaping, page 32), then cover and let rest while you preheat the pan.

Place a 10- to 12-inch nonstick or cast-iron skillet over medium heat until a few water drops flicked on the surface sizzle and almost immediately evaporate.

Recipe continues

MEANWHILE, ROLL THE DOUGH: Working with one piece of dough at a time on a well-floured surface, roll out the dough into a 6- to 7-inch round about ⅛ inch thick. Using a pastry brush, brush off any excess flour from the top and bottom of the round, then dock the round thoroughly with the tines of a fork.

Transfer the round to the preheated pan and cook until lightly golden brown around the edges and in spots, about 1 minute. Flip and continue cooking on the second side until the bottom is lightly golden brown around the edges and in spots, about 1 minute. Stack the cooked tunnbröd on a clean kitchen towel, wrapping to cover. This keeps the flatbread pliable and warm. Repeat with the remaining dough, stacking the flatbreads in the towel as you go.

Eat warm or cool completely before storing them in an airtight container at room temperature for up to 2 days. Freeze for longer storage.

VARIATION

LARGE-FORMAT SWEDISH RYE CRACKERS:

Make the dough as directed above. While the dough rests, preheat the oven to 450°F with a baking stone or steel on a rack in the top third of the oven. Use a plastic bowl scraper to gently ease the dough out of the bowl onto a lightly floured work surface. Divide the dough into 8 equal portions (each about 60 grams). Gently preshape each piece into a round (see Preshaping, page 32). Working with one piece of dough at a time on a well-floured surface, roll out the dough into a 9-inch round about 1/16 inch thick. Using a pastry brush, gently brush off any excess flour from the top and bottom of the round, then dock the round thoroughly with the tines of a fork. Gently transfer the rolled-out dough to a lightly floured baker's peel or an inverted baking sheet to transfer the dough onto the stone. Bake one at a time until the edges and top and bottom are golden brown in spots, about 5 minutes. Using tongs or a peel, carefully remove the cracker from the oven and transfer to a rack to cool completely. Repeat with the remaining dough. Once cooled, break into irregular pieces; they will keep in an airtight container for up to 1 week.

LEFSE

NORWEGIAN POTATO PANCAKES

PREP THE POTATOES	MIX	SHAPE	REST	ROLL	COOK
40 MIN TO 1½ HOURS	5 MIN	5 MIN	15–20 MIN	25 MIN	16–24 MIN

········· TIME: ABOUT 2½ HOURS ·········

MAKES SIXTEEN 6- TO 7-INCH LEFSE

2 large russet potatoes (about 520 grams/18 ounces)

18 grams (1 tablespoon plus 1 teaspoon) unsalted butter, at room temperature, plus more for serving

90 grams (¾ cup) unbleached all-purpose flour, plus more for dusting

1 teaspoon sugar, plus more for serving

3 grams (½ teaspoon) fine salt

57 to 70 grams (¼ cup to 5 tablespoons) heavy cream

Jam (optional), for serving

Lefse are Norwegian flatbreads that typically (though not always) include potatoes in the dough. For our potato lefse, we use low-moisture, starchy russet potatoes, then microwave or bake them (rather than boil) to further dry out the flesh. Using a ricer or sieve to "mash" the potatoes—rather than a hand-held potato masher—gives the best results, as hand-mashing can leave lumps that make it hard to roll out the lefse thinly enough. Traditionally, lefse are rolled with a ridged rolling pin, which gives them their distinctive appearance, but a regular rolling pin works fine, too. Lefse are topped with all sorts of sweet (butter and granulated sugar, butter and jam) and savory (smoked salmon and cream cheese) preparations, then rolled up into cigar shapes and enjoyed—it's unlikely that anyone will eat just one.

Prick the potatoes all over with a fork, then place them in the microwave and cook until tender, about 8 minutes. (Alternatively, bake the potatoes on a parchment-lined baking sheet in a preheated 400°F oven until tender, about 45 minutes.) Let the potatoes cool until they can be handled, 3 to 5 minutes, then carefully use a paring knife to peel the skins off. Discard the skin. Roughly chop the potato flesh, then transfer to a ricer or medium-gauge wire sieve. Press the cooked potato through the ricer or sieve, then measure out 310 grams (about 2 cups) cooked potato and transfer to a medium bowl.

Add the butter to the riced potato and use a fork to lightly toss together to evenly distribute and melt the butter. Place the potato mixture in the refrigerator, uncovered, until cold, about 30 minutes.

MAKE THE DOUGH: Add the flour, sugar, salt, and 57 grams (¼ cup) heavy cream to the cold potato mixture, using a fork to toss and mix until a crumbly dough forms. Gently knead the dough by hand in the bowl

Recipe continues

until smooth; the dough will have the consistency of modeling clay and be just slightly tacky. If the dough seems dry or is cracking and not holding together after kneading, add a bit more heavy cream ½ teaspoon at a time just until the dough holds together.

DIVIDE AND SHAPE: Transfer the dough to an unfloured surface and divide into 16 equal portions (each about 30 grams). Gently form each piece of dough into a ball, then flatten and smooth into a puck that is about 2 inches in diameter and ½ inch thick. Place the pucks of dough in a single layer on

a parchment-lined baking sheet and refrigerate, uncovered, for 15 to 20 minutes.

Preheat a 10- to 12-inch nonstick skillet over medium heat until a few water drops flicked on the surface sizzle and almost immediately evaporate. (Alternatively, preheat an electric griddle to 400°F.)

ROLL THE LEFSE: Generously flour a work surface. Working with 1 puck of dough at a time and adding additional flour on top of and underneath the dough as needed to keep it from sticking, roll each puck into a 6- to 7-inch round. If the dough is cracking when you roll it, let it warm up for a few minutes before rolling. If, on the other hand, the dough feels too soft or sticky when rolling, refrigerate the pucks until firm again before trying to roll. The dough will be thin enough that you can see the work surface through it. With a pastry brush, gently brush off any excess flour.

COOK THE LEFSE: Using a bench knife or thin metal spatula, gently release the dough from the work surface and transfer it to the hot pan (or griddle). Cook the lefse until bubbles cover the surface and the bottom is browned in spots, 30 to 45 seconds. Carefully flip the lefse and continue cooking on the second side until browned in spots, an additional 30 to 45 seconds (begin rolling the second lefse while the first cooks). Wrap the lefse in a clean kitchen towel to keep them warm and pliable. Repeat until all the lefse have been cooked.

To serve, spread each lefse with some butter, then sprinkle with sugar or spread with jam and roll into a cigar shape.

Store cooled lefse well wrapped in the refrigerator for up to 3 days. To freeze, once the lefse are completely cooled, they can be stacked between parchment paper and then placed in a zip-top bag or wrapped in plastic wrap, then aluminum foil. Thaw in the fridge overnight, then reheat in a preheated skillet for 10 to 20 seconds on each side or a few seconds in the microwave.

KNÄCKEBRÖD

SWEDISH-STYLE RYE CRISPBREAD

MIX	BULK FERMENTATION	SHAPE	BAKE
30 MIN	1 HOUR	25 MIN	36–40 MIN

TIME: ABOUT 2½ HOURS

MAKES FIVE 8-INCH CRISPBREADS

120 grams (1 cup) unbleached bread flour, plus more for dusting

60 grams (½ cup plus 1 tablespoon) whole rye flour

3 grams (1 teaspoon) instant yeast

3 grams (½ teaspoon) fine salt

14 grams (1 tablespoon) unsalted butter, at room temperature

30 grams (scant ¼ cup) sunflower seeds

10 grams (generous 1 tablespoon) flaxseeds

11 grams (1½ teaspoons) honey

128 grams (½ cup plus 1 tablespoon) warm water (see Temperature, page 25)

Flaky sea salt, such as Maldon, for sprinkling (optional)

These thin, crisp Swedish flatbreads were typically baked for long storage: The hole in the center made it easy to string the breads up and store them in the rafters, where they'd continue to dry, lasting from grain harvest season through a long Swedish winter. Though their keeping quality is still one of knäckebröd's greatest qualities, that's actually irrelevant: These seedy crispbreads, sweetened with a bit of honey, are so good they tend to disappear quickly. Store-bought crispbreads can be cardboard-like, but these are remarkably flavorful and wonderfully crunchy.

MAKE THE DOUGH: In a medium bowl, combine the bread flour, rye flour, yeast, and salt. With your fingers or a pastry cutter, work the butter into the flour mixture until no visible pieces remain. Add the sunflower seeds, flaxseeds, honey, and water and mix with the handle of a wooden spoon until no dry patches remain and a soft, sticky dough forms. Cover with plastic wrap and let rest in the bowl for 20 minutes.

Transfer the dough to a lightly floured work surface and knead until smooth and springy, about 5 minutes. Add just enough flour to keep the dough from sticking. Use a bench knife to scrape the dough off your work surface as you knead, which will speed up the process and reduce the amount of flour required for kneading (adding too much flour at this stage can make your dough dry and difficult to roll out). Return the dough to the bowl, re-cover, and let rest at room temperature until the dough is slightly risen, about 1 hour.

Meanwhile, position racks in the top and bottom thirds of the oven and preheat the oven to 350°F. Line two 18 × 13-inch baking sheets with parchment paper.

Recipe continues

DIVIDE, SHAPE, AND ROLL THE KNÄCKEBRÖD:
Lightly flour a work surface. Use a plastic bowl scraper to ease the dough out of the bowl onto the work surface. Divide the dough into 4 equal portions (each about 87 grams). Gently shape them into rounds. Working with 1 piece of dough at a time, roll it into an 8¼- to 8½-inch round. Using an 8-inch plate or cardboard cake round as a template, cut an 8-inch round from the dough. Using a fork or skewer, prick the round about every ½ inch (this will prevent bubbles from forming during baking), then use a 1-inch round cutter to cut a hole out of the middle of the round. Save the scraps and the smaller center round of dough. Repeat with the remaining 3 pieces of dough. Gather all the scraps into a ball and knead briefly to combine, then roll and cut one final fifth circle.

BAKE: Transfer 2 circles of dough to each of the prepared baking sheets (you'll need to wait for the first four to bake before baking the fifth and final circle). Sprinkle with flaky salt, if using. Bake until the crispbreads are medium golden brown and firm, 18 to 20 minutes, switching racks and rotating the baking sheets front to back halfway through.

Let cool completely on the baking sheets (they'll continue to crisp as they cool). They will keep, stored in an airtight container, for weeks.

OLIVE OIL TORTAS

MIX	BULK FERMENTATION	SHAPE	BAKE
8 MIN	30 MIN	25 MIN	13-15 MIN

······· TIME: ABOUT 80 MINUTES ·······

MAKES TWELVE 4- TO 5-INCH TORTAS

DOUGH

120 grams (1 cup) unbleached all-purpose flour, plus more for dusting

3 grams (1 teaspoon) instant yeast

1.5 grams (¼ teaspoon) fine salt

36 grams (3 tablespoons) olive oil

52 grams (scant ¼ cup) warm water (see Temperature, page 25)

TOPPING

3 grams (1½ teaspoons) anise seeds

50 grams (¼ cup) sugar

1 large egg white (35 grams)

Somewhere between a cracker and a cookie, these flatbreads are flaky and crisp, made with an olive oil–enriched dough and topped with anise seed sugar. Spanish in origin, they have a long history: Tortas are mentioned in *Don Quixote*. While the spiced sugar is a traditional topping, there are other options: For a savory version, top them with chopped fresh rosemary leaves, a sprinkle of smoked paprika, or sesame seeds. Instead of anise sugar, you could dust the tortas with cinnamon sugar instead. They're very good as a vehicle for a smear of soft cheese (sweet plus salty!) or alongside a cup of coffee or tea.

MAKE THE DOUGH: In a medium bowl, combine the flour, yeast, and salt. Add the oil and water and mix until no dry patches of flour remain. Transfer the dough to a clean work surface, then knead until the dough smooths out and becomes elastic, about 5 minutes. Note that the dough will not be completely smooth after kneading; this is normal. Return the dough to the bowl, cover, and let rest at room temperature for 30 minutes.

Meanwhile, position racks in the upper and lower thirds of the oven and preheat the oven to 350°F. Line two rimmed baking sheets with parchment paper.

MAKE THE TOPPING: Finely grind the anise seeds in a coffee/spice grinder or mortar and pestle. Transfer to a small bowl and add the sugar; stir to combine. Place the egg white in a small bowl and beat with a fork until lightly frothy.

DIVIDE AND SHAPE THE TORTAS: Divide the dough into 12 equal portions (each about 17 grams). Gently preshape each piece of dough into a round (see Preshaping, page 32). On a lightly floured surface, roll each piece of dough into a 4- to 5-inch round. It's necessary to roll the tortas thinly to ensure they bake up crisp; dust your work surface with flour to prevent sticking. Using a bench knife to aid you, transfer the rounds to the prepared baking sheets, 6 per pan, spacing them evenly.

Prick each round all over with the tines of a fork; this will prevent bubbles from forming during baking.

BAKE THE TORTAS: Lightly brush each round with egg white, then sprinkle with a generous teaspoon of anise sugar, pressing lightly so the sugar adheres. Bake the tortas until crisp and golden brown in spots, 13 to 15 minutes, switching racks and rotating the pans front to back halfway through.

Transfer to a rack to cool completely. Store leftover tortas in an airtight container for up to 5 days.

SEEDY CRACKER BREAD

MIX	REST	SHAPE	BAKE
5 MIN	10 MIN	5 MIN	50–60 MIN

TIME: ABOUT 1 HOUR 20 MINUTES

MAKES ONE 18 × 13-INCH PAN; THIRTY-TWO 3 × 2-INCH CRACKERS

80 grams (¾ cup) whole rye flour

70 grams (¾ cup plus 1 tablespoon) old-fashioned rolled oats

30 grams (¼ cup) pumpkin seeds

35 grams (¼ cup) sunflower seeds

26 grams (3 tablespoons) flaxseeds

26 grams (3 tablespoons) sesame seeds

15 grams (1 tablespoon) chia seeds

9 grams (1 tablespoon) poppy seeds

6 grams (1 teaspoon) fine salt

14 grams (2 teaspoons) honey

12 grams (1 tablespoon) olive oil

270 grams (1 cup plus 3 tablespoons) boiling water (212°F)

We debated whether crackers could technically be considered flatbreads, but we didn't want anyone to miss out on these crunchy, seedy crackers. They are a nutty, incredible canvas: Use them to scoop up dips or spread them with soft cheese or mashed avocado. The precise combination of seeds isn't terribly important; you'll need 1 cup in total, but you can vary the combination to suit your taste.

Arrange racks in the upper and lower thirds of the oven and preheat the oven to 325°F. Line a 18 × 13-inch baking sheet with parchment paper, folding or trimming the paper as necessary so that it sits flat against the pan.

MAKE THE DOUGH: In a medium bowl, combine the pumpernickel flour, oats, pumpkin seeds, sunflower seeds, flaxseeds, sesame seeds, chia seeds, poppy seeds, and salt, mixing to evenly distribute the ingredients. Add the honey, oil, and boiling water, stirring well to combine. (Alternatively, in a stand mixer bowl, combine the dry ingredients and, using the paddle, mix on low speed. Add the honey, oil, and water, mixing on low speed until well combined.) Let stand, uncovered, for 10 minutes at room temperature. The mixture will thicken to a spreadable consistency.

SPREAD THE DOUGH: Dollop 6 to 8 spoonfuls of the mixture onto the prepared baking sheet, spacing them evenly. Using a small offset or silicone spatula, evenly spread the mixture into the pan; it will be a thin layer. With a bench knife or the flat edge of a metal spatula, score the mixture into thirty-two 3 × 2-inch pieces.

BAKE THE CRACKERS: Bake until they are deep golden brown, fragrant, and firm to the touch, 50 minutes to 1 hour, switching between the top and bottom racks and rotating the pan front to back every 10 minutes. Turn off the oven and let the crackers cool completely in the oven. Carefully break the crackers along the scored lines, then store in an airtight container for up to 1 month.

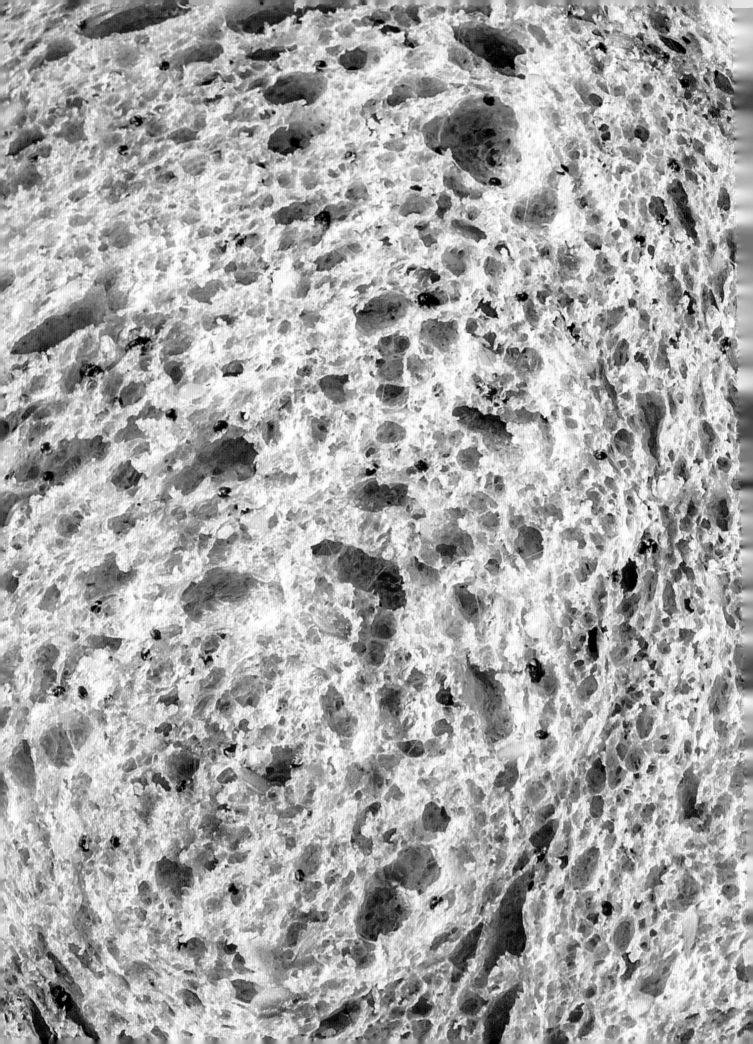

Pan Breads

(NOT SO) BASIC WHITE SANDWICH BREAD

MIX	BULK FERMENTATION	SHAPE	2ND RISE	BAKE
25 MIN	1–2 HOURS	5 MIN	1½–2 HOURS	30–35 MIN

TIME: ABOUT 5 HOURS

MAKES 1 LOAF

360 grams (3 cups) unbleached all-purpose flour, plus more for dusting

25 grams (2 tablespoons) sugar

7.5 grams (1¼ teaspoons) fine salt

6 grams (2 teaspoons) instant yeast

57 grams (4 tablespoons) unsalted butter, melted

142 grams (½ cup plus 2 tablespoons) warm milk (see Temperature, page 25), whole preferred

127 grams (½ cup plus 1 tablespoon) warm water (see Temperature, page 25)

This simple white sandwich bread is the perfect foundation for just about anything: a superlative grilled cheese, a classic PB&J, or truly wonderful cinnamon toast (see Cinnamon Toast Deluxe, page 411). Made with pantry staples, this bread is slightly sweet but not overly so, and the addition of butter and milk give it an especially soft and tender crumb. The dough is slightly sticky but can be mixed by hand or in a stand mixer.

MAKE THE DOUGH: In a medium bowl, combine the flour, sugar, salt, yeast, butter, milk, and water and mix with the handle of a wooden spoon until no dry patches of flour remain and a soft, sticky dough forms. Cover and let rest for 15 minutes.

Transfer the dough to a lightly floured surface and knead until a tacky, springy dough forms, about 5 minutes. The dough will be sticky at first but will smooth out quickly; to make it easier to handle, use a bench knife to scrape the dough off your work surface as you knead, which will speed up the process and reduce the amount of flour required for kneading. (Adding too much flour at this stage can make your bread denser.) Return the dough to the bowl, cover, and let rise at room temperature until puffy though not necessarily doubled in size, 1 to 2 hours.

Alternatively, in a stand mixer fitted with the dough hook attachment, mix the dough on medium-low speed until no dry patches of flour remain. Increase speed to medium and mix until smooth, elastic, and pulling away from the sides of the bowl, about 5 minutes. Cover and let rise at room temperature until puffy though not necessarily doubled in bulk, 1 to 2 hours.

Grease an 8½ × 4½-inch loaf pan with pan spray.

Recipe continues

NOTE: For a bread with nuttier flavor and boosted nutrition, golden wheat flour can be substituted for up to half (170 grams/1½ cups) of the all-purpose flour in this recipe.

SHAPE THE DOUGH AND LET IT RISE: Lightly flour a work surface, then use a plastic bowl scraper to ease the dough out of the bowl onto the work surface. Gently deflate the dough and pat it into a 12 × 8-inch rectangle. Shape the dough into a log by bringing the short sides toward the center, overlapping them slightly. Flatten the dough into an even layer, then starting from the top, gently roll the dough toward you to form a log (see Shaping, page 34) and pinch the seam to seal, then place it seam side down into the prepared pan. Cover and let rise at room temperature until the loaf crowns about 1 inch over the edge of the pan (see Proofing, page 44), 1½ to 2 hours.

Toward the end of the rising time, preheat the oven to 350°F.

BAKE: Bake the bread until the crust is golden brown and the internal temperature reaches 190°F, 30 to 35 minutes. Remove the loaf from the oven and immediately turn it out of the pan and onto a rack; doing this right away helps the bread come out of the pan easily and preserves the crust. Let cool completely before slicing. (For storage information, see Storing Bread, opposite.)

STORING BREAD

You've made a beautiful loaf of bread. Now you might be wondering how to keep it fresh. Here are some tips:

SLICING: When your bread has cooled and you're ready to cut it, slice the loaf in half crosswise, cut a slice from one of the halves, then press the two halves back together before wrapping. This way, no open surface will be exposed—which means less chance of moisture evaporating, causing your bread to dry out.

STORING YEASTED BREADS: Store your bread for a day or so at room temperature, wrapped in plastic or foil (rather than cloth). Breads wrapped in plastic or foil stay moist (though the crust will also soften), while loaves wrapped in cloth tend to develop a hard crust and a dried-out interior. And room temperature is preferable to the fridge: Chilling bread encourages the liquid in your loaf to continue migrating to the bread's surface, where it evaporates—and your bread quickly becomes stale.

STORING SOURDOUGH BREADS: An exception to the general practice of wrapping bread for storage is large boules or bâtards, particularly those made with sourdough culture. Sourdough bread will naturally stay fresh longer than bread made from yeasted dough. Sourdough's low pH (high acidity) creates an unfriendly environment for mold spores. In addition, this acidity keeps the loaf's crumb soft by slowing a process called starch retrogradation: the tendency of the starch in your bread's flour to revert to its original state, releasing any liquid it absorbed while being turned into a loaf of bread. The more liquid released by starch, the drier (staler) your bread will be, since this released liquid quickly exits your bread via evaporation. So sourdough's slowdown of this retrogradation helps keep your bread fresh. Crusty sourdough boules and bâtards can be stored for a couple of days unwrapped, cut side down on the counter. No wrapping means their crust will stay relatively crisp. A round loaf has less surface area than a longer loaf, limiting moisture evaporation. And a large loaf simply takes longer to dry out, especially if you shield its cut side by placing it flush with a solid surface to block airflow.

FREEZING: If you can't finish a loaf within a few days, your best option is to freeze it. Once your loaf is totally cool, cut off whatever portion you won't be eating within a couple of days. Slice and wrap the slices airtight in plastic: 4 to 6 slices to a packet (or however many you think you and your family will eat in one day). Place these individual packets in a plastic bag, seal tightly, and place in the freezer, preferably in the coldest part (away from the door). When you want bread, simply remove one packet, unwrap it, and store the slices in a zip-top plastic bag. Soft sandwich breads can be served as is; crusty breads will benefit by toasting, or at least reheating until warm. Heating bread releases starch's hold on its liquid, allowing moisture to circulate freely throughout the loaf just as it did when freshly baked.

ENGLISH MUFFIN TOASTING BREAD

MAKES 1 LOAF

PREFERMENT

57 grams (¼ cup) cool water (60°F to 70°F)

60 grams (½ cup) unbleached all-purpose flour

Pinch of instant yeast

DOUGH

300 grams (2½ cups) unbleached all-purpose flour, plus more for dusting

12 grams (1 tablespoon) sugar

9 grams (1 tablespoon) instant yeast

9 grams (1½ teaspoons) fine salt

1.5 grams (¼ teaspoon) baking soda

28 grams (2 tablespoons) unsalted butter, melted

284 grams (1¼ cups) warm milk (see Temperature, page 25), whole preferred

29 grams (3 tablespoons) yellow cornmeal, for the pan and top

This ultrasimple dough requires no special handling—in fact, it requires almost no handling at all. The soft, batter-like dough is mixed in a stand mixer bowl, then scooped into the pan. Because it's a stiff and sticky dough, mixing by hand is difficult (though not impossible—you'll just need to use some elbow grease). A preferment (see page 193) adds depth of flavor to the loaf, and the addition of baking soda results in a coarse, more open crumb than is typical for most pan loaves, reminiscent of the nooks and crannies of traditional English muffins. Coating both the pan and the top of the loaf with cornmeal gives the loaf a bit of crunch. As with traditional English Muffins (page 307), this bread is best toasted.

DAY 1

MAKE THE PREFERMENT: The evening before you want to bake, in a small bowl, combine the water, flour, and yeast. Stir together until no dry spots remain. Cover and let stand at room temperature overnight, 12 to 16 hours.

DAY 2

MAKE THE DOUGH: In a stand mixer bowl, combine the preferment, flour, sugar, yeast, salt, and baking soda. Add the melted butter and milk and, using the paddle, mix on medium-low speed until thoroughly combined. Increase the speed to medium, mixing until the dough is smooth and elastic, 2 to 3 minutes.

SHAPE THE DOUGH AND LET IT RISE: Lightly grease an 8½ × 4½-inch loaf pan with pan spray and sprinkle the bottom and sides with cornmeal; tap out any excess cornmeal, reserving it to sprinkle on top of the loaf. Scoop the soft dough into the pan, smoothing and leveling the top of the loaf. Cover and let rise at room temperature until the loaf crowns about 1 inch over the edge of the pan (see Proofing, page 44), 45 minutes to 1 hour.

Toward the end of the rise, preheat the oven to 400°F.

BAKE: Sprinkle a thin, even layer of cornmeal over the top of the loaf. Bake the bread until golden brown and the internal temperature reaches at least 190°F, 25 to 27 minutes.

Remove the loaf from the oven and immediately turn it out of the pan and onto a rack; doing this right away helps the bread come out of the pan easily and preserves the crust. Let cool completely before slicing. (For storage information, see Storing Bread, page 123.)

SOURDOUGH SANDWICH LOAF

MIX	BULK FERMENTATION	SHAPE	2ND RISE	BAKE
20–23 MIN	1½–2 HOURS	5 MIN	1–1½ HOURS	35 MIN

MAKE THE PREFERMENT (12–16 HOURS BEFORE)

············· TIME: ABOUT 21 HOURS ·············

MAKES 1 LOAF

PREFERMENT

31 grams (generous
2 tablespoons) sourdough culture
(see page 187)

66 grams (generous ½ cup)
unbleached all-purpose flour

66 grams (generous ¼ cup) cold
water (55° to 60°F)

DOUGH

345 grams (2¾ cups plus
2 tablespoons) unbleached
all-purpose flour, plus more for
dusting

29 grams (2 tablespoons plus
1 teaspoon) sugar

7.5 grams (1¼ teaspoons) fine salt

3 grams (1 teaspoon) instant yeast

33 grams (2 tablespoons plus
1 teaspoon) unsalted butter, at
room temperature

219 grams (scant 1 cup) warm
milk (see Temperature, page 25),
whole

If you've mastered some of the simpler yeasted loaves but have some sourdough culture (see page 187) that you're eager to press into service, this loaf is a good place to start. Slightly enriched with butter and sweetened with a touch of sugar, this bread is every bit as much a crowd-pleaser as the (Not So) Basic White Sandwich Bread (page 120). The preferment (see page 193) adds some acidity to the dough, which adds flavor to the bread and helps it last longer than a loaf made with yeast alone.

DAY 1

MAKE THE PREFERMENT: The evening before you want to bake, in a large bowl, mix the sourdough culture, flour, and water together with the handle of a wooden spoon until no dry patches of flour remain. Cover and let stand at room temperature overnight, 12 to 16 hours.

DAY 2

MAKE THE DOUGH: To the preferment, add the flour, sugar, salt, yeast, butter, and milk and mix with the handle of a wooden spoon until no dry patches of flour remain. Cover and let rest for 15 minutes. Transfer the dough to a lightly floured surface and knead until the dough is smooth and springy, 5 to 8 minutes. The dough will be sticky at first but will smooth out quickly. Scraping the work surface clean of any sticky dough will speed up the process and reduce the amount of flour required for kneading. Return the dough to the bowl, cover, and let rise at room temperature until doubled in size, 1½ to 2 hours.

Alternatively, in the bowl of a stand mixer, combine the preferment, flour, sugar, salt, yeast, butter, and milk. Using the dough hook attachment, mix on medium-low speed until no dry patches of flour remain. Increase speed to medium and mix until smooth, elastic, and pulling away from the sides of the bowl, 5 to 8 minutes. Cover and let rise at room temperature until doubled in size, 1½ to 2 hours.

Recipe continues

SHAPE THE DOUGH AND LET IT RISE: Lightly flour a work surface, then use a plastic bowl scraper to ease the dough out of the bowl onto the work surface. Gently deflate the dough, then press it into a 12 × 8-inch rectangle. Shape the dough into a log by bringing the short sides toward the center, overlapping them slightly. Flatten the dough into an even layer, and then, starting from the top, gently roll the dough toward you to form a log (see Shaping, page 34) and pinch the seam to seal, then place it seam side down in the prepared pan. Cover and let rise at room temperature until the loaf crowns about 1 inch over the rim of the pan (see Proofing, page 44), 1 to 1½ hours.

Toward the end of the rising time, preheat the oven to 375°F.

SCORE AND BAKE: Just before loading the bread into the oven, use a sifter to lightly dust the top of the loaf with flour, then score if desired (see Scoring, page 46). Bake the bread until the crust is golden brown, the sides of the loaf feel firm, and the internal temperature reaches 190°F, about 35 minutes.

Remove the loaf from the oven and immediately turn it out of the pan and onto a rack; doing this right away helps the bread come out of the pan easily and preserves the crust. Let cool completely before slicing. (For storage information, see Storing Bread, page 123.)

EVERYDAY BREAD

MAKES 1 LOAF

226 grams (2 cups) whole wheat flour

150 grams (1¼ cups) unbleached all-purpose flour, plus more for dusting

7.5 grams (1¼ teaspoons) fine salt

6 grams (2 teaspoons) instant yeast

42 grams (2 tablespoons) honey

28 grams (2 tablespoons) unsalted butter, at room temperature

284 grams (1¼ cups) warm milk (see Temperature, page 25), whole preferred

28 grams (¼ cup) wheat germ, for coating (optional)

While we typically endorse letting dough rest after it's mixed but before it's kneaded (see Autolyse, page 24), it's particularly important in this loaf, as it gives the bran in the whole wheat flour time to hydrate and soften, which makes the dough less sticky and easier to mix by hand (though, if you prefer, the dough can also be made in a stand mixer). While this bread has some whole wheat heartiness, it's still tender and yielding, without any of the density or bitterness that plagues some whole wheat breads. Quick and simple to make, it's the loaf we throw together at home whenever we realize we're low on bread and want a nutritious loaf, fast.

MAKE THE DOUGH: In a large bowl, combine the whole wheat flour, all-purpose flour, salt, and yeast. Add the honey, butter, and milk and mix with the handle of a wooden spoon until no dry patches of flour remain and a soft dough forms. Cover and let rest 15 minutes. This rest gives the flours a chance to absorb the water in the dough and will make kneading by hand easier and less sticky. Transfer the dough to a lightly floured surface and knead until a tacky, springy dough forms, 5 to 8 minutes. Return the dough to the bowl, cover, and let rise until puffy but not necessarily doubled in volume, 1 to 1½ hours.

Alternatively, in a stand mixer bowl, combine the whole wheat flour, all-purpose flour, salt, yeast, honey, butter, and milk. Using the dough hook attachment, mix the dough on medium-low speed until no dry patches of flour remain. Increase speed to medium and mix until smooth, elastic, and pulling away from the sides of the bowl, 5 to 8 minutes. Cover and let rise at room temperature until puffy but not necessarily doubled in volume, 1 to 1½ hours.

Grease an 8½ × 4½-inch loaf pan with pan spray.

Recipe continues

SHAPE AND COAT THE DOUGH: Lightly flour a work surface, then use a plastic bowl scraper to gently ease the dough out of the bowl onto the surface. Gently deflate the dough and pat it into a 12 × 8-inch rectangle. Shape the dough into a log by bringing the short edges toward the center, overlapping them slightly. Flatten the dough into an even layer, then starting from the top, gently roll the dough toward you to form a log (see Shaping, page 34) and pinch the seams to seal.

If coating the dough, spread the wheat germ on a rimmed baking sheet in an even layer the length of the dough log. Wet a clean kitchen towel, then wring it out; it should still be pretty damp. Roll the dough log over the towel to moisten it, then roll the log of dough in the wheat germ, turning to coat (see How to Coat a Loaf with Seeds, page 218).

LET THE DOUGH RISE: Place the dough seam side down in the prepared pan. Cover and let rise at room temperature until the loaf crowns about 1 inch over the edge of the pan (see Proofing, page 44), 1½ to 2 hours.

Toward the end of the rising time, preheat the oven to 350°F.

BAKE: Bake the loaf until the top is golden brown and the internal temperature is at least 190°F, 35 to 40 minutes. If the loaf is browning too quickly, tent it loosely with foil and continue baking.

Remove the loaf from the oven and immediately turn it out of the pan and onto a rack; doing this right away helps the bread come out of the pan easily and preserves the crust. Let cool completely before slicing. (For storage information, see Storing Bread, page 123.)

PAIN DE MIE

MIX	BULK FERMENTATION	SHAPE	2ND RISE	BAKE
7 MIN	1–1½ HOURS	5 MIN	40 MIN	35 MIN

TIME: ABOUT 3 HOURS

MAKES ONE 13 × 4-INCH LOAF (PULLMAN PAN)

690 grams (5 ¾ cups) unbleached all-purpose flour, plus more for dusting

14 grams (2¼ teaspoons) fine salt

12 grams (1 tablespoon) sugar

9 grams (1 tablespoon) instant yeast

78 grams (5 tablespoons plus 1½ teaspoons) unsalted butter, at room temperature

227 grams (1 cup) warm milk (see Temperature, page 25), whole preferred

227 grams (1 cup) warm water (see Temperature, page 25)

This yields a perfectly square-edged oversize loaf, with a tender, tight crumb and thin, soft crust: In other words, the quintessential white bread of our childhood dreams. This makes delicious toast, but it's also the bread of choice for a BLT or tender tea sandwiches (though we believe cutting off crusts is criminal!). Because this dough is enriched with butter, it can't be effectively mixed by hand; you'll need a stand mixer to properly develop the dough and incorporate the fat.

MAKE THE DOUGH: In a stand mixer bowl, combine the flour, salt, sugar, yeast, butter, milk, and water and, using the dough hook attachment, mix on medium-low speed for 1 to 2 minutes until a shaggy dough forms. Scrape down the bowl as needed, then increase the speed to medium and mix until the dough is smooth and elastic, 3 to 5 minutes more. Cover and let the dough rise at room temperature until very puffy and doubled in size, 1 to 1½ hours.

Grease a 13 × 4-inch Pullman loaf pan and the lid with pan spray.

SHAPE THE DOUGH AND LET IT RISE: Lightly flour a work surface, then use a plastic bowl scraper to ease the dough out of the bowl onto the work surface. Gently deflate the dough, then press it into a 20 × 8-inch rectangle. Shape the dough into a log by bringing the short sides toward the center. Flatten the dough into an even layer, and then, starting from the top, gently roll the dough toward you to form a log (see Shaping, page 34) and pinch the seam to seal, then place it seam side down in the prepared pan. Cover with the pan lid and let rise at room temperature until it is about 1 inch below the top edge of the pan (see Proofing, page 44), about 40 minutes.

Meanwhile, preheat the oven to 400°F.

BAKE: Bake the loaf with the lid on for 30 minutes. Then carefully remove the lid and continue baking until the crust is golden brown and the internal temperature reaches at least 200°F, an additional 5 minutes.

Remove the loaf from the oven and immediately turn it out of the pan and onto a rack; doing this right away helps the bread come out of the pan easily and preserves the crust.

The bread can be eaten as soon as it has cooled but slices best after resting for a day. (For storage information, see Storing Bread, page 123.)

SUPER SEED LOAF

SOAKER	MIX	BULK FERMENTATION	SHAPE	2ND RISE	BAKE
20 MIN	25 MIN	1½–2 HOURS	5 MIN	45–60 MIN	40 MIN

TIME: ABOUT 4½ HOURS

MAKES 1 LOAF

SOAKER

24 grams (2 tablespoons) quinoa

24 grams (¼ cup) old-fashioned rolled oats

21 grams (2 tablespoons) yellow cornmeal

20 grams (2 tablespoons) flaxseeds (brown, golden, or a combination)

10 grams (1 tablespoon) poppy seeds

10 grams (1 tablespoon) sesame seeds (white, black, or a combination)

3 grams (½ teaspoon) fine salt

170 grams (¾ cup) boiling water (212°F)

DOUGH

225 grams (1¾ cups plus 2 tablespoons) unbleached bread flour, plus more for dusting

212 grams (1¾ cups plus 2 tablespoons) whole wheat flour

6 grams (2 teaspoons) instant yeast

6 grams (1 teaspoon) fine salt

42 grams (2 tablespoons) honey

25 grams (2 tablespoons) olive oil

170 grams (¾ cup) warm water (see Temperature, page 25)

One day in the test kitchen we got to talking about "California" sandwiches, the kind you find at health food stores, even far outside of California. We debated the fillings—sprouts, of course, and avocado, but cheddar cheese? Hot sauce? Hummus? We all had our own ideas on the ultimate combination. We agreed, however, on the bread—a super-seedy whole wheat loaf, sturdy and a tiny bit sweet—and immediately set out to develop our own version. You can use the mix we suggest or your favorite combination of grains, finely chopped nuts, and seeds for the soaker (you'll need about 113 grams/¾ cup total). We rinse the quinoa because its outer layers are covered with saponin (a plant-derived organic chemical), which has a bitter taste that's removed by rinsing. For a vegan bread, use maple syrup in place of honey.

MAKE THE SOAKER: Rinse the quinoa by placing it in a fine-mesh sieve and running it under cool water for 20 to 30 seconds. Press on the quinoa to release any excess water. In a medium bowl, combine the rinsed quinoa, oats, cornmeal, flaxseeds, poppy seeds, sesame seeds, and salt. Add the boiling water, stirring to combine. Set the mixture aside to cool slightly and allow the grains and seeds to hydrate and absorb most of the water, about 20 minutes.

MAKE THE DOUGH: In a stand mixer bowl, combine the soaker, bread flour, whole wheat flour, yeast, salt, honey, olive oil, and water. Using the dough hook attachment, mix on medium-low speed until no dry patches of flour remain and a slightly sticky dough forms, about 2 minutes. Cover and let rest for 15 minutes. Continue mixing with the dough hook on medium speed until a tacky, springy dough that cleans the sides of the bowl forms, about 5 minutes. Cover and let rise at room temperature until puffy but not necessarily doubled in volume, about 1½ to 2 hours.

Alternatively, in a large bowl, combine the soaker, bread flour, whole wheat flour, yeast, salt, honey, olive oil, and water and mix with the

Recipe continues

handle of a wooden spoon until a shaggy dough forms. Cover and let rest 15 minutes. This short rest allows the flours to hydrate and will make hand-kneading easier and less sticky. Transfer the dough to a floured surface and knead, adding just enough flour to keep the dough from sticking and using your bench knife to scrape up any dough stuck to the work surface, until the dough is slightly tacky, smooth, and elastic, about 8 minutes. Return the dough to the bowl. Cover and let rise at room temperature until puffy but not necessarily doubled in size, 1½ to 2 hours.

Grease an 8½ × 4½-inch loaf pan with pan spray.

SHAPE THE DOUGH AND LET IT RISE: Lightly flour a work surface, then use a plastic bowl scraper to ease the dough out of the bowl onto the work surface. Gently deflate the dough and pat it into a 12 × 8-inch rectangle. Shape the dough into a log by bringing the short sides toward the center, overlapping them slightly. Flatten the dough into an even layer, and then, starting from the top, gently roll the dough toward you to form a log (see Shaping, page 34) and pinch the seam to seal, then place it seam side down in the prepared pan. Use a baker's lame or razor blade to score the top of the loaf with three to four diagonal cuts (see Scoring, page 46). Cover and let rise at room temperature until the loaf crowns about 1 inch over the edge of the pan (see Proofing, page 44), 45 minutes to 1 hour.

Toward the end of the rising time, preheat the oven to 375°F.

BAKE: Bake until the top is deep golden brown, the edges feel firm, and the internal temperature is at least 190°F, about 40 minutes. If the loaf is browning too quickly, tent it loosely with foil and continue baking.

Remove the loaf from the oven and immediately turn it out of the pan and onto a rack; doing this right away helps the bread come out of the pan easily and preserves the crust. Let cool completely before slicing. (For storage information, see Storing Bread, page 123.)

MOLASSES-OAT BREAD

MIX	BULK FERMENTATION	SHAPE	2ND RISE	BAKE
20 MIN	1–1½ HOURS	5 MIN	1–1½ HOURS	35–40 MIN

TIME: ABOUT 4 HOURS

MAKES 1 LOAF

119 grams (1⅓ cups) rolled oats, divided

63 grams (3 tablespoons) molasses (not blackstrap)

42 grams (3 tablespoons) unsalted butter, at room temperature

9 grams (1½ teaspoons) fine salt

255 grams (1 cup plus 2 tablespoons) boiling water (212°F)

240 grams (2 cups) unbleached bread flour, plus more for dusting

85 grams (¾ cup) whole wheat flour

6 grams (2 teaspoons) instant yeast

This oat-topped bread has a tawny, deep golden color, with a tender, sweet crumb thanks to the addition of molasses to the dough. Molasses is a bossy ingredient: Though this recipe contains only a small amount, it adds its distinctive flavor (and rich color) to the bread. Soaking the oats is an important step; by prehydrating the flakes, they won't pull moisture from the dough when they're added to the mix. Both molasses and soaked oats are also heavy ingredients. They add body to the bread but also have the potential to weigh down the dough, impacting its rise, so we use bread flour in combination with whole wheat flour to give the dough more strength and structure.

MAKE THE DOUGH: In a medium bowl, combine 89 grams (1 cup) of the oats, the molasses, butter, and salt. Pour the boiling water over the oat mixture, stirring briefly to ensure the oats are submerged. Soak, uncovered, for 10 minutes.

Stir in the bread flour and whole wheat flour, then the yeast. Mix to form a shaggy dough; it will appear slightly dry. Transfer the dough to a clean surface and begin kneading. The dough will become slightly sticky. Using a bench knife, scrape up any dough that's sticking to the work surface, then add just enough flour to your work surface to keep the dough from sticking. Continue kneading by hand until you have a soft, slightly tacky dough that bounces back when gently pressed with a floured finger, about 5 minutes. Return the dough to the bowl, cover, and let rise at room temperature until very puffy, 1 to 1½ hours.

Alternatively, in a stand mixer bowl, combine the soaked oats, bread flour, whole wheat flour, and yeast. Using the dough hook attachment, mix the dough on medium-low speed until no dry patches of flour remain. Increase the speed to medium and mix until smooth, elastic, and pulling away from the sides of the bowl, about 5 minutes. Cover and let rise at room temperature until very puffy, 1 to 1½ hours.

Recipe continues

Grease an 8½ by 4½-inch loaf pan with pan spray.

SHAPE THE DOUGH AND LET IT RISE: Lightly flour a work surface, then use a plastic bowl scraper to ease the dough out of the bowl onto the work surface. Gently deflate the dough, then shape it into a 12 × 8-inch rectangle. Shape the dough into a log by bringing the short sides toward the center, overlapping them slightly. Flatten the dough into an even layer, and then, starting from the top, gently roll the dough toward you to form a log (see Shaping, page 34) and pinch the seam to seal.

Roughly chop the remaining 30 grams (⅓ cup) oats, then spread on a baking sheet or piece of parchment in an even layer the length of the dough log. Wet a clean kitchen towel, then wring it out; it should still be pretty damp. Roll the dough log over the towel to moisten it, then roll into the chopped oats to coat (see How to Coat a Loaf with Seeds, page 218). Place the loaf seam side down in the prepared pan. Use a baker's lame or sharp knife to score three diagonal cuts across the top of the loaf (see Scoring, page 46), if desired. Cover and let rise at room temperature until the loaf crowns about 1 inch over the edge of the pan (see Proofing, page 44), 1 to 1½ hours.

Toward the end of the rising time, preheat the oven to 350°F.

BAKE: Bake the loaf until the top is golden brown and the internal temperature reaches at least 190°F, 35 to 40 minutes.

Remove the loaf from the oven and immediately turn it out of the pan and onto a rack; doing this right away helps the bread come out of the pan easily and preserves the crust. Let cool completely before slicing. (For storage information, see Storing Bread, page 123.)

SESAME SEMOLINA LOAF

MIX	BULK FERMENTATION	SHAPE	2ND RISE	BAKE
30 MIN	1½–2 HOURS	5 MIN	1½–2 HOURS	35 MIN

································· TIME: ABOUT 5 HOURS ·································

MAKE 1 LOAF

380 grams (2⅓ cups) semolina flour

60 grams (½ cup) unbleached bread flour, plus more for dusting

25 grams (2 tablespoons) sugar

9 grams (1½ teaspoons) fine salt

4.5 grams (1½ teaspoons) instant yeast

57 grams (4 tablespoons) unsalted butter, at room temperature

1 large egg (50 grams)

227 grams (1 cup) warm milk (see Temperature, page 25), whole preferred

36 grams (¼ cup) sesame seeds, unhulled preferred, for coating

1 large egg white (35 grams), lightly beaten

Semolina, a coarse grind of durum wheat (see page 142), brings a golden hue to this loaf, and its relatively high protein level gives the bread a pleasant chewiness. We favor the toasty flavor and nutty crunch of unhulled sesame seeds and use them to coat the exterior of the bread. For the highest-rising loaf, we recommend using a stand mixer to make this dough, which gives the sticky dough necessary strength. If you don't have a stand mixer, increase the yeast to 6 grams (2 teaspoons) and be sure to knead for at least 8 to 10 minutes by hand for the best possible rise.

MAKE THE DOUGH: In a stand mixer bowl, combine the semolina flour, bread flour, sugar, salt, and yeast. Add the butter, whole egg, and milk and, using the dough hook attachment, mix on medium-low speed, scraping the bowl as necessary, until a soft, sticky dough forms, about 3 minutes. Cover and allow to rest at room temperature for 20 minutes.

After the dough has rested, return to mixing with the dough hook on medium speed until the dough is smooth and elastic and clears the sides of the bowl, about 5 minutes. Cover and let rise at room temperature until puffy but not necessarily doubled in size, 1½ to 2 hours.

Alternatively, in a large bowl, combine the semolina flour, bread flour, sugar, salt, 6 grams (2 teaspoons) yeast, butter, egg, and milk and mix with the handle of a wooden spoon until a shaggy dough forms. Cover and let rest 20 minutes. This short rest allows the flours to hydrate and will make hand-kneading easier and less sticky. Transfer the dough to a floured surface and knead, adding just enough flour to keep the dough from sticking and using your bench knife to scrape up any dough stuck to the work surface, until the dough is slightly tacky, smooth, and elastic, about 8 to 10 minutes. Return the dough to the bowl, cover, and let rise at room temperature until puffy but not necessarily doubled in size, 1½ to 2 hours.

Recipe continues

Grease an 8½ × 4½-inch loaf pan with pan spray.

SHAPE THE DOUGH AND LET IT RISE: Lightly flour a work surface, then use a plastic bowl scraper to ease the dough out of the bowl onto the work surface. Gently deflate the dough, then pat the dough into a 12 × 8-inch rectangle. Shape the dough into a log by bringing the short sides toward the center, overlapping them slightly. Flatten the dough into an even layer, and then, starting from the top, gently roll the dough toward you to form a log (see Shaping, page 34) and pinch the seam to seal.

Spread the sesame seeds on a rimmed baking sheet in an even layer the length of the dough. Brush the shaped loaf all over with the egg white (you won't use all of it), then roll in the sesame seeds, turning to coat. Place the log seam side down in the prepared pan. Cover and let the loaf rise at room temperature until it crowns about 1 inch above the edge of the pan (see Proofing, page 44), 1½ to 2 hours.

Toward the end of the rising time, preheat the oven to 350°F.

BAKE: Bake the loaf until the crust is deep golden brown and the internal temperature registers at least 190°F, about 35 minutes.

Remove the loaf from the oven and immediately turn it out of the pan and onto a rack; doing this right away helps the bread come out of the pan easily and preserves the crust. Let cool completely before slicing. (For storage information, see Storing Bread, page 123.)

DURUM WHEAT

Durum wheat is the hardest of the hard wheats, in a category by itself. It is an ancient wheat variety and doesn't create the elastic gluten characteristic of more modern hard wheats (see Flour Primer, page 443). Durum wheat berries are so hard that they splinter when milled, resulting in a coarser flour called semolina, a golden-colored granulated flour with the consistency of Cream of Wheat, or a more finely milled flour called durum wheat flour. Semolina is used primarily for pasta and by bakers in the Indian subcontinent, or to keep pizza dough from sticking to the peel. But semolina can also be used in tandem with other wheat flour in breads (like the Sesame Semolina Loaf on page 141) or cakes, where it adds nutty flavor and a yellow hue.

PICKLE RYE

MIX	BULK FERMENTATION	SHAPE	2ND RISE	BAKE
30 MIN	1½–2 HOURS	5 MIN	1–1½ HOURS	35–40 MIN

TIME: ABOUT 5 HOURS

MAKES 1 LOAF

DOUGH

285 grams (2¼ cups plus 2 tablespoons) unbleached bread flour, plus more for dusting

141 grams (1⅓ cups) whole rye flour

12 grams (1 tablespoon) sugar

12 grams (1 tablespoon) yellow mustard seeds

3 grams (1 teaspoon) caraway seeds

7.5 grams (1¼ teaspoons) fine salt

7 grams (generous 2 teaspoons) instant yeast

3 grams (1 teaspoon) dill seeds

153 grams (⅔ cup) warm dill pickle juice (see Temperature, page 25)

142 grams (½ cup plus 2 tablespoons) warm water (see Temperature, page 25)

45 grams (scant ¼ cup) olive oil

TOPPING

Egg wash: 1 large egg (50 grams) beaten with ⅛ teaspoon fine salt

6 grams (2 teaspoons) caraway seeds

3 grams (1 teaspoon) flaky sea salt, such as Maldon

This is a classic deli rye, made with a combination of bread flour and whole rye flour, with a fun twist: We add a little pickle juice to the dough, which contributes some sour, briny flavor. We also load the loaf with caraway, mustard, and dill seeds, which are typically included in the brine used for pastrami, then coat the exterior of the loaf with more caraway and flaky salt. This bread begs to be used for a Reuben sandwich or toasted, buttered, and served alongside eggs. Because this bread contains a decent amount of rye flour, which is low in gluten, we recommend mixing this dough by machine to build strength.

MAKE THE DOUGH: In a stand mixer bowl, combine the bread flour, rye flour, sugar, mustard seeds, caraway seeds, fine salt, yeast, and dill seeds. Add the pickle juice, water, and oil. Using the dough hook attachment, mix on medium-low speed until no dry patches of flour remain and a soft, sticky dough forms. Cover and let rest 20 minutes. Mix the dough on medium speed until the dough cleans the sides of the bowl and is slightly tacky and smooth, about 7 minutes. Cover and let rise until puffy but not necessarily doubled in size, 1½ to 2 hours.

Alternatively, in a large bowl, combine the bread flour, rye flour, sugar, mustard seeds, caraway seeds, fine salt, yeast, dill seeds, pickle juice, water, and oil and mix with the handle of a wooden spoon until a shaggy dough forms. Cover and let rest 20 minutes. This short rest allows the flours to hydrate and will make hand-kneading easier and less sticky. Transfer the dough to a floured work surface and knead, adding just enough flour to keep the dough from sticking and using your bench knife to scrape up any dough stuck to the work surface, until the dough is slightly tacky, smooth, and elastic, 5 to 8 minutes. Return the dough to the bowl, cover, and let rise at room temperature until it's puffy but not necessarily doubled in size, 1½ to 2 hours.

Grease an 8½ × 4½-inch loaf pan with pan spray.

Recipe continues

SHAPE THE DOUGH AND LET IT RISE: Lightly flour a work surface, then use a plastic bowl scraper to ease the dough out of the bowl onto the work surface. Gently deflate the dough and press it into a 12 × 8-inch rectangle. Shape the dough into a log by bringing the short sides toward the center, overlapping them slightly. Flatten the dough into an even layer, and then, starting from the top, gently roll the dough toward you to form a log (see Shaping, page 34) and pinch the seam to seal. Place the loaf seam side down in the prepared pan.

Cover and let rise at room temperature until the loaf crowns about 1 inch over the edge of the pan (see Proofing, page 44), 1 to 1½ hours.

Toward the end of the rising time, preheat the oven to 350°F.

TOP THE LOAF AND BAKE: Lightly brush the top of the loaf with a thin layer of egg wash, then sprinkle with the caraway seeds and flaky salt. Bake the bread until the crust is golden brown and the internal temperature reaches 190°F, 35 to 40 minutes.

Remove the loaf from the oven and immediately turn it out of the pan and onto a rack; doing this right away helps the bread come out of the pan easily and preserves the crust. Cool completely before slicing. (For storage information, see Storing Bread, page 123.)

PICKLED JALAPEÑO AND CHEDDAR BREAD

MIX	BULK FERMENTATION	SHAPE	2ND RISE	BAKE
10 MIN	1½ HOURS	5 MIN	1–1½ HOURS	30–35 MIN

TIME: ABOUT 4 HOURS

MAKES 1 LOAF

178 grams (1½ cups) unbleached bread flour, plus more for dusting

180 grams (1¼ cups plus 3 tablespoons) durum flour

66 grams (6½ tablespoons) fine yellow cornmeal, divided

19 grams (1½ tablespoons) sugar

9 grams (1½ teaspoons) fine salt

6 grams (2 teaspoons) instant yeast

227 grams (1 cup) warm water (see Temperature, page 25)

57 grams (4 tablespoons) unsalted butter, at room temperature

85 grams (¾ cup) grated cheddar cheese

38 grams (3 tablespoons) chopped pickled jalapeños

This slightly spicy bread gets its heat and tang from pickled jalapeño peppers and its salty richness from the addition of cheddar cheese; choose a sharp or aged one for a more intense flavor. The addition of cornmeal (both in the dough and on the exterior of the loaf) is a nod to cornbread and gives the bread some welcome texture. Unlike other pan loaves in this chapter, this bread has a crusty exterior, which is achieved by adding steam to the oven as the loaf bakes. Be sure to score the loaf before proofing; if you score after, it will cause the loaf to collapse.

MAKE THE DOUGH: In a stand mixer bowl, combine the bread flour, durum flour, 24 grams (2½ tablespoons) of the cornmeal, the sugar, salt, and yeast. Add the water and butter and, using the dough hook attachment, mix on medium-low speed until no dry patches of flour remain, then increase the speed to medium-high and mix until the dough is smooth and elastic, 5 to 8 minutes. Add the cheddar and jalapeños, mixing on medium-low speed to combine. Cover the bowl and let rest at room temperature for 45 minutes.

Use a wet hand to grab a section of dough from one side, lift it up, then press it down firmly into the middle. Repeat these 8 to 12 times or until the dough resists stretching (see Bowl Fold, page 30). Cover and let rest at room temperature until puffy though not necessarily doubled in size, about 45 minutes.

Grease an 8½ × 4½-inch loaf pan with pan spray.

SHAPE THE DOUGH: Lightly flour a work surface, then use a plastic bowl scraper to ease the dough out of the bowl onto the work surface. Gently deflate the dough and pat it into a 12 × 8-inch rectangle. Shape the dough into a log by bringing the short edges toward the center, overlapping

Recipe continues

them slightly. Flatten the dough into an even layer, then starting from the top, gently roll the dough toward you to form a log (see Shaping, page 34) and pinch the seam to seal.

SCORE THE DOUGH AND LET IT RISE: Spread the remaining 39 grams (¼ cup) cornmeal into a rimmed baking sheet in an even layer the length of the dough log. Wet a clean kitchen towel, then wring it out; it should still be pretty damp. Roll just the top of the loaf across the wet towel, then into the cornmeal to coat (see How to Coat a Loaf with Seeds, page 218). Place the loaf cornmeal side up on your work surface and use a sharp knife or baker's lame to make eight 45-degree angled cuts spaced 1 inch apart the length of the loaf (see Scoring, page 46). Place the loaf scored side up in the prepared pan. Cover and let rise at room temperature until the loaf crowns about 1 inch over the edge of the pan (see Proofing, page 44), 1 to 1½ hours.

Toward the end of the rising time, arrange racks in the middle and bottom third of the oven and preheat the oven to 425°F. Place a cast-iron skillet on the lower rack to preheat (see Steaming, page 50).

Place the loaf pan on the middle rack, then pour about 227 grams (1 cup) of warm water into the skillet. Steam will billow upward to envelop the bread; be sure to wear good oven mitts to shield your hands and arms. Quickly close the oven door to trap the steam. Bake until the loaf is golden brown and feels firm and the internal temperature is 190°F, 30 to 35 minutes.

Remove the loaf from the oven and immediately turn it out of the pan and onto a rack; doing this right away helps the bread come out of the pan easily and preserves the crust. Let cool completely before slicing. (For storage information, see Storing Bread, page 123.)

MASA-HONEY TOASTING BREAD

MIX	BULK FERMENTATION	SHAPE	2ND RISE	BAKE
30 MIN	1½ HOURS	5 MIN	1–1½ HOURS	45 MIN

.... TIME: ABOUT 4½ HOURS ....

MAKES 1 LOAF

320 grams (2⅔ cups) unbleached bread flour, plus more for dusting

163 grams (1¾ cups) masa harina, divided

12 grams (2 teaspoons) fine salt

6 grams (2 teaspoons) instant yeast

368 grams (1½ cups plus 2 tablespoons) warm milk (see Temperature, page 25), whole preferred

84 grams (¼ cup) honey

57 grams (4 tablespoons) unsalted butter, at room temperature

This aromatic bread is made with a combination of bread flour and masa harina, which gives it a wonderful corn-y flavor. The thin, crispy crust yields to a moist, tender crumb, and, as the name suggests, it's especially good toasted. While we find it easiest to make this dough in a stand mixer, it can also be made by hand; just be mindful of the amount of flour added during kneading so that the nice tender crumb you're going for doesn't become too dense.

MAKE THE DOUGH: In a stand mixer bowl, combine the flour, 140 grams (1½ cups) of the masa, the salt, yeast, milk, honey, and butter. Using the dough hook attachment, mix on medium-low speed until a cohesive, stiff yet tacky dough forms, 1 to 2 minutes. Cover and let dough rest for 20 minutes.

Mix the dough on medium-high speed until the dough smooths out and slightly bounces back when pressed with a floured finger, about 5 minutes. Cover and let the dough rise at room temperature until puffy though not necessarily doubled in size, about 1½ hours.

Grease an 8½ × 4½-inch loaf pan with pan spray.

SHAPE THE DOUGH AND LET IT RISE: Lightly flour a work surface, then use a plastic bowl scraper to ease the dough out of the bowl onto the work surface. Gently deflate the dough and then press it into a 12 × 8-inch rectangle. Shape the dough into a log by bringing the short sides toward the center, overlapping them slightly. Flatten the dough into an even layer, and then, starting from the top, gently roll the dough toward you to form a log (see Shaping, page 34) and pinch the seam to seal.

Spread the remaining 23 grams (¼ cup) masa on a rimmed baking sheet in an even layer. Wet a clean kitchen towel, then wring it out; it should still be pretty damp. Roll the shaped log of dough over the damp towel, then into the masa, turning to coat. Place the dough seam side down in

Recipe continues

the prepared pan. Decoratively score the top of the loaf with a sharp knife or baker's lame, if desired (see Scoring, page 46). Cover and let the loaf rise at room temperature until it crowns about 1 to 1½ inches above the rim of the pan (see Proofing, page 44), 1 to 1½ hours.

Toward the end of the rising time, preheat the oven to 375°F.

BAKE: Bake until the loaf is deep golden brown and the internal temperature is at least 195°F, about 45 minutes.

Remove the loaf from the oven and immediately turn it out of the pan and onto a rack; doing this right away helps the bread come out of the pan easily and preserves the crust. Let cool completely before slicing. (For storage information, see Storing Bread, page 123.)

CINNAMON RAISIN SWIRL BREAD

MIX	BULK FERMENTATION	SHAPE	2ND RISE	BAKE
15 MIN	1–1½ HOURS	10 MIN	1½ HOURS	40 MIN

MAKE THE PREFERMENT (12–16 HOURS BEFORE)

TIME: ABOUT 20 HOURS

MAKES 1 LOAF

PREFERMENT (SEE NOTE)

111 grams/¾ cup raisins (golden, black, or a combination)

14 grams (1 tablespoon) sourdough culture (see page 187)

30 grams (¼ cup) unbleached bread flour

28 grams (2 tablespoons) cool water (60°F to 70°F)

DOUGH

300 grams (2½ cups) unbleached bread flour, plus more for dusting

12 grams (1 tablespoon) granulated sugar

6 grams (1 teaspoon) fine salt

3 grams (1 teaspoon) instant yeast

1 large egg (50 grams)

170 grams (¾ cup) warm milk (see Temperature, page 25), whole preferred

57 grams (4 tablespoons) unsalted butter, cut into small cubes, at room temperature

FILLING

53 grams (¼ cup packed) light brown sugar

Ingredients continue

Studded with raisins and showcasing a gooey brown sugar swirl through its center, this loaf is the ultimate breakfast bread. Made with a dough that is enriched with sugar, eggs, and butter, it has an especially soft crumb and toasts beautifully. This enriched dough requires the use of a stand mixer to produce a strong dough. This strength is important for the dough to hold its shape and produce a good rise. For a yeast-only version of this bread, see the Note on the following page.

DAY 1

SOAK THE RAISINS AND MAKE THE PREFERMENT: The evening before you want to bake, place the raisins in a small bowl, then pour 227 grams (1 cup) cold water over them. Cover and set aside to hydrate at room temperature overnight, 12 to 16 hours.

In a small bowl, combine the sourdough culture, flour, and water and mix until no dry patches of flour remain. Cover and let stand at room temperature overnight, 12 to 16 hours.

DAY 2

MAKE THE DOUGH: In a stand mixer bowl, combine the preferment, flour, granulated sugar, salt, yeast, egg, and milk. Using the dough hook attachment, mix on medium-low speed, scraping the mixer bowl as needed, until you have a firm yet tacky dough, 2 to 3 minutes. Increase the speed to medium and continue mixing until the dough is smooth and elastic, an additional 3 to 5 minutes.

Drain the raisins and have at the ready. With the mixer running, add the butter one piece at a time, mixing until the first piece is fully incorporated before adding the next. Continue mixing until the dough pulls away from the sides of the bowl and is soft, smooth, and elastic, 3 to

Recipe continues

5 grams (2 teaspoons) unbleached bread flour

4 grams (1½ teaspoons) ground cinnamon

Egg wash: 1 large egg (50 grams) beaten with ⅛ teaspoon fine salt

45 grams (¼ cup) turbinado sugar or 57 grams (¼ cup) sparkling sugar

NOTE: We like the flavor (and improved keeping qualities) that a sourdough preferment lends this bread, but if you don't have sourdough culture—or forgot to make the preferment—just add 37 grams (scant ⅓ cup) additional bread flour and 35 grams (2 tablespoons plus 1½ teaspoons) water to the final dough and increase the yeast to 6 grams (2 teaspoons).

5 minutes. With the mixer stopped, add the raisins, then mix until they are evenly distributed in the dough, 1 to 2 minutes. Cover and let rise at room temperature until doubled in size, 1 to 1½ hours.

MEANWHILE, MAKE THE FILLING: In a small bowl, combine the brown sugar, flour, and cinnamon.

Grease an 8½ × 4½-inch loaf pan with pan spray.

SHAPE THE DOUGH AND LET IT RISE: Lightly flour a work surface, then use a plastic bowl scraper to ease the dough out of the bowl onto the work surface. Gently deflate the dough, then roll it into a 15 × 8-inch rectangle with a short side facing you. Brush a light, even coat of the egg wash over the dough; you won't use all of it here but will use more for brushing the loaf before baking. Sprinkle the filling evenly over the dough, leaving a 1-inch-wide bare strip on the short side of the dough farthest away from you. Fold the outer ½ inch of each long edge in to enclose the edge of the filling. Gently press down to flatten. Starting with the short side closest to you, roll the dough into a log. Pinch the center seam closed, then pinch each end to seal. Place the log seam side down in the prepared pan. Cover and let the loaf rise at room temperature until it crowns about 1 inch over the rim of the pan (see Proofing, page 44), about 1½ hours.

Toward the end of the rising time, preheat the oven to 350°F.

BAKE: Lightly brush the top of the loaf with the reserved egg wash and sprinkle with the turbinado sugar, if using. Bake the bread until the crust is golden brown and the internal temperature reaches 190°F, about 40 minutes.

Remove the loaf from the oven, then turn it out of the pan and onto a rack right away; this helps the bread come out of the pan easily and preserves the crust. Let cool completely before slicing. (For storage information, see Storing Bread, page 123.)

SAVORY DUKKAH SWIRL BREAD

MIX	BULK FERMENTATION	SHAPE	2ND RISE	BAKE
15 MIN	1–1½ HOURS	10 MIN	1½ HOURS	40 MIN

MAKE THE PREFERMENT (12–16 HOURS BEFORE)

················ TIME: ABOUT 20 HOURS ················

MAKES 1 LOAF

PREFERMENT (SEE NOTE)

14 grams (1 tablespoon) sourdough culture (see page 187)

30 grams (¼ cup) unbleached bread flour

28 grams (2 tablespoons) cool water (60°F to 70°F)

DOUGH

300 grams (2½ cups) unbleached bread flour, plus more for dusting

12 grams (1 tablespoon) sugar

6 grams (1 teaspoon) fine salt

3 grams (1 teaspoon) instant yeast

1 large egg (50 grams)

170 grams (¾ cup) warm milk (see Temperature, page 25), whole preferred

57 grams (4 tablespoons) unsalted butter, cut into small cubes, at room temperature

DUKKAH FILLING

¼ teaspoon fennel seeds

½ teaspoon coriander seeds

½ teaspoon cumin seeds

44 grams (5 tablespoons) whole hazelnuts, toasted and cooled

Dukkah is an Egyptian condiment made of crushed toasted nuts and spices. It can be sprinkled on everything from eggs to roasted vegetables to fish and also used as a dip—pieces of bread are first dunked in olive oil, then into the dukkah. Here, we've reimagined it as a savory swirl inside a loaf of bread. We liked the combination of hazelnuts, pistachios, and sesame seeds, but you could substitute other nuts if you prefer. The addition of egg to the filling helps the spiral hold together when slicing the baked loaf. As with the Cinnamon Raisin Swirl Bread (page 153), this dough requires the use of a stand mixer.

DAY 1

MAKE THE PREFERMENT: The evening before you want to bake, in a small bowl, combine the sourdough culture, flour, and water and mix until no dry patches of flour remain. Cover and let stand at room temperature overnight, 12 to 16 hours.

DAY 2

MAKE THE DOUGH: In a stand mixer bowl, combine the preferment, flour, sugar, salt, yeast, egg, and milk. Using the dough hook attachment, mix on medium-low speed, scraping the mixer bowl as needed, until you have a firm yet tacky dough, 2 to 3 minutes. Increase the speed to medium and continue mixing until the dough is smooth and elastic, an additional 3 to 5 minutes. With the mixer running, add the butter one piece at a time, mixing until the first piece is fully incorporated before adding the next. Continue mixing until the dough pulls away from the sides of the bowl and is soft, smooth, and elastic, 3 to 5 minutes. Cover and let rise at room temperature until doubled in size, 1 to 1½ hours.

MEANWHILE, MAKE THE FILLING: In a small skillet over medium-low heat, combine the fennel, coriander, and cumin seeds and toast until they are fragrant and one to two shades darker than when you started,

Ingredients continue

Recipe continues

23 grams (3 tablespoons) whole shelled pistachios, toasted and cooled

26 grams (3 tablespoons) sesame seeds (white, black, or a combination), unhulled preferred, toasted and cooled

3 grams (½ teaspoon) fine salt

Egg wash: 1 large egg (50 grams) beaten with ⅛ teaspoon fine salt

TOPPING

36 grams (¼ cup) sesame seeds (white, black, or a combination), unhulled preferred

NOTE: We like the flavor (and improved keeping qualities) that a sourdough preferment lends this bread, but if you don't have sourdough culture—or forgot to make the preferment—just add 37 grams (scant ⅓ cup) additional bread flour and 35 grams (2 tablespoons plus 1½ teaspoons) water to the final dough and increase the yeast to 6 grams (2 teaspoons).

30 seconds to 1 minute. Let cool, then transfer to a small bowl and add the hazelnuts, pistachios, and sesame seeds.

When all the nuts and spices are at room temperature, pulse them in a coffee/spice grinder or food processor until finely chopped; taking care not to process so long that the mixture turns to nut butter (it can happen!). Return the mixture to the bowl, add the salt and 14 grams (1 tablespoon) of the egg wash to the nut mixture, mixing to form a coarse paste about the consistency of wet sand. (Reserve the remaining egg wash to brush on the dough.)

Grease an 8½ × 4½-inch loaf pan with pan spray.

SHAPE THE DOUGH AND LET IT RISE: Lightly flour a work surface, then use a plastic bowl scraper to ease the dough out of the bowl onto the work surface. Gently deflate the dough, then roll it into a 15 × 8-inch rectangle with a short side facing you. Brush a light, even coat of the egg wash over the dough; you won't use all of it. Sprinkle the filling evenly over the dough, leaving a 1-inch-wide bare strip on the short side of the dough farthest away from you. Gently press the filling onto the dough. Fold the outer ½ inch of each long edge in to enclose the edge of the filling. Gently press down to flatten.

Starting with the short side closest to you, roll the dough into a log. Pinch the center and end seams closed. Spread the sesame seeds on a rimmed baking sheet in an even layer about the length of the dough log. Brush the shaped loaf all over with the remaining egg wash, then roll into the seeds, turning to coat (see How to Coat a Loaf with Seeds, page 218). Place the log seam side down in the prepared loaf pan. Cover and let rise at room temperature until the loaf crowns about 1 inch over the edge of the pan (see Proofing, page 44), about 1½ hours.

Toward the end of the rising time, preheat the oven to 350°F.

BAKE: Bake the bread until the crust is golden brown and the internal temperature reaches 190°F, about 40 minutes.

Remove the loaf from the oven and immediately turn it out of the pan and onto a rack; doing this right away helps the bread come out of the pan easily and preserves the crust. Let cool completely before slicing. (For storage information, see Storing Bread, page 123.)

FRENCH ONION SWIRL BREAD, PAGE 160

MEXICAN CHOCOLATE SWIRL BREAD, PAGE 158

SAVORY DUKKAH SWIRL BREAD, PAGE 155

LEMON SWIRL BREAD, PAGE 162

MEXICAN CHOCOLATE SWIRL BREAD

MIX	BULK FERMENTATION	SHAPE	2ND RISE	BAKE
15 MIN	1–1½ HOURS	10 MIN	1–1½ HOURS	40–45 MIN

MAKE THE PREFERMENT (12–16 HOURS BEFORE)

TIME: ABOUT 20 HOURS

MAKES 1 LOAF

PREFERMENT (SEE NOTE)

14 grams (1 tablespoon) sourdough culture (see page 187)

30 grams (¼ cup) unbleached bread flour

28 grams (2 tablespoons) cool water (60°F to 70°F)

DOUGH

300 grams (2½ cups) unbleached bread flour, plus more for dusting

12 grams (1 tablespoon) sugar

6 grams (1 teaspoon) fine salt

3 grams (1 teaspoon) instant yeast

1 large egg (50 grams)

170 grams (¾ cup) warm whole milk (see Temperature, page 25)

57 grams (4 tablespoons) unsalted butter, cut into small cubes, at room temperature

44 grams (¼ cup) mini semisweet chocolate chips

FILLING

50 grams (¼ cup) sugar

5 grams (1 tablespoon) cocoa powder

¼ teaspoon fine salt

This bread is reminiscent of Mexican hot chocolate, which is often spiked with cinnamon and chile powder. The swirl at its center is a combination of cocoa powder, cinnamon, and chipotle powder, which gives it a bit of smokiness and some gentle, lingering heat. We think it's a dynamite combination, but you can omit the chile powder for a more straightforward chocolate-cinnamon spice profile. Mini chocolate chips are added to the dough, which amps up the chocolate flavor and gives the bread some nice texture. Toast a slice, and the chips melt into molten pockets of chocolate. This enriched dough requires the use of a stand mixer.

MAKE THE PREFERMENT: The evening before you want to bake, in a small bowl, combine the sourdough culture, flour, and water and mix until no dry patches of flour remain. Cover and let stand at room temperature overnight, 12 to 16 hours.

DAY 2

MAKE THE DOUGH: In a stand mixer bowl, combine the preferment, flour, sugar, salt, yeast, egg, and milk. Using the dough hook attachment, mix on medium-low speed, scraping the mixer bowl as needed, until you have a firm yet tacky dough, 2 to 3 minutes. Increase the speed to medium and continue mixing until the dough is smooth and elastic, an additional 3 to 5 minutes. With the mixer running, add the butter one piece at a time, mixing until the first piece is fully incorporated before adding the next. Continue mixing until the dough pulls away from the sides of the bowl and is soft, smooth, and elastic, 3 to 5 minutes.

With the mixer stopped, add the chocolate chips, then mix until they are evenly distributed in the dough, 1 to 2 minutes. Cover and let rise at room temperature until doubled in size, 1 to 1½ hours.

½ teaspoon ground cinnamon

¼ teaspoon chipotle chile powder

Egg wash: 1 large egg (50 grams) beaten with ⅛ teaspoon fine salt

DAY 1

NOTE: We like the flavor (and improved keeping qualities) that a sourdough preferment lends this bread, but if you don't have sourdough culture—or forgot to make the preferment—just add 37 grams (scant ⅓ cup) additional bread flour and 35 grams (2 tablespoons plus 1½ teaspoons) water to the final dough and increase the yeast to 6 grams (2 teaspoons).

MEANWHILE, MAKE THE FILLING: Combine the sugar, cocoa powder, salt, cinnamon, and chipotle powder in a small bowl.

Grease an 8½ × 4½-inch loaf pan with pan spray.

SHAPE THE DOUGH AND LET IT RISE: Lightly flour a work surface, then, using a plastic bowl scraper, gently ease the dough out of the bowl onto the work surface. Gently deflate the dough, then roll it into a 15 × 8-inch rectangle with a short side facing you. Brush a light, even coat of the egg wash over the dough; you won't use all of it here but will use more for brushing the loaf before baking. Sprinkle the filling evenly over the dough, leaving a 1-inch-wide bare strip on the short side of the dough farthest away from you. Fold the outer ½ inch of each long edge in to enclose the edge of the filling. Gently press down to flatten.

Starting with the short side closest to you, roll the dough into a log. Pinch the center seam closed, then pinch each end to seal. Place the log seam side down in the prepared pan. Cover and let rise at room temperature until the loaf crowns about 1 inch over the edge of the pan (see Proofing, page 44), 1 to 1½ hours.

Toward the end of the rising time, preheat the oven to 350°F.

BAKE: Brush the top of the bread with the remaining egg wash and bake until the crust is golden brown and the internal temperature reaches 190°F, 40 to 45 minutes.

Remove the loaf from the oven and immediately turn it out of the pan and onto a rack; doing this right away helps the bread come out of the pan easily and preserves the crust. Let cool completely before slicing. (For storage information, see Storing Bread, page 123.)

FRENCH ONION SWIRL BREAD

MIX	BULK FERMENTATION	SHAPE	2ND RISE	BAKE
15 MIN	1–1½ HOURS	10 MIN	1–1½ HOURS	40–45 MIN

MAKE THE PREFERMENT (12–16 HOURS BEFORE)

TIME: ABOUT 20 HOURS

MAKES 1 LOAF

PREFERMENT (SEE NOTE)

14 grams (1 tablespoon) sourdough culture (see page 187)

30 grams (¼ cup) unbleached bread flour

28 grams (2 tablespoons) cool water (60°F to 70°F)

DOUGH

300 grams (2½ cups) unbleached bread flour, plus more for dusting

12 grams (1 tablespoon) sugar

6 grams (1 teaspoon) fine salt

3 grams (1 teaspoon) instant yeast

1 large egg (50 grams)

170 grams (¾ cup) warm whole milk (see Temperature, page 25)

57 grams (4 tablespoons) unsalted butter, cut into small cubes, at room temperature

FILLING

1 large yellow onion (200 grams), finely chopped (about 1½ cups)

¼ teaspoon fine salt

¼ teaspoon freshly ground black pepper

A bowl of French onion soup, topped with a slice of crusty bread and lots of melty Gruyère cheese, is a very fine thing. This loaf tastes like that bistro stalwart, and features a swirl of caramelized onions, cheese, and fragrant thyme at its center. To avoid gaps in the swirl, it's key that you cook the onions until they are deeply caramelized and shred the cheese finely, using a rasp-style grater or the smallest holes on your box grater (and if gaps do occur, don't despair: the bread will still taste wonderful). Serve thick slices of this bread alongside your favorite soup or use it to make (double) grilled cheese sandwiches.

DAY 1

MAKE THE PREFERMENT: The evening before you want to bake, in a small bowl, combine the sourdough culture, flour, and water and mix until no dry patches of flour remain. Cover and let stand at room temperature overnight, 12 to 16 hours.

DAY 2

MAKE THE DOUGH: In a stand mixer bowl, combine the preferment, flour, sugar, salt, yeast, egg, and milk. Using the dough hook attachment, mix on medium-low speed, scraping the bowl as needed, until you have a firm yet tacky dough, 2 to 3 minutes. Increase the speed to medium and continue mixing until the dough is smooth and elastic, an additional 3 to 5 minutes. With the mixer running, add the butter one piece at a time, mixing until the first piece is fully incorporated before adding the next. Continue mixing until the dough pulls away from the sides of the bowl and is soft, smooth, and elastic, 3 to 5 minutes. Cover and let rise at room temperature until puffy and doubled in size, 1 to 1½ hours.

MEANWHILE, MAKE THE FILLING: Preheat the oven to 400°F. Line a rimmed baking sheet with parchment paper.

140 grams (1¼ cups) finely grated Gruyère cheese (see headnote)

2 tablespoons chopped fresh thyme leaves or 1 tablespoon dried thyme

Egg wash: 1 large egg (50 grams) beaten with ⅛ teaspoon fine salt

NOTE: We like the flavor (and improved keeping qualities) that a sourdough preferment lends this bread, but if you don't have sourdough culture—or forgot to make the preferment—just add 37 grams (scant ⅓ cup) additional bread flour and 35 grams (2 tablespoons plus 1½ teaspoons) water to the final dough and increase the yeast to 6 grams (2 teaspoons).

Toss the onions, salt, and pepper on the lined pan until combined. Bake until the onions are fragrant, softened, and well browned, even charred, in spots, 40 to 45 minutes, stirring and redistributing the onions every 10 minutes.

Transfer the onions to a measuring cup; you should have about 35 grams (a packed ¼ cup) of cooked onion. If you have much more than that, return the onions to the oven and continue to cook. Transfer the onions to a bowl and let cool. Add the Gruyère and thyme to the onions along with 28 grams (2 tablespoons) of the egg wash. Mix well to combine. Reserve the remaining egg wash for brushing the dough.

Grease an 8½ × 4½-inch loaf pan with pan spray.

SHAPE THE DOUGH AND LET IT RISE: Lightly flour a work surface, then use a plastic bowl scraper to gently ease the dough out of the bowl onto the work surface. Gently deflate the dough, then pat, roll, and stretch it into 15 × 8-inch rectangle with a short side facing you. Brush a light, even coat of the egg wash over the dough; you won't use all of it here but will use more for brushing the loaf before baking. Sprinkle the filling evenly over the dough, gently pressing down on it to adhere it to the dough, leaving a 1-inch-wide bare strip on the short side of the dough farthest away from you. Fold the outer ½ inch of each long edge in to enclose the edge of the filling. Gently press down to flatten. Starting with the short side closest to you, roll the dough into a log. Pinch the center seam closed, then pinch each end to seal. Place the log seam side down in the prepared pan. Cover and let rise at room temperature until the loaf crowns about 1 inch over the edge of the pan (see Proofing, page 44), 1 to 1½ hours.

Toward the end of the rising time, preheat the oven to 350°F.

BAKE: Lightly brush the top of the loaf with the reserved egg wash. Bake the bread until the crust is shiny and golden brown and the internal temperature reaches 190°F, 40 to 45 minutes.

Remove the loaf from the oven and immediately turn it out of the pan and onto a rack; doing this right away helps the bread come out of the pan easily and preserves the crust. Let cool completely before slicing. (For storage information, see Storing Bread, page 123.)

LEMON SWIRL BREAD

MIX	FERMENTATION	SHAPE	2ND RISE	BAKE
15 MIN	1–1½ HOURS	10 MIN	1½ HOURS	40–45 MIN

MAKE THE PREFERMENT (12–16 HOURS BEFORE)

TIME: ABOUT 20 HOURS

MAKES 1 LOAF

PREFERMENT (SEE NOTE)

14 grams (1 tablespoon) sourdough culture (see page 187)

30 grams (¼ cup) unbleached bread flour

28 grams (2 tablespoons) cool water (60°F to 70°F)

DOUGH

300 grams (2½ cups) unbleached bread flour, plus more for dusting

12 grams (1 tablespoon) granulated sugar

6 grams (1 teaspoon) fine salt

3 grams (1 teaspoon) instant yeast

1 large egg (50 grams)

170 grams (¾ cup) warm whole milk (see Temperature, page 25)

57 grams (4 tablespoons) unsalted butter, cut into small cubes, at room temperature

FILLING

60 grams (⅓ cup) turbinado sugar

7.5 grams (1 tablespoon) unbleached bread flour

1 packed tablespoon grated lemon zest (from 1 large lemon)

This bread, with its zippy swirl of lemon, is a great breakfast bread, particularly in the colder, darker months when you feel in need of some sunshine. Despite the fact that all the lemon flavor in this bread comes from just a tablespoon of zest, when combined with sugar it turns into a delightfully gooey spiral at the center of each slice that, in taste and texture, is like lemon curd.

DAY 1

MAKE THE PREFERMENT: The evening before you want to bake, in a small bowl, combine the sourdough culture, flour, and water and mix until no dry patches of flour remain. Cover and let stand at room temperature overnight, 12 to 16 hours.

DAY 2

MAKE THE DOUGH: In a stand mixer bowl, combine the preferment, flour, granulated sugar, salt, yeast, egg, and milk. Using the dough hook attachment, mix on medium-low speed, scraping the mixer bowl as needed, until you have a firm yet tacky dough, 2 to 3 minutes. Increase the speed to medium and continue mixing until the dough is smooth and elastic, an additional 3 to 5 minutes. With the mixer running, add the butter one piece at a time, mixing until the first piece is fully incorporated before adding the next. Continue mixing until the dough pulls away from the sides of the bowl and is soft, smooth, and elastic, 3 to 5 minutes. Cover and let rise at room temperature until doubled in size, 1 to 1½ hours.

MEANWHILE, MAKE THE FILLING: In a small bowl, stir together the turbinado sugar, flour, and lemon zest.

Lightly grease an 8½ × 4½-inch loaf pan with pan spray.

SHAPE THE DOUGH AND LET IT RISE: Lightly flour a work surface, then use a plastic bowl scraper to ease the dough out of the bowl onto the work surface. Gently deflate the dough, then roll it into a 15 × 8-inch rectangle with a short side facing you. Sprinkle the filling evenly over the

Egg wash: 1 large egg (50 grams) beaten with ⅛ teaspoon salt

49 grams (¼ cup) Swedish pearl sugar or 57 grams (¼ cup) sparkling sugar (optional)

NOTE: We like the flavor (and improved keeping qualities) that a sourdough preferment lends this bread, but if you don't have sourdough culture—or forgot to make the preferment—just add 37 grams (scant ⅓ cup) additional bread flour and 35 grams (2 tablespoons plus 1½ teaspoons) water to the final dough and increase the yeast to 6 grams (2 teaspoons).

dough, leaving a 1-inch-wide bare strip on the short side of the dough farthest away from you. Fold the outer ½ inch of each long edge in to enclose the edge of the filling. Gently press down to flatten. Starting with the short side closest to you, roll the dough into a log. Pinch the center seam closed, then pinch each end to seal.

Place the log seam side down in the prepared pan. Cover and let rise at room temperature until the loaf crowns about 1 inch over the rim of the pan (see Proofing, page 44), about 1½ hours. Brush the top of the loaf with egg wash, then sprinkle with pearl sugar or sparkling sugar, if using.

Toward the end of the rising time, preheat the oven to 350°F.

BAKE: Bake the bread until the crust is golden brown and the internal temperature reaches 190°F, 40 to 45 minutes.

Remove the bread from the oven and immediately turn it out of the pan and onto a rack; doing this right away helps the bread come out of the pan easily and preserves the crust. Let cool completely before slicing. (For storage information, see Storing Bread, page 123.)

FROM LEFT: CHOCOLATE MILK BREAD (PAGE 167),
JAPANESE MILK BREAD

JAPANESE MILK BREAD

MAKE TANGZHONG	MIX	BULK FERMENTATION	SHAPE	2ND RISE	BAKE
5 MIN	15 MIN	1–1½ HOURS	10 MIN	1½ HOURS	30 MIN

TIME: ABOUT 4 HOURS

MAKES 1 LOAF

TANGZHONG

11 grams (1½ tablespoons) unbleached bread flour

35 grams (2½ tablespoons) cold milk, whole preferred

35 grams (2½ tablespoons) cold water (55°F to 60°F)

DOUGH

240 grams (2 cups) unbleached bread flour, plus more for dusting

41 grams (3 tablespoons plus 1 teaspoon) sugar

11 grams (1½ tablespoons) nonfat dry milk powder (optional; see Note)

7.5 grams (1¼ teaspoons) instant yeast

5 grams (scant 1 teaspoon) fine salt

92 grams (¼ cup plus 2½ tablespoons) cold milk, whole preferred

1 large egg (50 grams), beaten

42 grams (3 tablespoons) unsalted butter, melted

Milk bread is a delightfully tender, slightly sweet bread, so soft and pillowy that you might wonder if you should eat it or take a nap on it. In Japan, where it's especially popular, it's known as shokupan. The bread gets its plush texture from an unusual technique called tangzhong, popularized in recent years by Taiwanese cookbook author Yvonne Chen. It involves cooking some of the flour in liquid prior to adding it to the remaining dough ingredients, and is related to the Japanese method known as yudane, though yudane typically uses a 1:1 ratio of flour to water. Bringing the temperature of the flour and liquid to 149°F pregelatinizes the flour's starches, which makes them more able to retain liquid—thus enhancing the resulting bread's softness and shelf life.

Milk bread dough is also highly enriched with sugar, milk, eggs, and butter, which gives the loaf its distinctive crumb; the bread pulls apart into feathery strands that almost melt in your mouth. Developing enough structure in the dough is critical to achieving a high-rising loaf, so a stand mixer is essential for this bread.

MAKE THE TANGZHONG: In a small saucepan, combine the flour, milk, and water and whisk together until no lumps remain. Bring to a boil, then reduce the heat to low and cook, whisking constantly, until the mixture is thickened enough that it does not flow back together when the whisk passes through, 3 to 5 minutes.

MAKE THE DOUGH: In a stand mixer bowl, combine the tangzhong, flour, sugar, milk powder (if using), yeast, salt, milk, 41 grams (3 tablespoons) of the beaten egg (reserving the rest to brush the loaf before baking), and melted butter. Using the dough hook attachment, mix on medium-low speed until a soft, sticky dough forms, scraping down the bowl as necessary. Increase the speed to medium-high and continue mixing until the dough forms a ball that is smooth and elastic. The dough will stick

Recipe continues

to the sides of the bowl for much of the mixing time. Every few minutes, scrape down the sides and bottom of the bowl, then continue mixing. Eventually the dough will strengthen enough to pull away from the sides of the bowl. This process will take about 15 minutes. Cover and let rise at room temperature until puffy and doubled in size, 1 to 1½ hours.

Lightly grease an 8½ × 4½-inch loaf pan with pan spray.

SHAPE THE DOUGH AND LET IT RISE: Lightly flour a work surface, then use a plastic bowl scraper to ease the dough out of the bowl onto the work surface. Gently form the dough into a square and divide it into 4 equal portions (each about 134 grams). Flatten each piece of dough into a 6 × 4-inch rectangle, then fold the short ends in to meet in the center. Flatten the folded pieces into rectangles again (this time about 5 × 3 inches) and, starting with a short side, roll each of them into a log about 3½ inches wide. Place the logs seam side down in the prepared pan, arranging them side by side in a row of four. Cover and let the loaf rise at room temperature until it crowns ¾ inch over the edge of the pan (see Proofing, page 44), 1½ hours.

Toward the end of the rising time, preheat the oven to 350°F.

BAKE: Lightly brush the top of the loaf with a thin layer of the remaining beaten egg. Bake until it's a glossy, deep golden brown on top and the internal temperature reaches at least 190°F, about 30 minutes.

Remove the loaf from the oven and cool briefly in the pan before turning it out of the pan and onto a rack to cool. Let cool completely before slicing. (For storage information, see Storing Bread, page 123.)

CHOCOLATE MILK BREAD

MAKE TANGZHONG	MIX	BULK FERMENTATION	SHAPE	2ND RISE	BAKE
7 MIN	15–20 MIN	1–1½ HOURS	10 MIN	1½ HOURS	30 MIN

TIME: ABOUT 4 HOURS

MAKES 1 LOAF

TANGZHONG

11 grams (2 tablespoons) black cocoa

11 grams (2 tablespoons) Dutch-process cocoa

11 grams (1½ tablespoons) unbleached bread flour

70 grams (¼ cup plus 1 tablespoon) cold milk, whole preferred

70 grams (¼ cup plus 1 tablespoon) cold water (55°F to 60°F)

DOUGH

218 grams (1¾ cups plus 1 tablespoon) unbleached bread flour, plus more for dusting

41 grams (3 tablespoons plus 1 teaspoon) granulated sugar

11 grams (1½ tablespoons) nonfat dry milk powder (optional; see Note on opposite page)

7.5 grams (2½ teaspoons) instant yeast

5 grams (scant 1 teaspoon) fine salt

46 grams (3 tablespoons) unsalted butter, melted

This is a chocolate-lover's version of tender milk bread. Black cocoa is used to give the bread the deepest, darkest color (more black than brown). Black cocoa is ultra-Dutch processed, meaning it is treated with an alkaline solution to reduce its acidity, which gives it a smooth texture, dark color, and deep chocolate flavor. You can, however, use additional Dutch-process cocoa if you don't have it. You need a stand mixer for this dough.

MAKE THE TANGZHONG: In a small saucepan, combine both cocoas, the flour, milk, and water and whisk together until no lumps remain. Bring to a boil, then reduce the heat to low and cook, whisking constantly, until the mixture has thickened enough that it does not flow back together when the whisk passes through, 7 minutes.

MAKE THE DOUGH: In a stand mixer bowl, combine the tangzhong, flour, granulated sugar, milk powder (if using), yeast, salt, melted butter, milk, and 41 grams (3 tablespoons) of the beaten egg (reserve the remaining egg to brush over the loaf before baking). Using the dough hook attachment, mix on medium-low speed until a soft, sticky dough forms, scraping down the bowl as necessary. Increase the speed to medium-high and continue mixing until the dough almost clears the sides of the bowl is smooth and elastic. The dough will stick to the sides of the bowl for much of the mixing time. Every few minutes, scrape down the sides and bottom of the bowl, then continue mixing. Eventually the dough will strengthen enough to mostly pull away from the sides of the bowl. This process will take 15 to 20 minutes and the dough will still be slightly sticky. Once the dough is homogeneous, knead in the chocolate chips by hand, then cover and let rise at room temperature until puffy and doubled in size, 1 to 1½ hours.

Lightly grease an 8½ × 4½-inch loaf pan with pan spray.

Ingredients continue

Recipe continues

70 grams (¼ cup plus 1 tablespoon) warm milk (see Temperature, page 25), whole preferred

69 grams (¼ cup plus 2½ tablespoons) semisweet chocolate chips

1 large egg (50 grams), beaten

OPTIONAL TOPPING

2 teaspoons coarse sparkling sugar or Swedish pearl sugar

SHAPE THE DOUGH AND LET IT RISE: Lightly flour a work surface, then use a plastic bowl scraper to gently ease the dough out of the bowl onto the work surface. Gently form the dough into a square and divide it into 4 equal portions (each about 155 grams). Flatten each piece of dough by gently pressing and stretching it into a 6 × 4-inch rectangle, then fold the short ends in toward one another to meet in the center. Flatten into rectangles again (this time about 5 × 3 inches) and, starting with a short end, roll each of them into a log about 3½ inches long.

Place the logs seam side down, side by side, in a row of four into the prepared pan. Cover and let the loaf rise at room temperature until it just crowns over the edge of the pan (see Proofing, page 44), 1½ hours.

Toward the end of the rising time, preheat the oven to 350°F.

BAKE: Lightly brush the top of the loaf with a thin layer of the remaining beaten egg and sprinkle with sparkling or pearl sugar, if desired. Bake until the loaf is fragrant, the top crust is firm, and the internal temperature is at least 190°F, about 30 minutes.

Remove the loaf from the oven and cool briefly in the pan before turning it out of the pan and onto a rack to cool. Let cool completely before slicing. (For storage information, see Storing Bread, page 123.)

TIGER MILK BREAD

MAKE
TANGZHONG | MIX | DIVIDE | BULK FERMENTATION | SHAPE | 2ND RISE | BAKE
3–5 MIN | 15 MIN | 5 MIN | 1½ HOURS | 15 MIN | 40–50 MIN | 50 MIN

TIME: ABOUT 4 HOURS

**MAKES ONE 9 × 4-INCH LOAF
(HALF PULLMAN PAN)**

TANGZHONG

14 grams (2 tablespoons) unbleached bread flour

43 grams (3 tablespoons) cold milk, whole preferred

43 grams (3 tablespoons) cold water (55°F to 60°F)

PLAIN DOUGH

300 grams (2½ cups) unbleached bread flour, plus more for dusting

50 grams (¼ cup) sugar

14 grams (2 tablespoons) nonfat dry milk powder (optional; see Note, page 166)

9 grams (1 tablespoon) instant yeast

6 grams (1 teaspoon) fine salt

113 grams (½ cup) cold milk, whole preferred

1 large egg (50 grams)

57 grams (4 tablespoons) unsalted butter, melted

Unsurprisingly, this bread is beloved by all children who taste it. Shaped like babka, the plain and chocolate milk bread doughs entwine together, giving each slice a beautiful, swirled, tiger stripe–like pattern. This loaf is easier to make than it looks, though: You make a single dough, color and flavor a portion of it with cocoa, then stack and twist the two together to give the bread its distinctive appearance. Both doughs are also highly enriched with sugar, milk, eggs, and butter, which gives the loaf its feathery crumb. Developing enough structure in the dough is critical to both shaping and achieving a high-rising loaf, so a stand mixer is essential for this bread. A Pullman pan (a lidded, square-sided pan named for its resemblance to a Pullman train car; see page 15) gives this bread its perfectly square shape, but you can also make a more organically shaped bread if you use an 8½ × 4½-inch loaf pan.

MAKE THE TANGZHONG: In a small saucepan, combine the flour, milk, and water and whisk together until no lumps remain. Bring to a boil, then reduce the heat to low and cook, whisking constantly, until the mixture has thickened enough that it does not flow back together when the whisk passes through, 3 to 5 minutes.

MAKE THE PLAIN DOUGH: In a stand mixer bowl, combine the tangzhong, flour, sugar, milk powder (if using), yeast, salt, milk, egg, and melted butter. Using the dough hook attachment, mix on medium-low speed until a soft, sticky dough forms. Increase the speed to medium-high and continue mixing until the dough forms a ball that is smooth and elastic. The dough will stick to the sides of the bowl for much of the mixing time. Every few minutes, scrape down the sides and bottom of the bowl, then continue mixing. Eventually the dough will strengthen enough to pull away from the sides of the bowl. This process will take about 15 minutes.

Ingredients continue

Recipe continues

CHOCOLATE DOUGH

9 grams (1 tablespoon plus 2 teaspoons) black cocoa (or another Dutch-process cocoa)

43 grams (3 tablespoons) cold milk (55°F to 60°F), whole preferred

64 grams (¼ cup plus 2 tablespoons) semisweet chocolate chips

NOTE: We tip the bread out of the pan for the last 5 minutes of baking so that it browns on all sides; this helps the extra moisture escape and will ensure that the loaf stays as squared-off as possible and doesn't get "side suck." Side suck happens when the sides of the bread literally suck in, giving bread an hourglass shape, which is caused when there is still moisture in the bread that has not escaped (because it's baked in a lidded pan). Because this bread is highly enriched, the step of cooling completely is even more important for keeping the loaf square.

MEANWHILE, FOR THE CHOCOLATE DOUGH: In a small saucepan, combine the cocoa and milk and whisk together until no lumps remain. Place the saucepan over low heat and cook, whisking constantly, until the mixture thickens and is about the consistency of heavy cream, 2 to 4 minutes. Transfer the mixture to a small bowl and cool to room temperature.

DIVIDE AND BULK FERMENT THE DOUGH: Lightly flour a work surface, then use a plastic bowl scraper to ease the dough out of the bowl onto the work surface. Using a bench knife or a knife, divide the dough into one roughly 230-gram piece and one roughly 420-gram piece (if you want to eyeball it, the larger piece should be roughly two-thirds of the total amount of dough). Place the larger piece of dough in a medium bowl, cover, and let rise at room temperature until puffy though not necessarily doubled in size, about 1½ hours.

Return the smaller piece of dough to the mixer bowl and add the cooked and cooled cocoa mixture. Mix with the dough hook on medium speed until the cocoa mixture is completely incorporated. Once the dough is homogeneous, add the chocolate chips and mix on medium-low until well distributed. The chocolate dough will be slightly more slack and stickier than the plain dough. Cover and let rise at room temperature until puffy though not necessarily doubled in size, about 1½ hours.

Grease a 9 × 4-inch half Pullman pan with pan spray.

SHAPE THE DOUGH AND LET IT RISE: Transfer both pieces of dough to a lightly floured surface, gently deflate, then pat each piece of dough into a 10 × 8-inch rectangle with a short side facing you. Stack the chocolate dough rectangle on top of the rectangle of plain dough, stretching the edges of the chocolate dough so it completely covers the plain dough. Gently press the two pieces of dough together to adhere.

Beginning at one short end, roll the dough into a log, then pinch the seam to seal. Orient the log of dough perpendicular in front of you with the seam side up. Using a bench knife or sharp knife, cut the log in half lengthwise along the seam. With the cut edges up, make an "X" with the two pieces of dough. Gently entwine the top, then the bottom ends together to form a twisted shape. Pinch and seal the ends, tucking them under slightly. Transfer the twist to the prepared pan. Grease the lid, then cover and let rise at room temperature until the loaf fills three-quarters of the pan (see Proofing, page 44), 40 to 50 minutes.

Recipe continues

Toward the end of the rising time, preheat the oven to 425°F.

BAKE: Bake the loaf with the lid on for 20 minutes, then reduce the oven temperature to 350°F and continue baking an additional 25 minutes. Meanwhile, line a baking sheet with parchment paper.

Gently remove the lid and tip the loaf out of the pan onto the lined baking sheet. Return the loaf (on the baking sheet) to the oven and continue baking until the loaf is a deep golden color and a digital thermometer inserted into the center reads at least 210°F, about 5 minutes more. Turn off the oven, crack the oven door, and allow the bread to cool to room temperature inside the oven.

Remove the bread from the oven. The bread slices best after resting, wrapped in plastic wrap or foil, overnight. (For storage information, see Storing Bread, page 123.)

GOLDEN MILK BREAD

MAKE TANGZHONG	MIX	BULK FERMENTATION	SHAPE	2ND RISE	BAKE
3–5 MIN	15 MIN	1½ HOURS	10 MIN	1½ HOURS	40 MIN

---- TIME: ABOUT 4 HOURS ----

MAKES 1 LOAF

TANGZHONG

14 grams (2 tablespoons) unbleached bread flour

½ teaspoon ground turmeric

¼ teaspoon ground cardamom

⅛ teaspoon ground cinnamon

⅛ teaspoon ground ginger

⅛ teaspoon ground nutmeg

⅛ teaspoon freshly ground black pepper

43 grams (3 tablespoons) cold water (55°F to 60°F)

45 grams (3 tablespoons) canned full-fat coconut milk, at room temperature and whisked until homogenous

DOUGH

330 grams (2¾ cups) unbleached bread flour, plus more for dusting

14 grams (2 tablespoons) coconut milk powder or nonfat dry milk powder (optional; see Note, page 166)

50 grams (¼ cup) sugar

9 grams (1 tablespoon) instant yeast

6 grams (1 teaspoon) fine salt

This bread is inspired by the Indian drink haldi doodh (in Hindi, haldi means "milk" and doodh is "turmeric"). It's the turmeric that gives this bread its brilliant hue, but its rich flavor comes from coconut milk, which we use in place of the cow's milk that is typically used in milk bread doughs. Generously spiced with fragrant cardamom, cinnamon, ginger, nutmeg, and black pepper, the bread has layered complexity.

MAKE THE TANGZHONG: In a small saucepan, combine the flour, spices, water, and coconut milk and whisk until no lumps remain. Bring to a boil, then reduce the heat to low and cook, whisking constantly, until the mixture has thickened enough that it does not flow back together when the whisk passes through, 3 to 5 minutes.

MAKE THE DOUGH: In a stand mixer bowl, combine the tangzhong, flour, milk powder (if using), sugar, yeast, salt, coconut milk, egg, and coconut oil. Using the dough hook attachment, mix on medium-low speed until a soft, sticky dough forms. Increase the speed to medium-high and continue mixing until the dough forms a ball that is smooth and elastic. The dough will stick to the sides of the bowl for much of the mixing time. Every few minutes, scrape down the sides and bottom of the bowl, then continue mixing. Eventually the dough will strengthen enough to pull away from the sides of the bowl. This process will take about 15 minutes. Cover and let rise at room temperature for 1½ hours.

Lightly grease an 8½ × 4½-inch loaf pan with pan spray.

SHAPE THE DOUGH AND LET IT RISE: Lightly flour a work surface, then use a plastic bowl scraper to ease the dough out of the bowl onto the work surface. Gently deflate the dough, then divide it into 4 equal portions (each about 170 grams). Flatten each piece of dough into an 8 × 5-inch rectangle, then fold the short ends in toward one another to meet in the center. Flatten the folded pieces into rectangles again (this

Ingredients continue

Recipe continues

113 grams (scant ½ cup) canned full-fat coconut milk, at room temperature and whisked until homogeneous

1 large egg (50 grams)

57 grams (4 tablespoons) unrefined coconut oil, melted

TOPPING

Egg wash: 1 large egg (50 grams) beaten with ⅛ teaspoon fine salt

2 teaspoons nigella seeds (optional)

time about 6 × 3 inches) and, starting with a short end, roll each of them into a 4-inch-long log. Place the logs seam side down and side by side in the prepared loaf pan. Cover and let the rise at room temperature until the loaf crowns about ¾ inch over the edge of the pan (see Proofing, page 44), about 1½ hours.

Toward the end of the rising time, preheat the oven to 350°F.

BAKE: Lightly brush the loaf with a thin layer of egg wash and sprinkle with nigella seeds, if desired. Bake the loaf until it's golden brown on top and the internal temperature reaches 190°F, about 40 minutes.

Remove the loaf from the oven and immediately turn it out of the pan and onto a rack; doing this right away helps the bread come out of the pan easily and preserves the crust. Let cool completely before slicing. (For storage information, see Storing Bread, page 123.)

GÂTEAU VOYAGE

FRUIT AND NUT TRAVEL BREAD

MAKES TWO 5¼ × 3-INCH LOAVES

PREFERMENT

38 grams (scant 3 tablespoons) sourdough culture (see page 187)

254 grams (2¼ cups) whole wheat flour

205 grams (¾ cup plus 2½ tablespoons) cold water (55° to 60°F)

DOUGH

193 grams (1½ cups) dried fruit (see headnote), chopped into raisin-size pieces

193 grams (1½ cups plus 3 tablespoons) nuts (see headnote), chopped into raisin-size pieces

103 grams (¼ cup plus 3½ tablespoons) hot water (115°F to 120°F)

12 grams (2 teaspoons) fine salt

1.5 grams (¼ teaspoon) baking soda

27 grams (3 tablespoons) sesame seeds, preferably black or unhulled white

This is the original power bar, a hearty loaf of nut-and-fruit-studded bread barely held together with tangy whole wheat dough. We've experimented with various combinations of nuts and fruit, from "single varietal" loaves with walnuts and prunes to clean-out-the-pantry loaves using an assortment of fruit and nuts, including golden and black raisins, dried cranberries, currants, apricots, peaches, pears, nectarines, pecans, and almonds. Every combination works, yielding a slightly different loaf each time. Whatever combination you choose, to make slicing the loaf easier, cut the nuts and fruit into raisin-size pieces so they integrate well with the dough. One of this bread's most compelling characteristics is its lasting power—it will remain moist and tasty for a week or more on your countertop (or in your backpack, earning it its name, "travel cake"). Note that you'll need two 5¼ × 3-inch mini loaf pans for this recipe; disposable aluminum pans will work.

DAY 1

MAKE THE PREFERMENT: The evening before you want to bake, in a large bowl, combine the sourdough culture, flour, and water and mix until no dry patches of flour remain. Knead until a stiff, smooth dough forms, 1 to 2 minutes. Cover and let stand at room temperature overnight, 12 to 16 hours.

DAY 2

Preheat the oven to 450°F.

MAKE THE DOUGH: In a medium bowl, combine the fruit, nuts, and hot water. In a small bowl, stir together the salt and baking soda. Sprinkle the salt and baking soda mixture over the fruit and nut mixture, stirring to combine. Add the fruit and nut mixture to the preferment, then

Recipe continues

squeeze, pinch, and fold the mixture together with your hands until it is homogeneous, about 3 minutes. The finished dough will have an airy, loose, almost batter-like consistency, with a generous ratio of nuts and fruit to dough.

Generously grease two 5¼ × 3-inch mini loaf pans with pan spray. Divide the batter evenly between the two pans (about 500 grams per pan). Using wet fingers, gently press and smooth the dough evenly into each pan. Sprinkle the top of each loaf generously with sesame seeds, pressing gently to help them adhere.

Let the loaves rest, uncovered at room temperature, for about 10 minutes to give the baking soda a chance to activate. The loaves may puff slightly during this time, which is normal.

BAKE: Transfer the pans to the oven and immediately reduce the oven temperature to 425°F. Bake the loaves until they are deeply colored and firm and the internal temperature reaches 210°F, 35 to 40 minutes.

Remove the loaves from the oven and let cool in the pans for 10 minutes before turning out onto a wire rack to cool completely. If necessary, run an offset spatula or table knife around the edges of the loaves to help them release. Let cool completely. To serve, slice very thinly.

VARIATION

GATEÂU VOYAGE CRACKERS: This bread makes killer crackers. Bake the bread as directed and cool. Preheat the oven to 200°F. Slice the bread as thinly as possible, arrange on a baking sheet in a single layer, then brush each slice lightly with melted butter and sprinkle with a bit of sugar. Bake until crisp and slightly caramelized, about 1 hour, flipping them halfway through baking.

RÚGBRAUÐ

ICELANDIC RYE

MAKES ONE 9 × 4-INCH LOAF (HALF PULLMAN PAN)

318 grams (3 cups) whole rye flour

170 grams (1½ cups) whole wheat flour

16 grams (4 teaspoons) baking powder

12 grams (2 teaspoons) fine salt

6 grams (1 teaspoon) baking soda

454 grams (2 cups) low-fat buttermilk, cold

336 grams (1 cup) golden syrup

We deviate from tradition when it comes to baking this Icelandic bread. It's usually baked for a long time in a relatively cool oven, often overnight, but we've adjusted its preparation so it's baked a bit hotter, and for a shorter-but-still-long time (nearly 2 hours!). This bread is often made entirely with rye flour, but our version contains a bit of whole wheat, which gives the crumb a pleasant chew. Despite the differences in recipes, this bread, like the classic, is a dense, moist loaf with a tight crumb and a delicate sweetness, and relies on baking powder, rather than yeast or sourdough culture, for its rise. After side by side tasting, we found we preferred rúgbrauð made with golden syrup, which is Icelanders' sweetener of choice for this bread; it has caramelized sugar notes, balancing the sweetness with a bit of bitterness. If you can't find it, you can substitute a combination of 168 grams (½ cup) honey mixed with 170 grams (½ cup) old-fashioned molasses (not blackstrap); or 312 grams (1 cup) dark corn syrup.

Serve this bread thinly sliced, topped with smoked, creamed, or pickled fish and fresh or pickled vegetables, or just with cream cheese or a thick layer of good butter.

Arrange a rack in the center of the oven and preheat the oven to 325°F. Grease a 9 × 4-inch half Pullman pan with pan spray.

MAKE THE DOUGH: In a large bowl, whisk together the whole rye flour, whole wheat flour, baking powder, salt, and baking soda. In a medium bowl, whisk together the buttermilk and golden syrup.

Pour the wet ingredients into the dry ingredients, stirring to form a thick batter. Transfer the batter to the prepared pan and smooth the top. Lightly grease the pan lid and slide the lid on the pan.

Recipe continues

BAKE: Bake the bread for 2 hours. The loaf will be deep brown and fragrant. Turn off the oven and remove the lid from the pan. Leave the loaf in the still-warm oven for an additional 15 minutes, then remove from the oven and turn out of the pan onto a rack to cool completely.

This bread tastes and slices best when allowed to rest, wrapped in plastic wrap or foil, overnight. To serve, slice thinly. (For storage information, see Storing Bread, page 123.)

VOLLKORNBROT

GERMAN WHOLE GRAIN RYE

MIX	SHAPE	RISE	BAKE	REST
10 MIN	10 MIN	1–1½ HOURS	1½ HOURS–1 HOUR 45 MIN	24 HOURS

MAKE THE PREFERMENT AND SOAKER (12–16 HOURS BEFORE)

TIME: ABOUT 3 DAYS

MAKES ONE 9 × 4-INCH LOAF (HALF PULLMAN PAN)

PREFERMENT

14 grams (1 tablespoon) sourdough culture (see page 187)

339 grams (3 cups plus 3 tablespoons) whole rye flour

339 grams (1½ cups) cool water (60°F to 70°F)

SOAKER

242 grams (2 cups) rye chops (see Note)

242 grams (1 cup plus 1 tablespoon) cool water (60°F to 70°F)

DOUGH

61 grams (¼ cup plus 3 tablespoons) sunflower seeds

182 grams (scant 1¾ cups) whole rye flour, plus more for dusting

95 grams (¼ cup plus 3 tablespoons) hot water (115°F to 120°F)

15 grams (2½ teaspoons) fine salt

7.5 grams (2½ teaspoons) instant yeast

This traditional German bread, made entirely with rye flour, is dense, hearty, moist, and chewy, perfect for slicing thinly and using as the base for an open-faced sandwich, similar to but less sweet than the Rúgbrauð (page 179). Because the dough is quite sticky, we recommend mixing the dough in a stand mixer, and use well-floured hands and a quick, light touch to shape the loaf. Once it's baked, let it cool completely and then rest for at least 24 hours before slicing. Unlike most other breads, Vollkornbrot actually improves upon sitting, and will keep, wrapped at room temperature, for 1 week. It also freezes beautifully.

DAY 1

MAKE THE PREFERMENT: The evening before you want to bake, in a large bowl, combine the sourdough culture, whole rye flour, and water. Mix until no dry patches of flour remain; the mixture will be thick. Cover and let rest at room temperature overnight, 12 to 16 hours.

MAKE THE SOAKER: In a large bowl, combine the rye chops and water, mixing well to ensure the rye chops are hydrated. There will not be much excess water remaining in the bottom of the bowl. Cover and let rest at room temperature overnight, 12 to 16 hours.

DAY 2

TOAST THE SUNFLOWER SEEDS: Preheat the oven to 350°F.

Place the sunflower seeds on a rimmed baking sheet and bake until fragrant and lightly brown, 5 to 8 minutes. Let cool to room temperature.

MAKE THE DOUGH: In a stand mixer bowl, combine the preferment, soaker, sunflower seeds, whole rye flour, hot water, salt, and yeast. Using the paddle attachment, mix on medium-low speed until a sticky dough

Recipe continues

forms. Scrape down the bottom and sides of the bowl along with the paddle. Continue mixing on medium-low speed until well combined, 3 to 5 minutes. The thick dough will be somewhat compact and sticky.

Grease a 9 × 4-inch half Pullman pan with pan spray, then dust lightly with whole rye flour.

SHAPE THE DOUGH AND LET IT RISE: Generously flour a work surface with whole rye flour. Transfer the dough to the prepared surface, then gently pat and roll the dough into a log. Coat any exposed dough in flour by rolling the log in the remaining flour on the work surface. Place the log in the prepared pan. Using the long edge of a plastic bowl scraper or a 4- to 5-inch spatula, gently pat the dough into the sides and corners of the pan, then dome the top of the loaf by angling the scraper against the dough and sides of the pan. With the short edge of the scraper or a 4-inch-wide kitchen spatula, score two large Xs about ½ inch deep on top of the loaf. Cover and let rise at room temperature until the loaf just crowns over the edge of the pan (see Proofing, page 44), 1 to 1½ hours.

Toward the end of the rising time, arrange a rack in the center of the oven and preheat the oven to 375°F.

BAKE: Bake the loaf until the top is browned and firm and the internal temperature reaches 210°F, 1 hour 30 minutes to 1 hour 45 minutes. If the loaf is browning too quickly, tent with foil.

Remove the loaf from the oven and turn it out of the pan and onto a rack to cool completely. Cover and let rest at least 24 hours before thinly slicing. This bread will keep well wrapped at room temperature for 1 week.

NOTES:

Rye chops—cracked rye berries, similar in appearance to steel-cut oats—can usually be found at health food stores in bulk bins; they are not the same as rye flakes, which are more akin to rolled oats.

For a slightly sweeter version, add 155 grams (1 cup plus 1 tablespoon) currants with the sunflower seeds when mixing the final dough.

Sourdough Primer

Sourdough baking is both craft and science, which is what makes it fascinating—and, sometimes, frustrating. When we talk about sourdough, what we're really talking about are breads that use a sourdough culture (in lieu of or in addition to commercial yeast) for rise and flavor. Sourdough may be the more familiar term, but naturally leavened is more accurate, because many sourdough breads aren't actually sour at all. In other words, all sourdoughs are naturally leavened, but not all naturally leavened breads are sour.

While made with simple ingredients—often just flour, water, and salt—naturally leavened breads can nevertheless sometimes be tricky to make, as each element of the process can be manipulated, and each manipulation (human-made or environmental) will result in a different outcome from day to day, batch to batch. Even in a professional bakery setting, no two loaves of bread are ever exactly the same.

Every loaf of naturally leavened bread is an expression of the ingredients, a record of the environmental conditions the day it was baked, and, of course, a reflection of the skill and preferences of the baker. That's the craft element of baking, and craft has no horizon.

Think about the process of making naturally leavened bread as a journey without end, one that begins now (or in about a week, when your culture is ripe and ready to use) and stretches on for as long as you choose to bake. Some days, your loaf might be flatter than you want; then again, you may knock it out of the park, pulling from your oven burnished bâtards or boules with blistered crusts and open, airy interiors. These extremes might exist in the same week! Though—and it pains us to say this—rarely do home bakers make a wonderful loaf of naturally leavened bread on the first try.

But with practice and patience comes improvement. So, if there's one piece of advice we have for you before you start baking sourdough, it's this: Don't give up. The more frequently you bake bread and the longer you keep at it, the more you will develop your senses and intuition. You'll know when to feed your culture, just from a glance. Your hands will develop a feel for the pillowy, marshmallow-like texture of perfectly proofed dough. And you will have figured out what oven setup works the best for you (see Baking, page 48), ensuring loaves with exceptional crusts.

As with everything, but especially with naturally leavened breads, with practice, you'll see your bread improve. And in the meantime, take heart that even the flattest, homeliest loaves of sourdough taste good toasted and buttered.

STARTING A SOURDOUGH
CULTURE (AKA "STARTER")

The first thing you need to bake naturally leavened breads is natural leaven, aka sourdough culture. There are several ways to acquire one. You can ask a baker friend for a bit of theirs (you only need a table-spoon or so), or show up, jar in hand, at your favorite bakery and ask for a spoonful—many will happily give you some. You can also buy sourdough starter. Or, with just flour, water, and some patience, you can make your own at home.

WHAT IS SOURDOUGH CULTURE AND HOW DOES IT WORK?

Sourdough culture is a simple combination of flour and water, stirred together and then left at room temperature until it becomes bubbly.

But let's back up a minute and start with wheat. As it grows, wheat collects naturally occurring bacteria and yeast. Those bacteria and yeast survive the drying and milling processes, remaining ever present in the flour (as well as on our hands and in the air). When we add water to flour, we unlock some of the starches in the flour, making them available for the yeast and bacteria to eat. Mixing water into flour also activates the proteins in the flour, which then form a web of strands and connectors. As the yeast and bacteria eat, they produce carbon dioxide, which gets caught in the sticky, glutenous web, making the sourdough culture bubbly (which, in turn, causes the bread dough to rise).

The by-products of this feeding frenzy, in addi-tion to the carbon dioxide, are acetic and lactic acids. They give culture its sour flavor. Note that we're saying these acids give the *culture* a sour flavor; there is little relationship between the taste of your starter and the flavor of your baked loaf of bread, which has much more to do with how, and for how long, the dough is fermented (we'll get to this later in the chapter).

To create a culture, all you need to do is combine flour and water, give the microorganisms the right environment in which to thrive, and wait, offering the yeast and bacteria (that are naturally present on the flour) a fresh supply of food when they're hungry.

MAKING YOUR OWN SOURDOUGH CULTURE

There's no one way to make a sourdough culture, but this method, developed by the King Arthur team, honed over many years, is a good place to begin. While not foolproof (we are, after all, dealing with fickle microorganisms), it is fool-resistant, and very likely to give you success. (And if it doesn't, we prob-ably have a solution; see page 196 for troubleshooting tips.)

As elsewhere in this book, we highly recom-mend measuring by weight, rather than volume, for the most successful results. When first making your starter, you'll use whole-grain flour, because it naturally has a higher concentration of microorgan-isms (yeast and bacteria) than all-purpose flour. This helps establish the culture more quickly. If you don't have whole-grain flour, you can use unbleached all-purpose; you just may find the culture simply takes a little longer to get going. On Day 2 (see details on the next page) you'll switch to all-purpose for the culture's regular daily feedings.

Making a starter requires no special training or tools: All you do is stir together flour and water and wait. In about a week, what began as an unpromising, sludgy mixture will, with some feeding, turn into a bubbly, happy home for wild yeast, a ripe sourdough culture. And from there, your baking journey really begins.

To start your culture, you'll need:
75 grams/$\frac{1}{2}$ cup plus 3 tablespoons whole wheat flour or whole rye flour
75 grams/5 tablespoons cool water

DAY 1

Combine the flour and water in a wide-mouth non-reactive quart container that's taller than it is wide. We like to use clear containers because they allow you to easily see the activity beneath the surface. When feeding, mark the culture's level and the time on the outside of the container with a piece of tape, then keep an eye on it as it grows. This makes it simple to determine whether your culture is doubling or tripling within 6 to 8 hours of feeding, which is a good indication of activity in your culture.

Stir the flour and water together thoroughly; make sure there's no dry flour. Cover the container loosely, either with plastic wrap or by resting a lid on top, and let the mixture sit at warm room temperature (about 70°F) for 24 hours. The colder the environment, the more slowly your starter will grow. If the normal temperature in your home is below 68°F, we suggest finding a warm spot to develop your starter, like setting the starter atop your water heater, refrigerator, or another appliance that might generate ambient heat.

DAY 2

After 24 hours, you may see a bit of growth or bubbling, or you may see no activity at all. Either way, you're going to discard all but 50 grams (about 3½ tablespoons) of the culture, then add, or feed it 50 grams (about 6 tablespoons) all-purpose flour and 50 grams (about ¼ cup) cool water (if your house is warm) or lukewarm water (if it's cold). Mix well, cover loosely, and let the mixture rest at warm room temperature for another 24 hours.

DAY 3

By the third day, you'll likely see some activity—bubbling; a fresh, fruity aroma; and some evidence of expansion. It's now time to begin feeding the culture twice a day, spacing the feedings about 12 hours apart: Once in the morning and again before you go to bed works well. For each feeding, weigh out and reserve 50 grams culture and discard the rest (it can be composted or thrown in the trash, but avoid throwing it down the drain, because it can cause clogs). Add, or feed, the reserved culture 50 grams all-purpose flour and 50 grams water.

DAYS 4 AND 5

Feed the culture twice a day, using the same amounts and instructions for Day 3.

BEWARE CULTURE FAKE OUT

Sometimes you'll find that in the first few days after mixing, your culture is going gangbusters, doubling in volume and seeming very active. Then, suddenly, it stops. Is it dead? No. The rising you see in those first days is caused by a sudden rush of activity as all the wild yeasts and bacteria in the mix start to feed voraciously. But as your culture begins to ripen it becomes more acidic, and a whole complex battle takes place, as microbes throw different molecules meant to kill their competitors and leave more food for themselves at one another. A portion of these microorganisms just can't hang on. As they die off, the culture takes on the sudden appearance of inactivity.

But with more time and feeding, a robust yeast colony will become established (only the strong survive!), which is when you'll begin to see predictable rising and falling again after each feeding, along with bubbles.

DAYS 5 AND 6

Now it's time to begin giving your starter a closer look. About 8 to 12 hours after the second feeding on Day 5, the culture should have at least doubled in volume. You'll see lots of bubbles; there may be some little "rivulets" on the surface, full of finer bubbles, all evidence that the yeast and bacteria are feasting away and producing carbon dioxide. Also, the starter should have a tangy aroma—pleasingly acidic, but not overpowering.

WHAT IF NOTHING IS HAPPENING?

If, by Day 6, your starter hasn't risen much and isn't showing lots of bubbles, don't give up. Just keep feeding it twice daily (about every 12 hours) on Days 6 and 7, and for additional days, if necessary—as long as it takes until your culture is doubling (or more) in volume within 6 to 8 hours of a feeding and is noticeably bubbly. A good way to check its growth is by putting a rubber band around your container of culture. Position the band so it marks the height of your culture right after feeding; then you'll easily be able to see its growth (this is also why it's nice to use a vessel for your culture that you can see into).

FEEDING SOURDOUGH STARTER

In general, the starter is ready after a week to 10 days, but this is not always the case—sometimes, it can take longer. If, after a week of scheduled feedings, your starter isn't looking bubbly or doubling in volume after feedings, try moving it to a warmer place (even in temperatures around 70°F, yeast can be sluggish), or replace some of the all-purpose flour you use for feeding with some whole-grain flour, which, with its higher concentrations of naturally occurring yeast and bacteria, is like espresso for sourdough culture.

The timeline described here is a guideline; watch your culture, not the calendar. Don't be discouraged if it takes longer to get your fledgling starter going; in almost every case the patient sourdough steward is rewarded, even if it takes longer than they'd like.

Note: The culture recipe above is for what is considered a 100 percent hydration culture, meaning that it's made with equal amounts (by weight) of flour and water; it's sometimes also referred to as a liquid levain, or liquid starter. Throughout this book, we refer to it simply as sourdough culture.

HOW DO I KNOW WHEN MY CULTURE IS READY FOR BAKING?

Once your culture is bubbly and reliably doubling or tripling in volume (and then falling) 6 to 8 hours after each feeding, the culture is now ready to bake with, and you can do one of two things: Keep it at room temperature, continuing to feed it twice daily, or, if you bake less frequently, store it in the refrigerator, feeding it once a week (for more details, read on).

MAINTAINING A SOURDOUGH CULTURE

AT ROOM TEMPERATURE (BEST FOR FREQUENT BAKERS)

If you're planning to use your culture frequently (that is, every few days), you can store it at room temperature. The nice thing about keeping your starter at room temperature and feeding it regularly is that you'll always have starter that's "ripe"—that is, ready for baking. The downside is you'll need to feed it twice a day. You can always move it to the refrigerator (see next page), but if you're a new parent to a sourdough culture, you'll learn a lot about how it behaves by watching it more closely and feeding it more regularly. The only way to know if your starter is healthy and at its best is to know how it looks and behaves when it *is* at its best. And the only way to get it to its best is to feed it regularly, twice daily, for at least a few weeks.

Feed the culture every 12 hours at roughly the same time of day: Stir the culture well and discard all but 50 grams. To that remaining 50 grams add 50 grams each water and all-purpose flour, mix until smooth, and cover. If your kitchen is very warm (above 85°F), you should store your culture in the refrigerator.

IN THE REFRIGERATOR (BEST FOR LESS-FREQUENT BAKERS)

If you plan to bake sourdough occasionally (or if your kitchen is very hot, above 85°F), it's best to store your culture in the refrigerator. The upside of refrigerator storage is that you don't need to feed your culture as frequently; the downside is that when you do want to use your culture for baking, you have to plan a few days ahead. Instead of the twice-daily feedings for a starter kept at room temperature, starter stored in the refrigerator should be fed at least once a week: Remove it from the refrigerator and discard all but 50 grams of culture. To that remaining 50 grams add 50 grams each all-purpose flour and water. Stir together, then cover loosely and let the culture rest at warm room temperature (about 70°F) for at least 2 hours; this gives the yeast a chance to warm up and get feeding.

After about 2 hours, the culture should show some signs of activity, at which point you can cover the container and return it to the refrigerator. Repeat weekly. The more consistent you are with feeding your refrigerated culture, the less time and effort it takes to get your culture ripe and ready for baking.

GETTING REFRIGERATED CULTURE READY FOR BAKING

Let's say you feed your refrigerated culture each week on Tuesday, but now it's Sunday and you want to bake with it. After 5 days without a fresh food source, the yeasts in your culture are going to be pretty hungry. And because they haven't eaten for a while, they won't be producing the carbon dioxide that makes your culture (and your bread) bubbly. Instead, you might notice that your culture looks different from the way it did right after feeding. It might look very thin and pourable, almost like pancake batter, or have a layer of liquid (sometimes dark in color) on top, all indications that it's in need of feeding.

If you tried to take that hungry culture right out of the refrigerator and use it for baking, chances are good that the results wouldn't be great. Before you bake with it, you need to feed it.

PREPARING A REFRIGERATED STARTER FOR BAKING

If your culture has been in the refrigerator and fed regularly (at least once a week), take the starter out of the fridge, discard all but 50 grams, and feed with 50 grams all-purpose flour and 50 grams water (whether this is one day after your "regular" weekly feeding day or six doesn't matter; the process is the same). Cover loosely and let stand at room temperature. Depending on its vitality, it may start to bubble and expand quickly, or it may take up to 12 hours to show signs of vigor.

A starter is considered "ripe" and ready for baking when it doubles or triples in volume within 6 to 8 hours. If your starter does not double or triple in this time, feed it every 12 hours until it does, at which point it's ready to use for baking.

Spoon out what you need for the recipe and set it aside. Transfer 50 grams of what remains to a jar and feed with 50 grams all-purpose flour and 50 grams water. Mix until smooth and let the starter rest for about 2 hours at room temperature before returning it to the refrigerator.

DO I HAVE TO DISCARD MY DISCARD?

It may seem odd (and wasteful) to discard a portion of your culture each time you feed it. But if you didn't, not only would you soon have a large volume of culture but it would also become too acidic. Reducing the volume gives the microorganisms more food to eat each time you feed the culture; it's not fighting with quite so many other little yeast and bacteria cells to get enough to eat. The recipes in this book call for a small amount of culture, which is all you need. But if you want to "build up" the volume of your culture at any time, it's easy to do so: Just feed your culture equal amounts (by weight) of flour and water, without discarding any.

Once you have an established culture, you can begin saving your discard. You can give it to a friend, or add it to muffins, quick breads, or crackers, where it will contribute depth of flavor (though have little to no leavening power). Sourdough discard will keep for 2 to 3 weeks in the refrigerator. You can combine discard from different days together in a single jar.

SOURDOUGH DISCARD CRACKERS

MAKES ABOUT 5 DOZEN 1½-INCH SQUARE CRACKERS

These super-simple crackers are an excellent way to use up surplus discard. The seasoning is up to you— we've found that a small amount of seasoning (try ½ teaspoon turmeric, ¾ teaspoon black pepper, or 1¼ teaspoons smoked paprika) goes a long way.

227 grams (1 cup) sourdough culture discard

57 grams (4 tablespoons) unsalted butter, melted

½ to 3 teaspoons of your favorite seasoning(s) (see headnote)

3 grams (½ teaspoon) fine salt

2 to 3 teaspoons sesame seeds, poppy seeds, or flaky salt, for topping (optional)

Preheat the oven to 325°F and arrange a rack in the center. Line a baking sheet with parchment paper. In a medium bowl, combine the discard, melted butter, seasoning(s), if using, and salt, stirring vigorously with a spatula until evenly combined. Transfer the batter to the prepared pan and use a small offset spatula to spread it into a thin rectangle, about 15 x 11 inches in size. Sprinkle the top of the crackers with the toppings of your choice, if using. Bake the crackers for 15 minutes, then remove them from the oven and use a pizza wheel or bench knife to cut the crackers into 1- to 1½-inch squares (don't separate them, just cut them).

Return the baking sheet to the oven and bake for an additional 35 to 45 minutes, rotating the pan halfway through, until the crackers in the middle are golden brown and firm to the touch. Remove the crackers from the oven and allow them to cool completely on the baking sheet before breaking them apart and serving. The crackers will keep in an airtight container at room temperature for several weeks.

REVIVING A NEGLECTED CULTURE

If your culture has been in the refrigerator or stored at room temperature and you have *forgotten* to feed it regularly (it happens!), all is not lost—it just may take a few days at room temperature, with feedings every 12 hours, to revive it. If you've neglected it for a long, long time (may we see a show of hands?), you may find that the time it takes to restore it to full health and vigor is about the same amount of time it might take to start a new culture altogether, so you can make a choice about what you prefer to do. And if you've pulled a neglected starter from the fridge and are wondering if it's dead, see Sourdough Culture Troubleshooting (page 196) for answers.

PRESERVING CULTURE

If you'd like to preserve your starter for a couple of weeks, a month, or even years without worrying about feeding it regularly, the best thing to do is to dry it. Before you do so, however, feed it for as many days and as many times as necessary until it's showing signs of ripeness: doubling or tripling every 6 to 8 hours, nice and bubbly.

TO DRY A CULTURE

Line a rimmed baking sheet with parchment paper. Dump your starter out onto the parchment and spread it in an even layer as thinly as possible. Let the starter sit at room temperature until it's completely dry. Depending on the weather, this could take as little as 1 day or up to 4 or 5 days. If you'd like to hasten the process, you can place the pan in the oven with the oven light on (don't turn on the oven; it will get too hot and may kill your starter).

Completely dry starter should peel easily off the parchment; when you pick up a piece, it will be brittle and easily snap between your fingers. Break the starter into small chips and store in an airtight container in a cool, dry place.

TO REVIVE A DRIED CULTURE

Place the dried starter chips in a 1-pint container and add enough lukewarm water to just cover the chips; tamp them down, if necessary. Stir the mixture occasionally until it dissolves completely. This may take up to 3 hours.

Once the mixture is fairly smooth, with perhaps just a couple of small undissolved chips, feed it 50 grams of unbleached all-purpose flour. Cover it lightly and place somewhere warm for 24 hours.

You should see some bubbles starting to form; if your room temperature is cool, this may take longer.

Without discarding any of the starter, feed it 50 grams lukewarm water and 50 grams unbleached all-purpose flour. Cover and wait; eventually you should see some bubbling (this could take 8 to 10 hours).

Feed the starter again with 50 grams lukewarm water and 50 grams unbleached all-purpose flour. Again, you're not discarding any at this point. Cover and wait. After about 12 hours, your starter should have lots of tiny bubbles on the surface and have expanded. It's now ready for its regular feeding schedule: Discard all but 50 grams of the starter. Add 50 grams lukewarm water and 50 grams all-purpose flour and stir to combine. Cover and let stand until bubbly. Your starter has been successfully revived and is ready to use!

SOURDOUGH CULTURE, MYSTIQUE, AND LEGEND

There's a great deal of mystique surrounding sourdough cultures; you'll often hear bakers talking about the age of their starter, or telling some fabled tale about its origin. If you've gotten some vintage sourdough starter from a friend, you've been feeding it, and it's happy and bubbly, terrific! But there's nothing inherently better about an old starter, and, in truth, after a few feedings in its new home, even an inherited culture will become predominantly populated by whatever yeast and bacteria are present in the fresh flour added during each feeding. In other words, that ancient culture will mostly be new.

All of which is to say there's absolutely nothing wrong with a "new" culture (except, maybe, a more boring origin story), and no evidence to suggest that starters that are generations old perform any better than ones that are two weeks old. So should you neglect your culture for a long time, you may find it more efficient to simply start from scratch rather than try to revive an ailing one.

BUILDING TO BAKE: PREFERMENTS

Earlier in this section, we wrote about how you don't need a large volume of sourdough culture, even if you're a frequent sourdough baker. That's because most of the sourdough recipes in this book (and some that are made only with yeast, or with a combination of sourdough culture and yeast) begin with what is called a preferment.

A preferment is a mixture of flour, water, leavening (commercial yeast or sourdough culture), and time—a key ingredient! As this mixture ferments, there's a buildup of lactic and other flavorful acids and carbon dioxide. The gases enable the dough to rise and the acids give bread the deep flavor that is the signature of each recipe.

Preferment is the general term that encompasses other terms you may have heard, like biga, poolish, levain, pâte fermentée, or even desem, all of which are different types of preferments. Preferments not only add flavor to your bread, they also improve its texture and keeping quality (that is, the time it takes for your loaf to go stale).

To easily distinguish among the common preferments, it helps to think of them in terms of their hydration and type of leavening.

Hydration, in baker's parlance, refers to the ratio of flour to liquid (see Hydration, page 54). A stiff preferment has low moisture and the consistency of bread dough. A liquid preferment has the consistency of pancake batter.

For leavening, we also divide preferments into two categories: those made with a sourdough culture, which contains wild yeast, and those made with commercial yeast.

We'll get to examples of each type in just a moment. For now, focus on the idea that most preferments fall into one of the four categories below:

	SOURDOUGH CULTURE	COMMERCIAL YEAST
LIQUID	Liquid preferment (also called liquid levain, levain liquide, lievito liquido)	Liquid yeasted (also called poolish)
STIFF	Stiff preferment (also called stiff levain, masa madre, lievito madre, mother, rye starter)	Stiff yeasted (also called biga or pâte fermentée)

It's easy to imagine the difference between a stiff and a liquid preferment, but is there really a difference in preferments if you use sourdough culture versus commercial yeast?

In short, yes. A sourdough culture is a symbiotic colony of bacteria and yeast (SCOBY). In broad terms, a SCOBY comprises bacterial and fungal populations living in symbiosis. The by-products of their activities bring complex flavors and aromas to the starter, dough, and resultant loaves.

Commercial yeast, in contrast, is not home to bacterial populations. The flavors associated with a yeasted preferment are delicious, but also gentler and less complex. It's not that one is better or worse than the other—they are simply different.

We use different styles of preferments in the recipes throughout this book, and in every case we'll refer to them interchangeably, simply as preferments. But having read the above, and by looking at the recipe, you'll know what type of preferment the recipe employs. Note that in every case, the preferment is made with a percentage of the *total amount* of the flour, water, and culture/yeast used in the recipe. In other words, given that the flour amount in a recipe is represented at 100%, if you use, say, 30% of that amount of flour in your preferment, the remaining 70% will be added when you mix the bread dough. For more about this, read the sections on Baker's Math (page 52) and Hydration (page 54).

LIQUID PREFERMENT: A liquid preferment is made with equal parts flour and water, and the two ingredients are simply stirred together. Liquid preferments have the consistency of pancake batter and, because of the relative hydration, ferment more quickly than stiff preferments. Poolish is a yeasted liquid preferment; liquid sourdough preferments are also commonly referred to as liquid levain.

STIFF PREFERMENT: Stiff preferments contain less water in relation to flour and are "dough consistency" levains that can be kneaded. In terms of function, stiff preferments ferment at a more controlled rate than liquid preferments (the extra water in a liquid preferment fuels extra activity). The difference in hydration also changes flavor. Biga, a stiff yeasted

preferment, and stiff sourdough preferments bring their own unique qualities to bread: a brighter, more floral profile that differs from liquid preferments, which tend to be sweeter and milder.

For the breads in this book that use a preferment, the preferment step is the first step in the recipe. In many cases, this means that the journey toward making your naturally leavened bread begins two or more days before you'll actually bake. On day one, you mix the preferment and let it sit overnight. The next day, that preferment is mixed into the bread dough, which then undergoes bulk fermentation (the "first rise") before being shaped and left to rise a second time, in some cases overnight. So, yes, adding a preferment to a bread recipe turns it, in most cases, into a multiday affair. But it's worth it, because adding a preferment to your dough will give it wonderful flavor, improve the bread's structure, contribute to a more richly colored crust, and improve the bread's keeping quality.

In essence, a sourdough preferment replicates the process that takes place when you feed your starter. The key difference is that you'll use the entire preferment mixture in your dough. You are building the preferment to bake the bread. And because a sourdough preferment typically uses a small amount of sourdough culture, it also allows you to maintain a smaller sourdough starter. Think of your sourdough culture like a bank: If you regularly make deposits (that is, feed your culture), when it comes time to make bread you can make a small withdrawal (the amount of culture you use to build your preferment) while still having enough money (that is, culture) for a rainy day (the next time you want to bake).

There are a few ways to incorporate preferments into dough. In some recipes, the remaining dough ingredients are simply added to the bowl containing the preferment and mixed (by hand or machine) until combined. In other recipes, the preferment is first squeezed between the fingers to incorporate it with the water, then vigorously mixed by hand until combined before the remaining dough ingredients are added.

SOURDOUGH CULTURE TROUBLESHOOTING

MY SOURDOUGH CULTURE...

...IS NOT RISING/HAS NO BUBBLES

If this is a new culture, it may just need more time. While most new cultures begin to bubble and rise and fall after about a week of feeding, sometimes it takes longer. To hasten fermentation, move your culture to a warm place (about 75°F or warmer) and feed it at the same times every day. If it's still sluggish, you can swap some whole-grain flour for all-purpose for a few feedings; whole-grain flour has more yeast and bacteria, which can help kick-start fermentation. If you're working with an established culture and notice that it's sluggish, you can do the same things (feed with whole-grain flour, warm it up).

...WAS FED AT THE WRONG TIME /TOO MUCH/TOO LITTLE

Missing a feeding (or not timing the feedings exactly 12 hours apart) won't even come close to killing your starter. Don't get up in the middle of the night to feed your starter! That said, if you miss too many feedings in a row, your culture is going to get hungry, and its performance will be degraded; you'll notice it'll be thinner, almost pourable in consistency, with few bubbles. A starter like that is not happy, and it's not going to make good bread! Spend some time getting your culture into fighting shape with regular feedings before using it to bake, rather than using a culture that's not ripe. (If you've *really* neglected your starter—say, left it in the fridge for six months without feeding it—it may take a week to revive it, at which point you may decide it's easier to just make a new starter from scratch.)

Feeding your culture the wrong amount of flour or water won't cause permanent damage, either. Your starter may seem too dry or too wet and may not bubble and expand the way you expect, but you can correct its consistency by adding a little more flour or water, and then using the correct amounts the next time you feed it.

...SMELLS BAD

Over the years we've heard lots of descriptors for the smell of culture, from the good, like yeasty and yogurty, to the bad, including nail polish or garbage. There is a range of smells that are perfectly normal for culture, but if your culture has a terrible odor, it's likely not super healthy—check it carefully for mold. If it's mold-free but stinky, try feeding it on a more regular schedule; it should soon start to smell better.

...IS MOLDY

A moldy culture is a neglected culture. Furry white or black mold is a sign that your culture isn't healthy. Nursing it back to health would likely take as long as starting a new culture from scratch, so we recommend tossing it and starting over.

If your starter has orange or pink mold, it means your culture is unsafe to use. Bad bacteria is generally indicated by an orange or pink tinge or streak; if you see this, your starter has lost its natural ability to ward off intruders, and it's time to throw it out.

...HAS BLACK (OR CLEAR) LIQUID FLOATING ON TOP

"Hooch" is the name for the liquid that collects on the top of your starter when it hasn't been fed in a while. This liquid is the alcohol given off as wild yeast ferments. The presence of hooch isn't a sign that your culture is in danger. However, it does indicate that your culture is hungry and needs to be fed.

When your starter is neglected for an extended period, the hooch tends to turn from clear to dark-colored. We get lots of calls from sourdough bakers worried about the safety or danger of various hooch hues. Is gray bad? What about brown or black? Happily, none of these colors indicates that your starter has spoiled. But because hooch is made primarily of sourdough waste products, we recommend pouring it off rather than stirring it in.

...IS VERY THICK/THIN

For a 100-percent hydration culture (that is, one with equal parts culture, flour, and water), you can expect the texture to be something like pancake batter. It will be thicker just after it's fed, become more bubbly and voluminous as it ripens, and get thinner and more liquid-y after it has passed through the window of optimal ripeness and is beginning to get hungry again. All perfectly normal! Naturally, if you change the hydration level (with either more water or flour), you'll also change the texture of your starter.

...HAS BEEN REFRIGERATED

If you don't bake sourdough frequently, the refrigerator is the best place to store your culture. To prepare it for baking, remove it from the fridge and feed it twice daily (about 12 hours apart), leaving it at room temperature between feedings, until it's bubbly and active and is rising and falling in a predictable pattern before using it to bake. Before you return it to the refrigerator for storage, feed it once more, let it stand for a couple hours to kick-start yeast activity, then return it to the fridge (for more information, see Maintaining a Sourdough Culture, page 189).

...HAS BEEN NEGLECTED

How long are we talking about? If you keep your starter in the refrigerator, it can tolerate some amount of neglect, but the longer you leave it unfed and untended in the refrigerator, the harder it will be to get it into baking shape. To revive it, remove it from the fridge, discard any liquid that has collected on the surface, then begin feeding it twice daily, leaving it at room temperature, until it looks healthy and bubbly.

...SEEMS WASTEFUL

There is some waste inherent in the sourdough culture feeding process. However, you can reduce waste by maintaining a smaller starter and, if you're not a frequent sourdough baker, by storing your starter in the refrigerator and feeding it just once a week.

...IS MAKING MY BREAD TOO SOUR/ NOT SOUR ENOUGH

It's logical to think that the flavor of your sourdough is imparted to your finished loaves, but that's not really true. A naturally leavened dough that has had a long cold fermentation, for example, like the Pain de Campagne (page 205), will result in a loaf that's more sour than one that fermented for a shorter period of time. The longer you allow raw dough to proof and ferment, the more lactic acid and acetic acid will develop, which will give the finished bread a more pronounced tang.

...IS CRUSTY

A little crust on top is fine; simply scrape off the crust and discard. Transfer the remaining starter to a container with a better fitting lid to avoid future crusts.

...IS RISING TOO MUCH

If it's especially warm where you live or you have a particularly active starter, you may find it doubles more quickly than we've suggested above. If that's the case, there are a few things you can do: Store your culture in a cooler location, which will slow down the yeast's feeding frenzy, or reduce the amount of starter you retain the next time you feed your culture. If, for example, you're following the recipe above, feeding 50 grams of culture with 50 grams each of unbleached all-purpose flour and water, you can reduce the culture amount to 25 grams (but keep the flour and water amounts at 50 grams), which will slow its growth. You can also feed your culture with cold water and chilled flour (an hour in the freezer will do the trick), both of which will help put the brakes on a racing culture.

...GOT TOO HOT

Yeast dies at 140°F, and it's likely that your sourdough starter will suffer at temperatures even lower than that. It's best to maintain your starter at comfortable room temperature (around 70°F), though a little higher or lower won't hurt it.

Hearth
Breads

PAIN AU LEVAIN

MIX	BULK FERMENTATION	PRESHAPE	SHAPE	2ND RISE	BAKE
5 MIN	2½ HOURS	25 MIN	5 MIN	2 HOURS	35–40 MIN

MAKE THE PREFERMENT (12–16 HOURS BEFORE)

·· TIME: ABOUT 22 HOURS ··

MAKES 2 LOAVES

PREFERMENT

28 grams (2 tablespoons) sourdough culture (see page 187)

150 grams (1¼ cups) unbleached all-purpose flour

76 grams (⅓ cup) cold water (55° to 60°F)

DOUGH

539 grams (2¼ cups plus 2 tablespoons) warm water (see Temperature, page 25)

630 grams (5¼ cups) unbleached all-purpose flour, plus more for dusting

53 grams (½ cup) whole rye flour (see headnote)

18 grams (1 tablespoon) fine salt

Pain au levain, or "bread with leaven," is the generic French name for sourdough bread. We use the term to refer to the quintessential classic loaf with its crisp crust and pleasantly chewy crumb. It's made almost entirely with all-purpose flour; a small amount of whole rye flour is added for the nutty flavor it contributes, but you could substitute medium rye, whole wheat flour, golden wheat, or even spelt flour for the rye. If you prefer a tangier, more deeply flavored loaf, rather than baking the bread on Day 2 (as directed below), you can instead refrigerate the loaves overnight on Day 2 and bake on Day 3.

DAY 1

MAKE THE PREFERMENT: The evening before you want to bake, in a large bowl, combine the sourdough culture, flour, and water and mix until a shaggy dough forms (see Mixing, page 20). Transfer the dough to a clean work surface and knead until no dry patches of flour remain and a stiff, smooth dough forms. Return the dough to the bowl, cover, and let stand overnight at room temperature, 12 to 16 hours.

DAY 2

MAKE THE DOUGH: Add the warm water to the preferment, then squeeze the preferment through your fingers to break it up. Holding your hand in a clawlike position, vigorously mix the preferment into the water until well combined. The mixture will look like thin pancake batter with a few small lumps. Add the all-purpose flour, whole rye flour, and salt to the bowl and mix with the handle of a wooden spoon until no dry patches of flour remain and a soft, sticky dough forms.

Bulk fermentation or the "first rise" (see page 25) will take 2½ hours. During that time you'll attend to the dough twice (directions follow), folding the dough first after 30 minutes and again after 1½ hours. Then the dough will rest, covered and undisturbed, for the final hour.

Recipe continues

BULK FERMENT THE DOUGH: Once you've mixed the dough, cover and let rest for 30 minutes. With a wet hand, perform 10 to 12 bowl folds (see Bowl Fold, page 30) until the dough begins to resist being pulled and smooths out. Cover and let rest at room temperature for 60 minutes. With a wet hand, perform 10 to 12 more bowl folds until the dough begins to resist stretching. Cover and let rise another 60 minutes.

PRESHAPE THE DOUGH: Lightly flour a work surface, then use a plastic bowl scraper to ease the dough out of the bowl onto the work surface. Gently deflate the dough and divide into 2 equal portions (each about 747 grams). Preshape each piece into a round (see Preshaping, page 32), then place the rounds seam side up on a floured surface. Cover and let rest for 20 minutes.

SHAPE THE DOUGH AND LET IT RISE: Generously dust two 9 × 3-inch round or oval proofing baskets with flour. After the 20-minute rest, shape each piece of dough into a boule or bâtard (see Shaping, page 34), then place them seam side up in the prepared baskets. (At this point, you can also refrigerate the shaped loaves overnight, which will give them a deeper, tangier flavor. Let the refrigerated loaves rise at room temperature for 1 hour before baking.) Cover and let rise until the dough feels light and almost marshmallowy, and when pressed with a floured finger, a small impression remains (see Proofing, page 44), about 2 hours.

TO BAKE ON A BAKING STONE OR STEEL:
PREHEAT: One hour before the loaves are finished rising, preheat the oven to 450°F with a baking stone or steel on the middle rack and an empty cast-iron skillet (or a cake pan filled with lava rocks) on the lower rack. If possible, adjust the stone and pan so that the skillet isn't directly under the stone, making it easier for steam to reach the baking bread (see Steaming, page 50).

Turn each loaf out of its proofing basket onto a sheet of parchment paper. Use a baker's lame or a razor blade to score the tops of the loaves (see Scoring, page 46).

BAKE: Using a baker's peel or an inverted baking sheet to aid you, transfer the loaves (still on the parchment) into the oven, placing them side by side on the stone or steel. Pour about 227 grams (1 cup) of warm water into the skillet. Steam will billow from the pan upward to envelop the bread; be sure to wear good oven mitts to shield your hands and arms. Quickly close the oven door to trap the steam. Bake the loaves until deep golden brown and the internal temperature reaches at least 200°F, 35 to 40 minutes.

Remove the loaves from the oven and transfer to a rack to cool completely before slicing. (For storage information, see Storing Bread, page 123.)

TO BAKE IN A COVERED BAKER:
PREHEAT: One hour before the loaves are finished rising, arrange a rack in the lower third of the oven and preheat the oven to 450°F, with the lidded baker set on the lower rack.

Turn one loaf out of its proofing basket onto a 9-inch round of parchment paper with a sling (see Transferring a Loaf to a Covered Baker, opposite). Keep the second loaf refrigerated while you bake the first. Use a baker's lame or razor blade to score the top of the loaf (see Scoring, page 46).

BAKE: Remove the covered baker from the oven, uncover, and, using the parchment paper sling, carefully lower the loaf into the pan, taking care not to burn your knuckles. Place the lid on the baker, return to the oven, and bake for 20 minutes.

Uncover and continue baking until the bread is deep golden brown and the internal temperature reaches at least 200°F, 15 to 20 minutes more.

Remove the pan from the oven, carefully lift out the loaf, and transfer to a rack to cool completely. Return the lidded baker to the oven and let heat for 30 minutes, then score and bake the second loaf as directed above. Let the bread cool completely before slicing. (For storage information, see Storing Bread, page 123.)

TRANSFERRING A LOAF TO A COVERED BAKER...

...WITHOUT BURNING YOUR KNUCKLES

One of the most high-stakes moments when baking in a covered baker is the moment you transfer your proofed dough to the preheated baker. We use a parchment paper sling to lower the loaf into the pan without burning our hands. To make one, trace a 9-inch circle on a piece of parchment paper, then draw two 5-inch tabs on opposite sides of the circle. Use scissors to cut out the sling. Turn one proofed boule out onto the parchment round. Score the loaf as desired. Carefully remove the hot baker from the oven. Using the tabs of the sling, carefully pick up the boule and place it in the hot baker. Place the lid on the baker and bake as directed. For a reusable option, you can also purchase silicone loaf lifters.

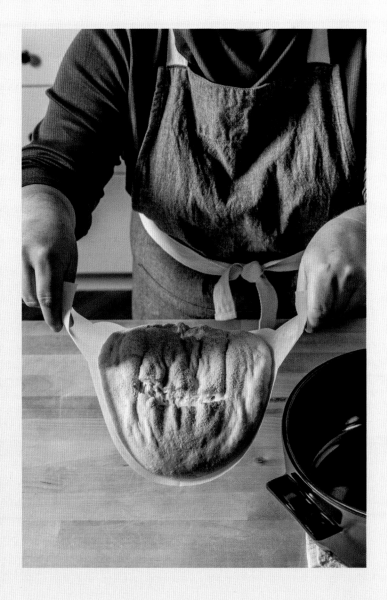

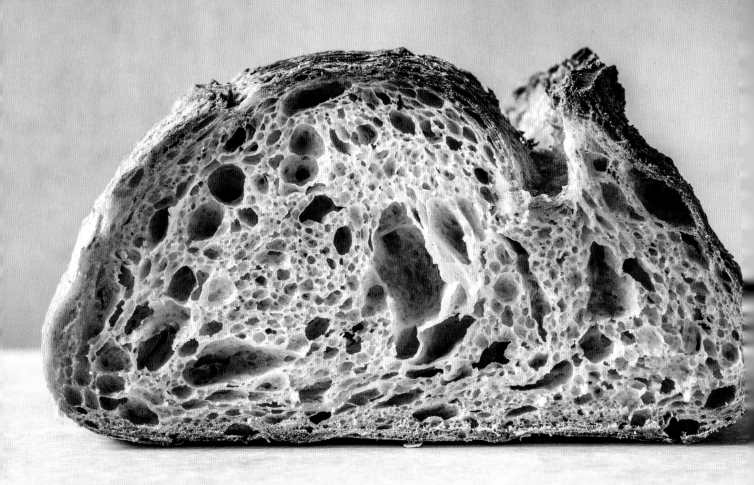

PAIN DE CAMPAGNE

MIX	BULK FERMENTATION	PRESHAPE	SHAPE	2ND RISE	BAKE
5 MIN	8–12 HOURS	20 MIN	5 MIN	8–12 HOURS	45 MIN

TIME: ABOUT 25 HOURS

MAKES 2 LOAVES

DOUGH

40 grams (3 tablespoons) sourdough culture (see page 187)

900 grams (7½ cups) unbleached bread flour, plus more for dusting

100 grams (¾ cup plus 2 tablespoons) whole wheat flour

20 grams (3¼ teaspoons) fine salt

800 grams (3½ cups plus 1 teaspoon) warm water (see Temperature, page 25)

There's a lot to love about this loaf, including its open crumb and crunchy crust. It's also very easy to make and is a great bread for bakers who are new to sourdough. The dough is mixed in the morning, proofed during the day, divided and shaped in the evening, and then refrigerated overnight, which deepens the bread's flavor (and also makes it an especially convenient loaf for someone who works a day job). After its overnight rest, the bread is ready to bake. If you're looking for a simple, low-fuss, flavorful sourdough bread, this is it.

DAY 1

MAKE THE DOUGH: The morning before the day you want to bake, in a large bowl, combine the sourdough culture, bread flour, whole wheat flour, salt, and water and mix with the handle of a wooden spoon until no dry spots remain (see Mixing, page 20).

Bulk fermentation or the "first rise" (see page 25) will take 8 to 12 hours. During that time you'll attend to the dough four times (directions follow), folding the dough every 15 minutes for the first hour. Then the dough will rest, covered and undisturbed, for the final 7 to 11 hours.

BULK FERMENT THE DOUGH: Once you've mixed the dough, cover and let rest for 15 minutes. Using a wet hand, perform 8 to 12 bowl folds (see Bowl Fold, page 30), or until the dough resists stretching. Round out the dough by cupping your hand and applying pressure toward the bottom of the dough, forcing it into the bottom and side of the bowl to create tension.

Cover and let rest for another 15 minutes. Using a wet hand, perform 6 to 8 more bowl folds, or until the dough resists stretching, then round out the dough again. Cover and let the dough rest for 15 minutes. Perform a third set of 6 to 8 bowl folds until the dough resists stretching, then

Recipe continues

round out the dough, cover it, and let it rest for 15 minutes before performing the fourth and final set of 6 to 8 bowl folds, or until the dough resists stretching.

Form the dough into a ball and transfer it to a large, preferably clear, container (a large plastic dough rising bucket—see Tools, page 15—is perfect), then mark the level of the dough on the outside of the container; this will help you gauge how much the dough has risen later. Cover and allow the dough to rest at room temperature until it has doubled in size, 7 to 11 hours. If you're baking in a warm climate or your sourdough starter is very active, the time it takes your dough to double will be closer to 7 hours. If you're baking in a cooler climate or your sourdough starter is sluggish, it will be closer to 11 hours. But the appearance of the dough is what you want to pay attention to, not the clock.

DIVIDE AND PRESHAPE: Generously dust two 9 × 3-inch round or oval proofing baskets with flour. Lightly flour a work surface, then use a plastic bowl scraper to ease the dough out of the container onto the work surface. Using a bench knife or a knife, divide the dough into 2 equal portions (each about 930 grams).

Gently pat each piece of dough to remove any large bubbles, then gently preshape into a round (see Preshaping, page 32) and place seam side down. Cover and let rest for 15 minutes.

SHAPE THE DOUGH AND LET IT RISE: Shape each piece of dough into a boule or bâtard (see Shaping, page 34). Transfer the shaped dough, seam side up, to the prepared proofing baskets, then cover.

If your dough doubled between 7 and 8 hours of bulk fermentation, transfer the loaves to the refrigerator. If it took closer to 11 to 12 hours to double (an indication that your dough is moving more slowly), let the loaves rise at room temperature for another hour before refrigerating. Refrigerate the loaves for 8 to 12 hours; at the end of this slow rise the dough should feel light, almost marshmallowy, and when pressed with a floured finger, a small impression should remain (see Proofing, page 44).

DAY 2

TO BAKE ON A BAKING STONE OR STEEL:

PREHEAT: Arrange racks in the center and bottom third of the oven and preheat the oven to 500°F with the baking stone or steel on the center rack and an empty cast-iron skillet (or a cake pan filled with lava rocks) on the lower rack. If possible, adjust the stone and pan so that the skillet isn't directly under the stone, making it easier for steam to reach the baking bread (see Steaming, page 50).

Turn each loaf out of its proofing basket onto a sheet of parchment paper. Use a baker's lame or razor blade to score the tops of the loaves (see Scoring, page 46).

BAKE: Using a baker's peel or an inverted baking sheet to aid you, transfer the loaves (still on the parchment) into the oven, placing them side by side on the stone or steel and pour about 227 grams (1 cup) of warm water into the skillet. Steam will billow from the pan upward to envelop the bread; be sure to wear good oven mitts to shield your hands and arms. Quickly close the oven door to trap the steam. Immediately reduce the oven temperature to 475°F. Bake the loaves for 25 minutes, then reduce the oven temperature to 450°F. Continue baking until the loaves are deeply browned and the crust is firm, about 20 minutes longer.

Remove from the oven and let cool completely on a wire rack before slicing. (For storage information, see Storing Bread, page 123.)

TO BAKE IN A COVERED BAKER:

PREHEAT: Arrange a rack in the lower third of the oven and preheat the oven to 500°F, with the lidded baker set on the lower rack. Allow the oven and baker to preheat for about 1 hour to ensure they're thoroughly heated.

Turn one loaf out of its proofing basket onto a 9-inch round of parchment paper with a sling (see Transferring a Loaf to a Covered Baker, page 203). Keep the second loaf refrigerated while you bake the first. Use a baker's lame or razor blade to score the top of the loaf (see Scoring, page 46).

BAKE: Remove the covered baker from the oven, uncover, and, using the parchment paper sling, carefully lower the loaf into the pan, taking care not to burn your knuckles. Place the lid on the baker,

return to the oven, and immediately reduce the oven temperature to 475°F. Bake the loaves for 25 minutes.

Uncover, reduce the oven temperature to 450°F, and continue baking until the loaf is deeply browned and the crust is firm, about 20 minutes longer.

Remove the pan from the oven, carefully lift out the loaf, and transfer to a wire rack to cool completely. (For storage information, see Storing Bread, page 123.)

Return the lidded baker to the oven and let heat for 30 minutes, then score and bake the second loaf as directed above.

EVERYDAY FRENCH LOAF

MIX	BULK FERMENTATION		PRESHAPE	SHAPE	2ND RISE	BAKE
5 MIN	2 HOURS		20 MIN	5 MIN	45 MIN–1 HOUR	32–38 MIN

MAKE THE PREFERMENT (12–16 HOURS BEFORE)

TIME: ABOUT 20 HOURS

MAKES 2 LOAVES

PREFERMENT

222 grams (1¾ cups plus 1½ tablespoons) unbleached all-purpose flour

1 gram (generous ¼ teaspoon) instant yeast or 14 grams (1 tablespoon) sourdough culture (see Note)

222 grams (scant 1 cup) cold water (55° to 60°F)

DOUGH

319 grams (1¼ cups plus 2½ tablespoons) warm water (see Temperature, page 25)

519 grams (4¼ cups plus 1 tablespoon) unbleached all-purpose flour, plus more for dusting

15 grams (2½ teaspoons) fine salt

2 grams (scant ½ teaspoon) instant yeast

Made with only four ingredients, this classic French bread has a thin, crisp crust with a soft and fluffy interior and open crumb structure; it's a fine example of a bread made with what's called a lean dough (that is, one without any added sugar or fat). Quotidian but not plain, this bread makes great toast, sandwiches, and Supreme Garlic Bread (page 399).

DAY 1

MAKE THE PREFERMENT: The evening before you want to bake, in a large bowl, combine the flour, yeast (or sourdough culture), and water and mix until no dry patches of flour remain. Cover and let stand at room temperature overnight, 12 to 16 hours.

DAY 2

MAKE THE DOUGH: Add the warm water to the preferment, then squeeze the preferment through your fingers to break it up. Next, holding your hand in a clawlike position, vigorously mix the preferment into the water until well combined. The mixture will look like foamy milk with some small pieces of preferment still visible. Add the flour, salt, and yeast, mixing well until no dry spots remain (see Mixing, page 20).

Bulk fermentation or the "first rise" (see page 25) will take 2 hours. During that time, you'll attend to the dough three times (directions follow), folding the dough every 20 minutes for the first hour. Then the dough will rest, covered and undisturbed, for the final hour.

BULK FERMENT THE DOUGH: Once you've mixed the dough, cover it and let it rest for 20 minutes. Using a wet hand, perform 8 to 12 bowl folds (see Bowl Fold, page 30) until the dough resists stretching. Round out the dough by cupping your hand and applying pressure toward the bottom of the dough, forcing it into the bottom and side of the bowl to create tension. Cover and let rest for another 20 minutes. Using a wet hand, perform 6 to 8 bowl folds, or until the dough resists stretching,

Recipe continues

then round out the dough again. Let the dough rest for 20 minutes. With wet hands, perform 2 to 3 coil folds (see Coil Fold, page 31) until the dough resists stretching. Round out the dough, then cover and let rest at room temperature until the dough is very puffy and marshmallowy, 1 hour.

DIVIDE AND PRESHAPE THE DOUGH: Lightly flour a work surface, then use a plastic bowl scraper to ease the dough out of the bowl and onto the work surface. With a bench knife, divide the dough into 2 equal portions (each about 650 grams). Gently preshape each piece of dough into a round (see Preshaping, page 32). Place seam side down, cover, and let rest on a lightly floured surface for 15 minutes.

SHAPE THE DOUGH AND LET IT RISE: Generously dust two 9 × 3-inch round or oval proofing baskets with flour. Shape each piece of dough into a boule or bâtard (see Shaping, page 34), then place them seam side up in the prepared proofing baskets. Cover and let rise until the dough looks and feels marshmallowy and a small indentation remains when pressed with a floured finger (see Proofing, page 44), 45 minutes to 1 hour.

TO BAKE ON A BAKING STONE OR STEEL:

PREHEAT: Arrange racks in the center and bottom third of the oven and preheat the oven to 475°F with a baking stone or steel on the center rack and an empty cast-iron skillet (or a cake pan filled with lava rocks) on the lower rack. If possible, adjust the stone

If you'd like, you can replace the 1 gram (generous 1/4 teaspoon) instant yeast in the preferment with 14 grams (1 tablespoon) sourdough culture for more flavor.

You can also substitute whole wheat flour for 25% of the all-purpose flour in the final dough without making any significant changes to hydration. To do this, make the preferment as written, then use 390 grams (3¼ cups) all-purpose flour and 130 grams (1 cup plus 2½ tablespoons) whole wheat flour in the dough.

and pan so that the skillet isn't directly under the steel, making it easier for steam to reach the baking bread (see Steaming, page 50).

Turn the loaves out of their proofing baskets onto a sheet of parchment paper, side by side and spaced a few inches apart. Use a baker's lame or razor blade to score the tops of the loaves (see Scoring, page 46).

BAKE: Using a baker's peel or an inverted baking sheet to aid you, transfer the loaves (still on the parchment) into the oven, placing them on the stone, and pour about 227 grams (1 cup) of warm water into the skillet. Steam will billow from the pan upward to envelop the bread; be sure to wear good oven mitts to shield your hands and arms. Quickly close the oven door to trap the steam. Bake the loaf until the crust is firm and medium golden brown, 32 to 38 minutes.

Transfer to a wire rack and let cool completely before slicing. (For storage information, see Storing Bread, page 123.)

TO BAKE IN A COVERED BAKER:

PREHEAT: Arrange a rack in the lower third of the oven and preheat the oven to 475°F, with the lidded baker set on the rack. Allow the oven and baker to preheat for about 1 hour to ensure they are thoroughly heated.

Turn one loaf out of its proofing basket onto a 9-inch round of parchment paper with a sling (see Transferring a Loaf to a Covered Baker, page 203). Keep the second loaf refrigerated while you bake the first. Use a baker's lame or razor blade to score the top of the loaf (see Scoring, page 46).

BAKE: Remove the covered baker from the oven, uncover, and, using the parchment paper as a sling, carefully lower one loaf into the pan, taking care not to burn your knuckles. Place the lid on the baker, return to the oven, and bake for 20 minutes.

Uncover and continue baking until the loaf is medium golden brown and the internal temperature reaches at least 200°F, 12 to 18 minutes more.

Remove the pan from the oven, carefully lift out the loaf, and transfer to a wire rack to cool completely. (For storage information, see Storing Bread, page 123.) Return the lidded baker to the oven and let heat for 30 minutes, then score and bake the second loaf as directed above.

CLASSIC MICHE

MIX	BULK FERMENTATION	SHAPE	2ND RISE	BAKE
5 MIN	3–4 HOURS	5 MIN	1 HOUR 15 MIN	1–1½ HOURS

MAKE THE PREFERMENT (12–16 HOURS BEFORE)

TIME: ABOUT 23 HOURS

MAKES 1 LARGE LOAF

PREFERMENT

30 grams (a generous
2 tablespoons) sourdough culture
(see page 187)

297 grams (2½ cups plus
2 tablespoons) whole wheat flour

198 grams (¾ cup plus
2 tablespoons) cold water (55° to
60°F)

DOUGH

415 grams (1¾ cups plus
2½ tablespoons) warm water (see
Temperature, page 25)

371 grams (3 cups plus
2 tablespoons) unbleached bread
flour

74 grams (½ cup plus
2 tablespoons) whole wheat
flour, plus more for dusting

19 grams (3⅛ teaspoons) fine salt

OPTIONAL TOPPING

40 grams (½ cup plus
2 tablespoons) coarse wheat
bran, for coating

We lovingly refer to this giant loaf as "The David," after King
Arthur's Editorial Director, David Tamarkin, who adores this bread.
But it's commonly known as a miche, a loaf characterized by its size
(large), shape (a bit lower profile than other loaves), and inclusion of
whole grains. Its size makes it great for a big dinner party, as there
will be plenty to go around. It also keeps exceptionally well, its flavor
almost improving in the first few days after baking, making it an
excellent everyday loaf. The amount of dough, along with its higher
hydration, makes this loaf a bit more challenging to shape. Expect
that it will stick to your hands a bit more, and try to use quick,
decisive moments when shaping; don't despair if it's not perfect.
Note that you'll need a large (10-inch-diameter) proofing basket or
sauté pan or skillet for proofing the loaf and that also, because of its
size, it won't fit in most covered bakers and so needs to be baked on
a baking stone or steel instead.

DAY 1

MAKE THE PREFERMENT: The evening before you want to bake, in a
large bowl, combine the sourdough culture, flour, and water. Mix, then
knead until a stiff, cohesive dough forms. Cover and let stand at room
temperature overnight, 12 to 16 hours.

DAY 2

MAKE THE DOUGH: Add the warm water to the preferment, then
squeeze the preferment through your fingers to break it up. Next, holding
your hand in a clawlike position, vigorously mix the preferment into the
water until well combined. The mixture will look like lumpy pancake
batter and be somewhat foamy. Add the bread flour, whole wheat flour,
and salt and mix well with the handle of a wooden spoon until no dry
spots remain (see Mixing, page 20).

Recipe continues

Bulk fermentation or the "first rise" (see page 25) will take 3 to 4 hours. During that time, you'll attend to the dough four times in the first 2 hours (directions follow), doing bowl folds every 30 minutes for the first hour, and coil folds every 30 minutes for the second hour. Then the dough will rest, covered and undisturbed, for the final 1 to 2 hours.

BULK FERMENT THE DOUGH: Once you've mixed the dough, cover and let rise for 30 minutes. Using a wet hand, perform 10 to 12 bowl folds (see Bowl Fold, page 30) or until the dough resists stretching. Round out the dough by cupping your hand and applying pressure toward the bottom of the dough, forcing it into the bottom and side of the bowl to create tension. Cover and let rest 30 minutes.

Using a wet hand, perform 6 to 8 bowl folds, or until the dough resists stretching. Round out the dough again. As you perform the folds, you'll notice the dough smooths out, gains strength, and becomes more elastic. Cover and let rest 30 minutes. Run wet hands around the outer edges of the dough to release it from the bowl, and perform 2 to 3 coil folds (see Coil Fold, page 31) until the dough resists stretching. Round out the dough, cover, and let rest another 30 minutes. Perform 2 to 3 more coil folds with wet hands, then round out the dough, cover, and let rest until the dough is very puffy and marshmallowy, 1 to 2 hours.

SHAPE THE DOUGH AND LET IT RISE: Dust a 10-inch proofing basket lightly with whole wheat flour, or line a 10-inch sauté pan or skillet with a kitchen towel and dust lightly with whole wheat flour. Spread the wheat bran on a rimmed baking sheet or piece of parchment paper. Wet a clean kitchen towel, then wring it out; it should still be pretty damp. Lightly flour a work surface with whole wheat flour, then use

a plastic bowl scraper to ease the dough out of the bowl onto the work surface. Shape the dough into a large boule (see Shaping, page 34). Roll the top and sides of the shaped loaf over the towel to moisten and then through the bran to coat. Transfer the loaf seam side up to the prepared proofing basket or sauté pan, then cover and let rest until puffy and marshmallowy (see Proofing, page 44), about 1 hour 15 minutes.

MEANWHILE, PREHEAT THE OVEN: Arrange racks in the center and bottom third of the oven and preheat the oven to 500°F with a baking stone or steel on the center rack and an empty cast-iron skillet (or a cake pan filled with lava rocks) on the lower rack. If possible, adjust the stone and pan so that the skillet isn't directly under the stone, making it easier for steam to reach the baking bread (see Steaming, page 50).

BAKE: Place a piece of parchment paper on top of the risen loaf, then top with a baker's peel or an inverted baking sheet. Invert the loaf onto the parchment. Score the loaf with a baker's lame or razor (see Scoring, page 46). Using the peel or an inverted baking sheet, transfer the bread (still on the parchment) onto the baking stone or steel and pour about 227 grams (1 cup) of warm water into the skillet. Steam will billow from the pan upward to envelop the bread; be sure to wear good oven mitts to shield your hands and arms. Quickly close the oven door to trap the steam. Reduce the oven temperature to 450°F and bake until the crust is deeply browned and firm and the internal temperature reaches at least 210°F, 50 to 60 minutes.

Turn off the oven, crack the oven door, and let the bread cool in the oven for 15 minutes, then transfer to a rack and cool completely before slicing. (For storage information, see Storing Bread, page 123.)

BIRDSEED BREAD

BULK FERMENTATION		PRESHAPE	SHAPE	2ND RISE	BAKE
8–12 HOURS		20 MIN	5 MIN	8–12 HOURS	45 MIN

MIX SOAKER AND DOUGH (24 HOURS BEFORE)

TIME: ABOUT 25 HOURS

MAKES 2 LOAVES

SOAKER

254 grams (about 2¼ cups) any combination of nuts, seeds, and/or grains (see headnote)

157 grams (½ cup plus 3 tablespoons) hot water (115°F to 120°F)

DOUGH

39 grams (scant 3 tablespoons) sourdough culture (see page 187)

470 grams (3¾ cups plus 3 tablespoons) unbleached bread flour, plus more for dusting

313 grams (2¾ cups) whole wheat flour

20 grams (3¼ teaspoons) fine salt

20 grams (1 tablespoon) honey

587 grams (2½ cups plus 1½ tablespoons) warm water (see Temperature, page 25)

CRUST

150 grams (about 1⅓ cups) grains, nuts, and/or untoasted seeds (see headnote)

For this seedy bread you can use any combination of grains, nuts, or seeds you have lying around in both the soaker (a mixture of soaked grains/nuts/seeds that goes into the dough itself) and as a coating on the exterior of the bread. Old-fashioned rolled oats, rye chops, flaxseeds, sunflower seeds, sesame seeds, or pumpkin seeds are all great additions; if you're including nuts, toast them lightly first and chop into bite-size pieces. (Note that while we use pumpkin seeds in the soaker, we don't recommend using them to coat the exterior of the loaf, because they burn more quickly than other seeds.) If you're a beginning sourdough baker, this incredibly delicious, wildly forgiving, and almost totally hands-off loaf is a great place to start.

DAY 1

PREPARE THE SOAKER: The morning of the day before you want to bake, in a medium bowl, combine your choice of nuts, seeds, or grains and cover with the hot water. Let stand at room temperature while you prepare the dough.

MAKE THE DOUGH: In a large bowl, combine the sourdough culture, bread flour, whole wheat flour, salt, honey, and water, mixing well until no dry spots remain (see Mixing, page 20).

Bulk fermentation or the "first rise" (see page 25) will take 8 to 12 hours. During that time, you'll attend to the dough four times (directions follow), folding the dough every 15 minutes for the first hour. Then the dough will rest, covered and undisturbed, for the final 7 to 11 hours.

BULK FERMENT THE DOUGH: Once you've mixed the dough, cover and let rest for 15 minutes. Using a wet hand, perform 8 to 12 bowl folds (see Bowl Fold, page 30) or until the dough resists stretching. Round out the dough by cupping your hand and applying pressure toward the bottom of the dough, forcing it into the bottom and side of the bowl to create tension.

Recipe continues

Cover and let rest for another 15 minutes. Using a wet hand, press indentations into the dough. Add the soaker, then perform 6 to 8 more bowl folds (to begin incorporating the soaked grains) until the dough resists stretching, then round out the dough again. Let the dough rest for 15 minutes. Perform a third set of bowl folds until the dough resists stretching, round out the dough, cover, and let rest for 15 minutes before performing the fourth and final set of bowl folds.

Transfer the dough to a large, preferably clear container (a plastic dough rising bucket—see Tools, page 15—is perfect), then mark the level of the dough on the outside of the container; this will help you gauge how much the dough has risen later. Cover and allow the dough to rest at room temperature until it is marshmallowy and doubled in size, 7 to 11 hours. If you're baking in a warm climate or your sourdough starter is very active, the time to double will be closer to 7 hours. If you're baking in a cooler climate or your sourdough starter is sluggish, it will be closer to 11 hours. But the appearance of the dough is what you want to pay attention to, not the clock.

Very lightly dust two 9 × 3-inch round or oval proofing baskets with flour. (You'll use less dusting flour here than with other loaves because of the seed crust.)

DIVIDE AND PRESHAPE THE DOUGH: Lightly flour a work surface, then use a plastic bowl scraper to ease the dough out of the container onto the work surface. Using a bench knife or a knife, divide the dough into 2 equal portions (each about 930 grams). Gently pat each piece of dough to remove any large bubbles, then gently preshape into a round (see Preshaping, page 32) and set seam side down. Cover and let rest for 15 minutes.

SHAPE THE DOUGH, ADD THE SEED CRUST, AND LET RISE: Shape each piece of dough into a boule or bâtard (see Shaping, page 34). Spread the seeds on a rimmed baking sheet or piece of parchment paper.

Wet a clean kitchen towel, then wring it out; it should still be pretty damp. Working with one loaf at a time, roll the top and sides of the shaped loaf over the towel to moisten the loaf, then through the seeds to coat (see How to Coat a Loaf with Seeds, page 218). Transfer the loaves seam side up to the prepared proofing baskets, then cover. If your dough doubled between 7 to 8 hours of bulk fermentation, transfer the loaves to the refrigerator. If it took closer to 11 to 12 hours to double (an indication that your dough is moving more slowly), let the loaves rise at room temperature for another hour before refrigerating.

Refrigerate the loaves for 8 to 12 hours; at the end of this slow rise the dough should feel light, almost marshmallowy, and when pressed with a floured finger, a small impression remains (see Proofing, page 44).

DAY 2

TO BAKE ON A BAKING STONE OR STEEL:

Arrange racks in the center and bottom third of the oven and preheat the oven to 500°F with the baking stone or steel on the center rack and an empty cast-iron skillet (or a cake pan filled with lava rocks) on the lower rack. If possible, adjust the stone and pan so that the skillet isn't directly under the stone, making it easier for steam to reach the baking bread (see Steaming, page 50).

Turn each loaf out of its proofing basket onto a sheet of parchment paper. Use a baker's lame or razor blade to score the tops of the loaves (see Scoring, page 46).

Using a baker's peel or an inverted baking sheet to aid you, transfer the loaves (still on the parchment) into the oven, placing them on the stone or steel side by side, and pour about 227 grams (1 cup) of warm water into the skillet. Steam will billow from the pan upward to envelop the bread; be sure to wear good oven mitts to shield your hands and arms. Quickly close the oven door to trap the steam.

Recipe continues

HOW TO COAT A LOAF WITH SEEDS

To add a seeded crust to a loaf (or rolls), first thoroughly wet a clean, non-lint kitchen towel and wring out some of the water, leaving it quite wet to the touch. Spread the towel flat on a rimmed baking sheet or tray. Pour a generous quantity of seeds (or oats, bran flakes, or rye chops—the method works the same way for all of them) onto a separate rimmed baking sheet or tray to make a thick, even layer. You can use a single type of seed or opt for a mixture.

If you want to seed only the top of your loaf, after shaping your bread, place what will become the top surface of your finished loaf on the damp kitchen towel, gently rocking it back and forth to moisten. Then place the moistened portion of the dough on the seed bed, rocking in a similar fashion to fully coat the loaf with the seeds. Let it sit for a few seconds on the seed bed to allow the seeds to adhere, then place the loaf in your proofing basket or pan. If using a proofing basket, the loaf should be placed seed side down; in a loaf pan, place it seed side up. If you want full seed coverage, first shape your bread, then roll it on the damp kitchen towel to moisten it all over before transferring it to your seed tray and rolling to coat on all sides with seeds.

Note that seeding your crust can make your loaf harder to score. Instead of a lame, you might need to use a pair of scissors or a serrated knife. Another risk, especially with higher-fat seeds like sunflower and pumpkin, is that the seed crust can burn. To avoid this, use raw, untoasted seeds or nuts (they'll toast as the bread bakes). For super seedy loaves, you may also need to drop your oven temperature by 10°F to 15°F; increase the bake time as needed until your loaf is a deep brown.

Immediately reduce the oven temperature to 475°F. Bake the loaves for 25 minutes, then reduce the oven temperature to 450°F. Continue baking until the loaves are deeply browned and the crust is firm, about 20 minutes longer. Remove from the oven and transfer to a wire rack to cool completely before slicing. (For storage information, see Storing Bread, page 123.)

TO BAKE IN A COVERED BAKER:

PREHEAT: Arrange a rack in the lower third of the oven and preheat the oven to 500°F, with the lidded baker set on the rack. Allow the oven and baker to preheat for about 1 hour to ensure they are thoroughly heated.

Turn one loaf out of its proofing basket onto a 9-inch round of parchment paper with a sling (see Transferring a Loaf to a Covered Baker, page 203). Keep the second loaf refrigerated while you bake the first. Use a baker's lame or razor blade to score the top of the loaf (see Scoring, page 46).

BAKE: Remove the covered baker from the oven, uncover, and, using the parchment paper as a sling, carefully lower one loaf into the pan. Immediately reduce the oven temperature to 475°F and bake the loaf for 25 minutes.

Uncover, reduce the oven temperature to 450°F, and continue baking until the loaf is deeply browned and the crust is firm, about 20 minutes longer.

Remove the pan from the oven, carefully lift out the loaf, and transfer to a wire rack to cool completely before slicing. (For storage information, see Storing Bread, page 123.) Return the lidded baker to the oven and let preheat for 30 minutes, then score and bake the second loaf as directed above.

SESAME WHEAT

MIX	BULK FERMENTATION	PRESHAPE	SHAPE	2ND RISE	BAKE
5 MIN	8–12 HOURS	20 MIN	5 MIN	8–12 HOURS	45 MIN

TIME: ABOUT 25 HOURS

MAKES 2 LOAVES

47 grams (generous
3 tablespoons) sourdough culture
(see page 187)

558 grams (4½ cups plus
2 tablespoons) unbleached bread
flour, plus more for dusting

372 grams (3¼ cups plus
1 tablespoon) whole wheat flour

23 grams (1 tablespoon plus
1 teaspoon) fine salt

23 grams (1 tablespoon) honey

93 grams (½ cup plus
2½ tablespoons) unhulled
sesame seeds

744 grams (3¼ cups plus
1½ teaspoons) warm water (see
Temperature, page 25)

CRUST

107 grams (¾ cup) unhulled
sesame seeds

Made with a considerable amount of whole wheat flour and nutty sesame seeds both in the dough and on the exterior, this bread is aromatic and flavorful and keeps well, too. It's also a mostly hands-off loaf with a long bulk fermentation period, making it an easy bread to fit into a busy schedule. One of our favorite ways to eat it is sliced, toasted, slathered with peanut butter and topped with sliced bananas.

DAY 1

MAKE THE DOUGH: The morning before you want to bake, in a large bowl, combine the sourdough culture, bread flour, whole wheat flour, salt, honey, sesame seeds, and water, mixing with the handle of a wooden spoon until no dry spots remain (see Mixing, page 20).

Bulk fermentation or the "first rise" (see page 25) will take 8 to 12 hours, during which time you'll attend to the dough four times (directions follow), folding the dough every 15 minutes for the first hour. Then the dough will rest, covered and undisturbed, for the final 7 to 11 hours.

BULK FERMENT THE DOUGH: Once you've mixed the dough, cover and let it rest for 15 minutes. Using a wet hand, perform 8 to 12 bowl folds (see Bowl Fold, page 30) or until the dough resists stretching. Round out the dough by cupping your hand and applying pressure toward the bottom of the dough, forcing it into the bottom and side of the bowl to create tension. Cover and let rest for another 15 minutes.

Using a wet hand, perform 6 to 8 bowl folds, or until the dough resists stretching, and round out the dough again. Cover and let the dough rest for another 15 minutes. Perform a third set of bowl folds until the dough resists stretching, then round out the dough, cover, and let rest for 15 minutes before performing the fourth and final set of bowl folds, once again folding until the dough resists stretching.

Flip the dough over so that the smooth side is up, then round out the dough. Transfer it to a large, preferably clear container (a plastic dough rising bucket—see Tools, page 15—is perfect), then mark the level of the dough on the outside of the container; this will help you gauge how much the dough has risen later. Cover and allow the dough to rest at room temperature until it is marshmallowy and doubled in size, 7 to 11 hours. If you're baking in a warm climate or your sourdough culture is very active, the time it takes your dough to double will be closer to 7 hours. If you're baking in a cooler climate or your sourdough culture is sluggish, it will be closer to 11 hours. But the appearance of the dough is what you want to pay attention to, not the clock.

Very lightly dust two 9 × 3-inch round or oval proofing baskets with flour. (You'll use less dusting flour here than with other loaves because of the seed crust.)

DIVIDE AND PRESHAPE THE DOUGH: Lightly flour a work surface, then use a plastic bowl scraper to ease the dough out of the container onto the work surface. Using a bench knife or a knife, divide the dough into 2 equal portions (each about 930 grams). Gently pat each piece of dough to remove any large bubbles, then gently preshape into a round (see Preshaping, page 32) and place seam side down. Cover and let rest for 15 minutes.

SHAPE THE DOUGH, ADD THE CRUST, AND LET RISE: Shape each piece of dough into a boule or bâtard (see Shaping, page 34). Spread the sesame seeds on a rimmed baking sheet or piece of parchment paper. Wet a clean kitchen towel, then wring it out; it should still be pretty damp. Working with one loaf at a time, roll the top and sides of the loaf over the towel to moisten, then through the seeds to coat (see How to Coat a Loaf with Seeds, page 218). Transfer seam side up to the prepared proofing baskets, then cover. If your dough doubled in 7 to 8 hours of bulk fermentation, transfer the loaves to the refrigerator. If it took closer to 11 hours to double (an indication

that your dough is moving more slowly), let the loaves rise at room temperature for another hour before refrigerating. Refrigerate the loaves for 8 to 12 hours. Allow any extra sesame seeds to dry completely before storing in an airtight container to use for your next loaves.

At the end of this slow rise the dough should feel light, almost marshmallowy, and when pressed with a floured finger, a small impression should remain (see Proofing, page 44).

DAY 2

TO BAKE ON A BAKING STONE OR STEEL:

PREHEAT: Arrange racks in the center and bottom third of the oven and preheat the oven to 475°F with a baking stone or steel on the center rack and an empty cast-iron skillet (or a cake pan filled with lava rocks) on the lower rack. If possible, adjust the stone and pan so that the skillet isn't directly under the stone, making it easier for steam to reach the baking bread (see Steaming, page 50).

Turn each loaf out of its proofing basket onto a sheet of parchment paper. Use a baker's lame or razor blade to score the tops of the loaves (see Scoring, page 46).

Using a baker's peel or an inverted baking sheet to aid you, transfer the loaves (still on the parchment) into the oven, placing them on the stone or steel side by side and pour about 227 grams (1 cup) of warm water into the skillet. Steam will billow from the pan upward to envelop the bread; be sure to wear good oven mitts to shield your hands and arms. Quickly close the oven door to trap the steam. Bake the loaves for 25 minutes, then reduce the oven temperature to 450°F. Continue baking until the loaves are deeply browned and the crust is firm, about 20 minutes longer.

Recipe continues

Remove from the oven, transfer to a rack, and let cool completely before slicing. (For storage information, see Storing Bread, page 123.)

TO BAKE IN A COVERED BAKER:

PREHEAT: Arrange a rack in the lower third of the oven and preheat the oven to 475°F, with the lidded baker set on the rack. Allow the oven and baker to preheat for about 1 hour to ensure they are thoroughly heated.

Turn one loaf out of its proofing basket onto a 9-inch round of parchment paper with a sling (see Transferring a Loaf to a Covered Baker, page 203). Keep the second loaf refrigerated while you bake the first. Use a baker's lame or razor blade to score the top of the loaf (see Scoring, page 46).

BAKE: Remove the lidded baker from the oven, uncover, and, using the parchment paper as a sling, carefully lower one loaf into the pan. Place the lid on the baker, return to the oven, and bake for 25 minutes.

Remove the lid, reduce the oven temperature to 450°F, and continue baking until the loaf is deeply browned and the crust is firm, about 20 minutes longer.

Remove the pan from the oven, carefully remove the loaf from the pan, and let cool completely on a wire rack before slicing. (For storage information, see Storing Bread, page 123.) Return the covered baker to the oven and let preheat for 30 minutes, then score and bake the second loaf as directed above.

TOURTE AU SEIGLE
RYE BREAD

MIX	BULK FERMENTATION	SHAPE	2ND RISE	REST	BAKE
5 MIN	45 MIN	5 MIN	30–45 MIN	20–30 MIN	40–45 MIN

MAKE THE PREFERMENT AND TOAST THE FLOUR (12–16 HOURS BEFORE)

TIME: ABOUT 18½ HOURS

MAKES 2 LOAVES

PREFERMENT

41 grams (3 tablespoons) sourdough culture (see page 187)

415 grams (scant 4 cups) whole rye flour

332 grams (scant 1½ cups) cold water (55° to 60°F)

DOUGH

311 grams (scant 3 cups) whole rye flour, plus more for dusting

498 grams (2 cups plus 3 tablespoons) warm water (see Temperature, page 25)

311 grams (2½ cups plus 1 tablespoon) unbleached bread flour

23 grams (3¾ teaspoons) fine salt

6 grams (2 teaspoons) instant yeast

62 grams (3 tablespoons) honey

This hearty bread, whose French name loosely translates to "pie of rye," is, unsurprisingly, made primarily with rye flour; it is used in both the preferment and the dough. Rye contributes tremendous nutty flavor to breads, especially when the flour is toasted first, as it is here. It's also one of the most sustainable grains there is: It's a phenomenal cover crop capable of preventing erosion, it fixes nitrogen (releasing it back into the environment after the plant dies, making it available as a fertilizer for neighboring plants), and is especially effective at sequestering carbon from the environment (for more, see Understanding Rye, page 228). Rather than scoring the breads before they bake (as we typically do for other hearth loaves), these rye breads are left to proof until natural cracks appear on the surface of the loaf, giving this bread its signature appearance.

DAY 1

MAKE THE PREFERMENT: The evening before you want to bake, in a large bowl, combine the sourdough culture, flour, and water and mix until no dry patches of flour remain. Cover and let stand at room temperature overnight, 12 to 16 hours.

TOAST THE RYE FLOUR FOR THE DOUGH: Preheat the oven to 350°F. Spread the rye flour on a parchment-lined rimmed baking sheet and toast in the oven, stirring every 5 minutes, until the flour is a shade darker and smells nutty, about 20 minutes. (Alternatively, toast the flour in a large skillet over high heat, stirring frequently, until the flour is a shade darker and smells nutty, 5 to 7 minutes.) Let cool completely, then transfer to a bowl and cover.

DAY 2

MAKE THE DOUGH: Add the warm water to the preferment, then squeeze the preferment through your fingers to break it up. Next, holding your hand in a clawlike position, vigorously mix the preferment into the water until well combined. The mixture will look like lumpy pancake batter.

Add the toasted rye flour, bread flour, salt, yeast, and honey and mix well until no dry spots remain (see Mixing, page 20). Cover and let rise until you see an increase in volume and the dough feels less dense, about 45 minutes.

Generously dust two 9 × 3-inch round proofing baskets with whole rye flour.

DIVIDE AND SHAPE THE DOUGH AND LET IT RISE: Heavily flour a work surface with rye flour, then use a plastic bowl scraper to ease the dough out of the bowl onto the work surface. Lightly flour the top of the dough and, using a bench knife or a knife that has been dipped in water, divide the dough into 2 equal portions (each about 1,000 grams). Pat each piece of dough flat, then gently form into rounds (they will not have the elasticity of a wheat-based dough; see Understanding Rye, page 228) and place seam side up in the prepared proofing baskets. Cover and let rise at room temperature until the dough feels less dense and is slightly puffy, 30 to 45 minutes.

TO BAKE ON A BAKING STONE OR STEEL:
PREHEAT: Arrange racks in the center and bottom third of the oven and preheat the oven to 450°F with a baking stone or steel on the center rack and an empty cast iron skillet (or a cake pan full of lava rocks) on the lower rack. If possible, adjust the stone and pan so that the skillet isn't directly under the stone, making it easier for steam to reach the baking bread (see Steaming, page 50).

Turn the loaves out of their proofing baskets onto a sheet of parchment paper, side by side and spaced a few inches apart. Cover and let rest until cracks begin to form on the surface of each loaf and they feel slightly puffy, 20 to 30 minutes.

BAKE: Transfer the loaves (still on the sheet of parchment) onto the stone or steel and pour about

227 grams (1 cup) of warm water into the empty cast-iron skillet. Steam will billow from the pan upward to envelop the bread; be sure to wear good oven mitts to shield your hands and arms. Quickly close the oven door to trap the steam. Bake the bread until the crust is deeply browned and firm, 40 to 45 minutes.

Remove from the oven and let cool completely on a wire rack before slicing. (For storage information, see Storing Bread, page 123.)

TO BAKE IN A COVERED BAKER:
PREHEAT: Arrange a rack in the lower third of the oven and preheat the oven to 450°F, with the lidded baker set on the rack. Allow the oven and baker to preheat for about 1 hour to ensure they are thoroughly heated.

Turn one loaf out of the proofing basket onto a 9-inch round of parchment paper with a sling (see Transferring a Loaf to a Covered Baker, page 203). Cover and let rest until cracks begin to form on the surface of the loaf and it feels slightly puffy, 20 to 30 minutes. Keep the second loaf refrigerated while you bake the first.

BAKE: Remove the lidded baker from the oven, uncover, and, using the parchment paper as a sling, carefully lower the loaf into the pan. Place the lid on the baker, return to the oven, and bake for 25 minutes.

Uncover and continue baking until the crust is deeply browned and firm and the internal temperature is at least 210°F, about 20 minutes more.

Remove the pan from the oven, carefully lift out the loaf, and transfer to a wire rack to cool completely before slicing. (For storage information, see Storing Bread, page 123.) Return the lidded baker to the oven and let preheat for 30 minutes, then bake the second loaf as directed above.

UNDERSTANDING RYE

Although rye contains about the same amount of protein as wheat does, it doesn't behave the same way in a dough. When it's mixed with water, it doesn't form gluten. As we noted earlier in the book (see Mixing, page 20), the glutinous web that results when wheat flour is mixed with liquid traps the carbon dioxide generated during fermentation, which in turn causes the dough to rise. Because rye contains much less gluten (and the gluten it does contain is less successful at trapping those carbon dioxide bubbles), breads that are made predominantly with rye flour tend to rise little and have a denser, tighter crumb.

Rye flour contains complex sugars called pentosans, which can absorb a lot of water, so rye bread doughs often require a higher proportion of liquid to flour than doughs made with wheat flour. Pentosans also break easily during mixing, resulting in stickier doughs that are difficult to handle; they can't be kneaded like bread doughs made primarily of wheat flour, and attempts by the baker to "solve" for the stickiness by adding additional flour only serve to make the bread even more dense. Instead, rye bread doughs are typically mixed by machine, or they're mixed briefly and then folded by hand during bulk fermentation.

In addition to pentosans, rye flour also contains enzymes called amylases. Amylase breaks starch down into sugar. In wheat bread doughs, it only partially breaks down those strong starches, adding a bit of sweetness to the bread without damaging its structure. But in rye doughs, which are naturally higher in starch because rye contains more starch than wheat, amylase really likes to party, breaking down so much of the starch that the structure of the bread is compromised and the resultant loaf has a gummy, unpleasant texture.

Happily, there is a way to counteract the deleterious effects of amylase in rye doughs. Amylase enzymes become inactive in a low-pH environment, so by acidifying rye bread dough—through the introduction of sourdough culture or by adding an ingredient like buttermilk or pickle juice (see Pickle Rye, page 143)—bakers can stop amylase in its tracks before it wreaks havoc on their nice rye doughs. When making naturally leavened rye bread doughs, it helps to use warmer water, which kick-starts and speeds up fermentation, causing the dough to more quickly develop the lactic acids that lower its pH.

Some rye breads that use a lower proportion of rye flour in tandem with wheat flour can be kneaded and shaped as you would any wheat flour dough. But rye breads with a higher proportion of rye flour relative to wheat flour (like the Rúgbrauð, page 179)—or with no wheat flour at all (like the Vollkornbrot, page 181)—are more batter-like in consistency; instead of being shaped, the batter is spooned into a pan and baked.

For all its relative fussiness, there's a very compelling reason to go through the extra effort to make rye bread: It's incredibly flavorful and keeps beautifully for many days without getting stale. The grain is naturally nutty, with deep malty notes, and adds wonderful complexity to breads, even if you're using only a small amount.

As with wheat flours, there are a few varieties of rye flour. The more rye kernel the flour contains, the darker it is.

WHITE RYE FLOUR: As the name implies, this is the lightest version of rye flour. It's also sometimes referred to as "light rye." In white rye flour, the bran and germ are completely removed, and the flour contains only the starchy endosperm of the rye kernel.

MEDIUM RYE FLOUR: This contains more of the bran than white rye, leading to a darker color and more robust rye flavor. It's not weighed down by the germ or too much bran as with darker rye flours, so it can still be used in delicate doughs.

WHOLE RYE FLOUR: This flour contains all of the bran, germ, and endosperm of the rye kernel. As a result, it has an even darker color than medium rye. With all the mineral-rich goodness of the whole rye berry, whole rye flour gives bread an assertive, complex flavor. This is also the kind of rye flour you'll usually find in sourdough recipes, as it's best for fermentation.

BREAKFAST PORRIDGE BREAD

MIX	BULK FERMENTATION	PRESHAPE	SHAPE	2ND RISE	BAKE
10 MIN	1½ HOURS	20 MIN	5 MIN	1½ HOURS	40–45 MIN

MAKE THE PREFERMENT AND PORRIDGE (12–16 HOURS BEFORE)

TIME: ABOUT 20 HOURS

MAKES 2 LOAVES

PORRIDGE

28 grams (¼ cup plus
1 tablespoon) old-fashioned
rolled oats

0.75 gram (⅛ teaspoon) fine salt

142 grams (½ cup plus
2 tablespoons) water

PREFERMENT

100 grams (¾ cup
plus 1 tablespoon) unbleached
bread flour

3 grams (½ teaspoon) fine salt

0.375 gram (⅛ teaspoon) instant
yeast

57 grams (¼ cup) cold water
(55° to 60°F)

DOUGH

425 grams (1¾ cups plus
2 tablespoons) warm water (see
Temperature, page 25)

507 grams (4¼ cups) unbleached
bread flour, plus more for dusting

125 grams (generous ½ cup)
cooked, cooled oatmeal porridge
(recipe above)

Ingredients continue

This bread gets its name because a portion of the grains in the loaf are first cooked until soft, like a bowl of oatmeal porridge, before being mixed into the final bread dough. In some cases, porridge breads can have a gummy interior, but this loaf is tender and moist, with a tight crumb (all the better for slathering the slices with butter and jam) and a nicely browned crust (thanks to the honey in the dough). And while you can cook some oatmeal with the express purpose of baking this bread, it also can be made with leftover oatmeal from breakfast; just substitute 125 grams (a generous ½ cup) cooled, unsweetened leftover cooked oatmeal.

This dough is a bit on the sticky side, and for that reason we recommend making this bread in a stand mixer rather than by hand.

DAY 1

MAKE THE PORRIDGE: The evening before you want to bake, in a small saucepan, combine the oats, salt, and water. Bring to a boil over medium heat and cook, stirring constantly, until the water is absorbed and the mixture is thickened, 2 to 3 minutes. Measure out 125 grams (generous ½ cup) porridge (any extra is a baker's snack!), transfer to a small bowl to cool to room temperature, and cover and refrigerate overnight. (Alternatively, you can use 125 grams/generous ½ cup leftover cooked oatmeal.)

MAKE THE PREFERMENT: In a stand mixer bowl, combine the flour, salt, yeast, and water. Mix by hand until no dry patches of flour remain, then knead by hand in the bowl until a stiff, smooth dough forms. Cover and let stand at room temperature overnight, 12 to 16 hours.

Recipe continues

122 grams (1¼ cups plus 2 tablespoons) old-fashioned rolled oats

104 grams (¾ cup plus 3 tablespoons) whole wheat flour

15 grams (2½ teaspoons) fine salt

2.5 grams (scant 1 teaspoon) instant yeast

67 grams (generous 3 tablespoons) honey

CRUST

67 grams (¾ cup) old-fashioned rolled oats

DAY 2

MAKE THE DOUGH: Add the water, bread flour, porridge, oats, whole wheat flour, salt, yeast, and honey to the preferment. Using the dough hook attachment, mix on medium-low speed until no dry spots remain (see Mixing, page 20), 1 to 2 minutes. Scrape down the bottom and sides of the bowl, then increase the speed to medium and continue mixing until the dough is elastic and cleans the sides of the bowl, about 8 minutes. The dough will be slightly sticky.

Bulk fermentation or the "first rise" (see page 25) will take 1½ hours, during which time you'll attend to it once. After a 45-minute rest, you'll perform one set of bowl folds (directions follow). Then the dough will rest, covered and undisturbed, for an additional 45 minutes.

BULK FERMENT THE DOUGH: Once you've mixed the dough, cover and let rest for 45 minutes. With a wet hand, perform 6 to 8 bowl folds (see Bowl Fold, page 30) or until the dough resists stretching. Cover and let rest until the dough is very puffy and marshmallowy, about 45 minutes.

Very lightly dust two 9 × 3-inch round or oval proofing baskets with flour. (You'll use less dusting flour here than with other loaves because of the oat crust.)

DIVIDE AND PRESHAPE THE DOUGH: Lightly dust a work surface with flour, then use a plastic bowl scraper to ease the dough out of the bowl and onto the work surface. With a bench knife, divide the dough into 2 equal portions (each about 763 grams). Gently preshape each piece of dough into a round (see Preshaping, page 32) and place seam side down on the work surface. Cover and let rest 15 minutes.

SHAPE THE DOUGH, ADD THE OAT CRUST, AND LET RISE: Gently shape each piece of dough into a boule or bâtard (see Shaping, page 34). Spread the oats on a rimmed baking sheet or piece of parchment paper. Wet a clean kitchen towel, then wring it out; it should still be pretty damp. Working with one loaf at a time, roll the shaped loaf over the towel to moisten the loaf, then into the oats to coat (see How to Coat a Loaf with Seeds, page 218). Transfer seam side up to the prepared proofing baskets. Cover and let rise until the dough feels light and marshmallowy and when pressed with a floured finger, a small impression remains (see Proofing, page 44), about 1½ hours.

TO BAKE ON A BAKING STONE OR STEEL:

PREHEAT: Arrange racks in the center and bottom third of the oven and preheat the oven to 475°F with a baking stone or steel on the center rack and an empty cast-iron skillet (or a cake pan filled with lava rocks) on the lower rack. If possible, adjust the stone and pan so that the skillet isn't directly under the stone, making it easier for steam to reach the baking bread (see Steaming, page 50).

Turn each loaf out of its proofing basket and onto a sheet of parchment paper. Use a baker's lame or razor blade to score the tops of the loaves (see Scoring, page 46).

Using a baker's peel or an inverted baking sheet to aid you, transfer the loaves (still on the parchment) into the oven, placing them on the stone or steel side by side, and pour about 227 grams (1 cup) of warm water into the skillet. Steam will billow from the pan upward to envelop the bread; be sure to wear good oven mitts to shield your hands and arms. Quickly close the oven door to trap the steam. Bake the bread until the crust is deeply browned and firm, 40 to 45 minutes.

Remove from the oven and let cool completely on a wire rack before slicing. (For storage information, see Storing Bread, page 123.)

TO BAKE IN A COVERED BAKER:

PREHEAT: Arrange a rack in the lower third of the oven and preheat the oven to 475°F, with the lidded baker set on the rack. Allow the oven and baker to preheat for about 1 hour to ensure they are thoroughly heated.

Turn one loaf out of its proofing basket onto a 9-inch round of parchment paper with a sling (see Transferring a Loaf to a Covered Baker, page 203). Keep the second loaf refrigerated while you bake the first. Use a baker's lame or razor blade to score the top of the loaf (see Scoring, page 46).

BAKE: Remove the lidded baker from the oven, uncover, and, using the parchment paper as a sling, carefully lower one loaf into the pan, taking care not to burn your knuckles. Place the lid on the baker, return to the oven, and bake the loaves for 20 minutes.

Uncover and continue baking until the loaves are deeply browned, the crust is firm, and the internal temperature is at least 210°F, about 20 to 25 minutes more.

Remove the pan from the oven, carefully lift out the loaf, and transfer to a wire rack to cool completely before slicing. (For storage information, see Storing Bread, page 123.) Return the covered baker to the oven and let preheat for 30 minutes, then score and bake the second loaf as directed above.

POLENTA, RICOTTA, AND ROSEMARY LOAF

MAKE THE POLENTA	MIX	BULK FERMENTATION	PRESHAPE	SHAPE	2ND RISE	BAKE
10 MIN	5 MIN	2 HOURS–2 HOURS 15 MIN	20 MIN	5 MIN	45 MIN–1 HOUR	35–40 MIN

TIME: ABOUT 4½ HOURS

MAKES 2 LOAVES

POLENTA

75 grams (¼ cup plus 3 tablespoons) polenta

15 grams (1 tablespoon) unsalted butter

2 grams (scant ½ teaspoon) fine salt

225 grams (1 cup) water

DOUGH

591 grams (4¾ cups plus 3 tablespoons) unbleached all-purpose flour, plus more for dusting

373 grams (1½ cups plus 2½ tablespoons) warm water (see Temperature, page 25)

118 grams (½ cup plus 1½ teaspoons) whole-milk ricotta cheese, at room temperature

15 grams (2½ teaspoons) fine salt

12 grams (1½ teaspoons) honey

5 grams (1¾ teaspoons) instant yeast

177 grams (½ cup plus 2½ tablespoons) cooked, cooled polenta (recipe above)

Ingredients continue

This aromatic, golden loaf is enriched with ricotta cheese and scented with rosemary. It has cooked polenta in the dough, which flavors the bread with a subtle hint of corn; a coating of cornmeal adds a bit of crunch and prevents the rising dough from sticking to the proofing basket. While this loaf is wonderful simply sliced and buttered, it also makes excellent crostini: Drizzle the slices with olive oil, toast them in the oven, then top with everything from herbed ricotta (to echo the cheese in the dough), to fat slices of tomato and burrata, to blue cheese and fresh figs.

MAKE THE POLENTA: In a small saucepan, combine the polenta, butter, salt, and water. Bring to a boil over medium heat, whisking constantly. Reduce the heat to low and continue cooking until the polenta is thick and does not flow back together when the whisk is drawn through it, 2 to 3 minutes. Weigh out 177 grams (½ cup plus 2½ tablespoons) of the polenta on a plate and set aside to cool; any extra is the baker's snack!

MAKE THE DOUGH: In a large bowl, combine the flour, water, ricotta, salt, honey, and yeast and mix with the handle of a wooden spoon until the dough is homogenous and no dry spots remain (see Mixing, page 20).

Bulk fermentation or the "first rise" (see page 25) will take 2 hours to 2 hours 15 minutes. During that time, you'll attend to the dough three times (directions follow), folding in the polenta and rosemary after the first 15 minutes, then letting it rest for another 15 minutes before performing a second set of folds. After a 45-minute rest, you'll perform a third and final round of bowl folds. Then the dough will rest, covered and undisturbed, for an additional 45 minutes.

BULK FERMENT THE DOUGH: Once you've mixed the dough, cover and let rest for 15 minutes. Add the cooled polenta and rosemary to

Recipe continues

9 grams (2 tablespoons) chopped fresh rosemary leaves (from 6 sprigs)

CRUST
78 grams (½ cup) finely ground yellow cornmeal

the dough and, with wet hands, pinch and squeeze them into the dough. Once they have been roughly incorporated, perform 6 to 8 bowl folds (see Bowl Fold, page 30) or until the polenta and rosemary are distributed throughout the dough and the dough resists stretching. Round out the dough by cupping your hand and applying pressure toward the bottom of the dough, forcing it into the bottom and side of the bowl to create tension, then cover and let rest for 15 minutes.

Perform another 6 to 8 bowl folds with a wet hand until the dough resists stretching, then round out the dough and cover. Let rest for 45 minutes, then perform a third and final round of bowl folds with a wet hand, until the dough resists stretching. Round out the dough, then cover and let rest, undisturbed, until the dough is very puffy and marshmallowy, 45 minutes to 1 hour.

DIVIDE AND PRESHAPE THE DOUGH: Lightly flour a work surface, then use a plastic bowl scraper to ease the dough out of the bowl and onto the work surface. With a bench knife or a knife, divide the dough into 2 equal portions (each about 650 grams). Gently preshape each piece of dough into a round (see Preshaping, page 32) and set seam side down on the work surface. Cover and let rest 15 minutes.

Very lightly dust two 9 × 3-inch round or oval proofing baskets with flour. (You'll use less dusting flour here than with other loaves because of the cornmeal crust.)

SHAPE THE DOUGH, ADD THE CORNMEAL CRUST, AND LET RISE: Shape each piece of dough into a boule or bâtard (see Shaping, page 34). Spread the cornmeal on a rimmed baking sheet or piece of parchment paper. Wet a clean kitchen towel, then wring it out; it should still be pretty damp. Working with one loaf at a time, roll the shaped loaf over the towel to moisten all over, then into the cornmeal to coat (see How to Coat a Loaf with Seeds, page 218). Transfer seam side up to the prepared proofing basket. Cover and let rise until the dough feels light and marshmallowy and when pressed with a floured finger, a small impression remains (see Proofing, page 44), 45 minutes to 1 hour.

TO BAKE ON A BAKING STONE OR STEEL:

PREHEAT: Arrange racks in the center and bottom third of the oven and preheat the oven to 500°F with the baking stone or steel on the center rack and an empty cast-iron skillet (or a cake pan filled with lava rocks) on the lower rack. If possible, adjust the stone and pan so that the skillet isn't directly under the stone, making it easier for steam to reach the baking bread (see Steaming, page 50).

Turn the loaves out of their proofing baskets onto a sheet of parchment paper side by side, leaving a few inches of space between them. Use a baker's lame or razor blade to score the top of each loaf (see Scoring, page 46).

BAKE: Load the loaves (still on the parchment) into the oven, placing them on the stone or steel, and pour about 227 grams (1 cup) of warm water into the skillet. Steam will billow from the pan upward to envelop the bread; be sure to wear good oven mitts to shield your hands and arms. Quickly close the oven door to trap the steam and reduce the oven temperature to 450°F. Bake until the crust is firm and deeply browned and the internal temperature reaches 200°F, about 35 minutes.

Remove from the oven and let cool completely on a wire rack before slicing. (For storage information, see Storing Bread, page 123.)

TO BAKE IN A COVERED BAKER:

PREHEAT: Arrange a rack in the lower third of the oven and preheat the oven to 500°F, with the lidded baker set on the rack. Allow the oven and baker to preheat for about 1 hour to ensure they are thoroughly heated.

Turn one loaf out of its proofing basket onto a 9-inch round of parchment paper with a sling (see Transferring a Loaf to a Covered Baker, page 203). Keep the second loaf refrigerated while you bake the first. Use a baker's lame or razor blade to score the top of the loaf (see Scoring, page 46).

BAKE: Remove the lidded baker from the oven, uncover, and, using the parchment paper as a sling, carefully lower one loaf into the pan. Place the lid on the baker, return to the oven, and immediately reduce the oven temperature to 450°F. Bake for 20 minutes.

Uncover and continue baking until the loaves are deeply browned, the crust is firm, and the internal temperature is at least 210°F, about 20 minutes more.

Remove the pan from the oven, carefully lift out the loaf, and transfer to a wire rack to cool completely before slicing. (For storage information, see Storing Bread, page 123.) Return the covered baker to the oven and let preheat for 30 minutes, then score and bake the second loaf as directed above.

LOADED BAKED POTATO BREAD

PREP THE POTATOES	MIX	BULK FERMENTATION	PRESHAPE	SHAPE	2ND RISE	BAKE
10–40 MIN	12 MIN	1½ HOURS	20 MIN	5 MIN	1 HOUR–1 HOUR 15 MIN	35 MIN

·········· TIME: ABOUT 4½ HOURS ··········

MAKES 2 LOAVES

2 medium russet potatoes
(392 grams/14 ounces)

571 grams (4¾ cups) unbleached all-purpose flour, plus more for dusting

63 grams (½ cup plus 1 tablespoon) whole wheat flour

32 grams (2 tablespoons plus 2 teaspoons) sugar

14 grams (2½ teaspoons) fine salt

6 grams (2 teaspoons) instant yeast

2.5 to 5 grams (1 to 2 teaspoons) coarsely ground black pepper

361 grams (1½ cups plus 2 tablespoons) warm water (see Temperature, page 25)

63 grams (1 small bunch) scallions, sliced (about 1 cup)

63 grams (generous ¼ cup) full-fat sour cream

We used baked potatoes as our inspiration here, loading the dough with chunks of roasted russets, generous amounts of black pepper, and scallions, and enriching it with sour cream. Because this bread is made entirely with yeast (rather than sourdough culture or a combination of the two), it is ready to bake about 2 hours after you mix the dough. For a roll version of this bread—which look, irresistibly, like baked potatoes—see the Variation that follows.

COOK THE POTATOES: Preheat the oven to 400°F. Line a baking sheet with parchment paper.

Cut the potatoes into 1-inch chunks and arrange on the lined baking sheet. Roast the potatoes until fork-tender and lightly golden brown, about 35 minutes. Remove from the oven and cool to room temperature. (Alternatively, prick the whole potatoes all over with a fork and cook on a microwaveable plate in the microwave until fork-tender, about 8 minutes. Remove and cool to room temperature, then cut into 1-inch chunks.) Weigh out 222 grams (about 2 cups) of roasted potato and set aside; snack on or save any surplus for another use.

MAKE THE DOUGH: In a stand mixer bowl, combine the roasted potato chunks, all-purpose flour, whole wheat flour, sugar, salt, yeast, pepper, water, scallions, and sour cream. Using the dough hook attachment, mix on medium-low speed for 1 minute, then stop and scrape down the bottom and sides of the bowl. Increase the speed to medium and continue mixing until a tacky, springy dough that cleans the sides of the bowl forms, about 10 minutes.

Bulk fermentation or the "first rise" (see page 25) will take 1½ hours. During that time you'll attend to the dough once (directions follow), folding the dough once after 45 minutes. Then the dough will rest, covered and undisturbed, for the final 45 minutes.

Recipe continues

BULK FERMENT THE DOUGH: Once you've mixed the dough, cover and let it rest for 45 minutes. With a wet hand, perform 6 to 8 bowl folds (see Bowl Fold, page 30) or until the dough resists stretching. Cover and let rest until the dough is puffy and nearly doubled in size, about 45 minutes more.

DIVIDE AND PRESHAPE THE DOUGH: Lightly flour a work surface, then use a plastic bowl scraper to ease the dough out of the bowl onto the work surface. Using a bench knife or a knife, divide the dough into 2 equal portions (each about 700 grams). Gently pat each piece of dough to remove any large bubbles, then lightly preshape into a round (see Preshaping, page 32) and place seam side down on the work surface. Cover and let rest for 15 minutes.

Generously dust two 9 × 3-inch oval or round proofing baskets with flour.

SHAPE THE DOUGH AND LET IT RISE: Shape each piece of dough into a boule or bâtard (see Shaping, page 34). Place the loaves seam side up in the prepared proofing baskets. Cover and let rise at room temperature until the loaves feel light, almost marshmallowy, and when pressed with a floured finger, a small impression remains (see Proofing, page 44), 1 hour to 1 hour 15 minutes.

TO BAKE ON A BAKING STONE OR STEEL:
PREHEAT: Arrange racks in the center and bottom third of the oven and preheat the oven to 450°F with the baking stone or steel on the center rack and an empty cast-iron skillet (or a cake pan filled with lava rocks) on the lower rack. If possible, adjust the stone and pan so that the skillet isn't directly under the stone, making it easier for steam to reach the baking bread (see Steaming, page 50).

Turn the loaves out of their proofing baskets onto a sheet of parchment paper side by side, spacing them a few inches apart. Use a baker's lame or razor blade to score the tops of the loaves (see Scoring, page 46).

BAKE: Using a baker's peel or an inverted baking sheet to aid you, transfer the loaves (still on the parchment) into the oven, placing them on the stone or steel, and pour about 227 grams (1 cup) of warm water into the skillet. Steam will billow from the pan upward to envelop the bread; be sure to wear good oven mitts to shield your hands and arms. Quickly close the oven door to trap the steam. Bake until the loaf is deeply browned, the crust is firm, and the internal temperature is at least 210°F, about 35 minutes. Remove from the oven and transfer to a rack to cool completely before slicing. (For storage information, see Storing Bread, page 123.)

TO BAKE IN A COVERED BAKER:
PREHEAT: Arrange a rack in the lower third of the oven and preheat the oven to 450°F, with the lidded baker set on the rack. Allow the oven and baker to preheat for about 1 hour to ensure they are thoroughly heated.

Turn one loaf out of its proofing basket onto a 9-inch round of parchment paper with a sling (see Transferring a Loaf to a Covered Baker, page 203). Keep the second loaf refrigerated while you bake the first. Use a baker's lame or razor blade to score the top of the loaf (see Scoring, page 46).

BAKE: Remove the lidded baker from the oven, uncover, and, using the parchment paper as a sling, carefully lower one loaf into the pan, taking care not to burn your knuckles. Place the lid on the baker, return to the oven, and bake for 20 minutes.

Uncover and continue baking until the loaf is deeply browned, the crust is firm, and the internal temperature is 210°F, about 15 minutes more.

Remove the pan from the oven, carefully lift out the loaf, and transfer to a wire rack to cool completely before slicing. (For storage information, see Storing Bread, page 123.) Return the lidded baker to the oven and let preheat for 30 minutes, then score and bake the second loaf as directed above.

BAKED POTATO ROLLS

Lovers of trompe l'oeil, these are for you. Shaped as oblong rolls and baked until deeply browned, they very closely resemble baked potatoes. Top them as you would a potato, with shredded cheese, cooked crumbled bacon, a dollop of sour cream, and a showering of finely sliced chives.

Make the dough according to the instructions on page 239. When it comes time to divide, use a bench knife or a knife to cut the dough into 12 equal portions (each about 116 grams). Preshape each into a round (see Preshaping, page 32) and place seam side down on the work surface. Cover and let rest for 15 minutes, then shape as blunt bâtards (see Shaping, page 34), each about 5 inches long. Place the shaped rolls, evenly spaced, on a sheet of parchment paper,

then cover and let rest until the rolls look puffy and feel marshmallowy, 45 minutes.

Bake the rolls at 450°F until deep brown, like a russet potato, 20 to 25 minutes.

Slide the rolls (still on the parchment) onto a rimmed baking sheet.

Allow the rolls to cool slightly, then cut a "V" shape out of the top of each roll. Sprinkle each roll with 14 grams (1 tablespoon) shredded cheddar cheese, then return to the oven to melt, about 5 minutes more. Remove the rolls from the oven and top with your favorite baked potato toppings: sour cream, crumbled cooked bacon, snipped chives, and another sprinkle of cheese.

MARBLED RYE

MIX	BULK FERMENTATION	SHAPE	2ND RISE	BAKE
20 MIN	1½ HOURS	30 MIN	2 HOURS	30–35 MIN

MAKE THE PREFERMENT (12–16 HOURS BEFORE)

TIME: ABOUT 21 HOURS

MAKES 2 LOAVES

PREFERMENT

44 grams (3 tablespoons) sourdough culture (see page 187)

145 grams (1⅓ cups) whole rye flour

73 grams (½ cup plus 2 tablespoons) unbleached bread flour

131 grams (½ cup plus 1 tablespoon) cold water (55°F to 60°F)

DOUGH

508 grams (4¼ cups) unbleached bread flour, plus more for dusting

36 grams (3 tablespoons) sugar

18 grams (1 tablespoon) fine salt

9 grams (1 tablespoon) caraway seeds

7 grams (2¼ teaspoons) instant yeast

298 grams (1⅓ cups) warm water (see Temperature, page 25), divided

2 large eggs (100 grams total)

73 grams (¼ cup plus 2 tablespoons) olive oil

22 grams (¼ cup) black cocoa

Ingredients continue

This is our version of the classic deli loaf, made with a rye preferment and enriched with olive oil and eggs. Commercially made marbled rye often has caramel color added to a portion of the dough. But we color and flavor our version naturally, with molasses and black cocoa (see page 167)—don't worry, it doesn't taste like chocolate! Though its fancy swirled appearance would suggest otherwise, it's easy to shape this bread. The plain and cocoa doughs are simply stacked together and then shaped into a loaf; when you cut into the loaf, the swirl appears. Don't skip the seedy, salty crust—it makes the bread.

DAY 1

MAKE THE PREFERMENT: The evening before you want to bake, in a stand mixer bowl, combine the sourdough culture, rye flour, bread flour, and water and mix by hand until no dry patches of flour remain. Knead by hand in the bowl until a compact, somewhat sticky dough forms. Cover and let stand at room temperature overnight, 12 to 16 hours.

DAY 2

MAKE THE DOUGH: Add the bread flour, sugar, salt, caraway seeds, yeast, 283 grams (1¼ cups) of the water, eggs, and olive oil to the bowl with the preferment. Using the dough hook attachment, mix on medium-low speed, stopping to scrape down the bowl as necessary, until a sticky dough with no dry patches of flour forms, about 2 minutes. Increase the speed to medium and mix until the dough cleans the sides of the bowl and is smooth and only slightly sticky, 8 to 10 minutes.

Lightly flour a work surface, then use a plastic bowl scraper to ease the dough out of the bowl onto the work surface. Using a bench knife or a knife, divide the dough into 2 unequal pieces: one 950 grams and one 570 grams. Place the larger piece of dough in a lightly greased medium bowl, cover, and set aside.

Recipe continues

20 grams (1 tablespoon) unsulphured molasses (not blackstrap)

CRUST

36 grams (¼ cup) caraway seeds

9 grams (1 tablespoon) coarse sea salt

Return the smaller piece of dough to the mixer bowl and add the remaining 15 grams (1 tablespoon) warm water, the black cocoa, and molasses. Continue mixing with the dough hook on medium-low speed until mostly combined, stopping to scrape down the bowl as necessary. Increase the speed to medium and mix until homogeneous, an additional 2 to 3 minutes. Place the cocoa dough in a lightly greased medium bowl, cover, and set aside.

Bulk fermentation or the "first rise" (see page 25) will take 1½ hours. During that time you'll attend to it once: After a 30-minute rest you'll perform one set of folds (directions follow) on each dough. Then each dough will rest, covered and undisturbed, for the final hour.

BULK FERMENT BOTH DOUGHS: Let both doughs rest for 30 minutes. Using a wet hand, perform 6 to 8 bowl folds (see Bowl Fold, page 30) on the plain dough and the cocoa dough or until the doughs resist stretching. Cover each dough and let rest for 1 hour.

DIVIDE AND SHAPE THE DOUGH, ADD THE SEED CRUST, AND LET RISE: Lightly flour a work surface, then use a plastic bowl scraper to ease the plain dough onto the work surface. Divide it into 2 equal portions (each about 475 grams). Stretch each portion of plain dough into a 7-inch square, then cover. Ease the cocoa dough onto a lightly floured surface and divide it into 2 equal portions (each about 285 grams). Stretch each piece of cocoa dough into a 5-inch square, then cover. Let both the plain and cocoa doughs rest for 10 minutes.

On a lightly floured work surface, roll one piece of plain dough into a 14 × 8-inch rectangle, then do the same with one piece of cocoa dough. Place the cocoa dough atop the plain dough, allowing the cocoa dough to contract slightly, so that it is slightly smaller and fits within the rectangle of plain dough. Fold the short sides of the dough in to meet in the middle, pressing to seal. The dough should now be roughly 8 × 7 inches. Starting with a long side, roll the dough into a log (see Shaping, page 34), pinching the ends to seal. Repeat this process with the remaining plain and cocoa dough to make a second loaf.

Lightly dust two 9 × 3-inch oval proofing baskets with flour.

For the crust, spread the caraway seeds and flaky salt on a rimmed baking sheet or piece of parchment paper. Wet a clean kitchen towel, then wring it out; it should still be pretty damp. Working with one loaf at a time, roll the top and sides of one loaf over the towel to moisten, then through the seeds and salt to coat. Place the loaf seam side up in the prepared proofing basket. Cover and let rise until they are puffy and marshmallowy and a small impression remains when pressed with a floured finger (see Proofing, page 44), about 2 hours.

BAKE: Arrange racks in the center and bottom third of the oven and preheat the oven to 450°F with a baking stone or steel on the center rack and an empty cast-iron skillet (or a cake pan filled with lava rocks) on the lower rack. If possible, adjust the stone and pan so that the skillet isn't directly under the stone, making it easier for steam to reach the baking bread (see Steaming, page 50).

Turn each loaf out of its proofing basket onto a sheet of parchment paper. Use a baker's lame or razor blade to score the top of each loaf (see Scoring, page 46).

Using a baker's peel or an inverted baking sheet to aid you, transfer each loaf (still on the parchment) into the oven, placing them on the stone or steel, and pour about 227 grams (1 cup) of warm water into the skillet. Steam will billow from the pan upward to envelop the bread; be sure to wear good oven mitts to shield your hands and arms. Quickly close the oven door to trap the steam. Bake the loaf until the crust is firm and deeply browned and the internal temperature is 210°F, 30 to 35 minutes.

Remove from the oven and let cool completely on a wire rack before slicing. (For storage information, see Storing Bread, page 123.)

TO BAKE IN A COVERED BAKER:

If you have an oval-shaped Dutch oven or covered baker, this bread can also be baked in that. Arrange a rack in the lower third of the oven and preheat to 450°F, with the lidded baker set on the rack. Allow the oven and baker to preheat for about 1 hour to ensure they are thoroughly heated.

Turn one loaf out of its proofing basket onto a sheet of parchment paper. (Keep the second loaf refrigerated while you bake the first.) Use a baker's lame or razor blade to score the top of the loaf (see Scoring, page 46).

BAKE: Remove the lidded baker from the oven, uncover, and, using the parchment paper as a sling, carefully lower one loaf into the pan. Place the lid on the baker, return to the oven, and bake for 20 minutes.

Uncover and continue baking until the loaf is browned, the crust is firm, and the internal temperature is 210°F, about 15 minutes more.

Remove the pan from the oven, carefully lift out the loaf, and transfer to a wire rack to cool completely before slicing. (For storage information, see Storing Bread, page 123.) Return the lidded baker to the oven and let preheat for 30 minutes, then score and bake the second loaf as directed above.

CHOCOLATE LEVAIN

MAKES 2 LOAVES

PREFERMENT

22 grams (1½ tablespoons) sourdough culture (see page 187)

216 grams (1¾ cups plus 1 tablespoon) unbleached bread flour

143 grams (½ cup plus 2 tablespoons) cold water (55°F to 60°F)

DOUGH

463 grams (2 cups plus 1 tablespoon) warm water (see Temperature, page 25)

447 grams (3¾ cups) unbleached bread flour, plus more for dusting

58 grams (½ cup) whole wheat flour

36 grams (¼ cup plus 3 tablespoons) Dutch-process cocoa, dark preferred

14 grams (2¼ teaspoons) fine salt

200 grams (1 cup plus 3 tablespoons) semisweet chocolate chips or roughly chopped disks (around 60% cacao)

Despite the addition of cocoa and semisweet chocolate, this dark loaf is more savory than sweet, with a well-balanced sour crumb with deep roasted coffee notes and a touch of bitterness. After the dough rests for 20 minutes, it's stretched and folded around chopped semisweet chocolate, which ensures the chocolate is surrounded by dough, preventing it from migrating to the exterior of the loaf where it would burn while baking. The dough is stretched on a moistened surface rather than a floured one, as the flour would leave white streaks in the dark dough.

DAY 1

MAKE THE PREFERMENT: The evening before you want to bake, in a large bowl, combine the sourdough culture, flour, and water and mix until no dry patches of flour remain, then knead in the bowl by hand until smooth. Cover and let stand at room temperature overnight, 12 to 16 hours.

DAY 2

MAKE THE DOUGH: Add the warm water to the preferment, then squeeze the preferment through your fingers to break it up. Next, holding your hand in a clawlike position, vigorously mix the preferment into the water until well combined. The mixture will look like lumpy pancake batter. Add the bread flour, whole wheat flour, cocoa, and salt and mix well until no dry spots remain (see Mixing, page 20).

Bulk fermentation or the "first rise" (see page 25) will take 3 to 3½ hours. During this time you'll attend to the dough three times (directions follow), folding the dough every 20 minutes for the first hour, then folding in the chocolate and letting the dough rest for an hour. You'll then fold the dough once more before it rests, covered and undisturbed, for the final 1 to 1½ hours.

Recipe continues

BULK FERMENT THE DOUGH: Once you've mixed the dough, cover and let rest for 20 minutes. Using a wet hand, perform 8 to 12 bowl folds (see Bowl Fold, page 30) until the dough resists stretching. Round out the dough by cupping your hand and applying pressure toward the bottom of the dough, forcing it into the bottom and side of the bowl to create tension. Cover and let rest for 20 minutes.

Perform a second set of bowl folds until the dough resists stretching, round out the dough, then cover and let rest for 20 minutes.

Moisten a 20-inch square area of your work surface by dipping your hand in water and spreading it across the surface. Use a plastic bowl scraper to ease the dough onto the moistened area and then stretch and pat it into a 16-inch square. Evenly sprinkle the chips or chopped chocolate over the dough.

Fold the dough like a business letter by first folding the left side toward the right, then the right side over the left so you have a rectangle that's about 16 × 4 inches with a short side facing you. Beginning at the top, roll up the dough; when you reach the end, pinch the seam and roll the log back and forth to develop some surface tension. Return the dough to the bowl and let rise, covered, for 1 hour. Uncover, perform 2 to 3 coil folds (see Coil Fold, page 31) until the dough resists stretching, then cover and let the dough rest until it is noticeably risen and marshmallowy, 1 to 1½ hours.

DIVIDE AND PRESHAPE THE DOUGH: Lightly flour a work surface, then use a plastic bowl scraper to ease the dough onto the work surface. With a bench knife, divide the dough into 2 equal portions (each about 800 grams). Gently preshape the dough into rounds (see Preshaping, page 32), then place it seam side down on the work surface, cover, and let rest for 20 minutes.

Heavily dust two 9 × 3-inch round or oval proofing baskets with flour.

SHAPE THE DOUGH AND LET IT RISE: Shape the dough into boules or bâtards (see Shaping, page 34) and transfer to the proofing baskets, seam side up. Cover and let rest at room temperature for 1 to 1½ hours, then transfer to the refrigerator and refrigerate overnight. At the end of this slow rise the dough should feel light and marshmallowy and when pressed with a floured finger, a small impression remains (see Proofing, page 44).

DAY 3

TO BAKE ON A BAKING STONE OR STEEL:

PREHEAT: Arrange racks in the center and bottom third of the oven and preheat the oven to 475°F with a baking stone or steel on the center rack and an empty cast-iron skillet (or a cake pan full of lava rocks) on the lower rack. If possible, adjust the stone and pan so that the skillet isn't directly under the stone, making it easier for steam to reach the baking bread.

Turn each loaf out of its proofing basket onto a sheet of parchment paper. Tuck in or remove any pieces of chocolate that are visible on the surface of the dough; otherwise, they might burn. Use a baker's lame or razor blade to score the tops of the loaves (see Scoring, page 46).

BAKE: Using a baker's peel or an inverted baking sheet to aid you, transfer each loaf (still on the parchment) into the oven, placing them on the stone or steel side by side, and pour about 227 grams (1 cup) of warm water into the skillet. Steam will billow from the pan upward to envelop the bread; be sure to wear good oven mitts to shield your hands and arms. Quickly close the oven door to trap the steam. Bake the loaf for 25 minutes, then reduce the oven temperature to 450°F and continue baking until the loaves are deeply browned, the crust is firm, and the internal temperature registers 210°F, 15 to 20 minutes longer.

Remove from the oven and let cool completely on a wire rack before slicing. (For storage information, see Storing Bread, page 123.)

TO BAKE IN A COVERED BAKER:

PREHEAT: Arrange a rack in the lower third of the oven and preheat the oven to 475°F, with the lidded baker set on the rack. Allow the oven and baker to preheat for about 1 hour to ensure both are thoroughly heated.

Turn one loaf out of its proofing basket onto a 9-inch round of parchment paper with a sling (see Transferring a Loaf to a Covered Baker, page 203). Keep the second loaf refrigerated while you bake the first. Tuck in or remove any pieces of chocolate that are visible on the surface of the dough; otherwise, they might burn. Use a baker's lame or razor blade to score the top of the loaf (see Scoring, page 46).

BAKE: Remove the lidded baker from the oven, uncover, and, using the parchment paper as a sling, carefully lower one loaf into the pan. Place the lid on the baker, return to the oven, and bake the loaf for 25 minutes.

Uncover, reduce the oven temperature to 450°F, and continue baking until the loaves are deeply browned and the crust is firm, 15 to 20 minutes longer.

Remove the pan from the oven, carefully lift out the loaf, and transfer to a wire rack to cool completely before slicing. (For storage information, see Storing Bread, page 123.) Return the covered baker to the oven and let preheat for 30 minutes, then score and bake the second loaf as directed above.

PECAN, CRANBERRY, AND RAISIN COURONNE

SOAKER	MIX		BULK FERMENTATION	PRE-SHAPE	SHAPE	2ND RISE	BAKE
	15 MIN	5 MIN	2–2½ HOURS	20 MIN	10 MIN	1 HOUR–1 HOUR 15 MIN	30–35 MIN

MAKE THE PREFERMENT (12–16 HOURS BEFORE)

·········· TIME: ABOUT 21 HOURS ··········

MAKES 2 LOAVES

PREFERMENT

23 grams (scant 2 tablespoons) sourdough culture (see page 187)

231 grams (2 cups plus 1 tablespoon) whole wheat flour

150 grams (½ cup plus 3 tablespoons) cold water (55°F to 60°F)

SOAKER

115 grams (1 cup plus 3 tablespoons) whole pecans

81 grams (¾ cup) dried cranberries

81 grams (½ cup plus 1 tablespoon) golden raisins

46 grams (generous 3 tablespoons) hot water (120°F)

DOUGH

228 grams (1 cup) warm water (see Temperature, page 25)

231 grams (1¾ cups plus 3 tablespoons) unbleached all-purpose flour

12 grams (2 teaspoons) fine salt

3 grams (1 teaspoon) instant yeast

Whole wheat flour, for dusting

This bread, loaded with fruit and nuts, is the perfect accompaniment to cheese, but is also wonderful sliced and buttered. The dough starts with a stiff whole-grain preferment, which gives the finished bread a pleasant floral aroma that complements the dried fruit. Because of the quantity of inclusions, this bread is not a high riser, but what it lacks in loft it makes up for in hearty flavor. We use a combination of dried cranberries, golden raisins, and pecans, which lend a buttery sweetness, but you can vary the dried fruit and nuts to suit your taste. Because of the shape of the loaves (the name *couronne*, which translates as "crown," refers to the curved shape), these can only be baked on a baking stone or steel, not in a covered baker.

DAY 1

MAKE THE PREFERMENT: The evening before you want to bake, in a large bowl, combine the sourdough culture, flour, and water and mix, then knead in the bowl by hand until a stiff, cohesive dough forms. Cover and let stand at room temperature overnight, 12 to 16 hours.

DAY 2

MAKE THE SOAKER: Preheat the oven to 350°F.

Spread the pecans on a rimmed baking sheet in an even layer. Bake until the nuts are lightly browned and fragrant, 8 to 10 minutes. Let cool and coarsely chop. In a medium bowl, combine the pecans, cranberries, and raisins and pour the hot water over. Let stand at room temperature while you prepare the dough.

MAKE THE DOUGH: Add the warm water to the preferment, then squeeze the mixture between your fingers to break it up. Holding your

Recipe continues

hand in a clawlike position, mix the preferment into the water until well combined. The mixture will look like lumpy pancake batter and be somewhat foamy. Add the flour, salt, and yeast and mix well until no dry spots remain (see Mixing, page 20).

Bulk fermentation or the "first rise" (see page 25) will take 2 to 2½ hours. During this time, you'll attend to the dough four times (directions follow), folding the dough every 15 minutes for the first hour. Then the dough will rest, covered and undisturbed, for the final 1 to 1½ hours.

BULK FERMENT THE DOUGH: Once you've mixed the dough, cover and let rest for 15 minutes. Using a wet hand, perform 8 to 12 bowl folds (see Bowl Fold, page 30) until the dough resists stretching. Round out the dough by cupping your hand and applying pressure toward the bottom of the dough, forcing it into the bottom and side of the bowl to create tension. Cover and let rest for another 15 minutes.

Using a wet hand, press indentations all over the dough and add the soaked nuts and fruit, plus any remaining soaking liquid, then perform 6 to 8 bowl folds until the dough resists stretching. Round out the dough again, cover, and let rest for 15 minutes. Perform a third set of bowl folds until the dough resists stretching, round out the dough, cover, and let rest for 15 minutes before performing the fourth and final set of bowl folds until the dough resists stretching. Cover and let the dough rest until the dough is noticeably puffy and feels marshmallowy, 1 to 1½ hours.

DIVIDE THE DOUGH: Lightly flour a work surface with whole wheat flour, then use a plastic bowl scraper to ease the dough out of the bowl onto the work surface. Using a bench knife or a knife, divide the dough into 2 equal portions (each about 600 grams).

SHAPE THE DOUGH AND LET IT RISE: Working with one piece of dough at a time, gently pat the dough

into a flat 9 × 5-inch rectangle to remove any large bubbles. Fold the short sides of the dough toward the center, gently patting to adhere. Starting from the top, gently roll the dough into a tube 6 to 7 inches long. Repeat with the second piece of dough. Place seam side down on the work surface, then cover and let rest for 15 minutes.

With the seam side down, flatten each piece of dough into a rectangle, then shape (1) as baguettes (see Shaping, page 34). Sift a light dusting of whole wheat flour over the loaf, then score a vertical cut in the middle of the loaf with a baker's lame or razor blade (2). Holding the lame at a 45-degree angle to the original vertical slash, score slashes along the entire rest of the loaf (3, 4, 5), about 1 inch apart (see Scoring, page 46). Repeat with the second piece of dough.

Curve the loaves into a horseshoe shape (6), then place side by side on a piece of parchment paper. Cover and let rise at room temperature until the bread feels light and puffy (see Proofing, page 44), 1 hour to 1 hour 15 minutes (it may not have gained much volume; this is normal).

Toward the end of the rising time, arrange racks in the center and bottom third of the oven and preheat the oven to 450°F with a baking stone or steel on the center rack and an empty cast-iron skillet (or a cake pan filled with lava rocks) on the lower rack. If possible, adjust the stone and pan so that the skillet isn't directly under the stone, making it easier for steam to reach the baking bread (see Steaming, page 50).

BAKE: Using a baker's peel or an inverted baking sheet to aid you, transfer the bread (still on the parchment) onto the stone or steel and pour about 227 grams (1 cup) of warm water into the empty cast-iron skillet. Steam will billow from the pan upward to envelop the bread; be sure to wear good oven mitts to shield your hands and arms. Quickly close the oven door to trap the steam. Bake the bread until the crust is deeply browned and firm, 30 to 35 minutes.

Remove the loaves from the oven and transfer to a rack to cool completely before slicing. (For storage information, see Storing Bread, page 123.)

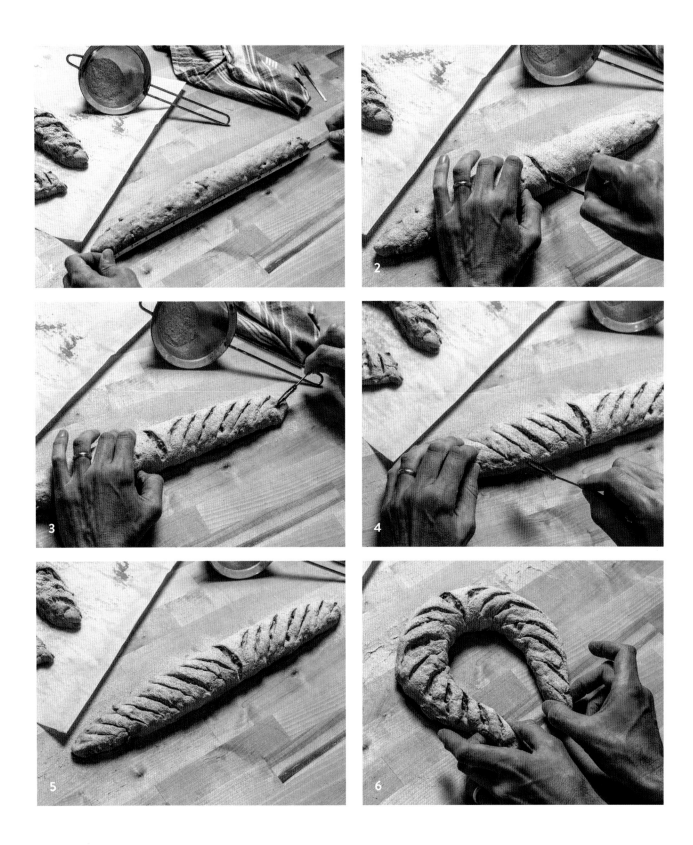

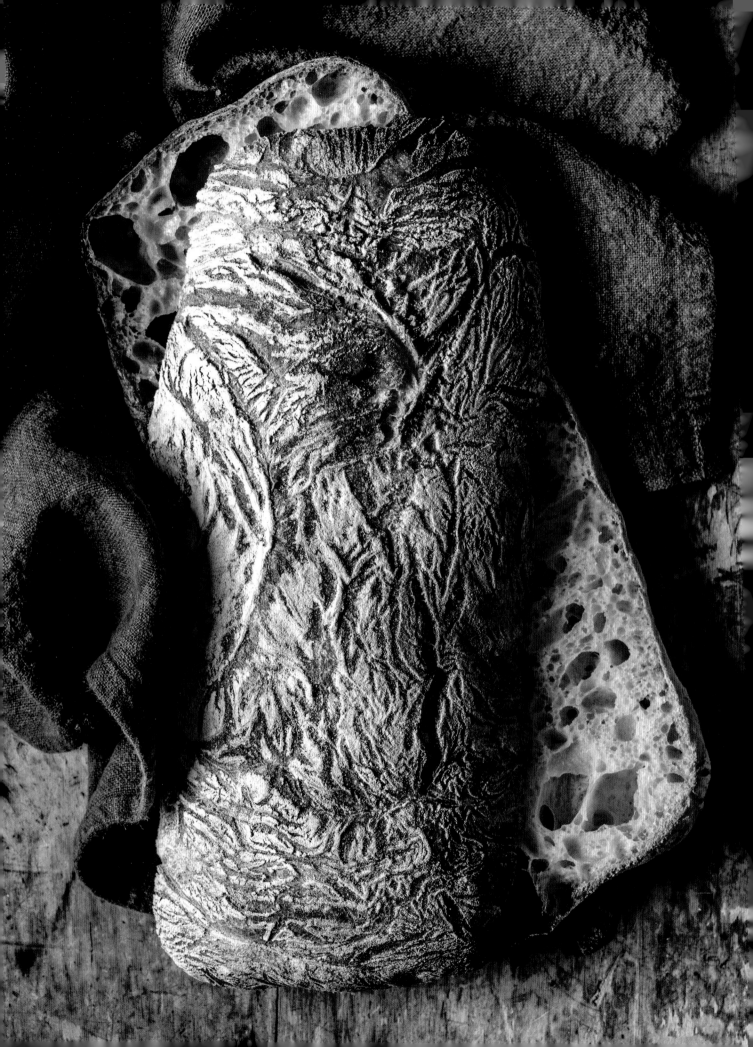

CIABATTA

MIX	BULK FERMENTATION	SHAPE	2ND RISE	BAKE
5 MIN	2–2½ HOURS	5 MIN	45–60 MIN	38–50 MIN

MAKE THE PREFERMENT (12–16 HOURS BEFORE)

············· TIME: ABOUT 21 HOURS ·············

MAKES 2 LOAVES

PREFERMENT

230 grams (1¾ cups plus 3 tablespoons) unbleached all-purpose flour

0.2 gram (pinch) instant yeast

129 grams (½ cup plus 1 tablespoon) cold water (55°F to 60°F)

DOUGH

397 grams (1¾ cups) warm water (see Temperature, page 25)

428 grams (3½ cups plus 2 tablespoons) unbleached all-purpose flour, plus more for dusting

13 grams (2⅛ teaspoons) fine salt

2 grams (generous ½ teaspoon) instant yeast

Ciabatta is made with a stiff, low-hydration preferment called a biga, which delicately scents the crumb with floral notes. And what a crumb it is! Wide open and airy, it's a beautiful contrast to the loaf's thick, crisp crust. Because this is a high-hydration dough (80%), it's very slack, making it a bit trickier to work with; don't be discouraged if it's not perfect on your first try, as it will still taste great (for more information, see Hydration, page 54). Practice makes better!

Generously coating the work surface (and the loaf) with flour will help prevent sticking; when you go to move the proofed loaves, use your hands like paddles, with all your fingers pressed together and hands held flat, moving quickly and decisively. Like baguettes, ciabatta are best the day they're made, and are just the right size and shape for oversize party sandwiches you can tote to the beach or on a picnic. For smaller rolls, see Ciabatta Rolls (page 257).

DAY 1

MAKE THE PREFERMENT: The evening before you want to bake, in a large bowl, combine the flour, yeast, and water and mix to form a dry, shaggy dough. The mixture will look like dry cheese curds and will not be cohesive. Transfer the dough to an unfloured surface and knead until no dry patches of flour remain and a very stiff, cohesive dough forms. Although the surface of the dough may not be smooth, there should not be any lumps remaining in the dough itself. Return to the bowl, cover, and let stand at room temperature overnight, 12 to 16 hours.

DAY 2

MAKE THE DOUGH: Add the warm water to the preferment, then squeeze the preferment through your fingers to break it up. Next, holding your hand in a clawlike position, vigorously mix the preferment into the water as best you can. The mixture will be very thin and slightly foamy

Recipe continues

with some pieces of preferment still visible. Add the flour, salt, and yeast and mix well with the handle of a wooden spoon until no dry spots remain (see Mixing, page 20).

Bulk fermentation or the "first rise" (see page 25) will take 2 to 2½ hours. During this time you'll attend to the dough three times (directions follow), folding the dough every 20 minutes for the first hour. Then the dough will rest, covered and undisturbed, for the final 1 to 1½ hours.

BULK FERMENT THE DOUGH: Once you've mixed the dough, cover and let rest for 20 minutes. Using a wet hand, perform 8 to 12 bowl folds (see Bowl Fold, page 30) or until the dough shows some resistance. Round out the dough by cupping your hand and applying pressure toward the bottom of the dough, forcing it into the bottom and side of the bowl to create tension. Cover and let rest for 20 minutes.

Uncover and perform 6 to 8 bowl folds, or until the dough shows slightly more resistance than it did after the first round of folding. Round out the dough and turn it seam side down, then cover and let rest for another 20 minutes.

Using a wet hand, work around the outside edge of the dough to release it from the bowl. Perform 2 to 3 coil folds (see Coil Fold, page 31), or until the dough resists being stretched. Round out the dough, cover, and let rest at room temperature until the dough is very puffy and some larger bubbles are visible, 1 to 1½ hours.

DIVIDE AND SHAPE THE DOUGH AND LET IT RISE: Generously flour a work surface, then generously dust the top of the dough with flour. Use a plastic bowl scraper to ease the dough out of the bowl onto the work surface. Dust the top of the dough with additional flour, then shape it into a 10-inch square by stretching and pushing the dough, working gently so you don't deflate the dough; those air bubbles are key to ciabatta's texture. Using a bench knife or a knife,

cut the dough in half to form two rectangles, each about 5 × 10 inches and 600 grams. Gently square off each rectangle.

Generously dust a couche or large kitchen towel with flour and set nearby. Generously flour your hands. Using your hands like paddles, with your fingers pressed together and hands flattened, carefully work your hands under the ends of one rectangle of dough to support it. Quickly and decisively lift the loaf and move it to the floured couche or towel. Repeat with the second loaf, placing it alongside the first but spaced several inches apart. Lightly cover with a floured kitchen towel (floured side against the bread) or overturned plastic box (do not cover with plastic wrap, because it will stick to the dough) and let rise until the loaves are puffy and large bubbles appear (see Proofing, page 44), 45 to 60 minutes. Depending on the humidity level where you're baking, the loaves may form a slight dry crust on top during this time; this is normal.

Meanwhile, arrange racks in the center and bottom third of the oven and preheat the oven to 500°F with a baking stone or steel placed on the center rack and an empty cast-iron skillet (or a cake pan filled with lava rocks) on the lower rack. If possible, adjust the stone and pan so that the skillet isn't directly under the stone, making it easier for steam to reach the baking bread (see Steaming, page 50).

BAKE: Gently invert each loaf onto a sheet of parchment paper by working your lightly floured hands underneath each loaf, then rolling them over onto the parchment. Use the sides of your hands to square up the loaves as necessary. Using a baker's peel or an inverted baking sheet to aid you, transfer the loaves (still on the parchment) into the oven, placing them on the stone or steel side by side, then pour about 227 grams (1 cup) of warm water into the skillet. Steam will billow from the pan upward to envelop the bread; be sure to wear good oven mitts to shield your hands and arms. Quickly close the oven door to trap the steam. Bake until deeply colored, 28 to 35 minutes. Turn the oven off, crack the oven door open, and leave the ciabatta in the oven for an additional 10 to 15 minutes. The loaves should feel light for their size.

Transfer to a rack to cool completely. Because of its crust-to-crumb ratio, ciabatta dries out quickly, so it's best eaten the same day it's made, though leftover ciabatta can be toasted to restore its crust.

CIABATTA ROLLS

Make the ciabatta dough and bulk ferment as directed. When it comes time to divide, generously flour a work surface, and generously dust the top of the dough with flour. Use a plastic bowl scraper to ease the dough out of the bowl onto the work surface. Dust the top of the dough with additional flour, then shape it into a 10-inch square.

TO SHAPE DINNER ROLLS:
Use a bench knife to score the square of dough into a grid of 16—4 in one direction and 4 in the other—then cut the dough into 4 strips vertically along the score marks, slightly separating the strips from each other as you go to prevent them from sticking back together. Then cut each strip horizontally into 4 pieces, again slightly separating them as you go. Each piece should be about 2½ × 2½ inches.

TO SHAPE PANINO-STYLE ROLLS:
Use a bench knife to score the square of dough into a grid of 6—3 in one direction and 2 in the other. Using a bench knife or sharp knife, cut the dough into 3 strips vertically along the score marks, slightly separating the strips from each other as you go to prevent them from sticking back together. Then cut each strip horizontally in half to form the rectangular rolls, again slightly separating them as you go. Each piece should be about 5 × 3¼ inches.

PROOF THE ROLLS: Generously dust a couche or lint-free kitchen towels with flour. Flour your hands. Using your hands like paddles, with your fingers pressed together and hands flat, carefully work your hands under a roll to support it. Quickly lift it and transfer to the couche or towel. Repeat with the remaining rolls, placing them several inches apart. Lightly cover with another floured kitchen towel, floured side against the dough, and let rise until they are puffy and large bubbles appear (see Proofing, page 44), 45 to 60 minutes.

While the rolls are rising, arrange racks in the center and bottom third of the oven and preheat the oven to 500°F with a baking stone or steel placed on the center rack and an empty cast-iron skillet on the lower rack. If possible, adjust the stone and pan so that the skillet isn't directly under the stone, making it easier for steam to reach the baking bread (see Steaming, page 50).

Gently invert the rolls by working your hands underneath each roll, then rolling them onto a sheet of parchment paper. For **DINNER ROLLS**, evenly space 8 rolls per sheet of parchment. For **PANINO-STYLE ROLLS**, evenly space 3 rolls per sheet of parchment. Use the sides of your hands to gently square up the rolls as necessary.

BAKE: Bake as directed above (keeping the second batch of rolls covered while you wait for the first batch to bake) until the rolls are deep golden brown and feel light for their size, 15 to 20 minutes for **DINNER ROLLS** and 20 to 25 minutes for **PANINO-STYLE ROLLS**. Transfer to a rack to cool completely. Let the baking stone or steel reheat for 10 to 15 minutes before baking the second batch of rolls with steam as before.

BAGUETTES TWO WAYS

If we were to compare bread baking to hiking, baguettes would be Kilimanjaro, the peak that, as our skills expand, we dream of climbing. In other words, if you're new to bread baking, this might not be the recipe to kick off your journey. But if you've made several recipes already and have some experience with shaping bread (see page 34) and assessing proof (see page 44), making baguettes at home can be a worthy challenge with astounding results: crisp-crusted golden-brown loaves with an almost creamy crumb and deep nutty flavor.

We're including two recipes here, one for baguettes made with a poolish, and a second for baguettes made with a sourdough preferment (see Building to Bake: Preferments, page 193). While we've talked about the importance of steam for crusty hearth breads (see Steaming, page 50), in many other recipes we're also able to suggest the workaround of baking loaves in a covered baker, which traps the steam that naturally escapes from the bread as it bakes. However, because of a baguette's long dimensions, a covered baker isn't possible here, so this is one place where we feel that unless you have an electric oven (which holds steam better than a gas oven), you may not even want to try. Baguettes baked in a gas oven will still be very tasty, but they won't have the thin, crispy crust and open crumb that are the signature of a baguette.

BAGUETTES AU LEVAIN

SOURDOUGH BAGUETTES

MIX	BULK FERMENTATION	PRESHAPE	SHAPE	2ND RISE	CHILL	BAKE
5 MIN	2½–3 HOURS	40 MIN	10 MIN	45–60 MIN	10–15 MIN	25–30 MIN

MAKE THE PREFERMENT (12–16 HOURS BEFORE)

TIME: ABOUT 22 HOURS

MAKES 3 BAGUETTES

PREFERMENT

10 grams (scant 1 tablespoon) sourdough culture (see page 187)

102 grams (¾ cup plus 2 tablespoons) unbleached all-purpose flour

102 grams (¼ cup plus 3 tablespoons) cold water (55°F to 60°F)

DOUGH

269 grams (1 cup plus 3 tablespoons) warm water (see Temperature, page 25)

406 grams (3¼ cups plus 2 tablespoons) unbleached all-purpose flour, plus more for dusting

10 grams (1½ teaspoons) fine salt

1.4 grams (½ teaspoon) instant yeast

DAY 1

MAKE THE PREFERMENT: The evening before you want to bake, in a large bowl, combine the sourdough culture, flour, and water and mix until no dry patches of flour remain. Cover and let stand at room temperature overnight, 12 to 16 hours.

DAY 2

MAKE THE DOUGH: Add the warm water to the preferment, then squeeze the mixture between your fingers to break it up. Holding your hand in a clawlike position, vigorously mix the preferment into the water until well combined. The mixture will look like thin pancake batter. Add the flour, salt, and yeast and mix with the handle of a wooden spoon until no dry spots remain (see Mixing, page 20).

Bulk fermentation or the "first rise" (see page 25) will take 2½ to 3 hours. During that time you'll attend to the dough three times (directions follow), folding the dough every 20 minutes for the first hour. Then the dough will rest, covered and undisturbed, for the final 1½ to 2 hours.

BULK FERMENT THE DOUGH: Once you've mixed the dough, cover and let rest for 20 minutes. Using a wet hand, perform 8 to 12 bowl folds (see Bowl Fold, page 30) or until the dough resists stretching. Round out the dough by cupping your hand and applying pressure toward the bottom of the dough, forcing it into the bottom and side of the bowl to create tension. Cover and let rest for another 20 minutes. Using a wet hand, perform 6 to 8 bowl folds, or until the dough resists stretching. Round out the dough again, cover, and let the dough rest for 20 minutes. With wet hands, perform 2 to 3 coil folds (see Coil Fold, page 31) until the dough resists stretching. Round out the dough, cover, and let rest until the dough is very puffy with some medium-size bubbles visible across the top, 1½ to 2 hours.

DIVIDE AND PRESHAPE THE DOUGH: Lightly flour a work surface, then use a plastic bowl scraper to ease the dough out of the bowl and onto the work surface. With a bench knife, divide the dough into 3 equal portions (each about 300 grams). Gently preshape each piece of dough into a tube about 5 ½ to 6 inches long (see Preshaping, page 32) and place seam side down on the work surface. Cover and let rest until the dough feels more relaxed—softer and less taut—about 30 minutes.

SHAPE THE DOUGH AND LET IT RISE: Generously dust a baker's linen (couche) or clean kitchen towel with flour. Shape each piece of dough into a 16- to 17-inch-long baguette (see Shaping, page 34) and transfer to the prepared linen or towel, seam side up. Gently fold about 1 inch of the linen up and place it against each baguette to support and separate them. Cover and let rest at room temperature until the dough feels light and when pressed with a floured finger, a small impression remains (see Proofing, page 44), 45 minutes to 1 hour. The dough may dry out slightly and form a thin crust during this time; this is normal.

Meanwhile, arrange racks in the center and bottom third of the oven and preheat the oven to 475°F with a baking stone or steel on the center rack and a cast-iron skillet (or a cake pan filled with lava rocks) on the lower rack. If possible, adjust the stone and pan so that the skillet isn't directly under the stone, making it easier for steam to reach the baking bread (see Steaming, page 50).

Use a transfer peel (page 18) to gently roll the baguettes onto a sheet of parchment paper so that the seam sides face down, spacing them a few inches apart. Slide the parchment (with the loaves) onto an inverted baking sheet and refrigerate, uncovered, for 10 to 15 minutes. This will allow the dough to chill and dry out slightly, making scoring easier. Use a baker's lame or razor blade to score the tops of the loaves (see Scoring, page 46).

BAKE: Load the loaves (still on the parchment) into the oven, placing them on the stone, and pour about 227 grams (1 cup) of warm water into the skillet. Steam will billow from the pan upward to envelop the bread; be sure to wear good oven mitts to shield your hands and arms. Quickly close the oven door to trap the steam. Bake the loaves until the crust is firm and deep golden brown, 25 to 30 minutes.

Remove from the oven and let cool on a wire rack. Baguettes are best eaten the day they are baked.

SHAPE A
BAGUETTE

YEASTED BAGUETTES

MIX	BULK FERMENTATION		PRESHAPE	SHAPE	2ND RISE	CHILL	BAKE
5 MIN	2½–3 HOURS		40 MIN	10 MIN	45–60 MIN	10–15 MIN	22–25 MIN

MAKE THE PREFERMENT (12–16 HOURS BEFORE)

TIME: ABOUT 22 HOURS

MAKES 3 BAGUETTES

PREFERMENT

101 grams (¾ cup plus 4½ teaspoons) unbleached all-purpose flour

0.5 gram (generous pinch) instant yeast

101 grams (¼ cup plus 3 tablespoons) cold water (55°F to 60°F)

DOUGH

282 grams (1¼ cups) warm water (see Temperature, page 25)

403 grams (3¼ cups plus 2 tablespoons) unbleached all-purpose flour, plus more for dusting

10 grams (generous 1½ teaspoons) fine salt

2 grams (generous ½ teaspoon) instant yeast

DAY 1

MAKE THE PREFERMENT: The evening before you want to bake, in a large bowl, combine the flour, yeast, and water and mix until no dry patches of flour remain. Cover and let stand at room temperature overnight, 12 to 16 hours.

DAY 2

MAKE THE DOUGH: Add the warm water to the preferment, then squeeze the preferment through your fingers to break it up. Next, holding your hand in a clawlike position, vigorously mix the preferment into the water until well combined. The mixture will be very thin and slightly foamy, with some pieces of preferment still visible (see photo on page 24). Add the flour, salt, and yeast and mix well with the handle of a wooden spoon until no dry spots remain (see Mixing, page 20).

Bulk fermentation or the "first rise" (see page 25) will take 2½ to 3 hours. During that time you'll attend to the dough three times (directions follow), folding the dough every 20 minutes for the first hour. Then the dough will rest, covered and undisturbed, for the final 1½ to 2 hours.

BULK FERMENT THE DOUGH: Once you've mixed the dough, cover and let rest for 20 minutes. Using a wet hand, perform 8 to 12 bowl folds (see Bowl Fold, page 30) or until the dough resists stretching. Cover and let rest for another 20 minutes. Using a wet hand, perform another set of 6 to 8 bowl folds, or until the dough resists stretching. Round out the dough, cover, and let the dough rest for 20 minutes. With wet hands, perform 2 to 3 coil folds (see Coil Fold, page 31) until the dough resists stretching. Cover and let rest until the dough is very puffy and marshmallowy, 1½ to 2 hours.

DIVIDE AND PRESHAPE THE DOUGH: Lightly flour a work surface, then use a plastic bowl scraper to gently ease the dough out of the bowl and onto the work surface. With a bench knife, divide the dough into 3 equal portions (each about 300 grams). Gently preshape each piece of dough into a 5½- to 6-inch tube (see Preshaping, page 32) and place seam side down on the work surface. Cover and let rest until the dough feels softer and less taut, about 30 minutes.

SHAPE THE DOUGH AND LET IT RISE: Generously dust a baker's linen (couche) or clean kitchen towel with flour. Shape each piece of dough into a 16- to 17-inch-long baguette (see Shaping, page 34) and transfer to the prepared linen or towel, seam side down. Gently fold about 1 inch of the linen up and place it against each baguette to support and separate them. Cover and let rest at room temperature until the dough feels light and marshmallowy and when pressed with a floured finger, a small impression remains (see Proofing, page 44), 45 minutes to 1 hour. The dough may dry out slightly and form a thin crust during this time; this is normal.

Meanwhile, arrange racks in the center and bottom third of the oven and preheat the oven to 475°F with a baking stone or steel on the middle rack and an empty cast-iron skillet (or a cake pan filled with lava rocks) on the lower rack. If possible, adjust the stone and pan so that the skillet isn't directly under the stone, making it easier for steam to reach the baking bread (see Steaming, page 50).

Use a transfer peel (page 18) to gently roll the baguettes onto a sheet of parchment paper so that the seam sides face down and space them a few inches apart. Slide the parchment (with the loaves) onto an inverted baking sheet and refrigerate, uncovered, for 10 to 15 minutes. This will allow the dough to chill and dry out slightly, making scoring easier. Use a baker's lame or razor blade to score the tops of the loaves (see Scoring, page 46).

BAKE: Using a baker's peel or an inverted baking sheet, transfer the loaves (still on the parchment) into the oven, placing them on the baking stone or steel, and pour about 227 grams (1 cup) of warm water into the skillet. Steam will billow from the pan upward to envelop the bread; be sure to wear good oven mitts to shield your hands and arms. Quickly close the oven door to trap the steam. Bake the loaves until the crust is firm and deep golden brown, 22 to 25 minutes.

Remove from the oven and let cool on a wire rack. Baguettes are best eaten the day they are baked.

SHAPE A
BAGUETTE

BLACK BREAD

MAKES 1 LARGE LOAF

PREFERMENT

50 grams (¼ cup) sourdough culture (see page 187)

227 grams (2 cups plus 2 tablespoons) whole rye flour

227 grams (1 cup) cold black coffee (55°F to 60°F)

¼ large yellow onion (64 grams), chopped (½ cup)

DOUGH

18 grams (2 tablespoons) caraway seeds

85 grams (¼ cup) molasses (not blackstrap)

25 grams (2 tablespoons) olive oil

12 grams (2 teaspoons) fine salt

200 grams (¾ cup plus 2 tablespoons) warm water (see Temperature, page 25)

480 grams (4 cups) unbleached all-purpose flour, plus more for dusting

This is an assertively flavored bread with a nice acidity and a deep chocolate-brown crumb. While the coffee in the preferment does contribute flavor, it also plays another role: Because it's slightly acidic, it strengthens the gluten network in this bread, making it easy to knead and shape.

DAY 1

MAKE THE PREFERMENT: The evening before you want to bake, in a large bowl, combine the sourdough culture, rye flour, coffee, and onion. Mix until no dry patches of flour remain, then cover and let stand at room temperature overnight, 12 to 16 hours.

DAY 2

MAKE THE DOUGH: In a small dry skillet, toast the caraway seeds over medium heat, swirling the pan to ensure even heat distribution, until the seeds are a shade darker and fragrant, 3 to 5 minutes. Transfer the seeds to a bowl to cool and set aside.

Add the molasses, oil, salt, toasted caraway seeds, and water to the preferment. Stir in the flour and mix until a cohesive, slightly sticky dough forms. Cover and let rest for 10 minutes. Turn the dough out onto a lightly floured surface and knead until smooth and springy, about 5 minutes, adding just enough additional flour to keep the dough from sticking to your hands and work surface. Use a bench knife to scrape up any dough that sticks to your work surface; this will reduce the amount of extra flour you need to add.

SHAPE THE DOUGH AND LET IT RISE: Generously dust a 9 × 3-inch round proofing basket with flour. After kneading the dough will already be in a round shape. Gently tighten the surface of the boule (see Shaping, page 34). Place the dough seam side up in the proofing basket. Cover and let rise until the dough feels light and marshmallowy and a small impression remains when pressed with a floured finger (see Proofing, page 44), 2 to 3 hours.

Recipe continues

TO BAKE ON A BAKING STONE OR STEEL:

PREHEAT: An hour before the loaf is finished rising, arrange racks in the center and bottom third of the oven and preheat the oven to 425°F with a baking stone or steel on the center rack and an empty cast-iron skillet (or a cake pan filled with lava rocks) on the lower rack. If possible, adjust the stone and pan so that the skillet isn't directly under the stone, making it easier for steam to reach the baking bread (see Steaming, page 50).

Turn the loaf out of its proofing basket onto a sheet of parchment paper. Use a baker's lame or razor blade to score the top of the loaf (see Scoring, page 46).

BAKE: Using a baker's peel or an inverted baking sheet to aid you, transfer the loaf (still on the parchment) into the oven, placing it on the stone or steel and pour about 227 grams (1 cup) of warm water into the skillet. Steam will billow from the pan upward to envelop the bread; be sure to wear good oven mitts to shield your hands and arms. Quickly close the oven door to trap the steam. Bake the loaf until deeply browned, the crust is firm, and the internal temperature is at least 210°F, 45 to 55 minutes.

Remove from the oven and transfer to a rack to cool completely before slicing. (For storage information, see Storing Bread, page 123.)

TO BAKE IN A COVERED BAKER:

PREHEAT: Arrange a rack in the lower third of the oven and preheat the oven to 425°F, with a lidded baker set on the rack. Allow the oven and baker to preheat for about 1 hour to ensure they are thoroughly heated.

Turn the loaf out of its proofing basket onto a 9-inch round of parchment paper with a sling (see Transferring a Loaf to a Covered Baker, page 203). Use a baker's lame or razor blade to score the top of the loaf (see Scoring, page 46).

BAKE: Remove the lidded baker from the oven, uncover, and, using the parchment paper as a sling, carefully lower the loaf into the pan, taking care not to burn your knuckles. Place the lid on the baker, return to the oven, and bake the loaf for 25 minutes.

Uncover and continue baking until the loaf is deeply browned, the crust is firm, and the internal temperature is at least 210°F, 20 to 30 minutes more.

Remove the pan from the oven, carefully lift out the loaf, and transfer to a wire rack to cool completely before slicing. (For storage information, see Storing Bread, page 123.)

WALNUT FICELLES

TOAST WALNUTS	MIX	BULK FERMENTATION	PRESHAPE	SHAPE	2ND RISE	BAKE
15 MIN	5 MIN	2 HOURS	20 MIN	10 MIN	1 HOUR	20-25 MIN

TIME: ABOUT 4 HOURS

MAKES THREE FICELLES

141 grams (1 cup plus 2 tablespoons) whole walnuts

353 grams (2¾ cups plus 3 tablespoons) unbleached bread flour, plus more for dusting

118 grams (1 cup plus 2 teaspoons) whole wheat flour, plus more for dusting

11 grams (scant 2 teaspoons) fine salt

5 grams (scant 2 teaspoons) instant yeast

282 grams (1¼ cups) warm water (see Temperature, page 25)

141 grams (½ cup plus 2 tablespoons) dry red wine (or water), at room temperature

Thinner than a baguette but with a similar crust-to-crumb ratio, a *ficelle* ("string" in French) is another classic bread shape. For our version, we hydrate the dough with a combination of water and red wine, which tints the loaf a beautiful lilac hue, and load it with toasted walnuts. Those inclusions make it a bread that is particularly well suited to a cheese board, whether you tear off pieces or thinly slice the bread and toast it.

TOAST THE WALNUTS: Preheat the oven to 350°F. Line a rimmed baking sheet with parchment paper.

Roughly chop the walnuts into marble-size pieces and arrange on the lined baking sheet. Bake for 5 minutes, then toss them with a spatula to redistribute on the pan and continue to bake until fragrant and lightly browned, 5 to 7 minutes more. Remove from the oven and allow to cool to room temperature.

MAKE THE DOUGH: In a large bowl, combine the bread flour, whole wheat flour, salt, yeast, water, and red wine and mix well until no dry spots remain (see Mixing, page 20).

Bulk fermentation or the "first rise" (see page 25) will take 2 hours. During that time you'll attend to the dough three times (directions follow), folding the dough every 20 minutes for the first hour. Then the dough will rest, covered and undisturbed, for the final hour.

BULK FERMENT THE DOUGH: Once you've mixed the dough, sprinkle the walnuts on top, cover, and let rest 20 minutes. Using wet hands, incorporate the walnuts by squeezing and pinching them into the dough and gently kneading the mixture. Flip the dough so that the seam side is down, then round out the dough by cupping your hand and applying pressure toward the bottom of the dough, forcing it into the bottom and

Recipe continues

side of the bowl to create tension before covering and resting for another 20 minutes.

Using a wet hand, perform 6 to 8 bowl folds (see Bowl Fold, page 30) or until the dough resists stretching. Round out the dough, place it seam side down in the bowl, cover, and let rest for 20 minutes. With wet hands, perform 6 to 8 bowl folds or until the dough resists stretching. Round out the dough again, place it seam side down in the bowl, cover, and let stand until the dough is very puffy and marshmallowy, about 1 hour.

DIVIDE AND PRESHAPE THE DOUGH: Lightly dust a work surface with bread flour, then use a plastic bowl scraper to ease the dough out of the bowl and onto the work surface. Cut the dough into 3 equal portions (each about 350 grams). Preshape each piece into a tube (see Preshaping, page 32) and place seam side down on a lightly floured surface, spacing the pieces at least 2 inches apart. Cover and let rest for 15 minutes.

SHAPE THE BREAD AND LET IT RISE: Generously dust a baker's linen (couche) or clean kitchen towel with whole wheat flour. On a work surface lightly dusted with bread flour, shape each piece of dough into a 13- to 15-inch-long baguette with tapered ends (see Shaping, page 34) and transfer seam side up to the prepared linen or towel. Gently fold about 1 inch of the linen up and place it against each ficelle to support and separate them. Cover and let rest at room temperature until the dough feels light and marshmallowy and when pressed with a floured finger, a small impression remains (see Proofing, page 44), about 1 hour.

Toward the end of the rising time, arrange racks in the center and bottom third of the oven and preheat the oven to 475°F with a baking stone or steel on the center rack and an empty cast-iron skillet (or a cake pan filled with lava rocks) on the lower rack. If possible, adjust the stone and pan so that the skillet isn't directly under the stone, making it easier for steam to reach the baking bread (see Steaming, page 50).

Use a transfer peel (page 18) to gently roll each ficelle seam side down onto a sheet of parchment paper, spacing them a few inches apart. Use a baker's lame or razor blade to score the top of the loaves (see Scoring, page 46).

BAKE: Using a baker's peel or an inverted baking sheet to aid you, transfer the loaves (still on the parchment) into the oven, placing them on the stone or steel, and pour about 227 grams (1 cup) of warm water into the skillet. Steam will billow from the pan upward to envelop the loaves; be sure to wear good oven mitts to shield your hands and arms. Quickly close the oven door to trap the steam. Bake the loaves until the crusts are firm and lightly browned, 20 to 25 minutes.

Remove from oven and let cool completely on a rack before slicing. Because of their high crust-to-crumb ratio, ficelles are best eaten the day they are baked. (For storage information, see Storing Bread, page 123.)

SHAPE A
BAGUETTE

OLIVE-ROSEMARY FOUGASSE

MIX	BULK FERMENTATION	PRESHAPE AND REST	SHAPE	BAKE
5 MIN	2½ HOURS	20 MIN	20 MIN	18–20 MIN

TIME: ABOUT 4 HOURS

MAKES 2 LOAVES

DOUGH

241 grams (2 cups) unbleached all-purpose flour, plus more for dusting

60 grams (½ cup) whole wheat flour

7 grams (1⅛ teaspoons) fine salt

2 grams (generous ½ teaspoon) instant yeast

238 grams (1 cup plus 1 tablespoon) warm water (see Temperature, page 25)

9 grams (generous 2 teaspoons) olive oil

90 grams (½ cup plus 2 tablespoons) drained, pitted kalamata olives, roughly chopped

2 grams (1 teaspoon) finely chopped fresh rosemary

Semolina flour or yellow cornmeal, for dusting

TOPPING

25 grams (2 tablespoons) extra-virgin olive oil

2 grams (1 teaspoon) finely chopped fresh rosemary

Flaky sea salt, such as Maldon

This Provençal bread is irresistibly chewy, wonderfully aromatic, and, when warm from the oven, slicked with olive oil, and garnished with flaky salt, pretty hard to stop eating. Fougasse is typically shaped into a triangle and slashed as described below, which gives the bread the appearance of a stalk of wheat. This bread can be made in a single afternoon and is best eaten the same day it's made (it's so good, you won't need to be convinced).

MAKE THE DOUGH: In a large bowl, combine the all-purpose flour, whole wheat flour, salt, yeast, water, and oil, mixing until no dry spots remain (see Mixing, page 20).

Bulk fermentation or the "first rise" (see page 25) will take about 2½ hours. During that time you'll attend to it four times (directions follow), folding the dough every 15 minutes for the first 1 hour. Then the dough will rest, covered and undisturbed, for the final 1½ hours.

BULK FERMENT THE DOUGH: Once you've mixed the dough, cover and let rest for 15 minutes. Using a wet hand, perform 8 to 12 bowl folds (see Bowl Fold, page 30) or until the dough resists stretching. Round out the dough by cupping your hand and applying pressure toward the bottom of the dough, forcing it into the bottom and side of the bowl to create tension. Cover and let rest for another 15 minutes.

Using a wet hand, press indentations all over the dough. Push the olives and rosemary into the dough, then fold 6 to 8 times, or until the dough resists stretching. Round out the dough, cover, and let rest for 15 minutes. Perform a third set of bowl folds until the dough resists stretching, then round out the dough, cover, and let rest for 15 minutes before performing the fourth and final set of bowl folds, until the dough resists stretching. Cover and let rest until the dough is noticeably risen and feels marshmallowy, about 1½ hours.

Recipe continues

Arrange a rack in the center of the oven and preheat the oven to 475°F with a baking stone or steel on the rack.

DIVIDE AND PRESHAPE THE DOUGH: Lightly flour a work surface with semolina flour, then use a plastic bowl scraper to ease the dough out of the bowl onto the work surface. Using a bench knife or a knife, divide the dough into 2 equal portions (each about 325 grams). Gently pat each piece of dough to remove any large bubbles, then form into a very loose preshaped round (see Preshaping, page 32). Sprinkle the round with semolina, then place seam side down, cover, and let rest for 15 minutes.

SHAPE THE DOUGH: On a semolina-dusted work surface, gently pat and stretch each round of dough into a 5- to 6-inch triangle, then cover and let rest another 15 minutes. Lightly dust a sheet of parchment paper with semolina, then transfer the pieces of dough to the parchment, arranging them side by side with a few inches of space between them. Starting 1 inch from the top point of a triangle, use a metal spatula or sharp knife to cut down the midline, stopping 1 inch from the base of the triangle (1). Then make three 45-degree angle cuts on each side of the midline (2), spacing them about 1 inch apart (a 3-inch-wide metal spatula or the short edge of a plastic scraper works great for this). Gently stretch the triangle to open the cuts (3), then repeat with the other piece of dough (4).

BAKE: Using a baker's peel or an inverted baking sheet to aid you, transfer the loaves (still on the parchment) to the stone or steel and bake until deep golden brown, 18 to 20 minutes.

MEANWHILE, MAKE THE TOPPING: In a small bowl, stir together the olive oil and rosemary.

Remove the fougasse from the oven and, while the loaves are still hot, brush all over with the olive oil/rosemary mixture and sprinkle with flaky salt to taste. Transfer to a wire rack to cool slightly, then serve warm or at room temperature. Fougasse are best eaten the same day they are made.

PRESERVED LEMON AND OLIVE BREAD

MIX	BULK FERMENTATION	PRE-SHAPE	SHAPE	2ND RISE	BAKE
5 MIN	2 HOURS 20 MIN–2 HOURS 50 MIN	20 MIN	5 MIN	12–16 HOURS	45 MIN

MAKE THE PREFERMENT AND QUICK-PRESERVED LEMONS (12–16 HOURS BEFORE)

······· TIME: ABOUT 36 HOURS ·······

MAKES 2 LOAVES

QUICK-PRESERVED LEMONS

1 large lemon, cut into ¼-inch-thick slices

12 grams (1 tablespoon) sugar

6 grams (1 teaspoon) fine salt

PREFERMENT

29 grams (2 tablespoons) sourdough culture (see page 187)

289 grams (2¼ cups plus 2 tablespoons) unbleached all-purpose flour

173 grams (¾ cup) cold water (55°F to 60°F)

DOUGH

470 grams (2 cups plus 1 tablespoon) warm water (see Temperature, page 25)

371 grams (3 cups plus 1 tablespoon) unbleached all-purpose flour, plus more for dusting

165 grams (1¼ cups plus 3 tablespoons) whole wheat flour

13 grams (2⅛ teaspoons) fine salt

Ingredients continue

This bread gets incredible flavor and fragrance from the addition of preserved lemons, which are whole lemons that have been cured in salt and sugar until the peel softens and the flesh becomes syrupy, a process that can take up to a month. Here, we've distilled it down to a simple overnight cure, which gives you some of the character of traditional preserved lemons, including their bright acidity and brininess, in a fraction of the time. Alternatively, you can substitute an equal amount of store-bought preserved lemons. The combination of lemon and olives is a classic one that's showcased brilliantly in this bread.

DAY 1

MAKE THE QUICK-PRESERVED LEMONS: The day before you make the dough, in a small microwaveable bowl, combine the lemon slices, sugar, and salt and toss to combine. Microwave for 3 minutes. Stir, then let cool to room temperature. Cover and let stand at room temperature overnight. Alternatively, in a small saucepan, combine the lemon slices, sugar, and salt. Set aside, uncovered, to macerate until the lemons have given off some of their juice, about 10 minutes. Bring the mixture to a boil over medium heat, then continue to cook until the peels are softened and the liquid has reduced slightly, 3 to 5 minutes. Transfer the lemon slices and any remaining liquid to a nonreactive container and cool to room temperature. Cover and let stand at room temperature overnight, 12 to 16 hours.

MAKE THE PREFERMENT: The evening before you make the dough, in a large bowl, combine the sourdough culture, flour, and water and mix until no dry patches of flour remain. Knead in the bowl by hand until a stiff, smooth dough forms. Cover and let stand at room temperature overnight, 12 to 16 hours.

Recipe continues

231 grams (1½ cups plus 2 tablespoons) drained, pitted kalamata olives, coarsely chopped

58 grams (¼ cup plus 1 tablespoon) finely chopped quick-preserved lemons (recipe above)

DAY 2

MAKE THE DOUGH: Finely chop the lemons. Measure out 58 grams (¼ cup plus 1 tablespoon) and set aside for the dough. (Save the remainder to add to pastas, grain salads, salad dressings, or braises. It will keep for up to 1 week in the refrigerator.)

Add the warm water to the preferment, then squeeze the preferment through your fingers to break it up. Next, holding your hand in a clawlike position, vigorously mix the preferment into the water until well combined. The mixture will look like lumpy pancake batter. Add the all-purpose flour, whole wheat flour, and salt and mix well with the handle of a wooden spoon until no dry spots remain (see Mixing, page 20).

Bulk fermentation or the "first rise" (see page 25) will take 2 hours 20 minutes to 2 hours 50 minutes. During that time you'll attend to it four times (directions follow), folding the dough every 20 minutes for the first 1 hour 20 minutes. Then the dough will rest, covered and undisturbed, for the final 1 to 1½ hours.

BULK FERMENT THE DOUGH: Once you've mixed the dough, cover and let rest for 20 minutes. Using a wet hand, perform 8 to 12 bowl folds (see Bowl Fold, page 30) or until the dough resists stretching. Round out the dough by cupping your hand and applying pressure toward the bottom of the dough, forcing it into the bottom and side of the bowl to create tension. Cover and let rest for another 20 minutes.

Using a wet hand, press indentations into the dough. Add the olives and reserved quick-preserved lemon, then fold the dough 6 to 8 times or until it resists stretching. Round out the dough again, cover, and let rest for 20 minutes. Perform a third set of bowl folds, until the dough resists stretching, then round out the dough, cover, and let rest for 20 minutes before performing the fourth and final set of bowl folds, until the dough resists stretching. Cover and let the dough rest until it is very puffy and marshmallowy, 1 to 1½ hours.

DIVIDE AND PRESHAPE THE DOUGH: Lightly flour a work surface with all-purpose flour, then use a plastic bowl scraper to ease the dough out of the bowl and onto the work surface. With a bench knife or a knife, divide the dough into 2 equal portions (each about 900 grams). Gently preshape each piece of dough into a round (see Preshaping, page 32) and place seam side down on the work surface. Cover and let rest 15 minutes.

SHAPE THE DOUGH AND LET IT RISE: Generously dust two 9 × 3-inch round or oval proofing baskets with all-purpose flour. Shape each piece of dough into boules or bâtards (see Shaping, page 34) and transfer to the prepared proofing baskets, seam side up. Cover and let rest at room temperature for 1 hour, then transfer to the refrigerator and refrigerate overnight, 8 to 12 hours. At the end of this slow rise the dough will feel light, almost marshmallowy, and when pressed with a floured finger, a small impression remains (see Proofing, page 44).

DAY 3

TO BAKE ON A BAKING STONE OR STEEL:

PREHEAT: Arrange racks in the center and bottom third of the oven and preheat the oven to 475°F with a baking stone or steel on the center rack and an empty cast-iron skillet (or a cake pan filled with lava rocks) on the lower rack. If possible, adjust the stone and pan so that the skillet isn't directly under the stone, making it easier for steam to reach the baking bread (see Steaming, page 50).

Turn each loaf out of its proofing basket onto a sheet of parchment paper. Use a baker's lame or razor blade to score the tops of the loaves (see Scoring, page 46).

BAKE: Using a baker's peel or an inverted baking sheet to aid you, transfer the loaves (still on the parchment) into the oven, placing them on the stone or steel side by side, and pour about 227 grams (1 cup) of warm water into the skillet. Steam will billow from the pan upward to envelop the bread; be sure to wear good oven mitts to shield your hands and arms. Quickly close the oven door to trap the steam. After 25 minutes, reduce the oven temperature to 450°F. Continue baking until the loaves are deeply browned, the crust is firm, and the internal temperature registers 210°F, about 20 minutes more.

Remove from the oven and transfer to a wire rack to cool completely before slicing. (For storage information, see Storing Bread, page 123.)

TO BAKE IN A COVERED BAKER:

PREHEAT: Arrange a rack in the lower third of the oven and preheat the oven to 475°F, with the lidded baker set on the rack. Allow the oven and baker to preheat for about 1 hour to ensure they are thoroughly heated.

Turn one loaf out of its proofing basket onto a 9-inch round of parchment paper with a sling (see Transferring a Loaf to a Covered Baker, page 203). Keep the second loaf refrigerated while you bake the first. Use a baker's lame or razor blade to score the top of the loaf (see Scoring, page 46).

BAKE: Remove the lidded baker from the oven, uncover, and, using the parchment paper as a sling, carefully lower one loaf into the pan, taking care not to burn your knuckles. Place the lid on the baker, return to the oven, and bake for 25 minutes.

Uncover, reduce the oven temperature to 450°F, and continue baking until the loaf is deeply browned, the crust is firm, and the internal temperature registers 210°F, about 10 to 20 minutes more.

Remove the pan from the oven, then remove the bread from the pan and transfer to a wire rack to cool completely before slicing. (For storage information, see Storing Bread, page 123.) Return the covered baker to the oven and preheat for 30 minutes, then score and bake the second loaf as directed above.

PUMPKIN SEED LEVAIN

MIX	BULK FERMENTATION	PRESHAPE	SHAPE	2ND RISE	BAKE
40 MIN	2 HOURS	20 MIN	5 MIN	1–1¼ HOURS	35–40 MIN

PREPARE THE INCLUSIONS, SOAKER, AND PREFERMENT (12–16 HOURS BEFORE)

TIME: ABOUT 22 HOURS

MAKES 2 LOAVES

INCLUSIONS

350 grams (12 ounces) peeled, seeded butternut or acorn squash (see Note), cut into ¾-inch cubes (scant 2½ cups)

146 grams (1 cup plus 2 tablespoons) pumpkin seeds

SOAKER

37 grams (scant ¼ cup) yellow cornmeal

37 grams (2½ tablespoons) cold water

PREFERMENT

14 grams (1 tablespoon) sourdough culture (see page 187)

172 grams (1¼ cups plus 3 tablespoons) unbleached bread flour

15 grams (2 tablespoons) whole wheat flour, plus more for dusting

113 grams (½ cup) cold water (55°F to 60°F)

DOUGH

308 grams (1¼ cups plus 2 tablespoons) warm water (see Temperature, page 25)

This golden, toothsome loaf gets its color from roasted squash, cornmeal, and semolina flour and its nutty flavor thanks to toasted pumpkin seeds in the dough. If you want to simplify the recipe, you can purchase prepeeled and cut butternut squash at the grocery store. If you've roasted your squash ahead and are using it directly from the refrigerator, increase the temperature of the water you use in the dough to compensate (see Temperature, page 25). Because this dough is sticky, we recommend mixing in a stand mixer rather than by hand.

DAY 1

PREPARE THE INCLUSIONS: The evening before you want to bake, preheat the oven to 400°F. Line two baking sheets with parchment paper.

Spread the squash on one of the prepared pans in a single layer and roast until very tender and browned in spots, about 30 minutes. Remove from the oven and let cool; reduce the oven temperature to 350°F. Spread the pumpkin seeds on the second lined pan. Bake the seeds until fragrant and lightly browned, 8 to 10 minutes. Remove from the oven and set aside to cool, then cover and store at room temperature.

Once the squash is cool, cover and refrigerate.

MAKE THE SOAKER: In a small bowl, mix the cornmeal and water until no dry spots remain. The mixture will look like wet sand. Cover and let stand at room temperature overnight, 12 to 16 hours.

MAKE THE PREFERMENT: In a stand mixer bowl, combine the sourdough culture, bread flour, and whole wheat flour. Add the water and mix by hand to form a dry, shaggy dough. Transfer the dough to an unfloured surface, then knead until no dry patches of flour remain and a stiff, cohesive dough forms. Although the surface of the dough may not be

Ingredients continue

Recipe continues

464 grams (3¾ cups plus 2 tablespoons) unbleached all-purpose flour, plus more for dusting work surface

58 grams (¼ cup plus 2 tablespoons) semolina flour

15 grams (2½ teaspoons) fine salt

0.75 gram (¼ teaspoon) instant yeast

smooth, there should not be any dry lumps remaining in the dough itself. Return to the bowl, cover, and let stand at room temperature overnight, 12 to 16 hours.

DAY 2

MAKE THE DOUGH: Add the warm water, all-purpose flour, semolina flour, and reserved 146 grams (a generous ½ cup) roasted squash to the mixer bowl with the preferment. Save any extra roasted squash for another use. Using the dough hook attachment, mix on medium-low speed until no dry spots remain (see Mixing, page 20). Add the salt, yeast, and soaker on top of the dough, but do not mix them in. Cover the bowl and let rest for 30 minutes.

Mix the dough on medium-low speed to incorporate the salt, yeast, and soaker, 1 to 2 minutes. Increase the speed to medium and continue mixing until the dough cleans the sides of the bowl and is shiny and elastic, 5 to 8 minutes. Add the toasted pumpkin seeds and mix on medium-low speed until well combined, 1 to 2 minutes.

Bulk fermentation or the "first rise" (see page 25) will take about 2 hours. During that time you'll attend to the dough twice (directions follow), folding the dough every 40 minutes for the first 1 hour 20 minutes. Then the dough will rest, covered and undisturbed, for the final 40 minutes.

BULK FERMENT THE DOUGH: Once the pumpkin seeds are mixed in, cover the dough and let rest for 40 minutes. Using a wet hand, perform 8 to 12 bowl folds (see Bowl Fold, page 30) or until the dough resists being stretched. Round out the dough by cupping your hand and applying pressure toward the bottom of the dough, forcing it into the bottom and side of the bowl to create tension, then turn it seam side down, cover, and let rest for 40 minutes. Uncover and perform 6 to 8 more bowl folds, or until the dough resists being stretched. Use a wet hand to round out the dough and turn it seam side down, then cover and let rest for the final 40 minutes.

DIVIDE AND PRESHAPE THE DOUGH: Lightly flour a work surface, then use a plastic bowl scraper to ease the dough out of the bowl onto the work surface. Using a bench knife or a knife, divide the dough into 2 equal portions (each about 760 grams). Gently pat each piece of dough to remove any large bubbles, then preshape into rounds (see Preshaping, page 32) and place seam side down on the work surface. Cover and let rest for 15 minutes.

SHAPE THE DOUGH AND LET IT RISE: Generously dust two 9 × 3-inch round proofing baskets with whole wheat flour. Shape each piece of dough into a boule (see Shaping, page 34). Transfer the shaped dough, seam side up, to the baskets, then cover. Let rise until puffy and a small indentation remains when the dough is pressed with a lightly floured finger (see Proofing, page 44), 1 to 1½ hours.

TO BAKE ON A BAKING STONE OR STEEL:

PREHEAT: Toward the end of the rising time, arrange racks in the center and bottom third of the oven and preheat the oven to 475°F with a baking stone or steel on the center rack and an empty cast-iron skillet (or a cake pan filled with lava rocks) on the lower rack. If possible, adjust the stone and pan so that the skillet isn't directly under the stone, making it easier for steam to reach the baking bread (see Steaming, page 50).

Turn each loaf out of its proofing basket onto a sheet of parchment paper. Use a baker's lame or razor blade to score the tops of the loaves (see Scoring, page 46).

BAKE: Using a baker's peel or an inverted baking sheet, transfer the loaves (still on the parchment) into the oven, placing them on the stone or steel side by side, and pour about 227 grams (1 cup) of warm water into the skillet. Steam will billow from the pan upward to envelop the bread; be sure to wear good oven mitts to shield your hands and arms. Quickly close the oven door to trap the steam. Bake the loaves until the crust is deep golden brown and crisp and the internal temperature registers 210°F, 35 to 40 minutes.

Transfer to a rack and let cool completely before slicing. (For storage information, see Storing Bread, page 123.)

TO BAKE IN A COVERED BAKER:

PREHEAT: Arrange a rack in the lower third of the oven and preheat the oven to 475°F, with the lidded baker set on the rack. Allow the oven and baker to preheat for about 1 hour to ensure they are thoroughly heated.

Turn one loaf out of its proofing basket onto a 9-inch round of parchment paper with a sling (see Transferring a Loaf to a Covered Baker, page 203). Keep the second loaf refrigerated while you bake the first. Use a baker's lame or razor blade to score the top of the loaf (see Scoring, page 46).

BAKE: Remove the lidded baker from the oven, uncover, and, using the parchment paper sling, carefully lower one loaf into the pan. Place the lid on the baker, return to the oven, and bake for 20 minutes.

Uncover and continue baking until the loaf is golden brown, the crust is firm, and the internal temperature registers 210°F, 15 to 20 minutes longer.

Remove the pan from the oven, carefully remove the loaf from the pan, transfer to a wire rack, and let cool completely before slicing. (For storage information, see Storing Bread, page 123.) Return the lidded baker to the oven and reheat for 30 minutes, then score and bake the second loaf as directed above.

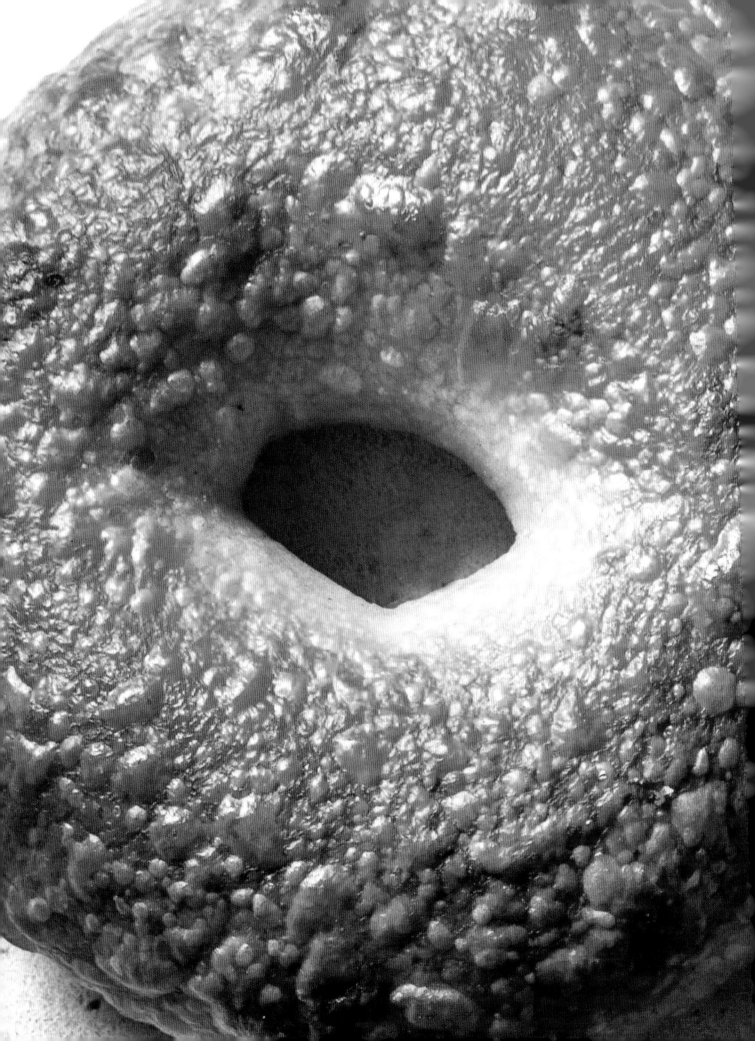

Buns, Bagels & Rolls

THE BEST BAGELS

MIX	BULK FERMENTATION	PRESHAPE	SHAPE	2ND RISE	BOIL	BAKE
5–18 MIN	1½–2 HOURS	20 MIN	15 MIN	15 MIN–16 HOURS	10 MIN	20–25 MIN

······ TIME: ABOUT 3–20 HOURS ······

MAKES 12 BAGELS

DOUGH

826 grams (6¾ cups plus 2 tablespoons) unbleached bread flour, plus more for dusting

17 grams (2¾ teaspoons) fine salt

3 grams (1 teaspoon) instant yeast

538 grams (2¼ cups plus 2 tablespoons) warm water (see Temperature, page 25)

Semolina flour or yellow cornmeal, for dusting

WATER BATH

1,816 grams (8 cups) water

42 grams (2 tablespoons) honey

18 grams (1 tablespoon) fine salt

OPTIONAL COATING

71 grams (about ½ cup) sesame seeds, poppy seeds, or everything bagel seasoning

We love these bagels. They are chewy and full-flavored with thin, blistered crusts, just right for spreading with cream cheese or using to make a superlative bacon, egg, and cheese sandwich. We much prefer the flavor and texture of bagels that have been shaped and then rested overnight, but if you're time-constrained, they can be made in a single day, though the texture and flavor won't be as good.

MAKE THE DOUGH: In a stand mixer bowl, combine the flour, salt, yeast, and water. Using the dough hook attachment, mix on medium-low speed until no dry patches of flour remain. Increase the speed to medium and mix until the dough is elastic and pulling away from the sides of the bowl, about 5 minutes. The exterior of the dough may not be completely smooth; that's OK. Cover and let rise until puffy and doubled in size, 1½ to 2 hours.

Alternatively, in a large bowl, combine the flour, salt, yeast, and water and mix to form a thick, sticky, cohesive dough with no dry spots. Cover and let rest 10 minutes. This rest allows the flour to hydrate and gluten formation to begin, making hand-kneading easier. Transfer the dough to a lightly floured surface and knead until a tacky, springy dough forms, 5 to 8 minutes. The dough will be sticky at first but will smooth out quickly; to make it easier to handle, use a bench knife to scrape the dough off the work surface as you knead, which will speed up the process and reduce the amount of flour required for kneading (adding too much flour at this stage can make your bagels denser). Return the dough to the bowl, cover, and let rise until puffy and doubled in size, 1½ to 2 hours.

DIVIDE AND PRESHAPE THE DOUGH: Lightly flour a work surface, then use a plastic bowl scraper to ease the dough out of the bowl onto the work surface. Divide the dough into 12 equal portions (each about 115 grams). Gently press out the bubbles from each piece. Preshape each piece of dough into a round (see Preshaping, page 32), place on a lightly floured surface seam side down, then cover and let rest for 15 minutes.

SHAPE THE BAGELS: Line two baking sheets with parchment paper, spray with pan spray, and lightly dust with semolina or cornmeal. Working with one piece of dough at a time, use your pointer finger to poke a hole into the center of the round. Gently expand the hole to 2 to 3 inches in diameter by twirling the dough in a circular motion around both of your index fingers. The bagel should be 1 to 1¼ inches thick around the entire ring. Evenly space 6 shaped bagels on each lined baking sheet.

At this point, if you are not cooking the bagels right away, cover the bagels lightly with greased plastic wrap and refrigerate overnight, 12 to 16 hours.

BOIL AND BAKE: Arrange racks in the upper and lower thirds of the oven and preheat the oven to 475°F. Cover the bagels and let them rest while you prepare the water bath.

In a shallow, wide, 6-quart pot, combine the water, honey, and salt and bring to a simmer over medium heat. If coating bagels with seeds, spread the seeds on a rimmed baking sheet or piece of parchment paper.

To transfer the bagels to the water bath, use one hand to hold down the parchment paper and the other hand to support the bagel as you lift it up and off the parchment to avoid pulling or stretching the bagel. Gently lower the bagel into the hot water. Repeat with 2 more bagels. Boil the bagels for 1 minute. Using a slotted spoon, tongs, or chopsticks, carefully flip each bagel and continue boiling for 1 more minute.

Remove the bagels from the water and return them to the parchment-lined baking sheets, spacing evenly. Repeat until all the bagels have been boiled, letting the water return to a simmer between batches. Let the bagels cool slightly before dipping the tops in seeds, if using. The tops of the bagels should still be tacky from the water bath. If they have dried, lightly brush the tops with water before dredging in seeds. Place the bagels seed side up on the baking sheets.

Bake the bagels until the outer crust is firm and deep golden brown, 20 to 25 minutes, switching racks and rotating the pans front to back halfway through.

Remove from the oven and transfer to a wire rack to cool. Store completely cooled bagels in an airtight container up to 3 days or freeze for longer storage.

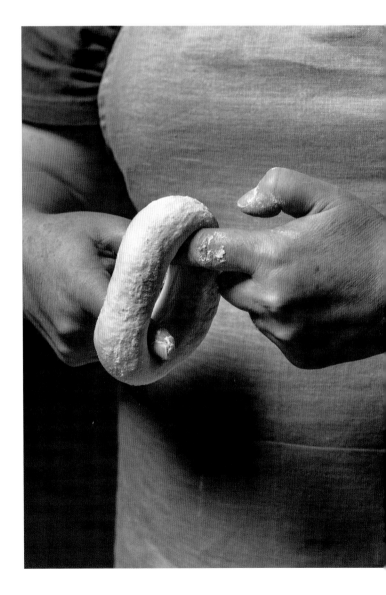

BIG-BATCH POTATO ROLLS

COOK POTATOES	MIX	BULK FERMENTATION	SHAPE	2ND RISE	BAKE
30–40 MIN	15 MIN	1½ HOURS	15 MIN	1–1½ HOURS	20–25 MIN

·······TIME: ABOUT 4½ HOURS·······

MAKES 20 ROLLS

2 medium Yukon Gold or russet potatoes (325 grams/11 ounces)

558 grams (4⅔ cups) unbleached all-purpose flour, plus more for dusting

67 grams (⅓ cup) sugar

13.5 grams (2¼ teaspoons) fine salt

7.5 grams (2½ teaspoons) instant yeast

2 large eggs (100 grams total)

85 grams (6 tablespoons) unsalted butter, at room temperature

28 grams (2 tablespoons) unsalted butter, melted, for brushing

This is a superlative dinner roll: super soft and excellent torn in half and slathered with softened butter. The dough contains boiled potatoes, which increases its starch content and allows it to retain more water. That translates to a soft bread with a long shelf life (although, let's be honest, a pan of hot-from-the-oven rolls isn't going to last long). You can choose Yukon Golds or russets, though the former give the rolls an attractive golden hue. If you want larger rolls, divide the dough into 16 pieces instead of 20.

COOK THE POTATOES: Peel the potatoes and cut into ½-inch cubes. Put in a medium saucepan, add cold water to cover, and then bring to a boil over medium-high heat. Once boiling, reduce the heat to medium-low and simmer until the potatoes are very tender, 15 to 20 minutes. Set a colander over a medium bowl and drain the potatoes into the colander, reserving the potato cooking water.

Pass the potatoes through a ricer or large-gauge wire sieve into a clean bowl. Weigh out 213 grams (about 1 cup) riced potatoes (any leftover riced potatoes can become the baker's treat or be saved for another use). Measure out 170 grams (¾ cup) of the reserved potato cooking water and set aside uncovered, along with the riced potatoes, until just warm, 15 to 20 minutes.

MAKE THE DOUGH: In a stand mixer bowl, combine the riced potatoes, potato cooking water, flour, sugar, salt, yeast, eggs, and the 85 grams (6 tablespoons) butter. Using the dough hook attachment, mix on medium-low speed until a shaggy dough forms, stopping to scrape down the bottom and sides of the bowl as necessary, 2 to 3 minutes. Increase the speed to medium-high and mix until a soft, elastic, and slightly sticky dough forms, about 10 minutes. The dough will mostly clear the sides but not the bottom of the bowl. Scrape the dough into a ball, cover, and let rise until puffy and doubled in size, about 1½ hours.

Recipe continues

DIVIDE AND SHAPE THE DOUGH AND LET RISE:
Spray the bottom and sides of a 13 × 9-inch baking pan with pan spray. Lightly flour a work surface, then use a plastic bowl scraper to ease the dough out of the bowl onto the work surface. Gently deflate the dough and divide it into 20 equal portions (each about 60 grams) or for larger rolls 16 equal portions (each about 75 grams). Preshape each piece into a round (see Preshaping, page 32), then place seam side down on a lightly floured surface. Using a cupped hand on an unfloured area of your work surface, shape each piece of dough into a taut round (see Shaping, page 34), then evenly space them seam side down in 4 rows of 5 in the prepared pan. Cover and let rise until puffy and when pressed with a floured finger, a small impression remains (see Proofing, page 44), 1 to 1½ hours. Meanwhile, preheat the oven to 350°F.

BAKE: Bake the rolls until the tops are evenly golden brown and the internal temperature reaches at least 190°F, 20 to 25 minutes.

Remove the rolls from the oven and brush with the 28 grams (2 tablespoons) melted butter. Let the rolls sit in the pan for 5 minutes, then turn out of the pan onto a rack. Flip so the rolls are buttered side up and let cool. Serve warm or at room temperature. (For storage information, see Storing Bread, page 123.)

BOLILLOS

MIX	BULK FERMENTATION	PRESHAPE	SHAPE	2ND RISE	BAKE
25 MIN	1 HOUR	20 MIN	10 MIN	30–45 MIN	25–30 MIN

······ TIME: ABOUT 3 HOURS ······

MAKES SIX 6-INCH ROLLS

500 grams (4 cups plus 3 tablespoons) unbleached all-purpose flour

25 grams (scant 2 tablespoons) lard or softened unsalted butter (see headnote)

15 grams (1 tablespoon plus ½ teaspoon) sugar

11 grams (scant 2 teaspoons) fine salt

9 grams (1 tablespoon) instant yeast

350 grams (1½ cups plus 1 tablespoon) warm water (see Temperature, page 25)

These rolls have a fluffy crumb and a crisp, thin crust that shatters when you bite into them. Also known as pan francés or pan blanco, they're made and eaten throughout Mexico and Central America (and anywhere else with a large Mexican or Central American community). Bolillo rolls are perhaps most famous as the bread of choice for tortas, those deliciously oversize pressed sandwiches filled with everything from ham and cheese to fried chicken cutlets and chiles. Turns out they're also perfect for "French Bread" Pizza (page 433).

Bolillos are traditionally enriched with lard, and we like that version the best, but if you prefer a vegetarian version, butter can be substituted. The rolls will be slightly less tender, but still very fluffy.

MAKE THE DOUGH: In a large bowl, combine the flour, lard, sugar, salt, yeast, and water and mix until no dry patches of flour remain and a soft, sticky dough forms. Cover and allow to rest for 15 minutes.

Transfer the dough to a lightly floured surface and knead until a tacky, springy dough forms, 5 to 8 minutes. The dough will be sticky at first but will smooth out quickly; to make it easier to handle, use a bench knife to scrape the dough off your work surface as you knead, which will speed up the process and reduce the amount of flour required for kneading (adding too much flour at this stage can make your rolls denser). Return the dough to the bowl, cover, and let rise until puffy and doubled in size, about 1 hour.

Alternatively, in a stand mixer bowl, combine the flour, lard, sugar, salt, yeast, and water. Using the dough hook attachment, mix on medium-low speed until no dry patches of flour remain. Increase the speed to medium and mix until smooth, elastic, and pulling away from the sides of the bowl, about 5 minutes. Cover and let rise until puffy and doubled in size, about 1 hour.

Recipe continues

DIVIDE AND PRESHAPE THE DOUGH: Lightly flour a work surface, then use a plastic bowl scraper to ease the dough out of the bowl onto the work surface. With a bench knife or a knife, divide the dough into 6 equal portions (each about 151 grams). Gently press down on each piece to remove any bubbles, then preshape them into 4-inch tubes (see Preshaping, page 32). Place the dough pieces seam side down and about 2 inches apart on a lightly floured surface. Cover and let rest for 10 minutes.

SHAPE THE DOUGH AND LET IT RISE: Place one piece of dough seam side up on a lightly floured surface. Gently deflate the dough, pressing it into a 5 × 3-inch rectangle. Shape the dough into a 6-inch bâtard with slightly tapered ends (see Shaping, page 34) and place it on a piece of parchment paper. Repeat with the remaining dough, evenly spacing them on the parchment. Cover and let rest at room temperature until very puffy (see Proofing, page 44), 30 to 45 minutes.

Meanwhile, arrange racks in the center and bottom third of the oven and preheat the oven to 450°F with a baking stone or steel placed on the center rack and an empty cast-iron skillet (or a cake pan filled with lava rocks) on the lower rack. If possible, adjust the stone and pan so that the skillet isn't directly under the stone, making it easier for steam to reach the baking rolls (see Steaming, page 50).

Use a baker's lame or razor blade to score a straight line vertically down the center of each roll (see Scoring, page 46).

BAKE: Using a baker's peel or an inverted baking sheet to aid you, transfer the rolls (still on the parchment) into the oven, then pour about 227 grams (1 cup) of warm water into the skillet. Steam will billow from the pan upward to envelop the rolls; be sure to wear good oven mitts to shield your hands and arms. Quickly close the oven door to trap the steam. Bake until the crust is firm, crisp, and deep golden brown and the rolls feel light for their size, 25 to 30 minutes.

Transfer to a rack to cool completely. These rolls are best enjoyed the day they are baked; the crust will soften and lose crispness if stored, but leftovers make amazing "French Bread" Pizzas (see page 433) and grilled sandwiches.

BUFFALO ROLLS

MIX	BULK FERMENTATION	SHAPE	2ND RISE	BAKE
5 MIN	2 HOURS	10 MIN	1–1½ HOURS	15–18 MIN

MAKE THE PREFERMENT (12–16 HOURS BEFORE)

TIME: ABOUT 20 HOURS

MAKES EIGHT 3- TO 4-INCH ROLLS

PREFERMENT

109 grams (¾ cup plus 2 tablespoons) unbleached all-purpose flour

0.5 gram (pinch) instant yeast

109 grams (scant ½ cup) cold water (55°F to 60°F)

DOUGH

157 grams (½ cup plus 3 tablespoons) warm water (see Temperature, page 25)

255 grams (2 cups plus 2 tablespoons) unbleached all-purpose flour, plus more for dusting

7.5 grams (1¼ teaspoons) salt

1 gram (generous ¼ teaspoon) instant yeast

FILLING

100 grams (¾ cup plus 2 tablespoons) shredded mozzarella cheese, whole milk preferred

100 grams (¾ cup) crumbled blue cheese

40 grams (2 tablespoons plus 2 teaspoons) Buffalo wings hot sauce

Yes, these rolls are inspired by a beloved bar snack. Yes, they're a little over the top. Crispy and chewy, with a spiral of hot sauce–spiked mozzarella and blue cheese, they're at once salty and tangy. If you want to amp up the flavor, brush the rolls with the (optional) hot sauce and butter mixture after they're baked. These rolls are irresistible on their own, but they're even better split and stuffed with fried chicken.

DAY 1

MAKE THE PREFERMENT: The evening before you want to bake, in a large bowl, combine the flour, yeast, and water and mix until no dry patches of flour remain. Cover and let stand at room temperature overnight, 12 to 16 hours.

DAY 2

MAKE THE DOUGH: Add the warm water to the preferment, then squeeze the preferment through your fingers to break it up. Next, holding your hand in a clawlike position, vigorously mix the preferment into the water until well combined. The mixture will look like foamy milk with some small pieces of preferment still visible. Add the flour, salt, and yeast, mixing well until no dry spots remain (see Mixing, page 20).

Bulk fermentation or the "first rise" (see page 25) will take 2 hours. During that time, you'll attend to it three times (directions follow), folding the dough every 20 minutes for the first hour. Then the dough will rest, covered and undisturbed, for the final hour.

BULK FERMENT THE DOUGH: Once you've mixed the dough, cover and let rest for 20 minutes. Using a wet hand, perform 8 to 12 bowl folds (see Bowl Fold, page 30) or until the dough resists stretching. Round out the dough by cupping your hand and applying pressure toward the bottom of the dough, forcing it into the bottom and side of the bowl to create tension. Cover and let rest for another 20 minutes.

OPTIONAL TOPPING

43 grams (3 tablespoons) unsalted butter, melted

30 grams (2 tablespoons) Buffalo wings hot sauce

Using a wet hand, perform 6 to 8 bowl folds, or until the dough resists stretching. Round out the dough, cover, and let the dough rest for 20 minutes. With wet hands, perform 2 to 3 coil folds (see Coil Fold, page 31) or until the dough resists stretching. Round out, cover, and let the dough rest at room temperature for 1 hour, or until the dough is very puffy and marshmallowy.

ADD THE FILLING AND SHAPE THE ROLLS: Line a rimmed baking sheet with parchment paper. Lightly flour a work surface, then use a plastic bowl scraper to ease the dough out of the bowl and onto the work surface. Lightly flour the top of the dough, then, with well-floured hands, pat and stretch the dough into an 8 × 14-inch rectangle with a short side in front of you. Sprinkle the mozzarella and blue cheeses evenly over the dough, leaving a ½-inch border along the short side closest to you. Drizzle the hot sauce over the cheese. Starting with the short side farthest from you, begin rolling the dough into a tight log. Pinch the seam to seal, then place the log seam side down in front of you. Using a bench knife or a knife, lightly score the log into 8 equal portions, each 1 to 1¼ inches thick. Then, using unflavored dental floss or a sharp serrated knife, cut the log into pieces following the score marks.

LET THE ROLLS RISE: Place the rolls cut side up on the prepared pan in a 3-2-3 pattern (two rows of 3 on the long sides of the pan, with a row of 2 between). Lightly dust your palm with flour, then gently flatten the rolls to ¾ inch thick. Cover and let rise until the rolls feel marshmallowy and when gently pressed with a floured finger, a small indentation remains (see Proofing, page 44), 1 to 1½ hours.

Meanwhile, arrange racks in the center and bottom third of the oven and preheat the oven to 450°F with a baking stone or steel on the center rack and an empty cast-iron skillet (or a cake pan filled with lava rocks) on the lower rack. If possible, adjust the stone and pan so that the skillet isn't directly under the stone, making it easier for steam to reach the baking bread (see Steaming, page 50).

BAKE: Using a baker's peel or an inverted baking sheet to aid you, transfer the rolls (still on the parchment-lined baking sheet) to the oven, placing them on the stone, then pour about 227 grams (1 cup) of warm water into the skillet. Steam will billow from the pan upward to envelop the rolls; be sure to wear good oven mitts to shield your hands and arms. Quickly close the oven door to trap the steam. Bake the rolls until the crust and exposed cheese are medium golden brown, 15 to 18 minutes.

Recipe continues

MEANWHILE, MAKE THE TOPPING, IF USING: In a small bowl, combine the melted butter and hot sauce and set aside. Remove the rolls from the oven and immediately brush all over with the butter mixture. Let the rolls cool slightly before serving (they're best when still warm).

To store, let cool completely, then transfer the rolls to an airtight container and store in the refrigerator for up to 3 days or freeze for longer storage. Let frozen rolls thaw to room temperature, then place on a parchment-lined baking sheet and heat in a preheated 350°F oven until warmed through, 8 to 10 minutes.

BUTTERMILK BUNS

MIX	BULK FERMENTATION	SHAPE	2ND RISE	BAKE
10 MIN	1–1½ HOURS	15 MIN	45 MIN–1 HOUR	20–25 MIN

TIME: ABOUT 3½ HOURS

MAKES 8 BURGER BUNS OR 12 HOT DOG BUNS

420 grams (3½ cups) unbleached all-purpose flour, plus more for dusting

37 grams (3 tablespoons) sugar

9 grams (1 tablespoon) instant yeast

7.5 grams (1¼ teaspoons) fine salt

1 large egg (50 grams)

241 grams (1 cup plus 1 tablespoon) warm low-fat buttermilk (see Temperature, page 25)

57 grams (4 tablespoons) unsalted butter, cut into small cubes, at room temperature

Egg wash: 1 large egg (50 grams) beaten with ⅛ teaspoon salt

18 grams (2 tablespoons) sesame or poppy seeds for topping (optional)

These buns have a subtle tang from the addition of buttermilk; a plush, tender crumb; and a glossy egg wash finish, and can be shaped as either burger or hot dog buns. You can make them well ahead of time, they're sturdy enough to load up with toppings and condiments, and they stay soft for days. While far superior to store-bought buns, they're pretty easy to make.

MAKE THE DOUGH: In a stand mixer bowl, combine the flour, sugar, yeast, and salt. Add the egg and buttermilk and, using the dough hook attachment, mix on medium-low speed until a cohesive dough forms, 2 to 3 minutes. Stop and scrape down the bowl as necessary. Increase the speed to medium-high and continue mixing the dough until it's smooth and elastic, about 5 minutes. Reduce the speed to medium-low, then add a few cubes of butter to the dough, allowing the first addition to incorporate fully before adding the next. Once all the butter has been incorporated, the dough will feel slightly tacky. Cover and let rise until very puffy, 1 to 1½ hours.

SHAPE THE BUNS AND LET THEM RISE: Lightly flour a work surface, then use a plastic bowl scraper to ease the dough out of the bowl onto the work surface and gently press it into a rectangle. Shaping into a rectangle as opposed to a round will make dividing and preshaping the dough easier.

FOR HAMBURGER BUNS: Line a rimmed baking sheet with parchment paper. Divide the dough into 8 equal portions (each about 100 grams). Loosely preshape the pieces of dough into rounds (see Preshaping, page 32), then use your cupped hand to create tension and shape smooth, taut rounds of dough (see Shaping, page 34). Evenly space the dough rounds on the prepared pan, then press down with your palm to flatten each into a disk that is about 4 inches in diameter and 1 inch thick. Cover and let rise until puffy and when pressed with a floured finger, a small indentation remains (see Proofing, page 44), 45 minutes to 1 hour.

Recipe continues

FOR HOT DOG BUNS: Line two rimmed baking sheets with parchment paper. Divide the dough into 12 equal portions (each about 68 grams). Loosely preshape the pieces of dough into 4-inch tubes (see Preshaping, page 32), then roll into 6-inch-long logs. Space 6 buns about 1 inch apart on each prepared pan. Cover and let rise until puffy and when pressed with a floured finger, a small indentation remains (see Proofing, page 44), about 45 minutes.

Toward the end of the rising time, preheat the oven to 375°F.

BAKE: Lightly brush the buns with egg wash and sprinkle with seeds, if using, then bake until the tops are deep golden brown and the internal temperature reaches 190°F, 20 to 25 minutes.

Remove the rolls from the oven, then transfer to a wire rack to cool completely before serving. Store leftover buns in an airtight container up to 3 days or freeze for longer storage.

CACIO E PEPE ROLLS

MIX	BULK FERMENTATION	SHAPE	2ND RISE	BAKE
10 MIN	1–1½ HOURS	10 MIN	30–45 MIN	25–30 MIN

MAKE THE PREFERMENT (1 HOUR BEFORE)

TIME: ABOUT 4 HOURS

MAKES 8 ROLLS

PREFERMENT

120 grams (1 cup) unbleached all-purpose flour

68 grams (¼ cup plus 2½ tablespoons) semolina flour

3 grams (1 teaspoon) instant yeast

300 grams (1¼ cups plus 1 tablespoon) warm water (see Temperature, page 25)

DOUGH

240 grams (2 cups) unbleached all-purpose flour

56 grams (½ cup plus 1 tablespoon) finely shredded pecorino Romano cheese

25 grams (2 tablespoons) olive oil

9 grams (1½ teaspoons) fine salt

3.5 grams (1½ teaspoons) freshly ground black pepper

TOPPING

56 grams (4½ tablespoons) olive oil

30 grams (¼ cup plus 1 tablespoon) finely shredded pecorino Romano cheese

2.5 grams (1 teaspoon) freshly ground black pepper

1.5 grams (¼ teaspoon) fine salt

These rolls capture all the salty, peppery flavors of the classic Roman pasta. There's pecorino Romano and black pepper both in the dough and coating the exterior of the rolls, so you get big flavor in every bite. Serve these rolls alongside salad, pasta, or soup—or even on the Thanksgiving table.

MAKE THE PREFERMENT: In a large bowl, combine the all-purpose flour, semolina flour, yeast, and water and mix until no lumps remain; the mixture will be thin. Cover and let stand at room temperature for 1 hour. The mixture will have increased some in volume and little bubbles will cover the surface.

MAKE THE DOUGH: Add the flour, pecorino Romano, olive oil, salt, and pepper to the preferment, mixing to form a cohesive dough. Transfer the dough to a lightly floured surface and knead until a tacky, springy dough forms, 5 to 8 minutes. The dough will be sticky at first but will smooth out quickly; to make it easier to handle, use a bench knife to scrape the dough off your work surface as you knead, which will speed up the process and reduce the amount of flour required for kneading (adding too much flour at this stage can make your rolls denser). Return the dough to the bowl, cover, and let rise until puffy and doubled in size, 1 to 1½ hours.

Alternatively, make the preferment in a stand mixer bowl, then cover and let stand for 1 hour. Add the flour, pecorino Romano, olive oil, salt, and pepper to the preferment and mix with the dough hook attachment on medium-low speed until no dry patches of flour remain. Increase speed to medium and mix until smooth, elastic, and pulling away from the sides of the bowl, about 5 minutes. Cover and let rise until puffy and doubled in size, 1 to 1½ hours.

DIVIDE AND SHAPE THE DOUGH AND LET RISE: Lightly flour a work surface, then use a plastic bowl scraper to ease the dough out of the

Recipe continues

bowl onto the work surface. With a bench knife or a knife, divide the dough into 8 equal portions (each about 103 grams). Gently press down on each piece to remove any bubbles, then preshape each piece into a round (see Preshaping, page 32) and place seam side down on a lightly floured surface. Using a cupped hand, shape each piece of dough into a taut round (see Shaping, page 34), then place seam side down and evenly spaced on a piece of parchment paper. Cover and let rest until puffy and when pressed with a floured finger, a small impression remains (see Proofing, page 44), 30 to 45 minutes.

Meanwhile, arrange racks in the center and bottom third of the oven and preheat the oven to 450°F with a baking stone or steel placed on the center rack and an empty cast-iron skillet (or a cake pan filled with lava rocks) on the lower rack. If possible, adjust the stone or steel and pan so that the skillet isn't directly under the stone or steel, making it easier for steam to reach the baking rolls (see Steaming, page 50).

BAKE: Using sharp scissors, snip small cuts along the top and sides of each roll; for a hedgehog-like appearance, make 12 small cuts. Using a baker's peel or an inverted baking sheet to aid you, transfer the rolls (still on the parchment) into the oven, then pour about 227 grams (1 cup) of warm water into the skillet. Steam will billow from the pan upward to envelop the rolls; be sure to wear good oven mitts to shield your hands and arms. Quickly close the oven door to trap the steam. Bake until the crust of the rolls is firm, crisp, and golden brown, 25 to 30 minutes.

MEANWHILE, MAKE THE TOPPING: In a large bowl, combine the olive oil, pecorino Romano, pepper, and salt, mixing well to combine.

Remove the rolls from the oven and, using tongs, carefully transfer them to the bowl with the topping. Toss the rolls in the topping until well coated. Return the rolls to the baking sheet and let cool slightly before serving. These rolls are best enjoyed the day they are baked; the crust will soften as they sit.

CLASSIC PRETZELS

MIX	BULK FERMENTATION	PRESHAPE	SHAPE	2ND CHILL	DIP	BAKE
10 MIN	1–1½ HOURS	30 MIN	15–20 MIN	1 HOUR	10 MIN	20–25 MIN

TIME: ABOUT 4 HOURS

MAKES 6 PRETZELS

DOUGH

360 grams (3 cups) unbleached bread flour, plus more for dusting

209 grams (¾ cup plus 3 tablespoons) warm water (see Temperature, page 25)

20 grams (1½ tablespoons) unsalted butter, at room temperature

7.5 grams (1¼ teaspoons) fine salt

4.5 grams (1½ teaspoons) instant yeast

DIPPING AND TOPPING

250 grams (1 cup plus 2 tablespoons) water

10 grams (scant 1 tablespoon) food-grade lye (see Note)

7 to 10 grams (1½ to 2 teaspoons) pretzel salt

Chewy, salty, and deep mahogany in color, these are *real* pretzels—and a far cry from what you might find at the mall. True pretzels are dipped in an alkaline solution of lye and water before being baked, which is what gives them their signature flavor and burnished color. Lye is caustic, meaning it can burn your exposed skin; for that reason, take great care when using it, and wear eye protection and rubber gloves to protect yourself. In case all that feels like too much of a hassle, we've given the method for a solution made with baking soda (see Note), which also yields good pretzels. But for the real McCoy, opt for the thrill of lye! For the thrill of sourdough, see the Variation below.

MAKE THE DOUGH: In a stand mixer bowl, combine the flour, water, butter, salt, and yeast. Using the dough hook attachment, mix on medium-low speed until a shaggy dough forms, about 1 minute. Scrape the bottom and sides of the bowl, then increase the speed to medium-high and continue mixing until the dough is smooth and elastic, about 5 minutes more. Cover and let rest until puffy though not necessarily doubled in size, 1 to 1½ hours.

Alternatively, in a large bowl, combine the flour, water, butter, salt, and yeast and mix by hand to form a shaggy dough. Transfer the dough to a lightly floured work surface and knead until the dough is smooth and elastic, 8 to 10 minutes. Return the dough to the bowl, cover, and let rest until puffy though not necessarily doubled in size, 1 to 1½ hours.

DIVIDE AND PRESHAPE THE DOUGH: Lightly flour a work surface, then use a plastic bowl scraper to ease the dough out of the bowl onto the work surface. Gently deflate the dough, then divide it into 6 equal portions (each about 100 grams). Preshape each piece of dough into a 4-inch tube (see Preshaping, page 32), place seam side down on the work surface, cover, and let rest for 20 minutes.

Recipe continues

With a bench knife, scrape the flour off your work surface, then roll each piece of dough out into an 18-inch log. To do this, place one hand in the center of the dough and begin rolling it back and forth under your hand so that the ends are thicker and the center thinner; it will resemble a dog bone. Next, place your hands next to each other in the center of the dough and apply pressure in a "down-and-out" motion, moving your hands away from each other to elongate the log; it should be the same thickness from end to end. Once you have rolled all the pieces to 18 inches, return to the piece you started with and use the same rolling motion to elongate each log to 24 to 26 inches; that brief rest will allow the dough to elongate more easily without snapping back.

SHAPE THE PRETZELS: Line a rimmed baking sheet with parchment paper and set nearby. To shape the pretzels, place one piece of dough in front of you in the shape of a "U" with the curved portion closest to you. Twist the two ends of the dough together twice. Then,  holding the ends, fold them down toward you so they overlap the curved piece of the dough, and press gently to adhere. Place the shaped pretzels on the lined baking sheet, then cover and refrigerate until cold and slightly firm, about 1 hour.

SHAPING PRETZELS

Meanwhile, preheat the oven to 425°F and arrange a rack in the center. Line a rimmed baking sheet with parchment and spray with pan spray. (Don't skip this step, or the pretzels will stick to the parchment!)

DIP THE PRETZELS: Set up your lye dipping station. Safety first! Be sure to wear goggles, an apron, closed-toed shoes, and rubber gloves when working with lye. Set a wire rack over a parchment-lined rimmed baking sheet and set nearby. Measure the water into a nonreactive medium bowl. Measure the lye into a separate small, nonreactive container. Slowly add the lye to the water, stirring with a nonreactive spoon or spatula until the lye is dissolved.

Working with one pretzel at a time, gently place the pretzel face down in the lye solution, then use a nonreactive slotted spoon or spider/skimmer to remove the pretzel from the solution. Place the pretzel face up on the wire rack and let any excess lye solution drip off, then gently transfer to the prepared baking sheet. Evenly space the pretzels in two rows of three, then sprinkle each with pretzel salt.

BAKE: Bake the pretzels until glossy, deep golden brown, and fragrant, 20 to 25 minutes, rotating the pan front to back halfway through.

Remove from the oven and let cool on the baking sheet. Pretzels are best eaten the day they are baked, as the salt will melt and make your pretzels soggy if stored.

VARIATION

SOURDOUGH PRETZELS: The night before you want to bake, make the preferment: In a small bowl, combine 33 grams (generous 2 tablespoons) sourdough culture, 71 grams (½ cup plus 2 tablespoons) unbleached bread flour, and 71 grams (¼ cup plus 1 tablespoon) cold water (55°F to 60°F). Mix until no dry spots remain, then cover and let rest at room temperature overnight, 12 to 16 hours. The next day, in a stand mixer, combine the preferment, 272 grams (2¼ cups) unbleached bread flour, 121 grams (½ cup plus 1 tablespoon) warm water, 20 grams (1½ tablespoons) room temperature unsalted butter, 7.5 grams (1¼ teaspoons) fine salt, and 3 grams (1 teaspoon) instant yeast. Follow the recipe as directed.

NOTE: No lye? No problem! For the water bath, combine 6 cups water and 36 grams (2 tablespoons) baking soda in a deep, wide pot. Bring to a boil, then reduce to a simmer. With a slotted spoon, lower the pretzels into the water and cook for 20 seconds each side. Remove from the water with a slotted spoon, then place on the prepared baking sheet. Top with salt and bake as directed.

ENGLISH MUFFINS

MAKES SIX 3½-INCH MUFFINS

PREFERMENT

190 grams (1½ cups plus 4 teaspoons) unbleached all-purpose flour

2.25 grams (¾ teaspoon) instant yeast

152 grams (½ cup plus 3 tablespoons) warm milk (90°F), whole preferred

102 grams (¼ cup plus 3 tablespoons) warm water (90°F)

DOUGH

120 grams (1 cup) unbleached all-purpose flour

6 grams (1 teaspoon) fine salt

4 grams (1 teaspoon) sugar

18 grams (1 tablespoon plus 1 teaspoon) unsalted butter, melted

20 to 30 grams (2 to 3 tablespoons) yellow cornmeal, for dusting

Slightly tangy and shot through with nooks and crannies, these homemade English muffins stand head and shoulders above store-bought. They're surprisingly easy to make at home—you don't even need to turn on the oven, as they're "baked" in a skillet on the stovetop. If you use a round cutter, you'll end up with 6 round English muffins with some scrap dough; if you don't mind a square muffin, you can use a bench knife or a knife to cut the dough and eliminate scraps altogether.

MAKE THE PREFERMENT: In a large bowl, whisk together the flour, yeast, milk, and water until smooth. The mixture will have the consistency of thick pancake batter. Cover and let rest at room temperature for at least 1 hour or up to 4 hours. After 1 hour the mixture will have grown a bit in volume and small bubbles will have appeared on top. After 4 hours, the preferment will have doubled in volume, have many small bubbles on the surface, and have a slightly sour aroma. The longer the mixture ferments, the more flavor the English muffins will have.

MAKE THE DOUGH: Add the flour, salt, sugar, and melted butter to the preferment, mixing by hand or with the handle of a wooden spoon to form a soft, sticky dough.

Bulk fermentation or the "first rise" (see page 25) will take 2 hours. During that time, you'll attend to the dough twice (directions follow), folding once right away and then again after the first hour. Then the dough will rest, covered and undisturbed, for the final hour.

BULK FERMENT THE DOUGH: Once you've mixed the dough, with a wet hand perform 6 to 8 bowl folds (see Bowl Fold, page 30) or until the dough resists stretching. Round out the dough by cupping your hand and applying pressure toward the bottom of the dough, forcing it into the bottom and side of the bowl to create tension. Cover and let rest at warm room temperature for 1 hour.

Recipe continues

With a wet hand, perform 6 to 8 more bowl folds until the dough resists stretching, then flip the dough over and round it out as before. Cover and let rest at warm room temperature until the dough is very puffy and marshmallowy, about 1 hour.

SHAPE THE DOUGH AND LET IT RISE: Lightly dust a work surface with cornmeal, then use a plastic bowl scraper to gently ease the dough out of the bowl onto the work surface. Gently deflate the dough and then sprinkle the top lightly with cornmeal. Pat the dough into a round that is ½ inch thick. Using a 3½-inch round cutter, cut 4 rounds out of the dough, keeping the spacing as close as possible to cut down on the amount of scrap dough left over. Gently bring the scrap dough together, pinching it to adhere. Flatten the dough to a ½ inch thickness again, if needed, then continue cutting rounds; you should be able to cut 2 more. Lightly dust a piece of parchment paper with cornmeal, then transfer the rounds of dough to the parchment. Cover and let rest until puffy, 20 to 30 minutes.

COOK THE ENGLISH MUFFINS: Preheat a 10- to 12-inch cast-iron or nonstick skillet over medium-low heat until a few water drops flicked on the surface sizzle, then take a moment to evaporate. (Alternatively, preheat an electric griddle to 350°F.)

Carefully transfer the muffins to the preheated pan (or griddle) and cook until the bottoms are lightly browned and the sides look matte, 10 to 15 minutes. The muffins will puff up to about 1 inch thick. Flip the muffins over and continue cooking on the second side until browned and the internal temperature registers at least 190°F, an additional 10 to 15 minutes.

Place the muffins on a wire rack to cool slightly before serving. For the ultimate "nook and cranny" experience, fork-split the muffins before toasting. (For storage information, see Storing Bread, page 123.)

JERUSALEM BAGELS

MIX	BULK FERMENTATION	PRESHAPE	SHAPE	2ND RISE	BAKE
20 MIN	1½–2 HOURS	25 MIN	20 MIN	20–30 MIN	20–25 MIN

TIME: ABOUT 4 HOURS

MAKES SIX 8-INCH BAGELS

DOUGH

558 grams (4½ cups plus 2 tablespoons) unbleached bread flour, plus more for dusting

28 grams (generous 2 tablespoons) sugar

12 grams (2 teaspoons) fine salt

3 grams (1 teaspoon) instant yeast

56 grams (generous ¼ cup) olive oil

410 grams (1¾ cups plus 1 tablespoon) warm milk (see Temperature, page 25), whole preferred

TOPPING

85 grams (¼ cup) pomegranate molasses

28 grams (2 tablespoons) warm water

150 grams (1 cup plus 1 tablespoon) sesame seeds, unhulled preferred

Unlike American-style bagels, the dough for Jerusalem bagels, also known as ka'ak, is enriched with sugar, oil, and milk, and they aren't boiled before baking, so instead of a crisp-chewy crust and dense crumb, they have a thin, crisp crust and an almost fluffy, soft crumb. They're also shaped differently; instead of a circle, they're pulled into an elongated oval. Before the bagels are baked they're dipped in pomegranate molasses, which gives the exterior a caramelized sweetness, then rolled in sesame seeds for a nutty finish. In Jerusalem they're often used as a vehicle for dips, like hummus, or served for breakfast with coffee.

MAKE THE DOUGH: In a large bowl, combine the flour, sugar, salt, yeast, olive oil, and milk and mix to form a thick, sticky, cohesive dough with no dry spots. Cover and let rest 10 minutes. This rest allows the flour to hydrate and gluten formation to begin, making hand-kneading easier. Transfer the dough to a lightly floured surface and knead until a tacky, springy dough forms, 5 to 8 minutes. The dough will be sticky at first but will smooth out quickly; to make it easier to handle, use a bench knife to scrape the dough off the work surface as you knead, which will speed up the process and reduce the amount of flour required for kneading (adding too much flour at this stage can make your bagels denser). Return the dough to the bowl, cover, and let rise until slightly puffy, 1½ to 2 hours. The dough will not expand much.

Alternatively, in a stand mixer bowl, combine the flour, sugar, salt, yeast, olive oil, and milk. Using the dough hook attachment, mix on medium-low speed until no dry patches of flour remain. Scrape down the bowl as needed, then increase speed to medium-high and mix until smooth and elastic, about 5 minutes. Cover and let rise until slightly puffy, 1½ to 2 hours. The dough will not expand much.

DIVIDE AND PRESHAPE THE DOUGH: Lightly flour a work surface, then use a plastic bowl scraper to ease the dough out of the bowl onto the

Recipe continues

work surface. Divide the dough into 6 equal portions (each about 177 grams). Preshape each piece of dough into a 5-inch tube (see Preshaping, page 32), place seam side down on a lightly floured surface, cover, and let rest for 20 minutes.

Arrange racks in the upper and lower thirds of the oven and preheat the oven to 450°F. Line two baking sheets with parchment paper.

MAKE THE TOPPING: In a 9-inch round or square baking pan, combine the pomegranate molasses and water. Spread the sesame seeds in an even layer on a rimmed baking sheet or sheet of parchment paper and have nearby.

SHAPE THE BAGELS AND LET THEM RISE: Working with one piece of dough at a time, place one hand in the center of the tube of dough. Begin rolling the dough on an unfloured surface until it resembles a dog bone, with a thinner center and thicker ends. Using both hands placed directly next to each other, continue rolling the dough into a log while applying light pressure and using a "down-and-out" motion as you roll your hands along the dough. Your right hand will move toward the right end of the log and your left hand will move toward the left end of the log as the log gets longer. If the dough is sliding around and difficult to roll (because of too much flour on the surface or the dough itself), wipe the work surface with a slightly damp cloth or kitchen towel. This will give the dough some tension and make it easier to roll out. Keep rolling until the log is 18 inches long with tapered ends. Pinch the ends of the log together, then gently roll over the seam by putting your hand through the center of the dough circle and using your palm to apply slight pressure to smooth and seal the seam. Gently stretch the bagel from opposite ends into an oval 7 to 8 inches long.

Using both hands to support the bagel, dip one side into the pomegranate molasses/water mixture, then into the sesame seeds to coat. Transfer to one of the lined baking sheets, seed side up, elongating it back into a 7- to 8-inch oval. Evenly space three bagels per baking sheet. Cover and let rise for 20 to 30 minutes. The bagels will not increase much in volume.

BAKE: Bake the bagels until the outer crust is firm and deep golden brown, 20 to 25 minutes, switching racks and rotating the pans front to back halfway through. If you have extra baking sheets, nest the pans of bagels into them; this double-thick protection will help prevent the bagel bottoms from overbrowning as they bake.

Remove from the oven and transfer to a wire rack to cool. Jerusalem bagels are best eaten the same day they're baked. Store leftover bagels in an airtight container at room temperature for up to 2 days. Rewarm in a low oven or the toaster until heated through.

OLIVE AND FETA POĞAÇA

MIX	BULK FERMENTATION	PRESHAPE	SHAPE	2ND RISE	BAKE
10 MIN	1–1½ HOURS	40 MIN	1 HOUR	30–45 MIN	25–30 MIN

·········· TIME: ABOUT 4½ HOURS ··········

MAKES 12 ROLLS

DOUGH

390 grams (3¼ cups) unbleached all-purpose flour, plus more for dusting

9 grams (1 tablespoon) instant yeast

7.5 grams (2 teaspoons) sugar

8 grams (1¼ teaspoons) fine salt

99 grams (½ cup) olive oil

1 large egg (50 grams)

227 grams (1 cup) warm milk (see Temperature, page 25), whole preferred

FILLING

130 grams (1 cup plus 2½ tablespoons) crumbled feta cheese

100 grams (½ cup plus 3 tablespoons) drained, pitted kalamata olives, chopped

4 grams (1½ tablespoons) chopped fresh oregano

4 grams (1½ tablespoons) chopped fresh parsley

3 grams (1½ teaspoons) grated orange or lemon zest (from ½ large orange or 1 large lemon)

These rosebud rolls are filled with an aromatic, salty, satisfying combination of feta cheese, pitted kalamata olives, and orange zest, with some red pepper flakes added for heat. Though the shaping makes the rolls look fancy, it's actually quite simple to do. These are a great meal on the go—who needs a sandwich?

MAKE THE DOUGH: In a large bowl, combine the flour, yeast, sugar, salt, olive oil, egg, and milk and stir until a soft, slightly sticky dough with no dry spots forms. Transfer the dough to a lightly floured surface and knead until a soft, smooth, springy dough forms, 5 to 8 minutes. The dough will be sticky at first but will smooth out quickly; to make it easier to handle, use a bench knife to scrape the dough off your work surface as you knead, which will speed up the process and reduce the amount of flour required for kneading (adding too much flour at this stage can make your rolls denser). Return the dough to the bowl, cover, and let rise until puffy and doubled in size, 1 to 1½ hours.

Alternatively, in a stand mixer bowl, combine the flour, yeast, sugar, salt, olive oil, egg, and milk. Using the dough hook attachment, mix on medium-low speed until no dry patches of flour remain. Scrape down the bowl as needed, then increase the speed to medium-high and mix until smooth and elastic, about 5 minutes. Cover and let rise until puffy and doubled in size, 1 to 1½ hours.

DIVIDE AND PRESHAPE THE DOUGH: Lightly flour a work surface, then use a plastic bowl scraper to gently ease the dough out of the bowl onto the work surface. Divide the dough into 12 equal portions (each about 65 grams). Preshape each piece of dough into a round (see Preshaping, page 32) and place seam side down on a lightly floured surface, then cover and let rest for 30 minutes.

Ingredients continue

Recipe continues

¼ teaspoon red pepper flakes (optional)

Egg wash: 1 large egg (50 grams), beaten with ⅛ teaspoon fine salt

MAKE THE FILLING: In a medium bowl, stir together the feta, olives, oregano, parsley, citrus zest, and pepper flakes (if using) until well combined. Cover and set aside.

Arrange racks in the upper and lower thirds of the oven and preheat the oven to 350°F. Line two rimmed baking sheets with parchment paper.

SHAPE THE DOUGH AND LET RISE: Lightly flour a work surface. Working with one piece of dough at a time, roll it out into a 5-inch-diameter circle. Using a bench knife or a paring knife, cut four 1½-inch slits around the round, spacing them evenly (1). Place about 20 grams (a generous tablespoon) of filling in the center of the circle (2), then wrap one flap of the dough around the filling (3), pulling the ends together at the bottom of the filling (4). The top of the filling will be exposed; imagine this as if you were wrapping a scarf around your shoulders and crossing it over in front of you. Slightly fold just the top of the dough back from the filling to begin forming a petal shape, as if folding the top of your scarf back like a collar.

Repeat the process with the flap of dough that's opposite to the one you just folded around the filling (5), pulling the ends of the dough together and slightly folding back the top of the dough to form another petal. Continue this pattern with the remaining two flaps of dough (6, 7). As you wrap the final flap of dough around the filling, pull the edges down and tuck them under the roll (8, 9). This will keep the roll from unfurling when rising and baking. Evenly space six rolls on each prepared pan. Cover and let rest until puffy and when pressed with a floured finger, a small impression remains (see Proofing, page 44), 30 to 45 minutes.

BAKE: Lightly brush the rolls all over with the egg wash, then bake until golden brown and the internal temperature reaches 190°F, 25 to 30 minutes.

Remove the rolls from the oven and transfer to a wire rack to cool for 10 minutes before serving warm. Store leftover cooled rolls in an airtight container in the refrigerator for up to 3 days. Rewarm rolls in a preheated 350°F oven for 5 to 8 minutes or until heated through.

BOLO BAO

CUSTARD-FILLED PINEAPPLE BUNS

MIX COOKIE	CUSTARD	MIX	BULK FERMENTATION	SHAPE	2ND RISE	BAKE
10 MIN	15 MIN	20 MIN	1–1½ HOURS	10 MIN	40–50 MIN	18–22 MIN

TIME: ABOUT 4 HOURS

MAKES 12 BUNS

These filled buns are a Chinese bakery classic—a fluffy, milk bread–based bun topped with a crackly, crunchy cookie topping—and get their name from their pineapple-like appearance. Though they're not always filled (or sometimes filled, most luxuriously, with only an unabashedly thick pat of salted butter), this version has a vanilla custard filling. The contrast of crunchy cookie topping, tender bun, and creamy custard is a triple threat. To fully develop this dough, it requires a long mix; for that reason, we recommend making the dough in a stand mixer rather than by hand.

COOKIE TOPPING

57 grams (4 tablespoons) unsalted butter, at room temperature

132 grams (⅔ cup) sugar

1 large egg yolk (14 grams)

14 grams (1 tablespoon) milk, whole preferred, plus more if needed

120 grams (1 cup) unbleached bread flour

28 grams (¼ cup) nonfat dry milk powder

1.5 grams (¼ teaspoon) baking soda

1 gram (¼ teaspoon) baking powder

1.5 grams (¼ teaspoon) fine salt

MAKE THE COOKIE TOPPING: In a stand mixer bowl, combine the butter and sugar. Using the paddle attachment, beat on medium speed until smooth, 1 to 2 minutes. Add the egg yolk and milk, then mix until smooth. Add the flour, milk powder, baking soda, baking powder, and salt. Mix until thoroughly combined. Add more milk, 1 teaspoon at a time, if the mixture seems dry.

Form the cookie dough into a log about 6 inches long and 1½ inches wide. Wrap tightly in parchment or plastic wrap and refrigerate until ready to use.

CUSTARD

2 large egg yolks (28 grams total)

50 grams (¼ cup) sugar

7.5 grams (1 tablespoon) unbleached bread flour

7 grams (1 tablespoon) cornstarch

1.5 grams (¼ teaspoon) fine salt

MAKE THE CUSTARD: In a medium bowl, whisk together the egg yolks, sugar, flour, cornstarch, salt, and 28 grams (2 tablespoons) of the milk.

In a medium saucepan, combine the remaining 142 grams (10 tablespoons) milk and the butter and bring to a simmer over medium-low heat. Once the milk mixture is simmering, slowly whisk half of the hot milk mixture into the egg mixture, whisking constantly to temper it. Then, pour the egg mixture through a fine-mesh sieve back into the remaining simmering milk. Cook, whisking constantly over medium-low heat, until the mixture is thick and pudding-like,

Ingredients continue

Recipe continues

170 grams (¾ cup) milk, whole preferred, divided

28 grams (2 tablespoons) unsalted butter

2.5 grams (½ teaspoon) pure vanilla extract

TANGZHONG

43 grams (3 tablespoons) water

43 grams (3 tablespoons) milk, whole preferred

14 grams (2 tablespoons) unbleached bread flour

DOUGH

300 grams (2½ cups) unbleached bread flour, plus more for dusting

14 grams (2 tablespoons) nonfat dry milk powder

50 grams (¼ cup) sugar

6 grams (1 teaspoon) fine salt

9 grams (1 tablespoon) instant yeast

113 grams (½ cup) cold milk, whole preferred

1 large egg (50 grams)

57 grams (4 tablespoons) unsalted butter, melted

Egg wash: 1 large egg yolk (14 grams), lightly beaten

3 to 4 minutes. Remove from the heat, whisk in the vanilla, and transfer to a bowl to cool. Cover and refrigerate until ready to use; the custard will keep for up to 3 days.

MAKE THE TANGZHONG AND DOUGH: In a small saucepan, combine the water, milk, and bread flour and whisk until no lumps remain. Place the saucepan over low heat and cook the mixture, whisking constantly, until thick and the whisk leaves lines on the bottom of the pan, 3 to 5 minutes.

Transfer the tangzhong to a stand mixer bowl. Add the flour, milk powder, sugar, salt, yeast, cold milk, egg, and melted butter. Using the dough hook attachment, mix on medium speed until the dough is smooth and elastic, about 15 minutes. Cover and let rest until puffy but not necessarily doubled in size, 1 to 1½ hours.

DIVIDE AND SHAPE THE DOUGH AND LET RISE: Line two baking sheets with parchment paper. Lightly flour a work surface, then use a plastic bowl scraper to ease the dough out of the bowl onto the work surface. Gently deflate the dough and divide it into 12 equal pieces (each about 55 grams). Shape each piece into a round (see Shaping, page 34) and place 6 buns on each of the lined pans, spacing them evenly. Cover and let rise until puffy and when pressed with a floured finger, a small impression remains (see Proofing, page 44), 40 to 50 minutes.

Toward the end of the rising time, preheat the oven to 350°F and remove the log of cookie topping from the refrigerator. Let rest on the counter for 10 to 15 minutes to make it easier to slice.

TOP THE BUNS: Slice the cookie log into 12 equal pieces (each about 31 grams) roughly ½ inch thick. Place one slice of cookie topping between two small pieces of parchment paper and flatten with your palm to form a 2½-inch disk. You can also use a rolling pin to form the round for a more precise cookie top, but it doesn't have to be perfect. Repeat with the rest of the dough.

Brush a dab of egg wash on the top center of each bun. (Brushing the entire surface will cause the cookie topping to shift during baking). Drape a disk of cookie topping over each bun and gently press down to secure the cookie topping to the bun; it won't cover the entire surface.

BAKE: Brush the cookie top of each bun with some of the beaten egg yolk. Transfer to the oven and bake until the topping is golden brown and crackly, 18 to 22 minutes.

Remove from the oven and transfer to a rack to cool completely.

FILL THE BUNS: Transfer the cooled custard to a piping bag fitted with a small, round tip or to a zip-top plastic bag with ½ inch of a corner snipped off. Gently invert the buns and use a paring knife or chopstick to poke a hole in the middle of the bottom of each bun so that it's large enough to fit the tip (or the end of your bag) about 1 inch deep. Fill each bun with about 2 tablespoons custard. Serve right away.

Baked buns can be stored, well wrapped and unfilled, at cool room temperature for 3 days. If you plan to make these ahead, store the custard and the buns separately and fill the buns just before serving.

CONCHAS

MIX	BULK FERMENTATION	MIX COOKIE	PRESHAPE	SHAPE	2ND RISE	BAKE
12 MIN	1–1½ HOURS	15 MIN	20 MIN	5 MIN	30–45 MIN	18–24 MIN

MAKE THE PREFERMENT (1 HOUR BEFORE)

TIME: ABOUT 4½ HOURS

MAKES 10 ROLLS

Conchas are one of a variety of Mexican pastries known as pan dulce. Literally translated as "sweet bread," it's a category that includes, by some estimates, up to 2,000 unique preparations. *Concha* means "seashell," and these sweet rolls are topped with a disk of cookie dough (like the Bolo Bao, page 317) that is scored in a gradient or spiral to mimic a shell's ridges. Once baked, it forms a decorative, crispy cap on each roll. Often, the cookie dough is colored and flavored; we've given a few options for how to customize your conchas below on page 322. Because this dough requires a long mix, it's best made in a stand mixer.

PREFERMENT

120 grams (1 cup) unbleached bread flour

6 grams (2 teaspoons) instant yeast

170 grams (¾ cup) warm water (see Temperature, page 25)

DOUGH

330 grams (2¾ cups) unbleached bread flour, plus more for dusting

99 grams (½ cup) sugar

7.5 grams (1¼ teaspoons) fine salt

2 large eggs (100 grams total)

43 grams (3 tablespoons) unsalted butter, at room temperature

1 large egg yolk (14 grams; reserve the white for the topping)

10 grams (2 teaspoons) pure vanilla extract

MAKE THE PREFERMENT: In a stand mixer bowl, combine the bread flour, yeast, and water and mix by hand until no dry spots remain. Cover and let rest for 1 hour, until bubbly.

MAKE THE DOUGH: Add the flour, sugar, salt, whole eggs, butter, egg yolk, and vanilla to the bowl with the preferment. Using the dough hook attachment, mix on medium-low speed until a shaggy dough forms, about 2 minutes. Scrape down the bottom and sides of the bowl well. Increase the speed to medium-high and continue mixing until the dough is smooth and elastic and pulls away from the sides of the bowl, 8 to 10 minutes. The dough will be sticky; scrape down the bowl as necessary. Cover and let rise in a warm place until the dough has doubled in size, 1 to 1½ hours.

COOKIE TOPPING

99 grams (½ cup) sugar

71 grams (5 tablespoons) unsalted butter, at room temperature

10 grams (2 teaspoons) pure vanilla extract

MEANWHILE, MAKE THE COOKIE TOPPING: In a medium bowl, mix together the sugar, butter, vanilla, and salt until smooth. Stir in the flour to form a soft, slightly tacky dough. Divide the dough into 10 equal portions (each about 26 grams). Flatten each portion into a 3- to 4-inch disk by placing each piece between two pieces of parchment or wax paper and rolling with a rolling pin. (A tortilla press works great here as well!) Set aside.

Ingredients continue

Recipe continues

1.5 grams (¼ teaspoon) fine salt

80 grams (⅔ cup) unbleached bread flour

Egg wash: 1 egg white, lightly beaten

DIVIDE AND PRESHAPE THE DOUGH: When the dough has fully risen, line two rimmed baking sheets with parchment paper. Lightly flour a work surface, then use a plastic bowl scraper to ease the dough onto the work surface. Divide the dough into 10 equal portions (each about 90 grams). Gently press down on each piece to remove any bubbles, then preshape them into rounds (see Preshaping, page 32) and place them seam side down on a lightly floured surface.

SHAPE THE DOUGH AND LET RISE: Using a cupped hand, shape each piece of dough into a taut round (see Shaping, page 34), then evenly space the balls of dough on the prepared baking sheets, 5 per sheet. Cover and let rest until noticeably puffy and when pressed with a floured finger, a small impression remains (see Proofing, page 44), 30 to 45 minutes.

Arrange racks in the upper and lower thirds of the oven and preheat the oven to 350°F.

Brush the top of each shaped concha with some of the beaten egg white, then lay on a disk of cookie topping. Use a sharp knife or a baker's lame to cut designs into the topping, being mindful not to cut into the dough below. If you have extra baking sheets, nest the pans of conchas into them; this double-thick protection will help prevent the conchas' bottoms from overbrowning as they bake.

BAKE: Bake until the conchas are golden brown, 18 to 24 minutes, switching racks and rotating the pan front to back halfway through.

Remove them from the oven and let them rest on the pan until they're cool enough to handle. Enjoy conchas warm or at room temperature. Store any leftover conchas, well wrapped, for 3 days at room temperature; freeze for up to 1 month.

CUSTOMIZE YOUR CONCHA COOKIE TOP

MANGO
Pulverize 20 grams (¼ cup plus 2 tablespoons) freeze-dried mango pieces by processing them in a coffee/spice grinder or small food processor until a smooth powder forms, then add to the butter mixture. Proceed with the recipe as directed.

STRAWBERRY/RASPBERRY
Pulverize 10 grams (¼ cup) freeze-dried strawberries or raspberries by processing them in a coffee/spice grinder or small food processor until a smooth powder forms, then sift the powder through a fine-mesh sieve to remove as many seeds as possible. Add the powder to the butter mixture. Proceed with the recipe as directed.

CAFÉ AU LAIT
Use 99 grams (scant ½ cup) brown sugar in place of the granulated sugar called for in the cookie topping. Dissolve 2.5 grams (1 teaspoon) espresso powder or instant coffee in the vanilla, then add it to the butter mixture. Proceed with the recipe as directed.

CHOCOLATE
Use a combination of 80 grams (½ cup plus 3 tablespoons) unbleached bread flour plus 20 grams (scant ¼ cup) cocoa powder in place of the bread flour in the cookie topping. Proceed with the recipe as directed.

CINNAMON
Add 5.2 grams (2 teaspoons) ground cinnamon to the butter mixture. Proceed with the recipe as directed.

KARDEMUMMABULLAR

CARDAMOM BUNS

MIX	BULK FERMENTATION	FILLING	PRESHAPE	CHILL	SHAPE	2ND RISE	BAKE
10–30 MIN	1 HOUR	5 MIN	10 MIN	10–15 MIN	30 MIN	1 HOUR–1 HOUR 15 MIN	15–20 MIN

TIME: ABOUT 4 HOURS

MAKES 8 BUNS

DOUGH

280 grams (2⅓ cups) unbleached all-purpose flour, plus more for dusting

57 grams (½ cup) whole wheat flour

31 grams (2½ tablespoons) sugar

7.5 grams (1¼ teaspoons) fine salt

6 grams (2 teaspoons) instant yeast

2 grams (¾ teaspoon) ground cardamom

113 grams (½ cup) warm water (see Temperature, page 25)

85 grams (¼ cup plus 2 tablespoons) warm milk (see Temperature, page 25), whole preferred

57 grams (4 tablespoons) unsalted butter, at room temperature

FILLING

99 grams (½ cup) sugar

5 to 8 grams (2 teaspoons to 1 tablespoon) ground cardamom

1½ teaspoons ground cinnamon

1½ teaspoons black cocoa

Ingredients continue

These Swedish-style twisted buns are made with an enriched dough and, while tender, are a bit denser in texture than American-style cinnamon buns. They are scented and flavored with cardamom—which is used in the dough, filling (along with sugar, cinnamon, black cocoa, and black pepper), and glaze—infusing the buns with its irresistible, slightly citrusy, resinous flavor.

MAKE THE DOUGH: In a stand mixer bowl, combine the all-purpose flour, whole wheat flour, sugar, salt, yeast, cardamom, water, milk, and butter. Using the dough hook attachment, mix for 1 to 2 minutes on low until combined, then increase to medium speed and knead until the dough is smooth and pulls away from the sides of the bowl, about 5 minutes. Cover and let rest until puffy and risen but not necessarily doubled in size, about 1 hour.

Alternatively, in a large bowl, combine the all-purpose flour, whole wheat flour, sugar, salt, yeast, cardamom, water, milk, and butter and mix to combine. Let the dough rest for 20 minutes (this will make it easier to knead by hand), then transfer to a lightly floured work surface and knead until smooth, 8 to 10 minutes. Return the dough to the bowl, cover, and let it rest until puffy and risen but not necessarily doubled in size, about 1 hour.

MAKE THE FILLING: In a small bowl, combine the sugar, cardamom, cinnamon, black cocoa, pepper, and salt. Set aside.

ROLL THE DOUGH: Line a rimmed baking sheet with parchment paper. On a lightly floured work surface, using a lightly floured rolling pin, roll the dough into a rectangle roughly 20 × 12 inches with a long side running parallel to the edge of your work surface.

Recipe continues

½ teaspoon freshly ground black pepper

¼ teaspoon fine salt

Egg wash: 1 large egg
(50 grams), beaten with 14 grams
(1 tablespoon) water

GLAZE

56 grams (¼ cup) water

25 grams (2 tablespoons) sugar

¼ teaspoon ground cardamom

Swedish pearl sugar, for sprinkling

Brush the entire surface of the dough with egg wash, reserving any excess. Sprinkle the filling mixture evenly over the entire surface of the dough. Fold the dough in thirds like a business letter: Starting on the right side, fold one third into the center, then the opposite third over the first. After the letter fold, the dough should measure about 12 × 6½ inches. Roll briefly to extend the length of the dough so that it measures roughly 12 × 8 inches long. Transfer the dough to the prepared baking sheet. Cover and refrigerate for 10 to 15 minutes; this will firm up the dough and make it easier to work with.

Gently transfer the dough to a lightly floured work surface and roll to elongate it to a 16 × 8-inch rectangle. Using a ruler and a pizza wheel or sharp knife, make small notches along a short side of the dough at 1-inch intervals. Repeat on the other short side of the dough. Align the ruler with the notches at both ends, placing it flat on the dough. Use it as a guide to cut 8 strips that are 1 inch wide and 16 inches long.

SHAPE THE DOUGH AND LET RISE: Working with one piece at a time, twist each end of the dough strip in opposite directions. The dough may start to form a tube, which is OK, but stop shy of twisting so tightly that a tube fully forms. (For the best rise, it is better to have a looser twist than a very tightly wound tube.) Loosely coil into a single layered spiral, tucking only the tip underneath at the end. Press gently to seal. Using both hands or a spatula, carefully place each spiral on the parchment-lined baking sheet. Cover the cardamom buns loosely and place them in a warm place until slightly puffy and risen, 1 hour to 1 hour 15 minutes. Toward the end of the rising time, preheat the oven to 450°F.

BAKE: Gently brush each cardamom bun with the reserved egg wash. Bake the cardamom buns until deep golden brown and the interior temperature reaches at least 190°F, 15 to 20 minutes.

MEANWHILE, MAKE THE GLAZE: In a small saucepan, stir together the water, sugar, and cardamom. Bring the mixture to a boil over medium heat, stirring until the sugar dissolves. Simmer until the mixture has thickened slightly, 5 to 7 minutes. Set aside until the buns are finished baking.

Remove the buns from the oven and immediately brush all over with the glaze. Quickly sprinkle with pearl sugar before the glaze dries.

The cardamom buns are best eaten warm the day they are baked.

PAN DE CRISTAL

MIX	BULK FERMENTATION	SHAPE	2ND RISE	BAKE
5 MIN	2½–3 HOURS	10 MIN	2 HOURS	1 HOUR

TIME: ABOUT 6 HOURS

MAKES FOUR 5 × 7-INCH ROLLS

12 grams (1 tablespoon) olive oil

500 grams (4 cups plus 2½ tablespoons) unbleached bread flour, plus more for dusting

10 grams (1¾ teaspoons) fine salt

2.5 grams (a generous ¾ teaspoon) instant yeast

500 grams (2 cups plus 3 tablespoons) warm water (see Temperature, page 25)

"Glass bread" is the translation for this traditional Catalan-style loaf, which has a thin, crisp crust and one of the airiest crumbs of the bread world. Because this is a very high-hydration dough, it's not the easiest to work with; when you first mix it, it will resemble pancake batter. But have faith! The dough stiffens during bulk fermentation and gains strength through folding. Before dividing, the dough is generously dusted with flour to prevent sticking; handle it as gently as possible to preserve its airiness. If your oven heats from the top, put your baking stone or steel on the bottom rack, rather than the middle, then move the breads to the middle rack for the second half of the bake; this will help prevent the breads from burning on top before they're baked through.

After baking, these rolls are light as a feather; cut them in half crosswise to reveal their beautiful webbed interior.

Grease a 2-quart, 10 × 7-inch rectangular baking dish (or 8- or 9-inch square pan) with the olive oil.

MAKE THE DOUGH: In a large bowl, combine the flour, salt, yeast, and water, mixing until thoroughly combined and no dry spots of flour remain (see Mixing, page 20). The dough will be very sticky, wet, and slack (not elastic).

Bulk fermentation or the "first rise" (see page 25) will take 2½ to 3 hours. During that time you'll attend to the dough four to five times (directions follow), folding the dough every 20 minutes for the first 1 hour 20 minutes to 1 hour 40 minutes. Then let the dough rest, covered and undisturbed, for the final 1 hour 20 minutes.

BULK FERMENT THE DOUGH: Scrape the dough into the prepared baking dish, cover, and let rest for 20 minutes. Using a wet hand, perform 8 to 12 bowl folds (see Bowl Fold, page 30). Cover and let the dough rest for 20 minutes. With wet hands, perform 4 to 5 coil folds (see Coil Fold, page 31), or until the dough resists stretching. Cover and let rest for 20 minutes. With wet hands, perform 4 to 5 more coil folds, or until the dough resists stretching. If your dough still feels slack and hard to handle, cover and allow it to rest 20 minutes, then perform 4 to 5 more coil folds, or until the dough resists stretching. If your dough feels relatively strong—elastic, holding its shape when folded, and easy to handle—cover and let rest until the dough is very puffy and marshmallowy, 1 hour 20 minutes. If the dough still feels slack, cover and let rest for 20 minutes, then perform a fifth and final set of coil folds before covering and letting rest until puffy and marshmallowy, 1 hour 20 minutes.

DIVIDE AND SHAPE THE DOUGH AND LET RISE: Heavily flour a work surface, then gently ease the dough out onto the surface. Very lightly stretch the corners to make an even-ish rectangle (don't press on the dough or manipulate it too aggressively, as this can cause it to deflate, compromising the open crumb). Sprinkle a generous amount of flour on the top and sides of the dough so that no sticky spots are exposed. Using a bench knife or a knife and working as gently as possible, divide the dough into 4 equal portions (each about 250 grams). Place 2 pieces on one sheet of parchment paper, leaving space between them. Repeat with the remaining 2 pieces of dough, placing them on a second piece of parchment. Let the loaves rest, uncovered, at room temperature for 2 hours; they may develop a slightly dry crust, which is OK.

Toward the end of the rising time, arrange racks in the lowest position and the upper third of the oven and preheat the oven to 475°F with a baking stone or steel on the lowest rack.

BAKE: Using a baker's peel or an inverted baking sheet to aid you, carefully slide the first 2 loaves (still on the parchment) into the oven onto the preheated stone or steel. Let the other 2 loaves rest either at room temperature (if your kitchen is on the cool side) or in the refrigerator (if your kitchen is on the warm side) while you bake the first.

Bake the loaves for 15 minutes. Transfer them to the rack in the upper third of the oven (moving them allows the baking stone or steel to become hot again in preparation for the next 2 loaves). Bake until the crust of the loaves is crisp and deep golden brown and the loaves feel light for their size, an additional 13 to 15 minutes; if they are browning too deeply, reduce the oven temperature slightly.

Remove the loaves from the oven and allow them to cool slightly on a wire rack.

Repeat the baking process with the remaining 2 loaves. For maximum crispness, cut in half crosswise and enjoy while still slightly warm. Pan de cristal is best eaten the same day it's baked.

CHOCOLATE PAN DE CRISTAL

MIX	BULK FERMENTATION	SHAPE	2ND RISE	BAKE
5 MIN	3 HOURS	10 MIN	2 HOURS	36–40 MIN

········· TIME: ABOUT 6 HOURS ·········

MAKES EIGHT 4 × 6-INCH ROLLS

12 to 24 grams (1 to 2 tablespoons) olive oil

500 grams (4 cups plus 2½ tablespoons) unbleached bread flour, plus more for dusting

21 grams (¼ cup) Dutch-process cocoa powder

10 grams (1¾ teaspoons) fine salt

2.5 grams (scant 1 teaspoon) instant yeast

520 grams (2¼ cups plus 1 tablespoon) warm water (see Temperature, page 25)

170 grams (1 cup) chopped semisweet chocolate or chocolate chips

Like traditional Pan de Cristal (page 330), these rolls have a wide-open crumb and a crisp crust, but here the dough contains cocoa and is studded with semisweet chocolate. You can use all Dutch-process cocoa, but for rolls with a darker color and deeper flavor, substitute black cocoa for half of the Dutch-process. We like these rolls split, toasted, and spread with salted butter for a fabulous breakfast, or topped with ricotta and cherry jam for a Black Forest–inspired version. If your oven heats from the top, place your stone or steel on the bottom rack, then move to the middle rack to finish baking, which will prevent the top of the bread from burning.

Grease a 2-quart, 10 × 7-inch rectangular baking dish (or 8- or 9-inch square pan) with 12 grams (1 tablespoon) of the olive oil. Set aside.

MAKE THE DOUGH: In a large bowl, combine the flour, cocoa, salt, yeast, and water, mixing until thoroughly combined and no dry spots of flour remain (see Mixing, page 20). The dough will be very sticky, wet, and slack (not elastic).

Bulk fermentation or the "first rise" (see page 25) will take 3 hours. During that time you'll attend to the dough five times (directions follow), folding the dough every 20 minutes for the first 1 hour 40 minutes. Then let rest, covered and undisturbed, for the final 1 hour 20 minutes.

BULK FERMENT THE DOUGH: Scrape the dough into the prepared baking dish, cover, and let rest for 20 minutes. Using a wet hand, perform 8 to 12 bowl folds (see Bowl Fold, page 30) or until the dough starts to show some elasticity. Cover and let the dough rest for 20 minutes. With wet hands, perform 4 to 5 coil folds (see Coil Fold, page 31) or until the dough resists stretching. Cover and let rest for 20 minutes. With wet hands, perform 4 to 5 more coil folds, or until the dough resists stretching. If your dough still feels slack and hard to handle, cover and allow it to rest 20 minutes, then perform 4 to 5 more coil folds, or until the dough resists stretching. If your dough feels relatively strong—elastic, holding its shape when folded, and easy to handle—cover and let rest for 20 minutes, then move on to incorporating the chocolate.

Lightly moisten a work surface by dipping your hand in water and spreading it across the surface (we use water on the surface instead of flour, as flour would leave streaks in the dark dough). Using a plastic bowl scraper and working as gently as possible to avoid deflating the dough, ease the dough out onto the surface and gently coax into a rectangle about 14 × 10 inches with a long side facing you. Sprinkle the chocolate evenly over the dough. Wet your hands and, using them like paddles (with your fingers extended and pressed together), fold the left side of the dough toward the center, then the opposite third over the first, like folding a business letter. Fold the dough a second time by bringing the top third of the dough down toward the center, then bringing the bottom third up over the top portion, again as if folding a business letter.

If necessary, add an additional 12 grams (1 tablespoon) oil to the pan to keep the dough from sticking. Return the dough to the oiled pan, cover, and let rise until puffy, about 1 hour 20 minutes.

DIVIDE AND SHAPE THE ROLLS AND LET RISE: Heavily flour a work surface and gently turn the dough out onto the surface. Very lightly stretch the corners to make an even-ish rectangle (don't press on the dough or manipulate it too aggressively, as this can cause it to deflate, compromising the open crumb). Sprinkle a generous amount of flour on the top and sides of the dough so that no sticky spots are exposed. Using a bench knife or a knife and working as gently as possible, divide the dough into 8 equal portions (each about 150 grams). Place 4 pieces on one sheet of parchment paper, leaving space between them. Repeat with the remaining 4 pieces of dough, placing them on a second piece of parchment. Tuck any visible pieces of chocolate into the dough to prevent them from burning. Let the rolls rest

uncovered at room temperature for 2 hours; they may develop a slightly dry crust, which is OK.

Toward the end of the rising time, arrange racks in the lowest position and the upper third of the oven and preheat the oven to 475°F with a baking stone or steel on the lowest rack.

BAKE: Using a baker's peel or an inverted baking sheet to aid you, carefully slide the 4 rolls (still on the parchment) into the oven onto the preheated stone or steel. Let the other 4 rolls rest either at room temperature (if your kitchen is on the cool side) or in the refrigerator (if your kitchen is on the warm side) while you bake the first.

Bake the rolls for 10 minutes, then transfer them to the rack in the upper third of the oven (moving them allows the baking stone or steel to become hot again in preparation for the next batch). Bake until the crust of the rolls is crisp and the rolls feel light for their size, 8 to 10 minutes more.

Remove the rolls from the oven and transfer to a rack to cool.

Repeat the baking process with the remaining rolls. For maximum crispness, cut and enjoy while still slightly warm. Pan de cristal is best eaten the same day it's baked.

MALLORCAS

MIX	BULK FERMENTATION	SHAPE	2ND RISE	BAKE
20 MIN	30 MIN	20 MIN	6–16 HOURS	20 MIN

TIME: ABOUT 8–18 HOURS

MAKES SIX 4½- TO 5-INCH MALLORCAS

DOUGH

93 grams (6½ tablespoons) lard or unsalted butter

360 grams (3 cups) unbleached bread flour, plus more for dusting

78 grams (⅓ cup plus 1 tablespoon) granulated sugar

3 grams (1 teaspoon) instant yeast

3 grams (½ teaspoon) fine salt

75 grams (⅓ cup) warm water (see Temperature, page 25)

57 grams (¼ cup) warm milk (see Temperature, page 25), whole preferred

4 large egg yolks (56 grams total)

TOPPING

28 to 42 grams (2 to 3 tablespoons) lard or unsalted butter, softened

Egg wash: 1 large egg (50 grams), beaten with 113 grams (½ cup) water

57 grams (½ cup) confectioners' sugar, for serving

These sweet, fluffy, oversize coiled buns originated on the Spanish island of Mallorca, where they are known as ensaïmadas; when immigrants made their way to Puerto Rico in the early twentieth century, they brought these buns, which were renamed for their place of origin. Lard is traditional, and gives them a plush, tender texture (and a slightly savory flavor), but you can substitute butter if you prefer. In either case, before serving, dust the mallorcas generously with confectioners' sugar and serve them for breakfast with jam alongside.

MAKE THE DOUGH: In a small saucepan, heat the lard or butter over gentle heat just until melted. (Alternatively, melt in a microwaveable bowl in the microwave.) Set aside to cool slightly.

In a stand mixer bowl, combine the flour, sugar, yeast, and salt and mix until well combined.

In a medium bowl, whisk together the water, milk, and egg yolks to combine. Add the wet ingredients all at once to the stand mixer bowl and, using the dough hook attachment, mix at low speed until a somewhat dry, shaggy dough forms, about 1 minute.

With the mixer running, slowly stream the melted lard or butter into the bowl. Stop the mixer once or twice to scrape down the sides of the bowl as needed. By this time, the dough will have no dry bits remaining. Once the lard or butter is incorporated, increase the mixer to medium speed and continue to mix until the dough cleans the sides of the bowl, gathers around the dough hook, and looks tight and feels bouncy, 10 to 15 minutes. Monitor the temperature of the dough so that it does not exceed 90°F to prevent the lard or butter from getting too soft; you can always pause and place the dough in the refrigerator for a few minutes before continuing to mix.

Recipe continues

Once fully kneaded, cover the dough and let rest at room temperature for 30 minutes. The dough will not rise much during this time.

Line a baking sheet with parchment paper.

DIVIDE THE DOUGH: Lightly flour a work surface, then use a plastic bowl scraper to ease the dough out of the bowl onto the work surface. Using a bench knife or a knife, divide the dough into 6 equal portions (about 120 grams each).

SHAPE THE DOUGH: For easiest shaping, complete the next four steps in a serialized way: Do one step for all the pieces, then move on to the next step for all pieces again, etc. The rest period between steps will allow the dough to relax, making it easier to roll to the stated dimensions.

Flatten each piece of dough with a rolling pin into a rectangle that's roughly 10 × 3 inches.

Starting with the first piece of dough you rolled, stretch the top corners to reinforce the 3-inch width and press down to adhere it to the work surface. Gently pull on the bottom of the now-anchored dough to stretch it toward you into a rectangle 12 to 16 inches long. (If it tears a bit, just keep going, or let the dough relax so that it becomes more extensible.) When the dough is the right size, press the bottom two corners down on the table to adhere them. Repeat with the remaining pieces of dough.

Use your hand to smear some of the 28 to 42 grams (2 to 3 tablespoons) softened lard or butter in a thin layer over the surface of each dough rectangle. Beginning with the first piece of dough that was stretched, roll it up into a log starting from one of the long sides, so you end up with a long rope of uniform thickness. Set aside and continue with the other pieces of dough.

Go back to the first log and use the palms of your hands to roll it gently from the center outward two or three times to seal the seam and lengthen it to about 18 inches. Loosely coil it like a snail, leaving room for the dough to rise, then tuck the end under the coil. (Avoid coiling the dough too tightly; a tight coil will rise upward instead of out.) Set on the prepared baking sheet.

Cover the mallorcas loosely with plastic wrap and let them rise at warm room temperature (ideally around 75°F) for at least 6 hours and up to 16 (overnight). When properly proofed, the mallorcas will look noticeably puffier, and the dough coils will fill out any of the empty space that was left during shaping.

Toward the end of the rising time, preheat the oven to 375°F with a rack in the center.

BAKE: Use a pastry brush to gently coat the mallorcas with egg wash. Bake until the buns are golden and the internal temperature registers 190°F, 20 minutes, rotating the pan front to back halfway through.

Let the mallorcas cool on the pan, then dust liberally with confectioners' sugar before serving.

Mallorcas can be stored in an airtight container at room temperature for up to 2 days, but wait to dust with confectioners' sugar until shortly before serving.

SHENG JIAN BAO

MUSHROOM AND CABBAGE PAN-FRIED BUNS

MIX	BULK FERMENTATION		SHAPE	COOK
10–15 MIN	1–1½ HOURS		40 MIN	20 MIN

TIME: ABOUT 2 HOURS 40 MIN

MAKES EIGHTEEN 3-INCH BUNS

DOUGH

360 grams (3 cups) unbleached all-purpose flour, plus more for dusting

74 grams (6 tablespoons) sugar

7 grams (2 heaping teaspoons) instant yeast

3 grams (½ teaspoon) fine salt

2 grams (½ teaspoon) baking powder

227 grams (1 cup) warm milk (see Temperature, page 25)

12 grams (1 tablespoon) vegetable oil

FILLING

12 grams (1 tablespoon) vegetable oil

1-inch piece fresh ginger (6 grams), peeled and finely chopped

2 garlic cloves (10 grams), finely chopped

227 grams (8 ounces) fresh shiitake mushrooms, stems trimmed, caps finely chopped (3 cups)

Ingredients continue

These plump, crispy-bottomed vegetarian buns are based on Shanghainese sheng jian bao. *Sheng jian bao* translates to "raw fried buns," which refers to the way they're cooked: The raw buns are first browned in an oil-slicked pan, then water is added and the pan is covered, trapping the steam within and cooking the buns to fluffy perfection. Sheng jian bao are traditionally filled with pork, but in this vegetarian version, the filling is a crunchy, umami-rich combination of mushrooms and cabbage.

MAKE THE DOUGH: In a stand mixer bowl, combine the flour, sugar, yeast, salt, baking powder, milk, and vegetable oil. Using the dough hook attachment, mix on medium speed until the dough is soft and elastic, 8 to 10 minutes. Cover and let rise in a warm place until it's nearly doubled in size, 1 to 1½ hours.

Alternatively, in a medium bowl, combine the flour, sugar, yeast, salt, baking powder, milk, and vegetable oil and mix the ingredients using the handle of a wooden spoon. Transfer to a lightly floured work surface and knead for 12 to 15 minutes. Return to the bowl, cover, and let it rise in a warm place until it's nearly doubled in size, 1 to 1½ hours.

MEANWHILE, MAKE THE FILLING: Place a large skillet over medium heat. When hot, add the oil, ginger, and garlic and cook, stirring frequently, until fragrant, about 30 seconds. Add the mushrooms, cabbage, five-spice powder, and pepper to taste. Cook, stirring occasionally, until the mushrooms and cabbage are soft and any liquid has evaporated, 5 to 6 minutes.

Add the soy sauce, sesame oil, and scallions and stir until combined, about 1 minute. Taste to check seasonings, adding salt if needed (this filling should be on the salty side to balance the sweetness of the bun).

Recipe continues

170 grams (2½ cups) shredded green cabbage

¼ teaspoon five-spice powder

Ground black pepper, to taste

10 grams (2 teaspoons) soy sauce

1 teaspoon toasted sesame oil

2 scallions (34 grams), thinly sliced

COOKING AND SERVING

12 to 25 grams (1 to 2 tablespoons) vegetable oil, for frying

114 grams (½ cup) water

1 scallion, thinly sliced

9 grams (1 tablespoon) toasted white sesame seeds

Chili oil or chili crisp (optional)

Black vinegar (optional)

Line a rimmed baking sheet with parchment paper and dampen a clean kitchen towel. Set both nearby. Preheat the oven to 200°F.

DIVIDE THE DOUGH AND SHAPE THE BUNS: After the dough has risen, divide it with a bench knife or a knife into 18 equal portions (each about 36 grams). Roll each piece into a ball and cover with a damp kitchen towel. Working with one ball at a time, place it on a lightly floured surface and flatten using the palm of your hand. Then use a rolling pin to roll the disk into a 3- to 3½-inch-diameter round, making sure the edges are thinner than the middle. (This will make it easier to pleat.) To achieve thin edges, hold the dough down with your nondominant hand, rotating it gradually as you roll out the edges of the round using a pin in your dominant hand. (A wooden dowel or a small tapered rolling pin is the best tool here.)

Add a little flour to your hand and fingers to prevent sticking, then take the dough round in your palm and place about 2 teaspoons of the filling in the center. Pleat the edges together, then twist to secure. Place on the prepared baking sheet, grouping the first 9 buns you shape together to ensure you cook those buns first, and cover with the damp towel.

COOK THE BUNS: Work in two batches, starting with the first 9 buns you shaped. Heat a 10-inch well-seasoned cast-iron or nonstick skillet over medium-high heat. When the pan is hot, reduce the heat to medium and add 1 to 2 teaspoons of the oil (it should be enough to coat the bottom of the pan) and place the first batch of buns in the pan, flat side down. The buns should be spaced slightly apart to give them room to expand.

Cook the buns until browned on only one side (no need to flip), 2 to 3 minutes, rotating the pan for even cooking and lifting the buns to check when the bottoms have turned golden brown. Add 57 grams (¼ cup) water to the pan and immediately cover with a lid. Cook until the buns are puffed, 5 to 6 minutes. Uncover, and if there is still water in the skillet, cook until it has evaporated. Remove the buns from the pan, transfer to a baking sheet, and place in the oven to keep warm while you fry the remaining buns, using the remaining oil and water for cooking, adjusting the heat as needed to avoid overbrowning.

To serve, top with sliced scallion and sesame seeds. If desired, serve with chili oil or chili crisp and black vinegar. These buns are best eaten right after they're cooked. Cooked buns can be stored in an airtight container in the fridge for up to 4 days or in the freezer for up to 3 months. To reheat, add the buns to a pan with a small amount of oil until recrisped, then add water, cover, and steam until the buns are warmed through and the dough is puffy again.

PETITS PAINS
MINI BAGUETTES

MIX	BULK FERMENTATION		PRESHAPE	SHAPE	2ND RISE	CHILL	BAKE
5 MIN	2½–3 HOURS		25 MIN	10 MIN	45 MIN–1 HOUR	10–15 MIN	42–55 MIN

MAKE THE PREFERMENT (12–16 HOURS BEFORE)

TIME: ABOUT 22 HOURS

MAKES NINE 6-INCH LOAVES

PREFERMENT

101 grams (¾ cup plus 4½ teaspoons) unbleached all-purpose flour

0.5 gram (pinch) instant yeast

101 grams (¼ cup plus 3 tablespoons) cold water (55°F to 60°F)

DOUGH

282 grams (1¼ cups) warm water (see Temperature, page 25)

403 grams (3¼ cups plus 2 tablespoons) unbleached all-purpose flour

10 grams (generous 1½ teaspoons) fine salt

2 grams (generous ½ teaspoon) instant yeast

Not only are these rolls exceptionally adorable but they also have the irresistible attributes of full-size baguettes, including a thin, crisp crust and an open crumb structure. A charming addition to a holiday bread basket, they're also just the right size and shape for sandwiches. The Parisian-style ham and butter sandwich is a particular favorite.

DAY 1

MAKE THE PREFERMENT: The evening before you want to bake, in a large bowl, combine the flour, yeast, and water and mix until no dry patches of flour remain. Cover and let stand at room temperature overnight, 12 to 16 hours.

DAY 2

MAKE THE DOUGH: Add the warm water to the preferment, then squeeze the preferment through your fingers to break it up. Next, holding your hand in a clawlike position, vigorously mix the preferment into the water until well combined. The mixture will be very thin and slightly foamy, with some pieces of preferment still visible. Add the flour, salt, and yeast, mixing well until no dry spots remain (see Mixing, page 20).

Bulk fermentation or the "first rise" (see page 25) will take 2½ to 3 hours. During that time you'll attend to the dough three times (directions follow), folding the dough every 20 minutes for the first hour. Then the dough will rest, covered and undisturbed, for the final 1½ to 2 hours.

BULK FERMENT THE DOUGH: Once you've mixed the dough, cover and let rest for 20 minutes. Using a wet hand, perform 8 to 12 bowl folds (see Bowl Fold, page 30) or until the dough resists stretching. Round out the dough by cupping your hand and applying pressure toward the bottom of the dough, forcing it into the bottom and side of the bowl to create

Recipe continues

tension. Cover and let rest for another 20 minutes. Using a wet hand, perform another set of 6 to 8 bowl folds, or until the dough resists stretching. Let the dough rest for another 20 minutes. With wet hands, perform 2 to 3 coil folds (see Coil Fold, page 31) until the dough resists stretching. Cover and let the dough rest 1½ to 2 hours, or until the dough is very puffy and marshmallowy.

DIVIDE AND PRESHAPE THE DOUGH: Lightly dust a work surface with flour, then use a plastic bowl scraper to ease the dough out of the bowl onto the work surface. With a bench knife or a knife, divide the dough into 9 equal portions (each about 99 grams). Tightly preshape each piece of dough into a 3-inch-long tube (see Preshaping, page 32), and place seam side down on the work surface. Cover and let rest until the dough feels more relaxed, softer, and less taut, about 15 minutes.

SHAPE THE DOUGH AND LET RISE: Slightly elongate each piece by placing your hands next to each other in the center of the cylinder and rolling in a "down-and-out" motion, slightly tapering the ends. The resulting loaf should be 6 inches long.

Generously dust a baker's linen or clean kitchen towel with flour and transfer the loaves to the prepared linen or towel, seam side up. Gently fold about 1 inch of the linen up and place it against each loaf to support and separate them. Cover and let rest at room temperature until the dough feels light and marshmallowy and when pressed with a floured finger, a small impression remains (see Proofing, page 44), 45 minutes to 1 hour.

Meanwhile, arrange racks in the center and bottom third of the oven and preheat the oven to 475°F with a baking stone or steel on the center rack and an empty cast-iron skillet (or a cake pan filled with lava rocks) on the lower rack. If possible, adjust the stone and pan so that the skillet isn't directly under the stone, making it easier for steam to reach the baking bread (see Steaming, page 50).

Using a transfer peel (see page 18), gently roll the loaves onto sheets of parchment paper so that the seam sides face down. Evenly space 4 or 5 of the loaves on each piece of parchment. Slide the loaves (still on the parchment) onto the backs of two baking sheets and refrigerate, uncovered, for 10 to 15 minutes. This will allow the dough to chill and dry out slightly, making scoring easier.

Use a baker's lame or a razor blade to score the tops of half the loaves (see Scoring, page 46). Keep the second batch of loaves refrigerated while the first batch bakes.

BAKE: Using a baker's peel or an inverted baking sheet to aid you, transfer the first batch of loaves (still on the parchment) into the oven, placing them on the stone, and pour about 227 grams (1 cup) of warm water into the skillet. Steam will billow from the pan upward to envelop the bread; be sure to wear good oven mitts to shield your hands and arms. Quickly close the oven door to trap the steam. Bake the loaves until the crust is firm and deep golden brown, 16 to 20 minutes.

Remove from the oven and let cool on a wire rack. Let the baking stone or steel reheat for 10 to 15 minutes before baking the second batch of loaves with steam as before. These are best eaten the day they are baked.

DUTCH CRUNCH ROLLS

MIX	BULK FERMENTATION	TOPPING	SHAPE	2ND RISE	BAKE
25 MIN	1 HOUR	5 MIN	10 MIN	30-40 MIN	25-30 MIN

·········· TIME: ABOUT 3 HOURS ··········

MAKES SIX 4-INCH ROLLS

DOUGH

250 grams (2 cups plus
1 tablespoon) unbleached all-
purpose flour

14 grams (1 tablespoon) unsalted
butter, at room temperature

8 grams (2 teaspoons) sugar

6 grams (1 teaspoon) fine salt

4.5 grams (1½ teaspoons) instant
yeast

175 grams (¾ cup plus
1 teaspoon) warm water (see
Temperature, page 25)

TOPPING

62 grams (¼ cup plus
3 tablespoons) white rice flour

11 grams (scant 1 tablespoon)
sugar

1.2 grams (scant ½ teaspoon)
instant yeast

0.5 gram (scant ⅛ teaspoon) fine
salt

57 grams (¼ cup) warm water
(90°F)

6 grams (1½ teaspoons) vegetable
or other neutral oil

Dutch crunch is ubiquitous in some places, absent in others. The earliest mention of a bread topped with a crispy rice flour topping comes from the Netherlands in the early part of the twentieth century, where it was called *tijgerbrood* (tiger bread). From there, its migratory pattern is unclear. You can find it in the UK (where it's often sold under the name giraffe bread, which, like tiger bread, is a reference to the pattern the rice flour topping develops as it bakes). But by the 1970s the bread had made its way to America, gaining a foothold in San Francisco; owing to its European origins, it was then renamed Dutch crunch. The Bay Area is still one of the few places in the United States where this bread can be found; there, it's a common option in delis and sandwich shops.

The rice flour slurry that's spread onto the rolls before baking makes the rolls special. Sweetened with a touch of sugar, the slurry spreads and cracks as it bakes, forming a mottled crust and adding a bit of texture to the soft roll. You can eat these rolls plain, or use them to make small sandwiches.

MAKE THE DOUGH: In a large bowl, combine the flour, butter, sugar, salt, yeast, and water and mix until no dry patches of flour remain and a soft, sticky dough forms. Cover and let rest for 15 minutes; this rest will make the dough easier to knead. Transfer the dough to a lightly floured surface and knead until a tacky, springy dough forms, 5 to 8 minutes. The dough will be sticky at first but will smooth out quickly; to make it easier to handle, use a bench knife to scrape the dough off your work surface as you knead, which will speed up the process and reduce the amount of flour required for kneading (adding too much flour at this stage can make your rolls denser). Return the dough to the bowl, cover, and let rise until puffy and doubled in size, about 1 hour.

Alternatively, in a stand mixer bowl, combine the flour, butter, sugar, salt, yeast, and water. Using the dough hook attachment, mix on medium-low

Recipe continues

speed until no dry patches of flour remain. Increase the speed to medium and mix until smooth, elastic, and pulling away from the sides of the bowl, 5 to 8 minutes. Cover the mixer bowl and let rise until puffy and doubled in size, about 1 hour.

MAKE THE TOPPING: In a small bowl, whisk together the rice flour, sugar, yeast, and salt. Add the water and oil, mixing well to form a thick paste. Cover and let rest at room temperature until ready to spread on the buns.

DIVIDE AND SHAPE THE DOUGH AND LET RISE: Line a rimmed baking sheet with parchment paper. Lightly flour a work surface, then use a plastic bowl scraper to gently ease the dough out of the bowl onto the work surface. With a bench knife or a knife, divide the dough into 6 equal portions (each about 75 grams). Gently press down on each piece to remove any bubbles, then preshape them into rounds (see Preshaping, page 32). Place seam side down on an unfloured area of your work surface. Working with one piece of dough at a time, use your cupped hand to create tension and form a smooth, taut round of dough (see Shaping, page 34). Place the roll on the prepared baking sheet. Repeat with the remaining pieces of dough, evenly spacing them on the baking sheet. Cover and let rest at room temperature until slightly puffy, 15 to 20 minutes.

Arrange a rack in the center of the oven and preheat the oven to 450°F.

Stir the topping mixture until smooth. Using a 1-tablespoon measure, dollop about 22 grams of topping on top of each roll. Using your finger or a small offset spatula, spread the topping evenly over the top and about halfway down all sides of each roll (if any of the topping drips down on the parchment paper, scoop it up and put it on top of the roll). Cover and let rise until the rolls are very puffy and when pressed with a floured finger, an indentation remains (see Proofing, page 44), an additional 15 to 20 minutes. If you have an extra baking sheet, nest the pan of rolls into it; this double-thick protection will help prevent the bottoms of the rolls from overbrowning as they bake.

BAKE: Bake the rolls until the topping is crisp, firm, and deep golden brown in spots, 25 to 30 minutes. The topping will have a leopard-like spotted pattern and the rolls should feel light for their size.

Transfer to a rack to cool completely. These rolls are best eaten the day they are baked; the crust will soften and lose crispness if stored.

FENNEL AND GOLDEN RAISIN ROLLS

MIX	BULK FERMENTATION	SHAPE	2ND RISE	BAKE
12 MIN	1½ HOURS	15 MIN	1 HOUR	20 MIN

TIME: ABOUT 3½ HOURS

MAKES 12 ROLLS

421 grams (3½ cups) unbleached all-purpose flour, plus more for dusting

49 grams (5 tablespoons) yellow cornmeal

10.5 grams (1¾ teaspoons) fine salt

6 grams (2 teaspoons) instant yeast

47 grams (3 tablespoons plus 1 teaspoon) unsalted butter, at room temperature

21 grams (1 tablespoon) honey

284 grams (1¼ cups) warm water (see Temperature, page 25)

121 grams (¾ cup plus 1 tablespoon) golden raisins

7 grams (1 tablespoon plus 1 teaspoon) fennel seeds

CRUST

40 grams (¼ cup) yellow cornmeal, for coating

These chewy yeasted rolls are infused with the flavor of fennel and punctuated with pockets of sweet golden raisins. There's cornmeal both in the dough and coating each roll, giving it a bit of subtle crunch; you can score each roll with a single diagonal slice, or use a pair of scissors to make small, shallow snips across the top, which gives the rolls a porcupine-like appearance. Baking the rolls on a baking stone or steel and adding some steam to the oven while they bake gives them a shiny, crispy crust.

MAKE THE DOUGH: In a stand mixer bowl, combine the flour, 49 grams (5 tablespoons) cornmeal, salt, yeast, butter, honey, and water. Using the dough hook attachment, mix on medium-low speed until a shaggy dough forms, about 1 minute. Scrape down the bottom and sides of the bowl, then increase the speed to medium and mix until a slightly sticky dough forms that releases from the sides but not the bottom of the bowl, 8 to 10 minutes. Add the raisins and fennel seeds and mix on medium-low speed until fully incorporated, 1 to 2 minutes more. The dough will be somewhat sticky. Cover and let rise until very puffy, about 1½ hours.

Place the 40 grams (¼ cup) cornmeal in a small bowl. Wet a clean kitchen towel, then wring it out; it should still be pretty damp. Place a sheet of parchment paper on the work surface near the moistened towel and cornmeal.

DIVIDE AND SHAPE THE ROLLS: Lightly flour a work surface, then use a plastic bowl scraper to ease the dough out of the bowl onto the work surface. Press gently to deflate the dough, then, with a bench knife or a knife, divide into 12 equal portions (each about 80 grams). Working with one piece of dough at a time, loosely preshape it into a round (see Preshaping, page 32). Place it seam side down on the work surface, then use your cupped hand to create tension and form a smooth, taut round of dough (see Shaping, page 34). Roll the bottom and lower sides of each piece of dough over the damp towel to moisten, then into the cornmeal

Recipe continues

to coat. When finished, the bottom and about ½ inch up the sides of the roll should be coated in cornmeal, with the top three-quarters of the roll uncoated.

Place the roll on the sheet of parchment, then continue shaping and coating the remaining rolls. Evenly space the rolls in a 4 × 3 grid on the parchment. Cover and let rise until the rolls are puffy and when pressed with a floured finger, an indentation remains (see Proofing, page 44), about 1 hour. Any leftover cornmeal can be saved and reused.

Toward the end of the rising time, arrange racks in the center and bottom third of the oven and preheat the oven to 450°F with a baking stone or steel on the center rack and an empty cast-iron skillet (or a cake pan filled with lava rocks) on the lower rack. If possible, adjust the stone and pan so that the skillet isn't directly under the stone, making it easier for steam to reach the baking rolls (see Steaming, page 50).

Just before baking, use a baker's lame or a sharp knife to score the top of each roll with one midline cut (you can also score them with scissors; see headnote).

BAKE: With a baker's peel or an inverted baking sheet to aid you, transfer the rolls (still on the parchment) into the oven and then pour about 227 grams (1 cup) of warm water into the skillet. Steam will billow from the pan upward to envelop the rolls; be sure to wear good oven mitts to shield your hands and arms. Quickly close the oven door to trap the steam. Bake until the rolls are deep golden brown and the crust is firm, about 20 minutes.

Remove from the oven and let cool slightly on a wire rack. The crust will soften as the rolls sit. Serve warm or at room temperature. Store leftover rolls in an airtight container at room temperature for up to 3 days or freeze for longer storage. To reheat rolls, place thawed rolls on a parchment-lined baking sheet and bake in a 350°F oven until heated through and slightly crisp, 5 to 8 minutes.

MULTIGRAIN BÂTONS

MIX	BULK FERMENTATION	PRESHAPE	SHAPE	2ND RISE	BAKE
5 MIN	1 HOUR	15 MIN	15 MIN	45 MIN–1 HOUR	25–30 MIN

MAKE THE PREFERMENT (12–16 HOURS BEFORE)

TIME: ABOUT 19 HOURS

MAKES 8 ROLLS

PREFERMENT

21 grams (1½ tablespoons) sourdough culture (see page 187)

85 grams (½ cup plus 3 tablespoons) unbleached all-purpose flour

85 grams (¼ cup plus 2 tablespoons) cold water (55°F to 60°F)

DOUGH

209 grams (¾ cup plus 3 tablespoons) warm water (see Temperature, page 25)

256 grams (2 cups plus · 2 tablespoons) unbleached all-purpose flour, plus more for dusting

85 grams (¾ cup plus 1 tablespoon) whole rye flour

11 grams (1¾ teaspoons) fine salt

3 grams (1 teaspoon) instant yeast

1½ teaspoons honey

35 grams (¼ cup) flaxseeds

SEED CRUST

120 grams (1 cup) rolled oats, rye chops, or untoasted seeds, such as flaxseeds, sunflower seeds, or a mixture

These seedy rolls can do anything you'd want a roll to do: act as a foundation for a small sandwich, be served alongside soup to turn it into a heartier meal, or be split, toasted, and lavished with butter and flaky salt (or topped with cheese for a breakfast that resembles one you might have in a European hotel). A portion of rye flour in the dough, along with flaxseeds, gives these bâtons a hearty nuttiness; coat the exterior of the rolls with additional flaxseeds, or use rolled oats or sunflower seeds, or, as is our preference, a mix of all three.

DAY 1

MAKE THE PREFERMENT: The evening before you want to bake, in a large bowl, combine the sourdough culture, flour, and water and mix until no dry patches of flour remain and a smooth dough forms. Cover and let stand at room temperature overnight, 12 to 16 hours.

DAY 2

MAKE THE DOUGH: Add the warm water to the preferment, then squeeze the preferment through your fingers to break it up. Next, holding your hand in a clawlike position, vigorously mix the preferment into the water until well combined. The mixture will look like lumpy pancake batter. Add the all-purpose flour, rye flour, salt, yeast, honey, and flaxseeds, mixing well until no dry spots remain (see Mixing, page 20).

BULK FERMENT THE DOUGH: Using a wet hand, perform 6 to 8 bowl folds (see Bowl Fold, page 30) or until the dough resists stretching. This dough is not as elastic as other more hydrated doughs. If you find the dough tears while pulling it up gently to fold, use slightly less strength when stretching before folding. Gently round out the dough and turn it seam side down. Cover and let rest until puffy though not necessarily doubled in size, 1 hour.

Recipe continues

DIVIDE AND PRESHAPE THE DOUGH: Lightly flour a work surface, then use a plastic bowl scraper to gently ease the dough out of the bowl onto the work surface. Gently deflate the dough, then divide with a bench knife or a knife into 8 equal portions (each about 100 grams). Working with one piece of dough at a time, loosely preshape it into a round (see Preshaping, page 32), placing them seam side down on a lightly floured surface. Cover and let rest for 10 minutes.

SHAPE THE DOUGH, ADD THE CRUST, AND LET RISE: Place the seed crust mixture on a parchment-lined rimmed baking sheet. Wet a clean kitchen towel, then wring it out; it should still be pretty damp. Place a sheet of parchment paper on the work surface near the moistened towel and seed mixture. Starting with the seam side up, shape each piece of dough into a 6-inch tube with slightly tapered ends (see Shaping, page 34). Roll all sides of each shaped roll over the towel to moisten, then into the seed mixture to coat the entire roll (see How to Coat a Loaf with Seeds, page 218). Place the rolls seam side down on the sheet of parchment, evenly spacing them in a 2 × 4 grid at an angle on the parchment. Cover and let rise until the rolls are puffy and when pressed with a floured finger, an indentation remains (see Proofing, page 44), 45 minutes to 1 hour.

Toward the end of the rising time, arrange racks in the center and bottom third of the oven and preheat the oven to 450°F with a baking stone or steel on the center rack and an empty cast-iron skillet (or a cake pan filled with lava rocks) on the lower rack. If possible, adjust the stone and pan so that the skillet isn't directly under the stone, making it easier for steam to reach the baking rolls (see Steaming, page 50).

Just before baking, use a baker's lame or a sharp knife to score the top center of each roll with one elongated cut (see Scoring, page 46).

BAKE: Using a baker's peel or an inverted baking sheet to aid you, transfer the rolls (still on the parchment) into the oven and then pour about 227 grams (1 cup) of warm water into the skillet. Steam will billow from the pan upward to envelop the rolls; be sure to wear good oven mitts to shield your hands and arms. Quickly close the oven door to trap the steam. Bake until the rolls are golden brown and the crust is firm, 25 to 30 minutes.

Remove from the oven and let cool slightly on a wire rack. The crust will soften as the rolls sit. Serve warm or at room temperature.

Store leftover rolls in an airtight container at room temperature for up to 3 days or freeze for longer storage. To reheat rolls, place thawed rolls on a parchment-lined rimmed baking sheet and bake in a 350°F oven until heated through and slightly crisp, 5 to 8 minutes.

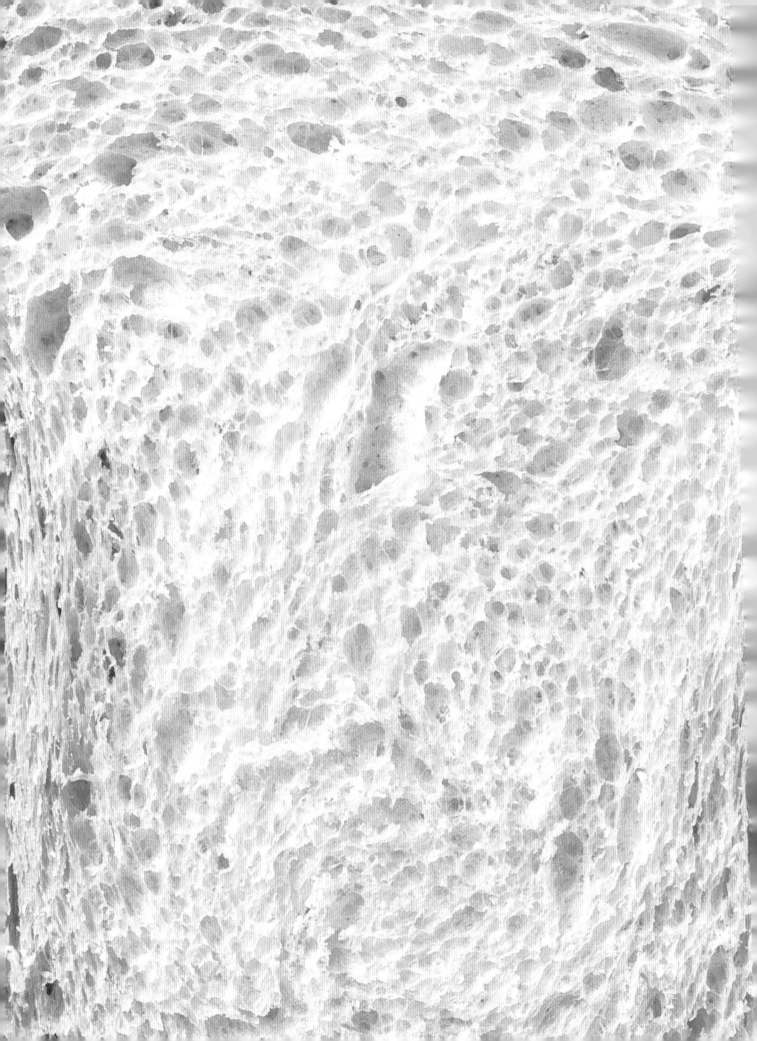

Fancy
Breads

BASIC BABKA DOUGH

MAKES 742 GRAMS

375 grams (3 cups plus
2 tablespoons) unbleached
all-purpose flour, plus more for
dusting

50 grams (¼ cup) sugar

9 grams (1 tablespoon) instant
yeast

7.5 grams (1¼ teaspoons) fine salt

71 grams (5 tablespoons) unsalted
butter, at room temperature

1 large egg (50 grams)

172 grams (¾ cup) warm milk
(see Temperature, page 25),
whole preferred

7.5 grams (1½ teaspoons) pure
vanilla extract

Babka was originally a vehicle for leftover dough—Jewish bakers would sprinkle some cinnamon sugar or chocolate on their scraps, then roll and twist it all into a simple treat. But in the past decade or so, babka has become less simple. Modern babka is richer, sweeter, and much more decadent than its forebears, and it begs for a dough that can keep up. Enter this recipe, a soft, tender bread dough that is sweeter and richer than challah, but not as buttery as brioche. It's the perfect middle ground of enriched doughs, which is why we use it not just for The Most Chocolatey Babka (page 355) and our honey and nut-studded Baklava Babka (page 359) but for our take on Stollen (page 361) as well. Because of its relatively high level of enrichment (that is, the amount of butter in the dough) and the long mix time needed to develop strength in the dough, this dough should be made in a stand mixer.

MAKE THE DOUGH: In a stand mixer bowl, combine the flour, sugar, yeast, salt, butter, egg, milk, and vanilla. Using the dough hook attachment, mix on medium-low speed until a shaggy dough forms, about 2 minutes. Scrape down the bottom and sides of the bowl, then increase the speed to medium-high and continue mixing until a slightly tacky, soft, springy dough forms, about 5 minutes. The dough will not be smooth, though it should mostly clear the sides of the bowl (some additional scraping may be necessary).

The dough is now ready to use in the recipes on the pages that follow.

THE MOST CHOCOLATEY BABKA

MIX	BULK FERMENTATION	SYRUP AND FILLING	SHAPE	2ND RISE	BAKE
10 MIN	1 HOUR	10 MIN	20 MIN	1–1½ HOURS	35–40 MIN

TIME: ABOUT 4 HOURS

MAKES ONE 12-INCH ROUND BABKA

Basic Babka Dough (recipe opposite)

Unbleached all-purpose flour, for dusting

SYRUP

75 grams (¼ cup plus 2 tablespoons) sugar

45 grams (3 tablespoons) water

15 grams (1 tablespoon) chocolate liqueur (optional)

FILLING

99 grams (½ cup) sugar

28 grams (⅓ cup) cocoa powder

Pinch of fine salt

57 grams (4 tablespoons) unsalted butter, melted

85 grams (½ cup) finely chopped semisweet chocolate

This yeasted bread has its origins in Eastern Europe and is typically filled with cinnamon, fruit, or, as in this version, chocolate. Ours is a decadent, moreish babka, containing both cocoa powder and chopped semisweet chocolate, so every bite is extra chocolatey. After the babka comes out of the oven it's brushed with a rich simple syrup, which gives the bread a bit of shine and keeps it moist for days (if it lasts that long).

MAKE THE DOUGH: Make the Basic Babka Dough as directed on page 354. Cover and let rise in a warm place until very puffy though not necessarily doubled in size, about 1 hour.

MAKE THE SYRUP: In a small saucepan, combine the sugar and water and heat over low, gently moving a heatproof spatula along the bottom of the pan in a back-and-forth motion (as if using a paintbrush) until the sugar is completely dissolved. Increase the heat to medium and bring the mixture to a low simmer. Cook until slightly thickened, 30 seconds to 1 minute. Remove from the heat and stir in the liqueur, if using. Let cool to room temperature.

MAKE THE FILLING: In a medium bowl, whisk together the sugar, cocoa powder, and salt. Add the melted butter, stirring to form a thick, granular paste with a matte finish; don't overmix, or the filling can separate. Set aside.

SHAPE THE BABKA: Lightly flour a work surface, then use a plastic bowl scraper to ease the dough out of the bowl onto the work surface. Gently press on the dough to deflate it; then, using a rolling pin, roll it out into a 16 × 12-inch rectangle. Position the dough so that a long side is facing you. Dollop the filling in small mounds over the dough, then use a small offset spatula or a knife to spread the filling in an even layer, leaving a 1-inch border of dough free from filling on the long side farthest away from you. Sprinkle the chopped chocolate over the filling in an even

Recipe continues

layer. Beginning with the long side closest to you, begin rolling up the dough into a log. Pinch the far edge to seal the log.

Line a baking sheet with parchment paper and set nearby. Arrange the log perpendicularly in front of you on the work surface with the seam facing up. Use a bench knife or a knife to cut the log in half lengthwise along the seam. With the cut sides facing up, make an "X" with the two pieces of dough, then twist the two pieces of dough together.

Transfer the dough to the prepared baking sheet. Bring the ends of the twist together to form a round wreath shape, pinching the ends to seal. (Alternatively, the babka can also be baked in a 9 × 4-inch half Pullman pan; follow the shaping instructions in the Baklava Babka recipe on page 359.) Cover and let rise until the dough is puffy and when pressed with a floured finger, a small indentation remains (see Proofing, page 44), 1 to 1½ hours.

Toward the end of the rising time, preheat the oven to 350°F.

BAKE: Bake the babka until golden brown and fragrant and the internal temperature reaches 200°F, 35 to 40 minutes.

Remove the babka from the oven, then brush all the syrup over the loaf. Cool completely on the baking sheet before slicing and serving. Store leftover babka in an airtight container at room temperature for up to 3 days or wrap tightly and freeze for longer storage.

SHAPING
A BABKA
WREATH

BAKLAVA BABKA

MIX	BULK FERMENTATION	SYRUP AND FILLING	SHAPE	2ND RISE	BAKE
10 MIN	1 HOUR	30 MIN	20 MIN	1–1½ HOURS	40–45 MIN

TIME: ABOUT 4 HOURS

MAKES ONE 9 × 4-INCH LOAF (HALF PULLMAN PAN)

Basic Babka Dough (page 354)

Unbleached all-purpose flour, for dusting

SYRUP

105 grams (¼ cup plus 1 tablespoon) honey

85 grams (¼ cup plus 2 tablespoons) water

7.5 grams (1½ teaspoons) fresh lemon juice

2.5 grams (½ teaspoon) rose water or pure vanilla extract

FILLING

60 grams (½ cup) pistachios

64 grams (½ cup) walnuts

37 grams (3 tablespoons) sugar

3.75 grams (¾ teaspoon) rose water or pure vanilla extract

Pinch of fine salt

2 large egg whites (70 grams total)

With its lightly sweetened striations of nut paste and honey syrup soak, this is a babka in baklava's clothing. Eat it fresh, or use day-old slices to make next-level French Toast (see page 400). Note that you need a 9 × 4-inch half Pullman pan (see page 15) for this recipe; it's too much dough for a standard loaf pan. No Pullman pan? Shape it into a circle instead; see shaping instructions for The Most Chocolatey Babka, page 355.

MAKE THE DOUGH: Make the Basic Babka Dough as directed on page 354. Cover and let rise until very puffy though not necessarily doubled in size, about 1 hour.

MAKE THE SYRUP: In a small saucepan, combine the honey, water, and lemon juice and bring to a boil over medium-high heat, stirring until the honey is dissolved. Reduce the heat to a low simmer and cook until the mixture is reduced and slightly thickened, about 8 minutes. You should have about 113 grams (⅓ cup) syrup. Remove from the heat and stir in the rose water or vanilla. Let cool to room temperature.

MAKE THE FILLING: In a food processor, pulse the pistachios until coarsely chopped. Add the walnuts, sugar, rose water or vanilla, and salt. Pulse until the mixture is finely chopped and looks like a coarse meal. (It's OK if some larger pieces of pistachios remain; take care not to overprocess the nut mixture, as it can quickly become nut butter if you're not paying attention.) Transfer the mixture to a bowl and stir in the egg whites to form a paste; it should have the consistency of natural peanut butter. Set aside.

SHAPE THE BABKA: Spray a 9 × 4-inch half Pullman loaf pan with pan spray. Lightly flour a work surface, then use a plastic bowl scraper to ease the dough out of the bowl onto the work surface. Gently press on the dough to deflate it. Using a rolling pin, roll it out into a 16 × 12-inch rectangle. Position the dough so that a short side is facing you. Dollop

Recipe continues

the filling in small mounds over the dough, then use a small offset spatula or a knife to spread the filling in an even layer, leaving a 1-inch border of dough free from filling on the short side of the dough farthest away from you. Beginning with the short side closest to you, roll up the dough into a log. Pinch the far edge to seal the log.

Place the log perpendicularly in front of you with the seam facing up. Use a bench knife or a knife to cut the log in half lengthwise along the seam. With the cut sides facing up, make an "X" with the two pieces of dough. Twist the two pieces of dough together, then pinch each end to seal. Gently tuck each end under the loaf to create a finished edge.

Place the loaf in the prepared pan, then cover and let rise until the crest of the loaf is about ¾ to 1 inch below the edge of the pan (see Proofing, page 44), 1 to 1½ hours. (Alternatively, the babka can be shaped into a circle; follow the shaping instructions for The Most Chocolatey Babka, page 355.)

Toward the end of the rising time, arrange a rack in the lower third of the oven and preheat the oven to 350°F.

BAKE: Bake the babka until the top crust is deep golden brown and the internal temperature reaches at least 200°F, 40 to 45 minutes. If the top is browning too quickly, tent the loaf with foil.

Remove the babka from the oven, then brush all the syrup over the top of the loaf. Let the loaf cool in the pan for 5 minutes, then remove from the pan and transfer to a wire rack to cool completely before slicing and serving. Store leftover babka in an airtight container at room temperature for up to 3 days or freeze for longer storage.

SHAPING A
BABKA LOAF

STOLLEN

MIX	BULK FERMENTATION	PRESHAPE AND REST	SHAPE	2ND RISE	BAKE
10 MIN	1 HOUR	20 MIN	30 MIN	45–60 MIN	35 MIN

SOAK THE FRUIT AND TOAST THE ALMONDS (12–16 HOURS BEFORE)

TIME: ABOUT 20 HOURS

MAKES 2 LOAVES

INCLUSIONS

186 grams (1¼ cups) raisins (dark, golden, or a combination)

32 grams (3 tablespoons) candied orange peel, homemade (page 389) or store-bought, cut into ¼-inch dice

32 grams (3 tablespoons) candied lemon peel, homemade (page 389) or store-bought, cut into ¼-inch dice

128 grams (½ cup plus 1 tablespoon) dark rum or apple juice

43 grams (¼ cup plus 2 tablespoons) slivered almonds, toasted

DOUGH

Basic Babka Dough (page 354)

10 grams (2 tablespoons) grated lemon zest (from 2 large lemons)

10 grams (2 teaspoons) pure vanilla extract

½ teaspoon ground cardamom

¼ teaspoon ground cinnamon

¼ teaspoon ground nutmeg

Unbleached all-purpose flour, for dusting

Ingredients continue

The dough for our version of this classic German holiday bread is flavored with citrus, studded with dried fruit and nuts, then formed around a log of almond paste, which creates a bull's-eye within each slice. After baking, the loaf is brushed with melted butter, dredged in granulated sugar, and showered with a snowdrift of confectioners' sugar.

fruit. Combine the raisins and candied peel in a medium bowl. Pour in the rum or apple juice, then cover and let stand at room temperature overnight, 12 to 16 hours.

DAY 2

MAKE THE DOUGH: Make the basic babka dough as directed on page 354. Once the dough comes together, add the lemon zest, vanilla, cardamom, cinnamon, and nutmeg and mix to incorporate.

Drain the dried fruit in a sieve set over a bowl, pressing gently on the fruit to push out as much liquid as possible (reserve the soaking liquid if desired—it makes a nice addition to a cocktail). Add the fruit to the dough along with the toasted almonds. Mix on medium-low speed until well incorporated, about 2 minutes. Cover and let rise until puffy though not necessarily doubled in size, about 1 hour.

MEANWHILE, MAKE THE FILLING: Roll the almond paste into two even 8-inch-long logs, each about 65 grams. Cover well to prevent them from drying out.

DIVIDE AND PRESHAPE THE DOUGH: Line a rimmed baking sheet with parchment paper. Lightly flour a work surface, then use a plastic bowl scraper to ease the dough out of the bowl onto the work surface. Divide the dough in half, each piece weighing about 550 grams. Gently deflate each piece, then preshape into 5-inch tubes (see Preshaping, page 32)

Recipe continues

130 grams (½ cup) almond paste

297 grams (1½ cups) granulated sugar

85 grams (6 tablespoons) unsalted butter, melted

Confectioners' or non-melting sugar, for dusting

DAY 1

SOAK THE FRUIT: The day before you want to bake, soak the dried

SHAPING STOLLEN

and place seam side down on the work surface. Cover and let rest for 15 minutes.

SHAPE THE STOLLEN: Position one piece of dough seam side up with a long side facing you. Press a rolling pin horizontally into the center of the dough to create a trough. Roll the center third of the dough to a thickness of ¼ inch, leaving the top and bottom edges of the dough thicker; the long side of dough closest to you should be slightly thicker than the long side farthest from you. Fold about ½ inch of dough from each short side in toward the center to square off the edges. Align the log of almond paste horizontally against the thicker edge of dough closest to you, then fold the top dough edge down and over the log of almond paste to almost meet the dough edge closest to you, offsetting it just slightly. With the flat edge of your hand or the handle of a wooden spoon held horizontally, make a slight indentation in the dough right beside the edge of the almond paste log to give the stollen its characteristic slightly humped shape. Repeat filling and shaping the second piece of dough. Evenly space the stollen on the prepared baking sheet and let rise until when pressed with a floured finger, a small indentation remains (see Proofing, page 44), 45 minutes to 1 hour.

Toward the end of the rising time, arrange a rack in the center of the oven and preheat the oven to 350°F. If you have an extra baking sheet, nest the pan of stollen into it; this double-thick protection will help prevent the bottom of the stollen from overbrowning as they bake.

BAKE: Bake the stollen until the crust is deep golden brown and the internal temperature reaches 200°F, about 35 minutes.

Meanwhile, spread the granulated sugar on a parchment-lined rimmed baking sheet and place nearby. Set the melted butter nearby as well.

Remove the stollen from the oven and immediately brush the melted butter all over the hot stollen, including the bottoms. Continue brushing until all the butter is used up. Dredge the butter-brushed stollen in the granulated sugar to coat, then transfer to a wire rack to cool completely.

Once cool, generously dust the stollen with confectioners' sugar. Store stollen well wrapped at room temperature for up to 1 week. If you plan to freeze the stollen, wait to dust them with confectioners' sugar until after thawing and right before serving.

BASIC CHALLAH DOUGH

MIX

12 MIN

BULK FERMENTATION

1–1½ HOURS

MAKE THE PREFERMENT (1 HOUR)

---------- TIME: ABOUT 3 HOURS ----------

MAKES 715 GRAMS

PREFERMENT

90 grams (¼ cup plus 2½ tablespoons) warm water (see Temperature, page 25)

50 grams (¼ cup plus 3 tablespoons) unbleached all-purpose flour

6 grams (2 teaspoons) instant yeast

DOUGH

325 grams (2½ cups plus 3 tablespoons) unbleached all-purpose flour, plus more for dusting

2 large eggs (100 grams total)

1 large egg yolk (14 grams; reserve the white for brushing)

64 grams (3 tablespoons) honey

56 grams (generous ¼ cup) vegetable or other neutral oil

11 grams (1¾ teaspoons) fine salt

Challah bakers are an opinionated bunch. Some believe that challah should be feathery and light; others don't call it challah unless it's sweet and almost as tight-crumbed as cake. But there's something that (almost) all challah bakers can agree on: The dough—which more often than not is braided, sometimes elaborately—should be a dream to work with. This one is just that. It's also sweetened lightly with honey and enriched with 2 eggs and an extra yolk, giving it a golden hue. It's perfect for the braided loaves that follow (see pages 366–68), but you should also keep it in mind for knotted, seeded rolls.

MAKE THE PREFERMENT: In a stand mixer bowl, whisk together the water, flour, and yeast and mix until no dry spots remain. The mixture will have the viscosity of pancake batter. Cover and let rest at room temperature for 1 hour. There will be many small bubbles on top and the mixture will have grown in volume.

MAKE THE DOUGH: Add the flour, whole eggs, egg yolk (reserve the white for brushing on later), honey, oil, and salt to the preferment. Using the dough hook attachment, mix on medium-low speed until a shaggy dough forms, about 2 minutes. Scrape down the bottom and sides of the bowl well, then increase the speed to medium-high and mix until the dough begins to pull away from the sides of the bowl and is shiny and smooth, 8 to 10 minutes. Scrape down the sides of the bowl; the dough will be sticky. Cover and let rise in a warm place until puffy though not necessarily doubled in size, 1 to 1½ hours.

The dough is now ready to use in the recipes on the pages that follow.

BRAIDED CHALLAH

MAKE DOUGH		PRESHAPE	SHAPE	2ND RISE	BAKE
3 HOURS		30 MIN	10 MIN	45 MIN	30 MIN

TIME: ABOUT 5 HOURS

MAKES 1 LARGE BRAIDED LOAF

Basic Challah Dough (page 365)

Unbleached all-purpose flour, for dusting

Reserved egg white (from Basic Challah Dough, page 365), lightly beaten

A golden loaf of braided challah is both delicious and symbolic. The soft, tender, eggy bread is traditionally baked on Fridays and served as an accompaniment to Shabbat dinner, though there's no reason you couldn't make it for any day of the week. Here, we've given instructions for a simple three-strand braid and a more elaborate six-strand one, too.

MAKE THE DOUGH: Make the Basic Challah Dough as directed on page 365. Line a rimmed baking sheet with parchment paper and set nearby.

DIVIDE AND PRESHAPE THE DOUGH: Lightly flour a work surface, then use a plastic bowl scraper to ease the dough out of the bowl onto the work surface. Divide the dough with a bench knife or a knife into 3 equal portions (each about 238 grams) for a 3-strand braid or 6 equal portions (each about 119 grams) for a 6-strand braid. Preshape each piece into a 4-inch tube (see Preshaping, page 32), place seam side down on the work surface, and cover and let rest for 15 minutes.

Working with one piece of dough at a time, place one hand in the center of the tube of dough. Begin rolling the dough until it resembles a dog bone, with a thinner center and thicker ends. Using both hands placed directly next to each other, continue rolling the dough into a log while applying light pressure and using a "down-and-out" motion as you roll your hands along the dough. Your right hand will move toward the right end of the log and your left hand will move toward the left end of the log as it gets longer. If the dough is sliding around and difficult to roll (because of too much flour on the work surface or on the dough itself), wipe the work surface with a slightly damp cloth or kitchen towel. This will give the dough some tension and make it easier to roll out. Roll each piece of dough into a log about 14 inches long with slightly tapered ends. If the dough resists stretching and shrinks back, set that piece aside and work on the other pieces before trying to roll it again. Even a short rest can help relax the gluten just enough to make shaping easier.

3-STRAND CHALLAH

6-STRAND CHALLAH

FOR A 3-STRAND BRAID: Place the three strands of dough vertically in front of you, spacing them so they're nearly but not quite touching. Beginning at the center, take the strand on the left and drape it over the strand in the middle (1). You don't need to pull or create tension; you're just draping one strand over the other. Next, take the strand on the right and drape it over the strand that is now in the middle (2). Continue braiding until you reach the end, then pinch the strands together (3, 4). Flip the loaf over so the unbraided half is facing you (5). Repeat the braiding process as described until you reach the end, then pinch the strands together (6, 7). If necessary, gently roll just the tips of the braid back and forth and tuck under to create clean-looking edges.

Recipe continues

FOR A 6-STRAND BRAID: Arrange the 6 strands of dough vertically in front of you, setting them side by side. Pinch the strands at the top into two sections of 3 each. Join the two sections together at the top into one and pinch firmly. Separate the strands into a single strand on either side and two sections of double strands in the middle. Cross the outer 2 strands. Now begin braiding: Bring the outer left strand to the center. Next, bring the second strand from the right to the outer left. Bring the outer right strand to the center. Bring the second strand from the left to the outer right. Repeat the process, starting with bringing the outer left strand to the center until you reach the end. Once you reach the bottom, tuck the ends under and pinch them together. Using the tips of your fingers, roll the loaf back and forth gently to secure the ends, then tuck the tail under the loaf.

LET THE LOAF RISE: Supporting the braid underneath with your hands and forearms, gently transfer it to the prepared baking sheet, setting it at an angle so it has room to grow. Cover and let rise until noticeably puffy and when the dough is pressed with a floured finger, a small indentation remains (see Proofing, page 44), about 45 minutes.

Preheat the oven to 375°F with a rack in the center.

BAKE: Generously brush the reserved beaten egg white all over the challah, taking care to brush some into the cracks of the braid. Bake until the crust is evenly deep golden brown (even where the strands cross) and the internal temperature reaches 190°F, about 30 minutes.

Remove the challah from the oven, then transfer to a wire rack to cool. Store leftover challah well wrapped at room temperature for up to 3 days or freeze for longer storage. Stale challah makes excellent French Toast (see page 400).

CARAMELIZED APPLE AND HONEY CHALLAH

TOAST SEEDS	MIX	BULK FERMENTATION	PRESHAPE	SHAPE	2ND RISE	BAKE AND GLAZE
10 MIN	15 MIN	1½ HOURS	30 MIN	15 MIN	45 MIN	35 MIN

.... TIME: ABOUT 5 HOURS ....

MAKES 1 LARGE ROUND LOAF

DOUGH

3 grams (2 teaspoons) coriander seeds or 2½ teaspoons ground coriander

Basic Challah Dough (page 365)

6 grams (1 tablespoon) grated orange zest (from ½ large orange; save to juice for glaze below)

1 large Granny Smith apple (250 grams)

Reserved egg white (from Basic Challah Dough, page 365), lightly beaten

GLAZE

63 grams (3 tablespoons) honey

14 grams (1 tablespoon) fresh orange juice

Apples and honey are traditional foods for Rosh Hashanah, and on that holiday, round challah replaces long braided loaves; the round shape represents continuity and the cycle of the seasons. This challah crown is studded with bits of tart apple and is flavored with citrusy coriander, which complements the glossy honey-orange glaze that gets brushed on the loaf after baking. Don't worry if some of the apple pieces pop out of the dough when shaping (they likely will). Just tuck them into the folds of the braid or scatter them over the top of the loaf, where they'll become deeply caramelized as the bread bakes.

TOAST THE CORIANDER SEEDS: In a small skillet, toast the seeds over medium heat until they are fragrant and a shade darker than when you began, 3 to 5 minutes. Transfer the seeds to a small bowl to cool to room temperature, then use a coffee/spice grinder or mortar and pestle to grind them into a fine powder. If using ground coriander, skip this step.

MAKE THE DOUGH: Make the Basic Challah Dough as directed on page 365, adding all the ground coriander and orange zest to the dough ingredients before mixing. Cover and let rise until slightly puffy, about 45 minutes.

Meanwhile, peel and core the apple, then cut into ¼- to ½-inch cubes.

Lightly flour a work surface, then use a plastic bowl scraper to ease the dough out of the bowl onto the work surface. Gently deflate the dough and pat it into a rectangle. Using a rolling pin, roll the dough out into a 16 × 11-inch rectangle, adding just as much flour as necessary to keep the dough from sticking.

Recipe continues

HOW TO SHAPE A 4-STRAND CHALLAH

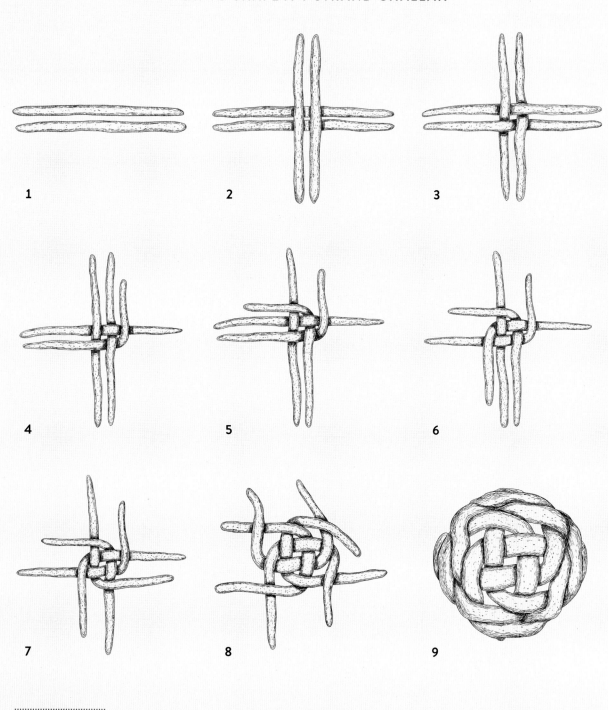

1

2

3

4

5

6

7

8

9

4-STRAND
CHALLAH

With a long side facing you, lightly score the dough crosswise into thirds, then sprinkle about one-third of the apple pieces evenly over the center third of the dough. Fold the left side of the dough up and over to cover the apples in the center, then press down on the dough to remove any air pockets trapped within the layer. Sprinkle half of the remaining apples on top of the folded dough, then fold the right side of the dough up and over to cover the apples. Press down on the dough to remove any air pockets. Sprinkle the remaining apples on top of the layered dough block, then fold the block in half to form a square, enclosing the apples. Press down on the dough to remove any air pockets, then gently pinch the edges to seal. Return the apple-filled dough square to the bowl, cover, and let rest an additional 45 minutes.

DIVIDE AND PRESHAPE THE DOUGH: Lightly flour a work surface, then use a plastic bowl scraper to gently ease the dough out of the bowl onto the work surface. Using a bench knife or a knife, divide the dough into 4 equal portions (each about 230 grams). Gently deflate each piece of dough and lightly preshape into tubes (see Preshaping, page 32). Some apples may be sticking out of the dough; this is OK. Cover and let rest for 20 minutes.

SHAPE THE CHALLAH: On a lightly floured work surface, roll each piece of dough out into a 14- to 16-inch log. To do this, place one hand in the center of the dough and begin rolling it back and forth under your hand so that the ends are thicker and the center thinner; it will resemble a dog bone. Next, place your hands next to each other in the center of the dough and apply pressure in a "down-and-out" motion, moving your hands away from each other to elongate the log. If the dough resists stretching and shrinks back, set that piece aside and work on the other pieces before trying to roll it again. Even a short rest can help relax the gluten just enough to make shaping easier. Some apple pieces may pop out of the dough when rolling it into logs. Tuck some of them back into the dough once you've rolled it to the required length. Save any other pieces of apple

to sprinkle on top of the bread once it's shaped. The logs will not look smooth at this point; this is normal. Additionally, the dough may thin or tear near the apple pieces; if this happens, just pinch the dough back together. If the dough sticks to the surface, use a bench knife to scrape up any residual dough and add just enough flour to keep the dough from sticking. If it is difficult to form the log because the dough is sliding on the surface, use a very lightly dampened kitchen towel to remove any excess flour from the surface and create some tension for the dough to roll more easily.

Place a piece of parchment paper on the work surface, then lightly dust with flour. Arrange 2 strands of dough horizontally on the parchment, spacing them about ½ inch apart (1). Place the remaining 2 strands of dough vertically on top of the horizontal strands, also about ½ inch apart (2). At this point the strands of dough should look similar to a number sign (#). At the center where the strands converge, they need to alternate in an under, over, under, over pattern (3), like weaving (or making a lattice pie crust). Braid your way clockwise around the loaf, weaving the strands so that the ones that were under are now over (4, 5, 6, 7). When you get back to where you started, reverse direction; again, the strands that are under are lifted over (8). When the strands become too short to weave, tuck the ends under (9). Don't worry if your loaf looks imperfect at this point; after proofing the imperfections will be hidden.

Once the loaf is shaped, evenly distribute any leftover apple pieces over the top, tucking them into the braided edges. Cover and let rise until noticeably puffy and when the dough is pressed with a lightly floured finger, a small indentation remains (see Proofing, page 44), about 45 minutes.

Toward the end of the rising time, preheat the oven to 375°F and arrange a rack in the center.

Recipe continues

Generously brush the challah all over with the reserved beaten egg white, taking care to brush some into the cracks of the braid. Bake until the crust is evenly deep golden brown (even where the strands cross) and the internal temperature reaches 190°F, about 30 minutes.

MEANWHILE, MAKE THE GLAZE: About 5 minutes before the challah is fully baked, in a small saucepan, combine the honey and orange juice and bring to a boil over medium heat. Cook for 30 seconds. Remove from the heat. Alternatively, combine the honey and orange juice in a microwavable measuring cup or bowl and microwave until the mixture comes to a boil, 30 seconds to 1 minute.

Remove the challah from the oven, then brush all over the top and sides with the hot glaze. Let the loaf cool for 10 minutes on the baking sheet, then transfer to a wire rack to cool. Serve the challah warm or at room temperature. Store leftover challah in an airtight container for up to 3 days or freeze for longer storage. Stale challah makes excellent French Toast (see page 400).

ONION AND POPPY STAR BREAD

MAKE DOUGH		PRESHAPE	SHAPE	2ND RISE	BAKE
3 HOURS		25 MIN	20 MIN	45 MIN	15–20 MIN

TIME: ABOUT 5 HOURS

MAKES 1 LOAF

Basic Challah Dough (page 365)

FILLING

2 medium yellow onions (about 361 grams/12 ounces), finely chopped (2½ cups)

25 grams (2 tablespoons) olive oil

¼ teaspoon fine salt

Scant ¼ teaspoon freshly ground black pepper

18 grams (2 tablespoons) poppy seeds

Unbleached all-purpose flour, for dusting

Reserved egg white (from Basic Challah Dough, page 365), lightly beaten

Flaky sea salt, such as Maldon, for sprinkling

The impressive appearance of this star-shaped bread belies its ease. This savory iteration is reminiscent of a bialy, with its filling of caramelized onions and poppy seeds. But whereas bialys are delightfully dense and chewy, this loaf is fluffy, soft, and a little sweet. Put it on a cheese board at a party, or tear it into wedges and serve alongside soup.

MAKE THE DOUGH: Make the Basic Challah Dough as directed on page 365.

MEANWHILE, MAKE THE FILLING: Preheat the oven to 400°F. Line a rimmed baking sheet with parchment paper.

Toss the onions, olive oil, salt, and pepper on the lined baking sheet until the onions are coated in oil. Roast until the onions are fragrant, softened, and well browned—almost charred—in spots, 30 to 40 minutes, stirring and redistributing the onions every 10 minutes. Remove from the oven, transfer to a shallow bowl, and let cool to room temperature. Stir in the poppy seeds.

DIVIDE AND PRESHAPE THE DOUGH: Lightly flour a work surface, then use a plastic bowl scraper to gently ease the dough out of the bowl onto the work surface. Using a bench knife or a knife, divide the dough into 4 equal portions (each about 178 grams). Lightly preshape each piece of dough into a round (see Preshaping, page 32), place seam side up on the work surface, cover, and let rest for 20 minutes.

SHAPE THE BREAD: On a floured work surface, roll one piece of dough into a 10-inch round. If the dough resists stretching and shrinks back, set that piece aside and work on the other pieces, then return to the first piece. Even a short rest can help relax the gluten just enough to make rolling easier. Place the round on a piece of parchment, then lightly brush with some of the reserved egg white. Evenly sprinkle

Recipe continues

about 25 grams (one-third) of the onion/poppy seed mixture over the dough, using a small offset spatula to spread it to the edges.

Roll out a second piece of dough, also into a 10-inch round to match the first piece, and place it on top of the first. Brush with reserved beaten egg white, then top with about 25 grams (half of the remaining) onion-poppy mixture, spreading it to the edges. Repeat the rolling, stacking, and spreading one more time, then top with the fourth round of dough.

Place a 2½- to 3-inch round cutter in the center of the top round of dough and leave it there as a guide as you move to the next step: With a bench knife or a knife, cut the round into 16 equal strips, cutting from the outer edge of the cutter to the edge of the round of dough, through all the layers. Remove the cutter.

Using two hands, pick up two adjacent strips and twist them in opposite directions twice so that the top side is facing up again. Repeat with the remaining strips of dough so that you end up with 8 pairs of strips. Pinch the pairs of strips together at the ends to create a star-like shape with 8 points.

Transfer the star (still on the parchment) to a rimmed baking sheet. Cover and let it rise until it becomes noticeably puffy and when the dough is pressed with a floured finger, a small indentation remains (see Proofing, page 44), about 45 minutes.

Preheat the oven to 400°F and arrange a rack in the center.

BAKE: Brush the top of the star with some of the reserved beaten egg white and sprinkle with flaky salt. Bake until it's deep golden brown and fragrant and the internal temperature reaches 190°F, 15 to 20 minutes. If the top is browning too quickly, tent it with foil.

Remove from the oven and let cool for about 10 minutes before serving warm or at room temperature. Store any leftovers in an airtight container at room temperature for 3 days or freeze for longer storage. To reheat, place the thawed loaf on a baking sheet in a preheated 350°F oven for 8 to 10 minutes, or until heated through.

SHAPING STAR
BREAD

BASIC BRIOCHE DOUGH

MIX	BULK FERMENTATION
25 MIN	12–16 HOURS

TIME: ABOUT 16 HOURS

MAKES 734 GRAMS

330 grams (2¾ cups) unbleached all-purpose flour, plus more for dusting

37 grams (3 tablespoons) sugar

9 grams (1 tablespoon) instant yeast

9 grams (1½ teaspoons) fine salt

3 large eggs (150 grams total), fridge-cold

57 grams (¼ cup) cold water (55°F to 60°F)

142 grams (10 tablespoons) cold unsalted butter, cut into pats (see Note)

NOTE: If your butter is very firm, you can make it pliable by pounding the pats with a rolling pin until they have the consistency of modeling clay. Using this method, the butter's temperature stays cold, but the softer consistency incorporates into the dough more easily.

Brioche is royalty among bread recipes, revered by bakers for its yeasty, slightly sweet, and ultrabuttery flavor. It's the richest of all breads—it's more decadent than both the challah and babka doughs in this chapter. Note the long dough mixing time and don't be tempted to shorten it; it's necessary for building strength in the dough and also allows time for the butter to become incorporated into the dough. (Because of this long mix, cold butter is added. Room temperature butter would become too warm during the mixing phase, resulting in a greasy dough.) Whatever you do, don't sleep on brioche's versatility: It's perfect for doughnut-like maritozzi (page 383) and grilled cheese (or chocolate!) sandwiches (page 419).

DAY 1

MAKE THE DOUGH: In a stand mixer bowl, combine the flour, sugar, yeast, salt, eggs, and water. Using the dough hook attachment, mix on medium-low speed until a shaggy dough forms, about 2 minutes. Scrape down the bottom and sides of the bowl, then increase the speed to medium-high and mix until the dough is smooth and elastic and cleans the sides of the bowl, 8 to 10 minutes. It may be necessary to scrape down the bowl in between; don't shorten the mixing time.

Add the butter 2 pats at a time, mixing on medium speed until the butter is completely incorporated before adding the next addition. Because you're starting with cold butter, this may take 1 to 2 minutes per addition. Once all the butter has been added, continue mixing the dough until it is shiny, smooth, and elastic, 1 minute longer. Spray a parchment-lined rimmed baking sheet with pan spray. Use a plastic bowl scraper to gently ease the dough out of the bowl onto the prepared pan. With lightly floured fingers, press the dough into an even 1-inch-thick layer. Cover tightly and refrigerate the dough overnight, 12 to 16 hours.

DAY 2

The dough is now ready to use in the recipes on the pages that follow.

SKY-HIGH NANTERRE

MAKES ONE 9 × 4-INCH LOAF (HALF PULLMAN PAN)

Basic Brioche Dough (page 377)

Unbleached all-purpose flour, for dusting

Egg wash: 1 large egg (50 grams), beaten with ⅛ teaspoon fine salt, for brushing

This recipe, for an impressively tall, incredibly rich loaf, is named for the Parisian suburb of Nanterre (presumably a nod to that city's famous skyscrapers). To make this French classic, the dough is divided into three pieces and rolled into balls. The balls are then nestled together in a pan, where they bake together into a handsome loaf. Note that you must use a 9 × 4-inch half Pullman loaf pan for this bread; the volume of dough is too much for a standard loaf pan. Brioche is wonderful toasted and spread with preserves, but it also is a delicious and perfect bread for Garlic Bread Egg in a Hole (page 403) or Vanilla Bread Pudding (page 439).

DAY 1

MAKE THE DOUGH: The day before you want to bake, make the basic brioche dough as directed. Cover and refrigerate overnight, 12 to 16 hours.

DAY 2

Spray a 9 × 4-inch half Pullman loaf pan with pan spray. Remove the brioche dough from the refrigerator and transfer it to a lightly floured work surface. If the dough sticks to the parchment, use a plastic bowl scraper to scrape up any dough and add it back to the dough mass. Divide the dough into 3 equal pieces (each about 244 grams).

SHAPE THE DOUGH AND LET RISE: Using lightly floured fingers, gently deflate each piece of dough to remove any bubbles, then shape into rounds. Using a cupped hand, shape each piece of dough into a taut round (see Shaping, page 34). Evenly space the 3 rounds of dough in the prepared pan. Cover and let rise until the loaf crests about 1 inch over the top of the pan (see Proofing, page 44), about 1 to 2 hours in a warm environment or 2 to 3 hours at cool room temperature.

Toward the end of the rising time, arrange a rack in the center of the oven and preheat the oven to 350°F.

Gently brush the top of the loaf with the egg wash, then bake until the loaf is deep golden brown and the internal temperature reaches at least 205°F, about 45 minutes. If the loaf is browning too quickly, tent it with foil.

Remove the loaf from the oven and let cool for 1 to 2 minutes in the pan before gently tipping it out of its pan and transferring it to a wire rack to cool completely. (For storage information, see Storing Bread, page 123.)

PLUM-HAZELNUT BRIOCHE COFFEE CAKE

STREUSEL   SHAPE   2ND RISE   ASSEMBLE   BAKE

| 10 MIN | 10 MIN | 45 MIN–3 HOURS | 10 MIN | 45–50 MIN |

MAKE THE DOUGH AND PASTRY CREAM (12–16 HOURS BEFORE)

TIME: ABOUT 20 HOURS

MAKES ONE 9-INCH COFFEE CAKE

½ batch (367 grams) Basic Brioche Dough (page 377)

PASTRY CREAM

37 grams (3 tablespoons) sugar, divided

15 grams (2 tablespoons) unbleached all-purpose flour

Pinch of fine salt

113 grams (½ cup) heavy cream

113 grams (½ cup) milk, whole preferred

1 large egg yolk (14 grams)

5 grams (1 teaspoon) vanilla bean paste or pure vanilla extract

STREUSEL AND ASSEMBLY

60 grams (½ cup) unbleached all-purpose flour, plus more for dusting

37 grams (3 tablespoons) sugar

Pinch of fine salt

28 grams (2 tablespoons) unsalted butter, at room temperature

40 grams (¼ cup plus 1 tablespoon) blanched hazelnuts, finely chopped

3 large plums (300 to 350 grams/⅔ to ¾ pound)

Buttery brioche forms the foundation of this custard, fruit, and streusel-topped coffee cake, which is a refined, not-too-sweet morning pastry. If you can't find ripe plums, you can substitute peaches, nectarines, or apricots, or try the gingery pear variation (below). Note that this recipe uses a half batch of brioche dough; shape the other half into buns and bake as directed in the Maritozzi recipe (page 383).

DAY 1

MAKE THE DOUGH: The day before you want to bake, make the basic brioche dough as directed. Cover and refrigerate overnight, 12 to 16 hours. Note that you're only using half of the dough for this recipe; reserve the other half for another use (see headnote).

MAKE THE PASTRY CREAM: Place the sugar, flour, and salt in a small pot, whisking to combine. Add the cream, milk, and egg yolk, whisking until no lumps or streaks of egg yolk remain. Heat the mixture over medium heat, whisking constantly, until the mixture comes to a boil. Continue cooking for 1 to 2 minutes, whisking constantly, until slightly thickened; it should have the consistency of plain (non-Greek) yogurt. Transfer the pastry cream to a clean medium bowl, then stir in the vanilla bean paste or extract. Place plastic wrap directly on the surface of the pastry cream, let cool to room temperature, then refrigerate overnight.

DAY 2

PREPARE THE STREUSEL: In a medium bowl, combine the flour, sugar, and salt. Work the butter into the flour mixture with your fingers or a fork until clumpy, irregular crumbs varying in size from a peppercorn to a pea form. Toss in the hazelnuts, mixing until evenly combined. Set aside.

Recipe continues

SHAPE THE DOUGH: Line a 9-inch round cake or springform pan with parchment paper and spray with pan spray. Remove the 367 grams of brioche dough from the refrigerator and, using lightly floured fingers, press it evenly into the prepared pan. Cover the pan and let rise until puffy and when the dough is pressed with a floured finger, a small indentation remains (see Proofing, page 44), about 45 minutes to 2 hours in a warm environment or 2 to 3 hours at cool room temperature.

Toward the end of the rising time, arrange a rack in the center of the oven and preheat the oven to 375°F.

ASSEMBLE AND BAKE: With lightly floured fingers, dimple the risen brioche round all over, pressing all the way to the bottom of the pan. Dollop the pastry cream on the dough, then use a small offset spatula to evenly spread it across the dough. Halve and pit the plums, then cut each half into 6 pieces. Arrange the plums, slightly overlapping, in a concentric circle atop the pastry cream layer. Sprinkle the streusel over the plums.

Bake the coffee cake until it is puffy, the fruit is bubbling, and the streusel is light golden brown, 45 to 50 minutes. The internal temperature should reach at least 200°F.

Remove the cake from the oven and let cool for 15 minutes in the pan before gently turning out of the pan and transferring to a wire rack to cool completely. Store leftovers refrigerated in an airtight container for up to 3 days or freeze for longer storage. Rewarm briefly in the microwave or a preheated 350°F oven for 5 minutes or until heated through before serving.

VARIATION

PEAR-GINGER COFFEE CAKE: On Day 1, make and chill the dough as directed. Omit the pastry cream. Instead, in a food processor, combine 58 grams (¼ cup plus 1 tablespoon) roughly chopped crystallized ginger and 62 grams (¼ cup plus 1 tablespoon) sugar and pulse until the ginger is very finely chopped. In a medium bowl, stir 128 grams (9 tablespoons) room-temperature cream cheese until smooth. Add the ginger sugar, mixing well to combine. Cover and refrigerate overnight; let come to room temperature before using.

On Day 2, make the streusel using walnuts in place of the hazelnuts. Follow the directions above for shaping the dough. When ready to assemble and bake, spread the ginger cream cheese on the dough in an even layer. In place of the plums, use 2 large (400 grams/14 ounces) ripe, unpeeled pears (we like Bartlett or d'Anjou best), coring and cutting them into ¼-inch wedges. Top with the streusel and bake as directed.

MARITOZZI

MAKES 12 CREAM-FILLED BUNS

Basic Brioche Dough (page 377)

Unbleached all-purpose flour, for dusting

227 grams (1 cup) heavy cream

35 grams (5 tablespoons) confectioners' sugar, plus more for garnish

Roman maritozzi have a charming history, both as an indulgence that was permitted during Lent and as a pastry that was often used in marriage proposals (complete with wedding ring hidden inside). Today they are beloved for their sublime simplicity: The two components—a fluffy roll (in this case, it's a mini brioche) and freshly whipped cream—are elemental on their own but together make a perfectly balanced treat that's light yet decadent, rich but not too sweet. If you want to take this to the next level, add a spoonful of jam (we like raspberry), lemon curd, or even chocolate ganache beneath the cream. Dust with confectioners' sugar, or to add texture and a burst of flavor, garnish with powdered freeze-dried fruit, chopped nuts, candied citrus peel, or chocolate.

If a dozen maritozzi is more than you need, make the full dozen brioche rolls, then freeze half for burgers, sandwiches, or a second round of maritozzi later on. If you're only planning to fill 6 buns, reduce the whipped cream amounts by half.

DAY 1

MAKE THE DOUGH: The day before you want to bake, make the basic brioche dough as directed on page 377. Cover and refrigerate overnight, 12 to 16 hours.

DAY 2

DIVIDE THE DOUGH, SHAPE THE BUNS, AND LET RISE: Line two baking sheets with parchment paper. Lightly flour a work surface, then remove the brioche dough from the refrigerator and transfer it to the work surface. If the dough sticks to the parchment, use a plastic bowl scraper to scrape up any dough and add it back to the dough mass. Divide the dough with a bench knife or a knife into 12 equal portions (each about 60 grams). Shape each piece into a tight ball (see Shaping, page 34). Evenly space the buns across the prepared baking sheets, cover lightly,

Recipe continues

and let rise until doubled and puffy and when the dough is pressed with a floured finger, a small indentation remains (see Proofing, page 44), 1 to 2 hours in a warm environment or 2 to 3 hours at cool room temperature.

Toward the end of the rise time, preheat the oven to 375°F. If you have an extra baking sheet, nest the pan of maritozzi into it; this double-thick protection will help prevent the bottoms of the maritozzi from over-browning as they bake.

BAKE: Bake the buns until they're golden brown and sound hollow when tapped, 15 to 20 minutes (tent with foil after 10 minutes if they're browning too quickly).

Remove them from the oven, let stand for 5 minutes, then transfer to a rack to cool completely.

MAKE THE WHIPPED CREAM: In a large bowl (or in a stand mixer with the whisk attachment), whisk the cream until soft peaks form. Add the confectioners' sugar and continue beating until stiff peaks form, being careful not to overbeat.

FILL THE BUNS: Use a serrated knife to make a slit lengthwise down the center of each bun while keeping it intact at the base. Open each bun slightly and spoon in 2 to 3 tablespoons whipped cream to create a cream-filled center about 1½ inches wide (if you're adding jam or lemon curd or chocolate ganache (see headnote), spoon about a tablespoon into the center of the split bun before adding the cream). Run an offset spatula over the top of the bun, keeping it flush with the edge to level the whipped cream and remove any excess that may have spilled over the edge. (Traditional maritozzi have a very clean finish.)

To garnish the maritozzi, generously dust the top of each bun with confectioners' sugar, or garnish with additional ingredients as you wish (see the headnote for some of our favorite options). Filled maritozzi are best served immediately, or at least the same day.

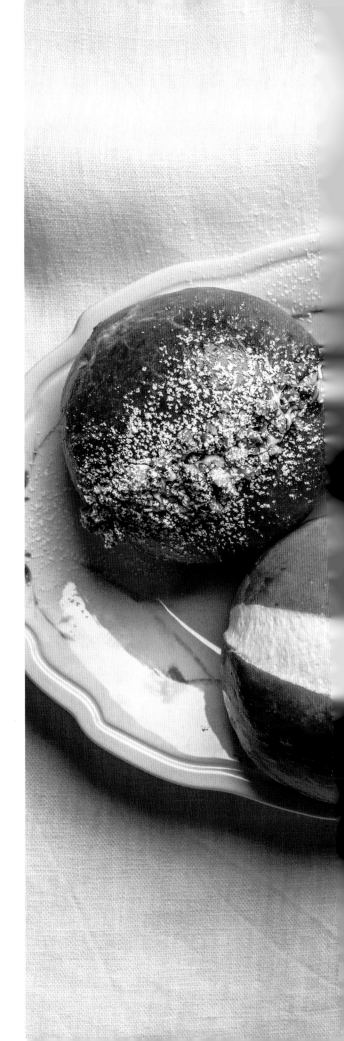

GIBASSIER

MIX	BULK FERMENTATION	PRESHAPE	SHAPE	2ND RISE	BAKE
15 MIN	1–1½ HOURS	30 MIN	20 MIN	1–1½ HOURS	15–18 MIN

TIME: ABOUT 4½ HOURS

MAKES 8 BUNS

DOUGH

275 grams (2¼ cups) unbleached all-purpose flour, plus more for dusting

25 grams (2 tablespoons) sugar

12 grams (1 tablespoon plus 1 teaspoon) instant yeast

6 grams (1 teaspoon) fine salt

1 large egg (50 grams), at room temperature

70 grams (¼ cup plus 1 tablespoon) warm milk (see Temperature, page 25), whole preferred

70 grams (¼ cup plus 1 tablespoon) warm water (see Temperature, page 25)

14 grams (1 tablespoon) orange blossom water or orange juice

12 grams (1 tablespoon) olive oil

43 grams (3 tablespoons) unsalted butter, at room temperature

47 grams (¼ cup) candied orange peel, homemade (page 389) or store-bought, cut into ¼-inch dice

2.5 grams (1 teaspoon) anise seeds

These plush buns, enriched with eggs and olive oil and flavored with candied orange and anise, are a Provençal breakfast treat. They manage to be both sturdy and light, and no matter how carefully you take a bite, invariably some of the sugar coating will rain down on your shirt. C'est la vie! Overachievers can make their own candied orange peel (see page 389), but a good-quality store-bought candied peel is fine, too. There are scores of different ways to shape these, from bear claw–like paddles to batons, but we like the simplicity of the S-shape.

MAKE THE DOUGH: In a stand mixer bowl, combine the flour, sugar, yeast, salt, egg, milk, water, orange blossom water, and olive oil. Using the dough hook attachment, mix on medium-low speed until a shaggy dough forms, about 1 minute. Scrape down the bottom and sides of the bowl, then increase the speed to medium-high and mix until the dough is smooth and elastic and cleans the sides of the bowl, about 7 minutes. Add the butter 1 tablespoon at a time, mixing on medium speed until the butter is completely incorporated before adding the next tablespoon. Once all the butter has been added, continue mixing the dough until it is shiny and smooth, 1 minute more.

Add the candied orange peel and anise seeds, mixing on medium-low speed until well combined, 1 to 2 minutes. Cover the dough and let rise until puffy though not necessarily doubled in size and when the dough is pressed with a floured finger, a small indentation remains (see Proofing, page 44), 1 to 1½ hours.

DIVIDE AND PRESHAPE THE DOUGH: Lightly flour a work surface, then use a plastic bowl scraper to gently ease the dough out of the bowl onto the work surface. Divide the dough with a bench knife or a knife into 8 equal portions (each about 75 grams). Deflate each piece of dough by pressing it into a 5-inch oval, then preshape it into a 3- to 4-inch-long tube (see Preshaping, page 32) and place seam side down. Cover and let

Ingredients continue

Recipe continues

TOPPING

1 teaspoon anise seeds

198 grams (1 cup) sugar

28 grams (2 tablespoons) unsalted butter, melted

rest 15 minutes in the refrigerator, which will make it easier to shape. The preshaped dough may be refrigerated up to 24 hours before shaping and baking.

SHAPE THE DOUGH AND LET RISE: Working with one piece of dough at a time, place one hand in the center of the tube of dough. Begin rolling the dough until it resembles a dog bone, with a thinner center and thicker ends. Using both hands placed directly next to each other, continue rolling the dough into a log while applying light pressure and using a "down-and-out" motion as you roll your hands along the dough. Your right hand will move toward the right end of the log and your left hand will move toward the left end of the log as it gets longer. If the dough is sliding around and difficult to roll (because of too much flour on the surface or on the dough itself), wipe the work surface with a slightly damp cloth or kitchen towel. This will give the dough some tension and make it easier to roll out. Roll each tube of dough out into a 16- to 18-inch-long log. If the dough resists stretching, cover the piece and set it aside for a few minutes while you work on other pieces. This rest gives the gluten time to relax and will make it easier to continue rolling to the desired length. If the dough sticks to the work surface, add just enough flour to prevent sticking.

Line a baking sheet with parchment paper. Shape each log of dough into a swirled "S": Starting with the left end of a log of dough, gently begin curling the dough clockwise around itself like a snail's shell, stopping just shy of the halfway point of the log. Repeat the process with the other end of the log to form an "S." Evenly space the gibassier on the lined baking sheet. Cover and let rise until puffy and when the dough is pressed with a lightly floured finger, a small indentation remains (see Proofing, page 44), 1 to 1½ hours.

MEANWHILE, MAKE THE TOPPING: Roughly grind the anise seeds in a coffee/spice grinder or with a mortar and pestle, then add them to the sugar, mixing well to combine. Place the anise sugar in a shallow, wide bowl. Set the melted butter nearby as well.

Toward the end of the rising time, preheat the oven to 375°F and arrange a rack in the center.

BAKE: Bake the gibassier until evenly deep golden brown and the internal temperature is 190°F, 15 to 18 minutes.

Remove the gibassier from the oven and brush all over (including the bottoms) with the melted butter, then dredge in the anise sugar. Serve warm or allow to cool to room temperature; they're best the day they are baked.

CANDIED CITRUS PEEL

BLANCH   CANDY   SUGAR AND DRY

40 MIN   **30–45 MIN**   **12–16 HOURS**

TIME: ABOUT 18 HOURS

MAKES ABOUT 100 GRAMS
(½ CUP PLUS 2 TABLESPOONS)

2 large oranges or lemons,
preferably unwaxed

340 grams (1½ cups) water

75 grams (¼ cup plus
2 tablespoons) sugar

227 grams (1 cup) water

COATING

50 grams (¼ cup) sugar

The process for candying lemon and orange peel is the same: First you blanch the peels in water, then cook them in a sugar syrup. It transforms the rind into a confection, with an incredible bright flavor and pleasant chewiness.

BLANCH THE CITRUS PEEL: Cut the oranges or lemons into quarters. Using a sharp knife, carefully cut off the fruit and enjoy as a baker's snack or save for another use. Cut the peel into ¼-inch-wide strips.

In a small pot, combine the citrus peel with 340 grams (1½ cups) water to cover. Bring to a boil over medium-high heat. Reduce the heat and simmer for 30 minutes. Drain the peels and set aside. If the peel has a significant amount of white pith remaining on it, use a sharp knife to carefully trim it away and discard.

CANDY THE PEELS: In the same pot, combine the sugar and 227 grams (1 cup) water. Heat over medium-low heat, stirring constantly until the sugar is dissolved. Add the peels to the pot, then increase the heat and bring the mixture to a boil. Reduce the heat to a low simmer. Simmer until the mixture is syrupy and the peel is mostly translucent, 30 to 45 minutes. Drain the peels in a sieve set over a bowl, reserving any of the leftover citrus syrup for sweetening tea, using in cocktails, or brushing on cakes. Using tongs or chopsticks, set the pieces of peel on a wire rack, leaving some space between them, to cool and dry slightly until tacky.

COAT THE PEELS: Line a rimmed baking sheet with parchment paper. Place the coating sugar in a shallow dish, then add the peel a few pieces at a time, tossing to coat. Spread the sugar-coated peel in a single layer on the lined baking sheet, then sprinkle with any remaining sugar. Let dry uncovered overnight (or longer if it is humid) to form a dry sugar crust.

Once dry, sift any excess sugar off the peel (save the sifted citrus-scented sugar for tea, add it to the anise sugar used to coat the Gibassier (page 387) or Stollen (page 361), or sprinkle on quick breads or muffins and store in an airtight container at room temperature for up to 2 weeks.

THE GIANT STICKY BUN

MIX	BULK FERMENTATION	TOPPING	FILLING	PRESHAPE	SHAPE	2ND RISE	BAKE
15 MIN	1–1½ HOURS	5 MIN	5 MIN	25 MIN	20 MIN	30 MIN–1 HOUR	30 MIN

TIME: ABOUT 4½ HOURS

MAKES ONE 9-INCH ROLL

Gibassier Dough (page 387), with modifications (see Make the Dough below)

TOPPING

146 grams (½ cup plus 3 tablespoons packed) light brown sugar

71 grams (5 tablespoons) unsalted butter, melted

63 grams (3 tablespoons) golden syrup (see Note) or light corn syrup

57 grams (¼ cup) heavy cream

1.5 grams (¼ teaspoon) fine salt

5 grams (1 teaspoon) pure vanilla extract

113 grams (1 cup) chopped pecans

FILLING

160 grams (¾ cup packed) light brown sugar

15 grams (2 tablespoons) unbleached all-purpose flour

0.75 gram (⅛ teaspoon) fine salt

57 grams (4 tablespoons) unsalted butter, melted

Ingredients continue

This multilayered treat has a lot going for it: plush dough striated with brown sugar, a caramel topping, and tons of toasted pecans.

If you want to bake this in the morning and serve it fresh, get ahead by making the dough the evening before you want to bake. Spray a piece of parchment paper with pan spray, then spread the dough into a rough rectangle about ½ inch thick. Cover tightly and refrigerate overnight. In the morning, preheat the oven while you roll, fill, and shape the dough as described below.

MAKE THE DOUGH: Make the dough for the gibassier as directed on page 387, with these changes: Omit the orange blossom water and replace it with 14 grams (1 tablespoon) warm milk. Omit the candied orange peel and anise seeds. Cover the dough and let rise until puffy though not necessarily doubled in size, 1 to 1½ hours.

MAKE THE TOPPING: Spray the bottom and sides of a 9-inch round cake or springform pan with pan spray. In a medium bowl, combine the brown sugar, melted butter, golden syrup, heavy cream, salt, and vanilla, stirring until a soft paste with no lumps forms. Spread the topping into the prepared pan, then sprinkle the pecans evenly over the topping. Set aside.

MAKE THE FILLING: In a medium bowl, combine the brown sugar, flour, and salt and whisk together, breaking up any lumps. Add the melted butter, water, and vanilla, mixing to form a soft, somewhat granular paste. Set aside.

Line a rimmed baking sheet with parchment paper. Lightly dust a work surface, then use a plastic bowl scraper to gently ease the dough out of the bowl onto the work surface. Using a rolling pin, roll the dough out into a 16 × 10-inch rectangle. If the dough resists stretching, cover it and set aside for a few minutes. This rest gives the gluten time to relax and

Recipe continues

14 grams (1 tablespoon) water

5 grams (1 teaspoon) pure vanilla extract

Unbleached all-purpose flour, for dusting

will make it easier to continue rolling to the desired size. If the dough sticks to the work surface, add just enough flour to prevent sticking and employ the use of a bench knife or a plastic bowl scraper to ease the dough off the surface. Transfer the dough to the prepared baking sheet, cover, and let rest 15 minutes in the refrigerator. Briefly chilling the dough will make it easier to shape.

Transfer the dough to a lightly floured work surface, gently rolling or stretching it into a 16 × 12-inch rectangle. Dollop the filling over the dough, then use a small offset spatula or silicone spatula to spread it in an even layer all over the dough to the edges. (If the filling has firmed up, heat it in the microwave in 5-second intervals until just soft enough to spread.)

Using a pizza wheel or sharp knife, cut the dough in half lengthwise so that you have two 12 × 8-inch pieces. Gently maneuver your hands, a bowl scraper, or a bench knife under the edges of one piece of dough and place it filling side up on top of the other piece of dough. You should now have a stacked 12 × 8-inch piece of dough/filling/dough/filling. Orient the rectangle so a long side is facing you.

SHAPE THE BUN: Using the pizza wheel or sharp knife, cut the dough crosswise into eight 1½-inch-wide strips. Starting at the end of one of the strips, loosely roll it up into a coil (as if you were rolling one cinnamon roll) and place it, flat side down, in the center of the pan on top of the pecans. This piece will form the center of the giant sticky bun. Working with the remaining strips one at a time, pick each one up and gently wrap it, filling side in, around the coiled center piece. Continue with the remaining strips, adding each new strip at the end of the previous one, gently pinching the ends together to seal as you go. Continue assembling this way until you have used all the strips. Be careful not to wrap the strips too tightly, as the dough will need some room to expand. There will be about ½ to 1 inch of space between the last strip of dough and the edge of the cake pan; this is normal. Cover and let rise in a warm place until puffy and when the dough is pressed with a lightly floured finger, a small indentation remains (see Proofing, page 44), 30 to 45 minutes. (If the dough has been chilled overnight, increase this time to 45 minutes to 1 hour.)

Toward the end of the rising time, preheat the oven to 350°F and arrange a rack in the center. Line a rimmed baking sheet with parchment paper.

BAKE: Place the sticky bun pan on the lined baking sheet to catch any drips, then transfer to the oven (still on the baking sheet) and bake until the bun is well puffed, the top is golden brown, and the internal temperature is at least 205°F, about 30 minutes.

Remove from the oven and transfer to a wire rack to cool in the pan for 5 minutes. Invert a large serving platter over the cake pan. Using oven mitts and holding the sheet pan in place over the cake pan, swiftly and decisively flip so the serving platter is now on the bottom and the cake pan is resting on top. Set the platter on your work surface, then slowly remove the cake pan. Some topping will trickle down the sides of the bun and pool at the bottom. Resist the urge to sneak a taste, as the topping is hot! Let the sticky bun cool for 30 minutes before slicing into wedges and serving.

Any leftover sticky bun can be stored in an airtight container at room temperature for up to 2 days or frozen for longer storage. Thaw any frozen sticky bun, place on a heatproof plate, then heat in the microwave in 5- to 10-second intervals until warm or place on a parchment-lined baking sheet in a preheated 350°F oven until heated through, 5 to 8 minutes.

NOTE: A staple in British kitchens, amber-colored golden syrup has a wonderful caramelized flavor, and because it's an invert sugar, the topping stays gooey, even hours (or days) after it's baked. If you can't find it, light corn syrup can be substituted.

Things to Make with Bread

CROUTONS

MAKES 4 CUPS

200 grams (7 ounces) bread (see headnote), torn into bite-size pieces or cut into ½-inch cubes (about 4 cups)

36 grams (3 tablespoons) olive oil

¼ teaspoon fine salt

¼ teaspoon freshly ground black pepper (optional)

Croutons are an essential food. Not only are they a terrific way to use up stale bread but they also take salads and soups from boring to brilliant. In our test kitchen, there was debate about whether the best croutons were made from torn bread or cubed; you can experiment with both and see which you prefer. Any bread can be croutoned, but enriched breads that contain sugar will brown more quickly and retain a softer character even when toasted. And if you use a flavored bread, the croutons may have more limited applications than those made from an unadorned loaf.

Preheat the oven to 350°F and arrange a rack in the center.

Combine the bread, olive oil, salt, and pepper (if using) on an unlined baking sheet and toss so the bread is coated in oil. Arrange in a single layer. Bake, stirring occasionally, until the croutons are golden brown and crisp, 12 to 14 minutes (they will continue to crisp as they cool).

Croutons will keep in an airtight container at room temperature for 2 to 3 days. If they become a bit soft, refresh them by baking in a 200°F oven until they re-crisp, about 5 minutes.

VARIATION

TOASTED BREAD CRUMBS: Toast the croutons as directed. Let them cool, then place in a zip-top plastic bag. Roll a rolling pin over the bag of croutons, crushing them as coarsely or as finely as you'd like. Coarser crumbs are perfect for topping pasta dishes (like macaroni and cheese) or tucking into the filling of an omelet. Finer crumbs are good for binding meatballs, breading eggplant or chicken, or thickening soups.

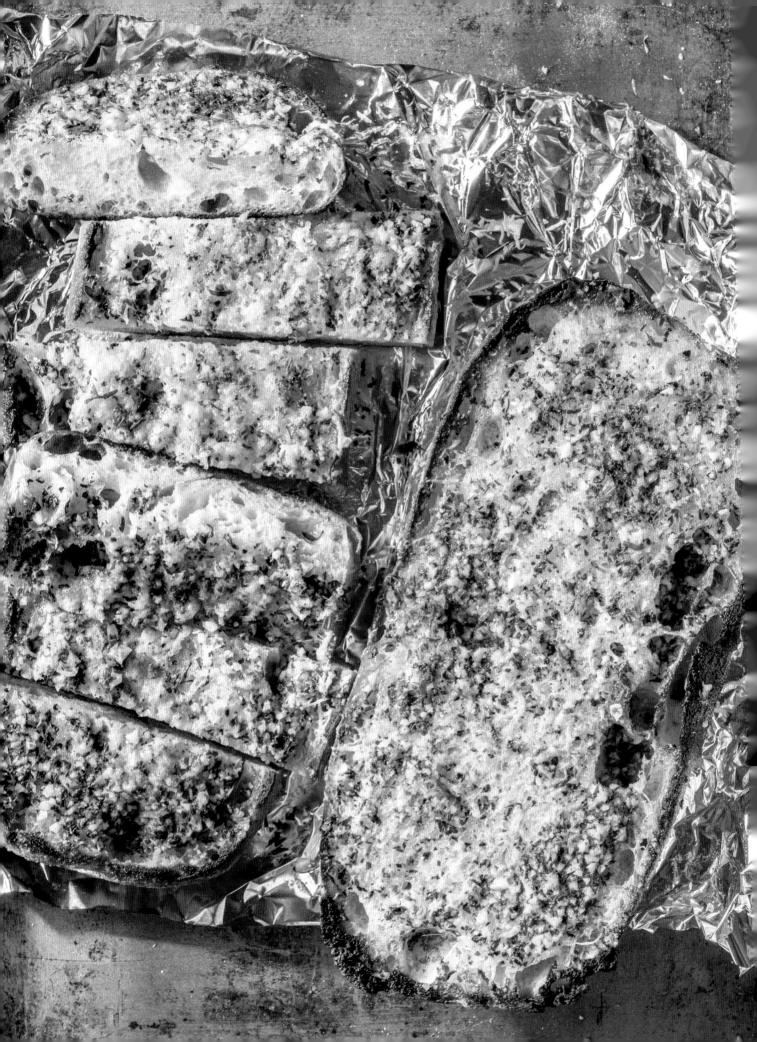

SUPREME GARLIC BREAD

MAKES 1 LARGE LOAF; SERVES 8
TO 10

113 grams (8 tablespoons)
unsalted butter, softened

4 large cloves garlic (25 grams/
2 tablespoons), minced

2 tablespoons fresh flat-leaf
parsley, finely chopped

Fine salt

Freshly ground black pepper

1 loaf Everyday French Loaf (page
208) or Ciabatta (page 255)

25 grams (¼ cup) grated
Parmesan cheese

Red pepper flakes, for sprinkling
(optional)

To make the ultimate garlic bread, you need three things: good bread, ample butter, and lots of garlic. Texture, too, is important—we bake the loaf first, wrapped in foil, until the garlic butter is melted and the bread is warmed through. Then we expose the buttered sides of the loaf to the heat of the broiler, so the bread browns and crisps.

Preheat the oven to 350°F and arrange racks in the center and upper third.

In a medium bowl, stir together the butter, garlic, and parsley until combined. Season to taste with salt and pepper. Cut the bread lengthwise into two planks and slather the cut sides with the butter, spreading evenly. Sandwich the bread back together, buttered sides touching, then wrap the loaf in foil.

Place the foil-wrapped loaf on a rimmed baking sheet and transfer to the oven. Bake for 10 minutes.

Remove the baking sheet, unwrap the loaf, and arrange the two halves side by side on top of the foil, buttered side up. Dividing evenly, sprinkle the buttered sides of the bread with the Parmesan. Sprinkle with pepper flakes to taste, if desired.

Preheat the broiler. Return the bread (still on the pan) to the top rack and broil until deep golden brown, watching carefully so the bread doesn't burn, 2 to 3 minutes.

Remove from the oven, transfer to a cutting board, and cut each half crosswise into thick batons. Serve warm.

FRENCH TOAST

28 grams (2 tablespoons) unsalted butter, divided

22 grams (2 tablespoons) vegetable oil, divided

3 large eggs (150 grams total)

170 grams (¾ cup) heavy cream

28 grams (2 tablespoons) rum (optional)

25 grams (2 tablespoons) granulated sugar

1 teaspoon pure vanilla extract

¼ teaspoon ground nutmeg

¼ teaspoon ground cinnamon

Pinch of salt

8 slices (¾ inch thick) day-old soft white bread, such as Challah (page 365), English Muffin Toasting Bread (page 124), Pain de Mie (page 132), Japanese Milk Bread (page 165), or Sky-High Nanterre (page 378)

FOR SERVING

Softened unsalted butter and warm maple syrup (optional, but not really)

Confectioners' sugar or cinnamon sugar, for dusting (optional)

Most people can make a version of French toast with their eyes closed: Whisk together an egg and some milk, dip some bread into it, and slap it in a hot pan. That's all good and fine, but we believe that if you want to make something seriously unforgettable, you need to go bigger. That means using heavy cream instead of milk; seasoning the custard with nutmeg and cinnamon and, yes, a shot of rum; and soaking, not dipping, the bread (for maximum custard absorption). You can make French toast from many types of bread, but sweet enriched breads like challah, pain de mie, milk bread, and brioche are particularly well suited to the task because they're slightly sweet, soak up large quantities of custard without falling apart, and can stand up to a generous pour of warm maple syrup.

Preheat the oven to 300°F. Line a baking sheet with parchment paper.

In a large, well-seasoned cast-iron or nonstick skillet, heat 14 grams (1 tablespoon) of the butter and 11 grams (1 tablespoon) of the oil over medium heat.

In a shallow casserole dish large enough to hold 2 pieces of bread snugly, whisk together the eggs, cream, rum (if using), sugar, vanilla, nutmeg, cinnamon, and salt until smooth but not foamy.

Place 2 pieces of bread in the dish; let them soak for about 30 seconds, then turn them over and let soak for about 30 seconds on the other side. You want the bread to absorb some of the liquid, but not to become soggy.

Place the bread in the skillet and fry until both sides are golden brown, about 2 minutes per side.

Transfer the French toast to the baking sheet and place it in the preheated oven. Keep in the oven while you cook the remaining pieces, adding more butter and oil to the skillet as necessary.

When all the pieces are cooked, transfer the French toast to warmed plates. Serve with softened butter and maple syrup, or dust with confectioners' sugar or cinnamon sugar.

GARLIC BREAD EGG IN A HOLE

SERVES 2 (EASILY SCALES UP)

2 slices (¾ inch thick) Pain de Mie (page 132), (Not So) Basic White Sandwich Bread (page 120), Sourdough Sandwich Loaf (page 127), Everyday Bread (page 129), or other bread of your choice

42 grams (3 tablespoons) mayonnaise

12 grams (2 tablespoons) grated Parmesan cheese, plus more for sprinkling

1 garlic clove, grated

1 tablespoon finely chopped fresh flat-leaf parsley, plus more for serving

Fine salt

Freshly ground black pepper

14 grams (1 tablespoon) unsalted butter

2 large eggs (100 grams total)

There are several different names for this egg preparation: toad-in-a-hole, eggs-in-a-basket, and framed eggs, to list a few. They're all essentially the same thing: A slice of bread with a hole cut in its center, into which an egg is cracked and cooked. We amped our version up by using a cheesy herbed garlic and mayonnaise mixture on the bread instead of butter for a fine twist on a beloved classic.

Use a 2-inch round cutter to cut a hole in the center of each slice of bread; reserve the center cutout.

In a small bowl, stir together the mayonnaise, Parmesan, garlic, and parsley. Season to taste with salt and pepper. Spread the mixture on both of sides of each slice of bread and both sides of the center cutouts.

In a large well-seasoned cast-iron or nonstick skillet, heat the butter over medium-low heat. Add the bread (including the cutouts; depending on the size of your skillet, you may need to do this in batches) and cook until the bread is starting to brown on the bottom, about 2 minutes. Crack 1 egg into each hole. Season the egg with salt and pepper and sprinkle with a bit of grated Parmesan. Let cook until the egg is mostly set, another 2 minutes, then flip and continue to cook until the underside is toasted and the egg whites are set but the yolk is still runny, 2 to 3 minutes, adjusting the heat as needed to achieve desired browning.

Serve warm, garnished with more parsley and Parmesan, if desired.

BOSTOCK

4 slices (¾ inch thick) day-old
Sky-High Nanterre (page 378),
Challah (page 365), or Japanese
Milk Bread (page 165)

FRANGIPANE (ALMOND CREAM)

85 grams (6 tablespoons)
unsalted butter, at room
temperature

99 grams (½ cup) granulated
sugar

¼ teaspoon salt

96 grams (1 cup) almond flour

23 grams (3 tablespoons)
unbleached all-purpose flour

1 large egg (50 grams), at room
temperature

2 teaspoons almond extract

SIMPLE SYRUP

50 grams (¼ cup) sugar

50 grams (¼ cup) water

1 vanilla bean (optional)

ASSEMBLY

22 grams (¼ cup) sliced almonds,
for sprinkling

Confectioners' sugar, for dusting

Leave it to the French to take something very good and make it even better. This breakfast pastry is made by soaking slices of day-old brioche (or challah or milk bread) with sugar syrup, slathering them with frangipane, then baking until puffed and golden brown. The recipe that follows is the simplest version, but you can dress it up further with a layer of jam (smear it on the bread before the frangipane) or by adding some fresh fruit, such as berries or thin slices of peaches or nectarines, on top of the frangipane before baking.

Arrange a rack in the center of the oven and preheat the oven to 350°F. Line a baking sheet with parchment paper.

Arrange bread slices in a single layer on the lined baking sheet and set aside.

MEANWHILE, MAKE THE FRANGIPANE: In a stand mixer bowl, combine the butter, sugar, and salt. Using the paddle attachment, beat on medium speed until pale and fluffy, about 1 minute. Add the almond flour, all-purpose flour, egg, and almond extract and mix until just combined. Set aside.

MAKE THE SIMPLE SYRUP: In a small saucepan, combine the sugar and water. If using the vanilla bean, split it lengthwise, scrape the seeds into the pan, and add the pod. Bring to a simmer, stirring, and cook just until the sugar dissolves. Remove the vanilla bean pod from the syrup, rinse, and let dry; once dried, it can be added to a jar of sugar to make vanilla-scented sugar.

ASSEMBLE AND BAKE THE BOSTOCK: Use a pastry brush to coat each piece of bread generously with the simple syrup. Flip the slices and brush on the remaining liquid until it's all used up. Spread a ⅛-inch-thick layer of frangipane over the entire surface of one side of each piece of bread. Evenly sprinkle 1 tablespoon sliced almonds on each piece.

Bake the bostock until the frangipane is golden brown around the edges and the bottom of the bread is evenly caramelized, 25 to 30 minutes. Serve bostock fresh from the oven with a dusting of confectioners' sugar

on top. Bostock are best enjoyed as soon as they're baked. Leftovers
can be stored in the refrigerator, covered, for up to 1 day. To reheat
refrigerated bostock, place slices on a wire rack on top of a baking sheet
and bake at 350°F for about 15 minutes.

MIGAS

SERVES 2

4 stale corn tortillas, store-bought or homemade (page 66)

36 grams (3 tablespoons) vegetable or other neutral oil

Fine salt

43 grams (3 tablespoons) unsalted butter

½ small (50 grams) white onion, finely diced

½ jalapeño or serrano pepper, minced

4 large eggs (200 grams total)

Freshly ground black pepper

FOR SERVING (OPTIONAL)

2 tablespoons chopped fresh cilantro

Refried beans, warmed

Sour cream

Sliced avocado

Lime wedges, for squeezing

Salsa or hot sauce

There are several versions of migas. In Spain, it's made from bits of bread that are toasted until crisp (*migas* means "crumbs"), then combined with scrambled eggs; in the Tex-Mex iteration, stale corn tortillas take the place of bread. If you're thinking that Tex-Mex migas sound a bit like chilaquiles, you're right—both contain tortillas and eggs. But chilaquiles is typically made with tortilla chips that are coated in salsa, then mixed with eggs, while migas use short strips of fried tortillas and are coated in eggs, with salsa offered as an optional condiment.

Migas is a humble yet satisfying breakfast (or late-night snack), a proven hangover cure, and a great way to use up stale corn tortillas. We've given options below for ways to dress up migas, but even in its simplest form it's still a wonderful way to start the day.

Cut the tortillas in half, then stack the half-moons and cut crosswise into ½-inch-wide strips.

Line a plate with paper towels and set nearby. In a medium skillet, heat the oil over medium-high heat. When the oil is hot, add the tortilla pieces and fry, stirring, until crispy and golden brown, about 5 minutes. With tongs, transfer to the paper towels to drain. Season with salt.

Use a paper towel to wipe out any excess oil remaining in the pan. Reduce the heat to medium and add the butter to the now-empty skillet. When the butter has melted, add the onion, jalapeño, and a generous pinch of salt and cook, stirring, until the onions have softened and are beginning to color, about 5 minutes.

In a large bowl, vigorously whisk the eggs and season generously with salt and black pepper. Return the tortilla strips to the skillet with the onions, then pour the eggs over. Cook, stirring, until the eggs are softly set, about 3 minutes.

Divide the migas between two serving plates. Sprinkle with the cilantro, if using. If desired, serve with refried beans, sour cream, avocado, a squeeze of lime, and some salsa or hot sauce alongside.

CHEDDAR-KIMCHI STRATA

SERVES 6

One 16-ounce (453-gram) jar medium-spicy kimchi

12 grams (1 tablespoon) vegetable or other neutral oil

1 bunch scallions (about 226 grams/8 ounces), thinly sliced, dark-green tops kept separate

Fine salt

9 large eggs (450 grams total)

510 grams (2¼ cups) milk, whole preferred

7.5 grams (1¼ teaspoons) fine salt

Softened unsalted butter, for the baking dish

400 grams crusty bread, such as Pain au Levain (page 201), Pain de Campagne (page 205), or Everyday French Loaf (page 208), cut into 1-inch cubes (about 6 cups)

113 grams (4 ounces) cheddar cheese, shredded (1 cup)

Tangy kimchi and sharp cheddar—both a great pairing with eggs—join forces in this hearty strata. Just as with bread pudding, the cubed bread gives the casserole body and heft; use a crusty bread with some structure, because the cubes soak in the custard overnight and the sturdier bread results in a nicely textured finished dish. Serve for brunch or as an easy, no-fuss supper.

Empty the kimchi into a large bowl. With clean hands, pick up fistfuls of the kimchi and squeeze, letting the brine fall back into the bowl. Transfer the squeezed kimchi to a cutting board and chop it roughly. Reserve the brine in the bowl.

In a large skillet, heat the vegetable oil over medium-high heat. Add the kimchi, scallion whites and light-green parts, and a pinch of salt and cook, stirring, until the scallions have softened and the kimchi has started to caramelize, 5 to 6 minutes. Turn off the heat, stir in the scallion tops, and set aside.

In a large measuring cup or bowl, whisk together the eggs, milk, and salt. Give the reserved kimchi brine a stir, then measure out ¼ cup and whisk it into the egg mixture.

Butter an 8-inch square baking dish. Add about half of the bread cubes to the dish, arranging them in an even layer. Top the bread with about half of the kimchi mixture, scattering it as evenly as possible, followed by half the cheddar. Repeat these layers once with the remaining bread, kimchi, and cheese. Pour the egg mixture over the bread. Wrap the strata tightly and refrigerate for about 8 hours or overnight.

Arrange a rack in the center of the oven and preheat the oven to 350°F. While it preheats, let the strata sit at room temperature.

Unwrap the strata and bake until it's a little puffy, the bread on top is crispy and golden, and there's little to no jiggling in the center when you wiggle the baking dish, about 40 minutes.

Let the strata cool for at least 10 minutes before serving. Eat warm or at room temperature.

CINNAMON TOAST DELUXE

SERVES 6

113 grams (8 tablespoons) softened butter

62 grams (5 tablespoons) sugar

6 grams (2 teaspoons) ground cinnamon

¼ teaspoon fine salt

6 thick-cut (¾-inch) slices Challah (page 365), Sky-High Nanterre (page 378), Japanese Milk Bread (page 165), or (Not So) Basic White Sandwich Bread (page 120)

How do you improve on classic cinnamon toast? It's not easy, but this recipe manages to do just that, rendering decadent, buttery toasts with a crispy coating of caramelized sugar and spice. To ensure success, cut your bread thick (¾ inch) and slather on the butter with gusto. This is a special-occasion cinnamon toast that's suitable for company—which is why it makes a batch that serves six.

Preheat the oven to 450°F and arrange a rack in the center.

In a medium bowl, combine the butter, sugar, cinnamon, and salt. Spread a generous tablespoon of the mixture on one side of each slice of bread.

Arrange the slices buttered side up on a baking sheet and slide into the oven. Bake the toasts until the edges and underside of the bread are deeply golden brown and the butter (which will bubble throughout baking) has settled into a layer of caramelized sugar, about 10 minutes. (If you can still see a thick-ish layer of butter on top of the bread, the toasts aren't ready yet.) Immediately transfer the toasts to a cooling rack and let them sit for 3 to 5 minutes; the sugar will firm up in this time and turn into a crispy shell. Smear a thin layer of the remaining cinnamon butter on each piece of toast and serve immediately.

THREE GREAT TOASTS

SEARED MUSHROOM TOAST WITH RICOTTA

SERVES 4

In a large skillet, heat a generous glug of EXTRA-VIRGIN OLIVE OIL over medium-high heat. Add 226 TO 284 GRAMS (8 TO 10 OUNCES) SLICED OR TORN MUSHROOMS, like shiitake, maitake, cremini, or a mix. Cook, undisturbed, until beginning to brown on the bottom, 2 to 3 minutes. Season with SALT, stir, and continue to cook the mushrooms until they're browned and starting to crisp. When the mushrooms are nearly finished, add a little more oil and sprinkle in SMOKED PAPRIKA, MILD CHILE FLAKES (like Aleppo-style), or OTHER SPICES of choice to taste. Spread WHOLE-MILK RICOTTA generously onto 4 PIECES OF THICK-CUT TOAST (¾ inch thick is perfect) and season with salt. Spoon mushrooms over top, then garnish with torn CILANTRO and a final drizzle of olive oil.

AVOCADO TOAST WITH WHIPPED FETA

SERVES 4

In a food processor or blender, combine 113 GRAMS (1 CUP) CRUMBLED FETA, 28 GRAMS (2 TABLESPOONS) CREAM CHEESE, 2 TEASPOONS EXTRA-VIRGIN OLIVE OIL, and 1 TEASPOON WATER until very smooth. Season to taste with LEMON ZEST, BLACK PEPPER, and, if you'd like, HONEY (which is especially good if your feta is ultra tangy). Spread generously onto 4 pieces of thick-cut toast (¾ inch thick is perfect), then top with thinly sliced avocado (you'll want about half an avocado per piece). Drizzle with olive oil and lemon juice, then season with pepper and garnish with torn herbs like basil and dill.

PAN CON TOMATE

SERVES 4

Core 1 LARGE RIPE TOMATO (ABOUT 200 GRAMS/7 OUNCES) and halve it. Set a box grater over a bowl. Grate the tomato halves on the large holes of the grater, letting the pulp fall into the bowl; discard the skin. To the tomato pulp add ¼ TEASPOON FINE SEA SALT and 1 TEASPOON SHERRY VINEGAR and stir to combine. Taste the mixture and adjust the seasoning; it should taste balanced and delicious. Coat a large nonstick or cast-iron skillet with a generous glug of EXTRA-VIRGIN OLIVE OIL. You're essentially shallow-frying the bread, so you want a good amount of oil. Heat the oil over medium heat until hot. Working in batches if necessary, add 4 THICK-CUT SLICES OF BREAD (about ⅔ inch thick is perfect), such as Pain au Levain (page 201), Pain de Campagne (page 205), or Everyday French Loaf (page 208). The bread should sizzle on contact with the oil. Fry the bread, turning once, until deep golden brown on one side, about 3 minutes. Flip and fry on the second side for 2 minutes more. Transfer to a plate. Rub 1 PEELED GARLIC CLOVE over one side of each slice of bread and sprinkle with some FLAKY SALT. Dividing evenly, spoon some of the seasoned tomato pulp on each piece of toast. If you'd like, drizzle each slice with a bit more olive oil.

PAN CON TOMATE

SEARED MUSHROOM
TOAST WITH RICOTTA

AVOCADO TOAST WITH
WHIPPED FETA

EXTREMELY CHEESY GRILLED CHEESE

MAKES 1 SANDWICH (EASILY SCALES UP)

2 slices (½ inch thick) Pickled Jalapeño and Cheddar Bread (page 147) or any other sandwich bread of your choosing, such as Sourdough Sandwich Loaf (page 127) or Everyday Bread (page 129)

14 grams (1 tablespoon) mayonnaise

14 grams (1 tablespoon) unsalted butter, softened

56 grams (2 ounces) sharp cheddar cheese, shredded (½ cup)

12 grams (2 tablespoons) finely grated Parmesan cheese (grated on a rasp-style grater or the small holes of a box grater)

The only thing that could make a grilled cheese better is more cheese. Here, it shows up in three forms. There's cheddar both in the bread (though you can use a different type of bread if you prefer) and filling the sandwich. Then the outside of the sandwich is coated with grated Parmesan cheese. As the sandwich toasts, it melts into an irresistibly crispy, lacy cheese layer on the exterior, adding texture and umami. We use mayonnaise on the exterior of the sandwich, since butter has a tendency to brown before the cheese is melted, but spread a bit of butter on the interior so its flavor comes through in the finished sandwich.

Spread one side of each slice of bread with the mayonnaise, spreading all the way to the edges. Spread the opposite side of each slice of bread with the butter. Arrange the slices buttered side up on your work surface. Top one of the slices with the shredded cheddar, then top with the second slice of bread, buttered side down. Coat the exterior of the sandwich on both sides with the grated Parmesan, pressing gently so the cheese adheres to the mayonnaise-coated bread.

Heat a small nonstick skillet over medium heat and add the sandwich to the pan. Cook until the bottom is golden brown and the Parmesan is crispy, about 3 minutes. Flip and cook on the second side until the cheddar is melted and the sandwich is deep golden brown, 3 to 4 minutes longer. If the Parmesan is browning before the cheddar has melted, reduce the heat and continue cooking the sandwich, flipping more frequently, until the cheddar is melty.

Transfer the sandwich to a cutting board, let stand for 1 minute, then cut diagonally in half. Serve hot.

GRILLED CHOCOLATE SANDWICH

MAKES 1 SANDWICH (EASILY SCALES UP)

2 slices (½ inch thick) bread, sourdough preferred

56 grams (2 ounces) chocolate (semisweet, bittersweet, or milk), finely chopped or grated (about ⅓ cup)

1 to 2 tablespoons raspberry (or other red) jam, apricot jam, or orange marmalade (optional)

28 grams (2 tablespoons) unsalted butter, softened

Flaky salt, such as Maldon, or cinnamon sugar (optional)

Though there is nothing very original about a grilled chocolate sandwich (you can find them in Italian cafés and versions of them in other cookbooks, including one by chocolate expert and cookbook author Alice Medrich, who brilliantly suggests dusting the finished sandwich with cinnamon sugar), there's still something that feels subversive about it. It's a sandwich—shouldn't it be filled with egg salad? Or sliced turkey? Or hot, melty cheese?

At first, we made grilled chocolate sandwiches exclusively with enriched breads like Challah (page 365), Brioche (page 377), and Pain de Mie (page 132), making something very dessert-like. But eventually we tried it with thick slices of sourdough (like the Pain au Levain, page 201) and the Sesame Wheat (page 220), and it was a revelation. Chocolate plays nicely with the tang and salt and crunch of griddled sourdough, and we've found we now prefer it for our chocolate sandwiches, as long as the bread is not too holey (in which case the molten chocolate escapes).

To make the world's best grilled chocolate, sandwich the bread around the chocolate. If you like, add a smear of jam. Spread softened butter on the outsides of the sandwich. In a small, heavy skillet, cook the sandwich over medium-low heat, occasionally pressing gently with a spatula, until the sandwich is golden and crispy on one side, 2 to 3 minutes. (Low and slow is the game here; if it's not ready, don't turn up the heat, just keep cooking and checking.) Flip the sandwich and cook the other side until golden and crispy and the chocolate has melted, 2 to 3 minutes more. If you'd like, sprinkle the sandwich with some flaky salt or cinnamon sugar; do not share.

THE MONTE CRISTO

SERVES 4

20 grams (4 teaspoons) Dijon mustard

8 slices (½ inch thick) sandwich bread, such as (Not So) Basic White Sandwich Bread (page 120), Sourdough Sandwich Loaf (page 127), or Everyday Bread (page 129)

170 grams (6 ounces) sliced Swiss cheese

170 grams (6 ounces) sliced turkey

170 grams (6 ounces) sliced ham

3 large eggs (150 grams total)

76 grams (⅓ cup) milk

56 grams (4 tablespoons) unsalted butter, divided

Confectioners' sugar, raspberry jam, or maple syrup, for serving (optional)

This battered and pan-fried ham, turkey, and Swiss cheese sandwich has been a mainstay of American diners since the 1960s, when it was featured on a menu at Disneyland. The whole sandwich is dredged in a combination of beaten eggs and milk, like French toast, then cooked in butter until browned. It's typically served with a side of jam or a dusting of confectioners' sugar (or both), a salty-sweet don't-knock-it-'til-you've-tried-it combination that somehow just makes sense. Given that we always have Vermont maple syrup in our test kitchen, we also tried drizzling the sandwich with that, for a delicious twist on a classic.

Preheat the oven to 200°F.

Spread 1 teaspoon of mustard onto each of 4 slices of bread. Dividing evenly, top each slice with Swiss cheese, turkey, and ham. Place a second slice of bread on top to make a sandwich.

Crack the eggs into a pie plate or cake pan, add the milk, and beat until well combined.

Heat a large nonstick or cast-iron skillet over medium heat and add 28 grams (2 tablespoons) of the butter. Working with one sandwich at time, dip the sandwich into the beaten egg mixture, turning to coat on both sides, then place the sandwich in the pan. Repeat with a second sandwich. Fry the sandwiches, turning once, until deeply browned and the cheese is melty, about 3 minutes per side. Transfer to a baking sheet and place in the oven to keep warm while you fry the remaining 2 sandwiches in the remaining 28 grams (2 tablespoons) butter.

When all the sandwiches have been cooked, transfer to a cutting board and cut on the diagonal into triangles. If desired, dust with confectioners' sugar or serve with jam or maple syrup alongside for spreading/dipping.

MOZZARELLA IN CARROZZA

SERVES 4

8 slices (½ inch thick) white sandwich bread, such as (Not So) Basic White Sandwich Bread (page 120) or Sourdough Sandwich Loaf (page 127), crusts removed

283 grams (10 ounces) low-moisture whole-milk mozzarella cheese, thinly sliced

1 to 2 teaspoons Calabrian chile paste (optional)

3 large eggs (150 grams total)

Fine salt

Freshly ground black pepper

75 grams (1¼ cups) panko breadcrumbs

Olive oil, for frying

Flaky sea salt, such as Maldon, for sprinkling

Mozzarella in carrozza, or "mozzarella in a carriage," is Italy's answer to grilled cheese. Mild, milky mozzarella is sandwiched between slices of crustless white bread, battered with egg and rolled in breadcrumbs, then pan-fried in a generous amount of olive oil until marvelously crisp and beautifully golden. Consider the (optional) smear of Calabrian chile paste, which offsets the mellow cheese with some fruity heat. Don't use preshredded mozzarella here; it falls out when you're breading the sandwiches and doesn't melt as nicely.

Dividing evenly, top 4 slices of the bread with the mozzarella, then dot it with a bit of the Calabrian chile paste (if using) and top with a second slice of bread.

In a pie plate or baking dish, beat the eggs until well combined and season with a few pinches of salt and pepper. Spread the panko in a second rimmed dish. Set a large plate or rimmed baking sheet nearby. Working with one sandwich at a time, dip it into the beaten eggs, turning to coat on both sides and letting the excess drip off. Transfer to the panko, pressing to coat, then flip the sandwich and coat with panko on the second side. Transfer to the plate or baking sheet and repeat with the remaining 3 sandwiches until ready to cook. The sandwiches can be prepared to this point up to 2 hours in advance; refrigerate until ready to fry.

Pour a generous slick of olive oil into a large nonstick or cast-iron skillet; you're essentially shallow-frying the sandwiches, so be generous with the oil. Heat the oil over medium heat. To test its temperature, drop in a panko breadcrumb; it should sizzle on contact with the oil.

When the oil is hot, add as many sandwiches as will fit in a single layer in the pan. Fry, turning once, until the cheese is melted and the sandwiches are deep golden brown on both sides, 5 to 6 minutes total. Using tongs, stand the sandwiches on their edges to brown them all over. Transfer to a wire rack and repeat with the remaining sandwiches.

When all the sandwiches have been fried, sprinkle with flaky salt and cut in half on the diagonal. Serve hot.

TOMATO PANZANELLA

SERVES 6

680 grams (1½ pounds) tomatoes, preferably a mix of cherry, heirloom, and beefsteak

Fine salt

1 medium red onion (about 170 grams/6 ounces), thinly sliced

28 grams (2 tablespoons) sherry vinegar or red wine vinegar

Extra-virgin olive oil

396 to 453 grams (14 to 16 ounces) crusty day-old bread, such as Everyday French Loaf (page 208), Pain au Levain (page 201), or Pain de Campagne (page 205), sliced 1 inch thick

1 small garlic clove, grated

½ teaspoon Dijon mustard

Handful of fresh basil leaves

1 small/medium cucumber (about 180 grams/6½ ounces), thinly sliced

226 grams (8 ounces) fresh mozzarella cheese (optional), torn or cut into bite-size pieces

Freshly ground black pepper

Saturated with the juice of ripe tomatoes and good olive oil, day-old bread takes on new life in this salad. For the most beautiful and flavorful dish, use a variety of tomatoes of different shapes, sizes, and colors. Frying the slices of bread on one side adds texture, richness, and flavor to the salad, and prevents the bread from becoming too soggy. Cucumber and mozzarella add crunchiness and creaminess, respectively.

PREPARE THE TOMATOES: Halve the cherry tomatoes and cut any heirloom and beefsteak tomatoes into 1-inch chunks or wedges. Transfer to a fine-mesh sieve set over a bowl; sprinkle with salt (which will help the tomatoes release some of their liquid), gently toss to combine, and set aside to drain for at least 15 minutes while you prepare the rest of the salad.

In a large serving bowl, combine the onion and vinegar. Season with salt, stir to combine, and set aside; this will temper the bite of the onion.

Add enough olive oil to a large skillet to coat the bottom and set over medium heat. When the oil is hot, add as many slices of bread as will fit in a single layer and cook until deliciously brown and toasted, 2 to 3 minutes. Cook only one side, then transfer to a cutting board and repeat with the remaining slices of bread. When all the bread has been cooked, cut into 1- to 2-inch cubes.

To the bowl with the onion and vinegar, add the garlic, mustard, 3 tablespoons olive oil, and the liquid that's drained from the tomatoes. Whisk until emulsified. Add the bread, tomatoes, basil, cucumber, and mozzarella and stir until the bread is saturated with dressing. Season with salt, pepper, and olive oil to taste.

Eat immediately. Leftovers can be refrigerated for up to 2 days (the bread will get softer as it absorbs the dressing and tomato juices, but what the salad loses in crispness it makes up for in flavor). Let the panzanella come to room temperature before eating.

FATTOUSH

SERVES 4 TO 6

DRESSING

2 teaspoons sumac

10 grams (2 teaspoons) hot water

85 grams (6 tablespoons) fresh lemon juice (from 2 large lemons)

26 grams (1 tablespoon plus 1 teaspoon) pomegranate molasses

½ teaspoon dried mint

1 garlic clove, minced

12 grams (2 teaspoons) fine salt, plus more to taste

1 teaspoon freshly ground black pepper, plus more to taste

48 grams (¼ cup) olive oil

LAVASH

2 sheets Lavash (page 71)

25 grams (2 tablespoons) olive oil

Fine salt and freshly ground black pepper

SALAD

340 grams (1 pint) cherry tomatoes, halved

3 Persian (mini) cucumbers (about 340 grams/12 ounces), halved lengthwise, then cut crosswise into ¼-inch half-moons

1 medium head romaine lettuce (about 600 grams/1¼ pounds), chopped

Ingredients continue

This salad originated in rural Lebanon, where fresh vegetables were combined with stale flatbread to make a filling meal (*fatteh* is the Arabic word for "crumbs"), though versions of it are found throughout the Middle East and beyond. What makes this salad so great are its contrasting flavors and textures: You've got juicy tomatoes, crunchy cucumber, and shards of toasted lavash, plus bright, fresh mint all dressed in a sumac, lemon juice, and pomegranate molasses vinaigrette. Note that if you use store-bought lavash, the toasting time will likely be shorter since they're much thinner than homemade. Purslane is a weed—a wild-growing edible plant—with succulent leaves. You might find it at the farmers' market (or growing in your backyard), but if not, you can substitute arugula, sorrel, or baby spinach.

MAKE THE DRESSING: In a small bowl, combine the sumac and hot water and let stand for 15 minutes. Add the lemon juice, pomegranate molasses, dried mint, garlic, salt, and pepper to the bowl and whisk to combine. Slowly whisk in the olive oil until the dressing is emulsified. Season to taste with additional salt and pepper.

PREPARE THE LAVASH: Preheat the oven to 350°F. Line a rimmed baking sheet with parchment paper.

Place the lavash on the lined pan and toast in the oven until browned and very crispy, 8 to 15 minutes depending on its thickness, flipping at the halfway point. Remove from the oven and brush each piece on both sides with the olive oil, then sprinkle on both sides with salt and pepper. (It is important to coat the bread in olive oil while warm. This keeps the lavash crispy and prevents them from absorbing too much of the dressing and becoming soggy.) Let cool completely and then break up the lavash up into 1-inch pieces. This can be done up to 1 day ahead; store in an airtight container.

MAKE THE SALAD: In a large bowl, combine the tomatoes, cucumbers, lettuce, scallions, parsley, mint, and purslane. Add the toasted lavash, drizzle on the dressing, then mix gently but thoroughly until combined. Season to taste with additional salt and pepper and serve right away.

1 bunch scallions (about 85 grams/3 ounces), chopped

1 bunch fresh flat-leaf parsley (about 57 grams/ 2 ounces), leaves stripped off stems

½ bunch fresh mint (about 45 grams/ 1½ ounces), leaves stripped off stems

113 grams (4 ounces) purslane, sorrel, baby arugula, or baby spinach

Fine salt and freshly ground black pepper

PAPPA AL POMODORO

Kosher salt

3 pounds ripe red tomatoes

75 grams (6 tablespoons) olive oil, plus more for drizzling

3 large leeks (about 750 grams/ 1 pound 10 ounces), white and light-green parts only, thinly sliced (about 4 cups)

2 garlic cloves, minced

113 grams (4 ounces) crustless bread, such as Pain au Levain (page 201) or Pain de Campagne (page 205), cut into 1-inch cubes (about 3½ cups)

Freshly ground black pepper

226 grams (8 ounces) burrata cheese (optional)

Flaky sea salt, such as Maldon, for garnish

Basil leaves, for garnish (optional)

We may think of tomato soup (and its loyal companion, the grilled cheese sandwich; see page 416) as winter food, but this Italian version, made with fresh tomatoes, thickened with bread, and topped with fresh burrata cheese, makes a case for eating soup on a summer's day, too. Super-ripe, juicy tomatoes will make the best soup; in a pinch, you can substitute 6 cups good-quality store-bought tomato puree for the fresh tomatoes.

Bring a large pot of salted water to a boil. Fill a large bowl with ice and water and set nearby. Remove the stems from the tomatoes and, with a sharp knife, cut a shallow "X" into the bottom of each tomato. Drop the tomatoes into the boiling water and cook for 30 seconds, until the skins begin to split at the X. With a slotted spoon, transfer the tomatoes to the ice bath. When cool enough to handle, peel the tomatoes, then halve them and pass them through the fine plate of a food mill. If you don't have a food mill, whiz the tomatoes in a food processor until pureed, then pass the puree through a sieve into a clean bowl; discard the seeds.

In a 4- or 5-quart saucepan, heat the olive oil over medium-low heat. Add the leeks and a generous pinch of salt and cook, stirring, until the leeks are translucent but not browned, about 5 minutes. Add the garlic and cook 1 minute more. Pour in the tomato purée, reduce the heat so the mixture is simmering gently, and cook, stirring occasionally, for 15 minutes.

Stir in the bread and continue cooking, stirring occasionally, until the bread breaks down and thickens the soup, about 15 minutes more. The texture should be like a thick porridge; if it's too thick, thin with a bit of hot water.

Season to taste with pepper and additional salt. Spoon into warmed bowls. If desired, tear the burrata into pieces and place a piece on top of each serving. Drizzle with a bit of olive oil, sprinkle with flaky salt, and garnish with a few basil leaves. Serve immediately.

SIMPLE RIBOLLITA

SERVES 6

36 grams (3 tablespoons) olive oil, plus more for drizzling

2 sprigs fresh rosemary, thyme, or a combination

1 medium carrot (105 grams/ 4 ounces), finely chopped

2 celery stalks (112 grams/ 4 ounces), finely chopped

1 large yellow onion (230 grams/ 8 ounces), finely chopped

Fine salt and freshly ground black pepper

4 garlic cloves, finely chopped

44 grams (3 tablespoons) tomato paste

1 large bunch lacinato or curly kale (300 grams/10 ounces), stems and ribs removed, leaves torn

Two 15-ounce (425-gram) cans cannellini or navy beans, drained and rinsed

1 medium Yukon Gold potato (225 grams/8 ounces), peeled and cut into ½-inch cubes

One 28-ounce (794-gram) can whole peeled tomatoes

1 small wedge Parmesan cheese with rind

190 to 284 grams day-old crusty bread, such as Pain au Levain (page 201) or Pain de Campagne (page 205), cut or torn into 1- to 1½-inch cubes (4 to 6 cups)

Lemon wedges, for serving

This rib-sticking vegetarian soup gets body and heft from beans, potatoes, and cubed stale bread, which you add at the end of the soup's cooking time. The cubes of bread soak up the broth and then begin to break down, thickening the soup. Like minestrone, it's loaded with vegetables, though not a lot of any one thing, so it's a good way to use up the bits and bobs that might be kicking around in your crisper drawer.

In a large pot, heat the olive oil over medium heat. Add the herbs and let sizzle until fragrant, about 30 seconds. Add the carrot, celery, and onion, season with salt and pepper, and stir to coat in oil. Reduce the heat to medium-low and cook, stirring occasionally, until the vegetables are very soft but not browning, 20 to 25 minutes.

Add the garlic and tomato paste and stir until fragrant, about 2 minutes. Add the kale, season with salt, stir to coat in oil, and cook until wilted, 3 to 4 minutes. Add the beans and potato and stir to coat. Add the tomatoes, crushing with a heavy spoon or cutting with kitchen shears to break them up. Then fill the empty tomato can with water and add that to the pot. Cut the rind off the wedge of Parmesan and add that, too.

Bring to a boil, then reduce the heat to maintain a gentle simmer. Partially cover and cook until the soup is flavorful and the potatoes are completely tender, 20 to 25 minutes.

Add the bread cubes, stir to submerge, and cook until soft, with some pieces beginning to disintegrate, 3 to 5 minutes. Add more water by the ½ cup until you achieve the consistency you'd like. (The bread will drink up a lot!) Season to taste with additional salt.

Spoon the ribollita into bowls and top with a squeeze of lemon juice, a drizzle of olive oil, and freshly ground black pepper. Grate a generous amount of Parmesan on top. Let leftover soup cool and then transfer to a lidded container and store in the refrigerator. Reheat over medium heat, thinning with water as needed to achieve your desired consistency (it will thicken considerably as it stands) and seasoning to taste with additional salt and pepper.

"FRENCH BREAD" PIZZA

SERVES 2 TO 4

50 grams (¼ cup) olive oil

½ teaspoon dried oregano

⅛ teaspoon red pepper flakes, plus more for garnish

1 garlic clove, grated or finely chopped

2 Bolillos (page 291), preferably day-old

170 grams (6 ounces) low-moisture whole-milk mozzarella cheese, shredded (1½ cups)

63 grams (4 tablespoons) store-bought pizza sauce

Grated Parmesan cheese, for sprinkling

For some, the phrase "French bread pizza" conjures up a childhood memory of a certain frozen pizza. As the name suggests, French bread pizza is made from a loaf of bread that's split lengthwise, then dressed up like pizza with tomato sauce and cheese. The name, however, misleads; a baguette has too great a ratio of crust to crumb and so isn't a good choice for these pizzas. Instead, we prefer to use individual bolillo rolls, which, when toasted, have a thin, shattering crust and a plush interior (as anybody who has had a good mollete knows). For a larger-format pizza, use a loaf of Everyday French Loaf (page 208) and double the other ingredients.

Arrange a rack in the upper third of the oven and preheat the oven to 425°F. Line a baking sheet with parchment paper or foil.

In a small saucepan, heat the olive oil, oregano, and pepper flakes over medium heat until the oil is warm and fragrant. Remove from the heat and stir in the garlic.

Halve the bolillos lengthwise. Use your hands to compress and flatten the halved rolls so that they're less likely to tilt in the oven. Place cut side up on the lined baking sheet. Brush the cut side of each roll generously with the seasoned oil.

Bake the rolls until the cut sides are golden and starting to dry out, 5 to 6 minutes.

Remove the baking sheet from the oven and evenly distribute half of the mozzarella across the rolls. Return to the oven until the cheese is melted, 2 to 3 minutes. Spread 1 tablespoon of pizza sauce on top of the melted cheese on each roll half, spreading it to the edges. Evenly sprinkle the remaining cheese over the top of the rolls. Return to the oven until the cheese is melted, 3 to 4 minutes. Broil the rolls, if desired, to further brown the cheese.

Sprinkle the pizzas with Parmesan and additional pepper flakes. Eat warm.

CLASSIC BREAD STUFFING

SERVES 8 TO 10

Two 1¼-pound (567-gram) loaves white sandwich bread, such as (Not So) Basic White Sandwich Bread (page 120) or Sourdough Sandwich Loaf (page 127)

113 grams (8 tablespoons) unsalted butter, plus more for the baking dish

1 large onion (226 grams/ 8 ounces), diced

4 celery stalks (200 grams/ 7 ounces), finely diced

1 garlic clove, minced

Fine salt

Freshly ground black pepper

908 grams (4 cups) turkey or chicken stock

15 grams (¼ cup) finely chopped fresh sage

15 grams (¼ cup) finely chopped fresh parsley

2 teaspoons Bell's Seasoning or poultry seasoning

2 large eggs (100 grams total)

There are plenty of recipes for stuffing: stuffing made with cornbread, stuffing studded with dried fruit and nuts, sausage stuffing, oyster stuffing, you name it. And while we've been curious to try some of these formulas over the years, we always return to this classic one. Note that we call for drying out fresh bread in the oven rather than using stale bread; we find that dried bread cubes are more absorbent, acting as sponges and soaking up the stock, resulting in the most flavorful stuffing. For the same reason, we also think that bread with a tight crumb, such as a white pan bread, makes better stuffing than a crusty hearth bread. We've provided instructions for baking the stuffing in a pan, though you could also use this in a turkey (just be sure to take the stuffing's temperature if you cook it inside the bird; it needs to reach at least 165°F). The optional addition of Bell's Seasoning, an additive-free blend of dried spices along with fresh herbs, gives this stuffing a classic flavor.

Arrange racks in the upper and lower thirds of the oven and preheat the oven to 275°F.

Cut the bread into 1-inch cubes. Divide the cubed bread between two rimmed baking sheets and spread into an even layer. Bake until the bread is completely dry, about 1 hour, stirring occasionally and rotating the pans halfway through. Remove from the oven and let cool; you should have about 8 cups of dried bread cubes. This step can be done a week ahead. Let the bread cool, then store in airtight containers until ready to use.

If you're planning to bake the stuffing now, increase the oven temperature to 350°F. Butter a 9 × 13-inch baking dish.

In a large Dutch oven or deep pot, melt the butter over medium heat. Add the onion, celery, and garlic and season generously with salt and pepper. Cook, stirring, until the vegetables have softened but are not browned, 6 to 7 minutes. Transfer to a very large bowl and add the cooled bread and 2 cups of the turkey stock.

Add the sage, parsley, and Bell's Seasoning or poultry seasoning to the bowl with the bread and toss well to combine. Taste the mixture and adjust the seasoning; you're likely going to need to add additional salt

and pepper. In a large measuring cup, whisk together the remaining 2 cups stock and the eggs until well combined. Pour over the bread and toss to combine. The mixture should be moist. Spoon the stuffing into the prepared baking dish and spread into an even layer. Cover the pan with foil. The stuffing can be prepared to this point and refrigerated for up to 2 days before baking.

Transfer to the oven and bake for 40 minutes. Uncover and bake until the top is well browned, another 15 to 20 minutes. Serve warm. Store leftover stuffing in the refrigerator for up to 3 days; rewarm in the microwave or a low oven until heated through.

SOURDOUGH LASAGNA

SERVES 8 TO 10

454 grams (1 pound) day-old crusty sourdough bread (about ½ loaf), such as Pain de Campagne (page 205), Preserved Lemon and Olive Bread (page 275), or Polenta, Ricotta, and Rosemary Loaf (page 235)

28 grams (2 tablespoons) olive oil, plus more for drizzling

Fine salt

½ large white onion (about 113 grams/4 ounces), finely diced

2 garlic cloves, minced

Two 10-ounce (283-gram) packages chopped frozen spinach, thawed

Freshly ground black pepper

85 grams (3 ounces) grated pecorino Romano cheese, divided

454 grams (16 ounces) whole-milk ricotta cheese

15 grams (¼ cup) finely chopped fresh basil

Two 26-ounce (750-gram) jars marinara sauce (or 6 cups homemade sauce)

454 grams (16 ounces) low-moisture whole-milk mozzarella cheese, shredded

In this bread lover's take on lasagna, thin slices of sourdough stand in for the pasta. It's a genius way to use days-old bread (the older the bread, the easier it is to thinly slice), but otherwise it's by the book: lots of cheese, lots of marinara. Because the bread absorbs more liquid than noodles, you need to start with lots of sauce. Even still, the texture of this is firmer than a traditional lasagna and slices easily; for anyone who has made lasagna only to end up with a soupy mess, this one's for you.

Arrange racks in the upper and lower thirds of the oven and preheat the oven to 350°F.

With a sharp knife, cut the bread as thinly as possible; ideally, the slices should be no more than ¼ inch thick. Arrange the slices on two rimmed baking sheets, then drizzle with olive oil and sprinkle with salt. Transfer to the oven and bake until the bread is dry and beginning to brown, 10 to 15 minutes, switching racks halfway through. Remove from the oven and set aside. Leave the oven on and increase the temperature to 400°F.

In a large skillet, heat 2 tablespoons olive oil. Add the onion, garlic, and a generous pinch of salt and cook, stirring, until the onions have softened, 4 to 5 minutes. Add the spinach and cook, stirring, until most of the moisture has evaporated from the spinach and it's beginning to stick to the pan, about 4 minutes. Remove from the heat and season to taste with salt and pepper. Let cool.

Set aside 50 grams (½ cup) of the grated Romano. In a medium bowl, combine the remaining Romano, the ricotta, and the basil and stir well to mix. Season to taste with salt and pepper.

BUILD THE LASAGNA: Spoon about 1 cup of marinara in the bottom of a 9 × 13-inch baking dish and spread into a thin, even layer. Arrange a layer of toasted bread slices on top in a single layer (if you need to cut or break the slices to fit them together, do so). Dollop half the ricotta mixture over the bread, then use an offset spatula or the back of a spoon to spread into an even layer. Top with half of the spinach mixture, spreading

Recipe continues

evenly, then spoon over 2 cups of the marinara sauce. Sprinkle one-third of the shredded mozzarella over the marinara. Repeat the layers a second time in this order: a layer of bread, the remaining ricotta, the remaining spinach, 2 more cups of the marinara, and half of the remaining mozzarella. Top with a third layer of bread, then spread the remaining 1 cup marinara directly over the bread. Combine the reserved Romano with the remaining mozzarella, then sprinkle over the top.

Cover the dish loosely with foil, transfer to the oven, and bake for 45 minutes. Remove from the oven, carefully uncover, then return the pan to the oven and bake until the top of the lasagna is well browned, 15 to 20 minutes.

Let the lasagna stand for 10 minutes before cutting into squares and serving.

VANILLA BREAD PUDDING

SERVES 6 TO 8

340 grams (1½ cups) heavy cream

170 grams (¾ cup) whole milk

1 vanilla bean

175 grams (6 ounces) soft white bread, such as Pain de Mie (page 132), Challah (page 365), Japanese Milk Bread (page 165), Sky-High Nanterre (page 378), or (Not So) Basic White Sandwich Bread (page 120), cut into 1-inch cubes (5 cups)

Softened unsalted butter, for the baking pan

3 large eggs (150 grams total)

112 grams (½ cup plus 1 tablespoon) sugar

¼ teaspoon fine sea salt

10 grams (2 teaspoons) pure vanilla extract

42 grams (¼ cup) coarsely chopped semisweet chocolate (optional)

The key to this ultra-silky bread pudding is a high ratio of custard to bread, using heavy cream for most of the liquid, and baking the bread pudding in a water bath. The water bath might seem a bit fussy, but its steady heat cooks the custard gently, giving the pudding its wonderfully smooth, creamy texture. We like to add a bit of chopped chocolate to our vanilla bread pudding. As it bakes it forms melty pockets that we seek out with our spoons. It could be omitted, of course, for a purely vanilla version. Bread pudding is also wonderful drizzled with caramel sauce or topped with seasonal fruit or fruit that has been sautéed in butter and sugar until caramelized.

In a medium saucepan, combine the heavy cream and milk. Split the vanilla bean lengthwise and use the tip of a knife to scrape the seeds into the pan, then add the pod, too. Set the pan over medium heat until small bubbles begin to form at the edge (don't let the mixture boil), about 5 minutes.

Remove the cream from the heat, cover, and let stand for 30 minutes at room temperature. Remove the vanilla pod, rinse, dry, and set aside for another use (add it to a jar of sugar to make vanilla sugar).

Butter an 8-inch square baking pan and spread the cubed bread in the pan in an even layer.

In a stand mixer fitted with the whisk attachment, whisk the eggs, sugar, and salt on medium-high speed until voluminous and pale, about 4 minutes. Add the cooled cream mixture and vanilla extract and mix on low to combine. Pour the mixture through a fine-mesh sieve over the cubed bread. Gently nudge the bread down into the liquid; the pan will be quite full, but it will settle some.

Sprinkle the chopped chocolate, if using, over the top of the custard and use your fingertip or a spoon to gently press it under the surface. Refrigerate the bread pudding for 30 minutes (this gives the bread some time to absorb the custard) while you preheat the oven.

Recipe continues

Preheat the oven to 350°F and arrange a rack in the center.

Set the 8-inch pan into a 9 × 13-inch baking pan. Add boiling water to the large pan until it comes halfway up the sides of the 8-inch pan. Transfer to the oven and bake until the pudding is just set and the top begins to take on some color, 20 to 25 minutes.

Remove the pan from the oven, then remove the bread pudding from the water bath and let it cool on a rack. (The bread pudding can be prepared to this point and refrigerated for up to 3 days before serving. Once cool, cover and refrigerate. When you're ready to serve, warm in a low oven until heated through, then broil the top as directed in the next step.)

Just before serving, preheat the broiler and toast the top of the pudding (it should be about 3 inches below the heating element) until nicely browned, watching constantly. Remove from the oven and let cool for 5 minutes before serving. Store leftovers, covered, in the refrigerator for up to 3 days.

Flour Primer

It would be impossible to write a book about bread without writing about its most foundational ingredient, flour, the pantry staple that makes it all possible.

Put simply, flour is what results from grinding whole grains, which are the edible seeds of cereal plants (mostly grasses), including wheat, rye, rice, oats, barley, millet, and maize. (The word "cereal" is derived from Ceres, who was the Roman goddess of agriculture and fertility—in other words, the original Earth mother.)

Grains can be grouped into two primary categories: true grains and pseudograins. True grains include rye, millet, oat, barley, rice, and corn, but the star of the true grain family is, of course, wheat, which is further subdivided into modern wheat and so-called ancient wheats, varieties that include spelt, Khorasan (also called Kamut), emmer, and einkorn. Ancient wheats are referred to as such not because they're no longer grown (they are!) but because their cultivation and consumption predates recorded human history.

Pseudograins include buckwheat, quinoa, and amaranth. They resemble grains in appearance but are more closely related, botanically speaking, to grasses. Like wheat, these grains and pseudograins can all be ground into flour and used for baking, though because of their chemical makeups and protein levels, some are better suited to bread baking than others.

What makes wheat flour so special, and so perfectly suited to bread, is that it contains high levels of two proteins, glutenin and gliadin. When a flour that contains these proteins is mixed with liquid, gluten is produced. Gluten gives the dough both cohesion and elasticity. Its weblike structure captures and contains the carbon dioxide bubbles produced by yeast (either commercial yeast or the yeast in sourdough culture). In short, gluten is the magic substance that allows a dough to rise (and stretch), and it is found in the greatest abundance in wheat flour. Like any protein, gluten is pliable until cooked; after baking, it becomes firm and holds its shape.

Wheat flour begins with the wheat berry (also called a wheat kernel), which comprises the endosperm, bran, and germ. The endosperm is the largest part of the berry and is where the starch, the majority of the protein, and the B vitamins (niacin, riboflavin, and thiamine) are stored. The bran is the outer layer of the kernel and is about 14% of the total kernel weight. It contains a small amount of protein, a large amount of B vitamins, and a hefty dose of fiber. The germ, or embryo, is the sprouting part of the berry, where the plant's fat and genetic material are stored.

After eons of isolating and breeding, there are more than 30,000 varieties of wheat today. In the United States, wheat is grouped into six classes: hard red winter, hard red spring, hard white, soft red winter, soft white, and durum. Regardless of classification, the makeup of the wheat berries is always the same (endosperm, germ, bran), though the resulting flour has different characteristics depending on the type of wheat and what parts of the berry are included in the flour blend.

HARD WHEAT

The majority of wheat grown in North America is hard wheat. Hard wheats are high-protein wheats (typically between 10% and 12% protein) and contain more gluten-producing proteins than soft wheats. Hard wheat berries can be either red or white, based on the color of the pigment in the bran, and can be grown in either winter or spring. The more protein in flour, the more gluten it will produce. The more gluten that is produced, the stronger the dough will be and the more structure it will have. Beyond the strength of the dough, protein content also impacts other functional properties of the flour and doughs made from that flour, including water absorption, elasticity, texture, volume, and crumb.

Practically speaking, that means that some flours are better suited to bread baking than others. Higher-protein hard wheat flours, including bread flour (12.7% protein) and golden wheat (12.2% protein), among others, have enough protein to produce strong doughs. Often, higher-protein wheats are used in bread recipes in tandem with other grain (and pseudograin) flours, and you'll see lots of evidence of that in the recipes in this book. By combining the two, we can take advantage of the functional superiority of strong wheat flour and the kaleidoscopic array of flavors other flours can bring to the party.

SOFT WHEATS

Soft wheats are typically winter wheats, planted in the fall and wintered over in a state of dormancy to begin growing the following spring. Soft wheats have a larger percentage of carbohydrates and less protein than hard wheats, and thus flour milled from soft wheat berries has less gluten-forming ability. Weaker wheat flours (as well as nonwheat flours, such as oat, rice, buckwheat, or corn) lack the protein necessary for producing a strong dough that will hold its structure, and so are not often used as the majority flour in bread doughs. But soft wheat flour (sold as cake or pastry flour) is ideal for other baked goods where tenderness and a delicate crumb are desired, like biscuits, cakes, and other pastries. And non-wheat, lower-protein flours are often used in tandem with strong flour. The strong flour gives the bread necessary structure, while the non-wheat flour contributes flavor.

MILLING

Of course, there's a critical step that transforms a wheat berry into flour: milling. Grain milling might be the oldest manufacturing process in the world. For almost all of recorded history—at least up until the end of the nineteenth century—grains were stone-milled. In stone mills a pair of heavy millstones, each etched on one side, are sandwiched together, etched sides touching. The bottom stone remains fixed; the top stone, which has a hole in its center through which grain is added, rotates slowly. The friction between the stones grinds the whole grains into flour. At first, stone mills lacked the technology to separate a wheat berry into its constituent parts (endosperm, germ, and bran), so the flour they milled contained the whole berry—germ, bran, and all. As stone-milling technology advanced, the coarse stone-milled flour was sifted to remove some of the bran and germ, then ground subsequent times until the flour was more finely milled.

There are still stone mills in operation throughout the United States, and there has been a resurgence of stone-milling in recent years that mirrors Americans' burgeoning enthusiasm for home bread baking. Often these regional mills specialize in milling locally grown grain as well as more unusual varietals.

Most commercial milling operations use the roller milling method. The wheat berries are first cleaned and tempered (soaked to bring them to a uniform moisture level, an unnecessary step in stone-milling) and then passed through a set of corrugated steel rollers, which smash the berries and separate them into their constituent parts: bran, germ, and endosperm. For white flour (also known as "straight" flour), the germ is removed, the majority of the bran is sifted out, and the endosperm is passed through a series of increasingly smooth rollers until it is finely milled into flour. For whole-grain flours, a portion of the germ and bran are added back into the flour. White flour, whole wheat flour, and golden wheat flour are all made from wheat berries; the difference is that white flour contains only the endosperm, while whole wheat and golden wheat flours contain the whole berry. Whole wheat flour is made from hard red winter wheat; golden wheat flour is ground from hard white spring wheat. Whole-grain flours are particularly flavorful because they contain the germ, which is where all of the wheat berry's fat (and therefore flavor) is contained.

STORING FLOURS AND GRAINS

HOW TO STORE FLOUR

Flours that don't contain the germ, such as all-purpose, bread, pastry, cake, and white rye can be stored for a long time in airtight containers in a cool, dry place.

Whole-grain flours are a different story. Once you rupture the oily germ of the berry by grinding it into flour, it's exposed to air and thus subject to oxidation, which can cause it to develop a musty flavor and aroma that persists even after it's baked. Freshly ground whole-grain flours stored in cool and dry conditions will keep for about 3 months; the refrigerator is a good idea. For longer storage, freezing is by far the best way to store whole-grain flours, but it won't stop oxidation entirely. It's better to buy small amounts and replenish your stock frequently. All grains are subject to insect infestation. If you're going to have flour around at room temperature for any length of time, tuck in a bay leaf to discourage insects.

HOW TO TELL IF YOUR FLOUR HAS SPOILED

Smell your flour. It should smell nutty, maybe a little malty. Past-prime flour will actually smell rancid and unpleasant, which is the indicator that it's time to toss it. Don't make the mistake of thinking you won't be able to taste stale flour once it's baked; in fact, baking seems to magnify the mustiness (and then you've devoted a lot of time to something you won't want to eat). Obviously, toss any flour that you discover is harboring insects.

ADDITIVES

After wheat flour has been milled, a number of things can be added to it. All-purpose flour usually has malted barley or enzymes to enhance its performance for yeast baking. The enzymes help convert the starch in the flour to sugars the yeast likes to eat.

During the 1940s (the heyday of Wonder Bread, the first sliced bread on the market), there was a temporary US Government mandate that white flour, then a foundational part of the American diet, be enriched with vitamins. Because white flour is made only from the endosperm of the berry and not the germ and bran, where all the vitamins are stored, white flour lacks those vitamins. The government's solution? Add small amounts of iron, niacin, thiamine, and riboflavin to white flour to replace the naturally occurring vitamins that had been stripped out in milling. These days, white flour is no longer required to be enriched, and most, including King Arthur's, are not.

And while Wonder Bread is no longer the only, nor the most popular, bread on the market, contemporary millers are still primarily in the business of making white flour. The first step in accomplishing this, as mentioned above, is to separate the bran and germ through the milling process itself. The next step is to "whiten" the remaining flour.

Given time and exposure to air, flour will slowly oxidize and whiten on its own. This rest period, around 2 weeks in the summer and up to 1 month in the winter, also changes flour's chemistry so that it will create a dough that is more elastic. But rather than using time as an agent, as King Arthur Baking Company does, many millers use chemicals to whiten flour almost instantly. As the flour comes off the line at the mill, bleaching and oxidizing chemicals are added in order to quicken or entirely replace the aging process.

Chlorine dioxide, benzoyl peroxide, and chlorine gas, all of which whiten and/or oxidize flour, are currently permissible additives (though King Arthur Baking Company flours do not contain any of them). Benzoyl peroxide leaves behind some benzoic acid, which can be mildly toxic to the skin, eyes, and mucous membranes. Some people with an acute sense of taste recognize benzoyl peroxide in baked goods because it has a bitter aftertaste, but its addition does not appreciably change its baking qualities.

Chlorine gas reacts with the flour to change its absorbency, flavor, pH, and, in the case of some cake flours, its performance. In baked goods where other ingredients do not mask it, it imparts a detectable flavor to people with sensitive palates.

The most controversial additive used today is

potassium bromate, which is still in use both as an oxidizer and an "improver," strengthening dough and allowing for greater oven spring and higher rising in the oven. It has come under scrutiny, however, as tests with it have indicated that it is carcinogenic in animals and probably in humans. Since 1991, flour sold in California containing potassium bromate has had to carry a warning label. It is banned in Canada, Europe, and Japan, and will likely someday be banned in the United States. Regardless, although there are scientists who claim that there is no harmful residue left in bromated flour after baking, King Arthur Baking Company flours do not contain potassium bromate.

FLOUR FROM THE GROUND UP

When we buy a bag of flour at the grocery store, we probably do so without considering it as an agricultural product. But wheat is one of the top three crops grown in North America (corn and soybeans hold the top two spots), and as a flour company we spend a lot of time thinking about how the wheat that's eventually milled into our flour is grown and harvested.

The double whammy of industrialization and climate change have impacted how wheat is grown now, and how it will be grown in the future. If large-scale monocropping seemed at one time a pretty great idea, some 80 years on we've come to see that while it delivered on efficiency and yield, it came with costs, for both farmers and the environment. Add to that a rapidly changing climate, and the need to produce wheat and flour as sustainably and nutritionally as possible becomes not just a business decision but an ethical imperative.

Regenerative agriculture, a practice that seeks to restore, renew, and enhance natural resources through a focus on healthy soils, ecosystems, and farming communities, is increasingly becoming adopted by modern wheat farmers. And while regenerative agriculture isn't new (it embodies principles foundational to long-standing Indigenous land traditions), its application on larger-scale farms is. Examples of regenerative agriculture practices include cover cropping and crop rotations, minimizing inputs, no/limited tillage, and affordability and accessibility of crops.

It differs from organic agriculture in a few notable ways: Regenerative focuses on outcomes and principles, while organic is a labeling term that indicates products were produced by practices verified by the USDA, primarily without the use of synthetic pesticides and fertilizers.

Regenerative agriculture is also dedicated to improving the well-being of farmers and creating a future in which farming communities are economically viable and able to invest in practices that support the land. The goal is to create a system where farming is healthy for both the planet and for the people farming it, the ultimate version of sustainability.

To support regenerative farming initiatives and research, King Arthur has deepened our partnership with Washington State University's Breadlab, an organization committed to grain innovation and research. They're working to breed climate-resilient wheat that can withstand the chaotic effects of climate change, like fluctuating temperatures and water levels. Our hope (and expectation) is that regeneratively grown, climate-resistant wheat will eventually be grown at scale, and that bakers will have easy, broad access to flour made from this wheat so they can bake sustainably and forever after.

TRUE GRAINS

Also called cereals, true grains are the edible seeds of certain grasses.

WHEAT: The undisputed MVP of the true grain family, there are 30,000 types of wheat. Spelt, khorasan (Kamut), Emmer (also known as farro), and einkorn are the most ancient varieties and are still grown today, along with dozens and dozens of modern varieties.

RYE: Rye contains about the same amount of protein as wheat, but, because of its chemical makeup, does not behave the same way in doughs (see Understanding Rye, page 228).

BARLEY: High in carbohydrates and low in gluten, barley is typically used to make flatbreads or in combination with a stronger flour to make bread.

MILLET: High in iron and calcium, millet is a staple grain in India and Africa. The tiny grains can be used in bread as an inclusion or crust treatment on the exterior of a loaf. Teff is one variety of millet, and is typically ground and fermented to make spongy injera bread.

OAT: Nutty and slightly sweet, oats contain more fat and protein than wheat, although the protein is not gluten-producing. Old-fashioned oats are steamed and flattened with steel rollers; steel-cut oats are the entire grain, cracked for faster cooking. Oat flour is a soft flour and can be used in breads along with a stronger flour.

PSEUDOGRAINS

Though they resemble true grains in appearance, pseudograins are botanically distinct from true grains and naturally gluten-free.

BUCKWHEAT: Most of the buckwheat grown in this country is grown as a cover crop, not a food source. But with its distinctive slightly bitter and nutty flavor, it's a wonderful grain to incorporate into your baking. Buckwheat flour is gray in color and naturally gluten-free, so it has to be used in conjunction with a stronger flour for bread baking.

QUINOA: Though not a true grain, quinoa is a complete protein and rich in vitamins. It's typically cooked or soaked and added to bread doughs. Because it contains no gluten, it needs to be added to a dough containing a stronger wheat flour.

AMARANTH: A staple crop of the Aztecs, amaranth is related to pigweed, and it grows quickly and is extremely hardy. The grains are tiny and can be cooked and eaten as a cereal, popped like popcorn, or ground into flour. Because it contains no gluten, it needs to be mixed with strong wheat flour for bread baking.

CORN: Most often used in its refined form, degermed and ground into cornmeal, polenta, or grits. Stone-ground cornmeal (made from the whole kernel) is more flavorful, but, like all whole-grain flours, can go rancid more quickly and is best stored in the refrigerator or freezer.

RICE: Rice flour (and glutinous rice flour, ground from short-grain rice) is gluten-free. It's used in Asian baking and in breads in tandem with stronger flours.

FREQUENTLY USED FLOURS AT A GLANCE

ALL-PURPOSE FLOUR (11.7% PROTEIN)

This versatile flour is milled from hard red winter wheat. It's strong enough to be used in many breads (especially yeasted breads), but not so strong that it can't also be used for cakes and cookies.

BREAD FLOUR (12.7% PROTEIN)

Bread flour is higher in protein than all-purpose flour and is a great choice for breads of all kinds, including pan breads and naturally leavened hearth breads. It's also frequently used in bread doughs in combination with other, weaker flours, like rye.

GOLDEN WHEAT FLOUR (13% PROTEIN)

Milled from hard white spring wheat (a lighter-colored grain than the traditional red wheat used in whole wheat flour), this flour has a similar nutritional profile to whole wheat but is mellower in flavor and lighter in color. It is often sold under the name white whole wheat flour.

WHOLE WHEAT FLOUR (14% PROTEIN)

Whole wheat flour is made by milling the entire wheat berry, including the inner germ and outer bran, which gives it more nutrition and a stronger, more robust flavor.

SEMOLINA FLOUR

Semolina flour is made from coarsely ground durum wheat. (Durum flour is also made from durum wheat, but is more finely ground than semolina flour.) Compared to the other major types of wheat (hard red, hard white, soft red, and soft white) that are used for most other flours, durum wheat is the "hardest" of them all, with a high protein content.

'00' FLOUR (11.5% PROTEIN)

This finely milled flour is made from a blend of soft and hard wheats. It's typically used for pizza dough and other flatbreads. The soft wheat contributes to a crisp crust, while the hard flour makes the dough especially extensible.

RYE FLOUR

See Understanding Rye, page 228.

SKY-HIGH NANTERRE, PAGE 378

ACKNOWLEDGMENTS

King Arthur Baking Company is a collaborative place. The employee-owners of our company are always helping one another out, in ways big and small, and so much of what we do—and are able to do—is because of that truly awesome collaboration. This book is no different; it was a team effort.

Our editor, Doris Cooper, joined us in bringing this book to life and, to our delight, became a bread baker along the way. Our agent, Janis Donnaud, helped keep the train on the tracks. The company leadership, including Karen Colberg, Bill Tine, and the late Ralph Carlton, enthusiastically supported this undertaking.

Without employee-owners and bakers Martin Philip and Melanie Wanders, this book would not exist; with patience and passion and grace they developed and tested and baked hundreds of loaves of bread and translated all their thoughts and notes into a brilliant guide for home bakers. The editorial team at King Arthur, including Kye Ameden, Rossi Anastopoulo, Tatiana Bautista, Lee Clark, Lydia Fournier, Sarah Jampel, Molly Marzalek-Kelly, Chris McLeod, Laura Scaduto, and David Turner tested recipes, provided guidance, stocked the pantry, and supported this project in every way. Editorial director David Tamarkin gave us unwavering encouragement as well as thoughtful edits all along the way; to show our gratitude we (almost) named a bread after him (see Classic Miche, page 213). And Jessica Battilana not only project-managed this book but also wrote nearly every word—and she somehow kept her signature sense of humor about her the whole time.

We were fortunate to get recipes and guidance from some amazing bakers, including several of King Arthur's own: Marc Levy (Breakfast Porridge Bread, page 231), Lucas Diggle (Pumpkin Seed Levain, page 278), Jennifer Rein, and Jessica Meyers. We also benefitted from the baking talents of Tara O'Brady (Aloo Paratha, page 86), Betty Liu (Sesame dà Bǐng, page 99, and Guō Kuī, page 96), Hetty Lui McKinnon (Scallion Pancakes, page 93, and Sheng Jian Bao, page 337), Reem Assil (Sfeeha Halaby, page 77), and Karen Ogrinc (Gözleme, page 75, and Fattoush, page 426).

We are grateful to Ed Anderson for the beautiful images in this book, as well as his patience and kindness. On set, we benefitted from the food styling talents of Rebecca Jurkevich and Kaitlin Wayne and the prop styling vision of Gerri Williams, as well as support from studio director Johnny Grasso.

Mia Johnson designed this book beautifully; King Arthur's creative director, Tomlynn Biondo, together with designer Michelle Chen, was instrumental in helping bring the vision to life. Julianna Brazill contributed helpful illustrations. We're especially grateful to employee-owners Barbara Alpern, Andrea Brown, Amber Eisler, and Jeff Yankellow, who read these pages as we reached the finish line and asked thoughtful questions and made smart suggestions. Finally, to all of our fellow employee-owners whose work has or will impact this book and its place in the world: Thank you.

Bread by Time

THREE-DAY BREADS

APPENDIX B:
Bread by Leavening

Index

Note: Italic page numbers refer to illustrations.

SIMON
ELEMENT

An Imprint of Simon & Schuster, LLC
1230 Avenue of the Americas
New York, NY 10020

First Simon Element hardcover edition October 2024

SIMON ELEMENT is a trademark of Simon & Schuster, LLC

Simon & Schuster: Celebrating 100 Years of Publishing in 2024

For information about special discounts for bulk purchases, please
contact Simon & Schuster Special Sales at 1-866-506-1949 or
business@simonandschuster.com.

The Simon & Schuster Speakers Bureau can bring authors to your
live event. For more information or to book an event, contact the
Simon & Schuster Speakers Bureau at 1-866-248-3049 or visit
our website at www.simonspeakers.com.

Interior design by Mia Johnson

Manufactured in China

1   3   5   7   9   10   8   6   4   2

Library of Congress Cataloging-in-Publication Data
has been applied for.

ISBN 978-1-6680-0974-1
ISBN 978-1-6680-0975-8 (ebook)

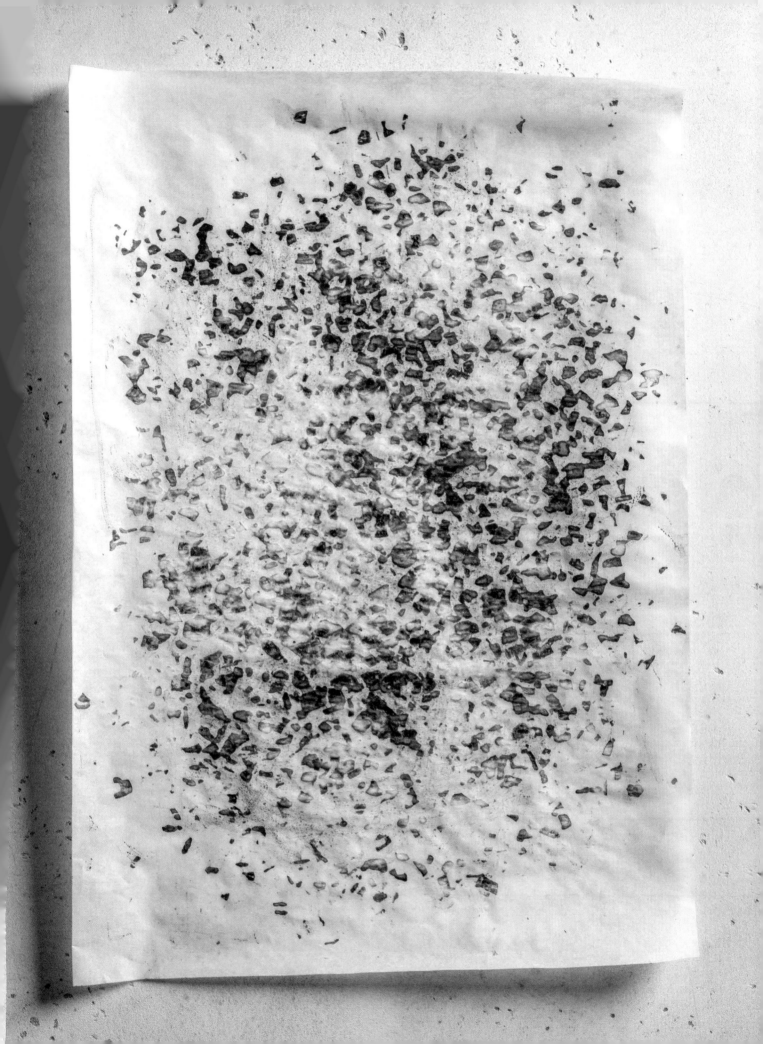